The Days of Reckoning Are at Hand

THE DAYS OF RECKONING ARE AT HAND

From Fig Leaf to Olive Branch to Laurel Wreath

James Venezia

The Christian Exceptionalism in Counseling Series™

EXULTANTIS PRESS

NEW YORK

The Days of Reckoning Are at Hand: From Fig Leaf to Olive Branch to Laurel Wreath.
Copyright TXu 1-944-558 © 2015 by James Venezia

The Christian Exceptionalism in Counseling Series™. Trademark 2015 by James Venezia

Published by EXULTANTIS PRESS, NEW YORK

All rights reserved, including the right to reproduce this book or portions thereof in any form whatsoever.

Available in print and electronic-book formats through Amazon.com:
    ISBN 978-0-9961181-5-6 (paperback)
    ISBN 978-0-9961181-2-5 (electronic book)

Unless otherwise noted, Scripture taken from the HOLY BIBLE, NEW INTERNATIONAL VERSION ®. Copyright © 1973, 1978, 1984 by International Bible Society. Used by permission of Zondervan. All rights reserved.

The author can be contacted at jamesvenezia@yahoo.com.

Second edition, 2016

Cover picture: *Ecce Homo*, Antonio Ciseri, c. 1880

Printed in the United States of America

The days of punishment are coming, *the days of reckoning are at hand*. Let Israel know this. Because your sins are so many and your hostility so great, the prophet is considered a fool, the inspired man a maniac. (Hosea 9:7, emphasis added)

The Christian Exceptionalism in Counseling Series™

Welcome, dear reader, to *The Christian Exceptionalism in Counseling Series*™. This material is written to be accessible to both the neophyte as well as to the counseling aficionado. The first book in the series, *Ask for the Ancient Paths: From Art to Artifice to Arisen*, serves as a comprehensive introduction to biblical counseling. It is written as an overview of the Bible's creation-fall-redemption paradigm. The second book, *What Agreement Is There Between the Temple of God and Idols?: The Accidence of Sin and Idolatry*, explores sin and idolatry so as to eradicate it. The third book, *The Days of Reckoning Are at Hand: From Fig Leaf to Olive Branch to Laurel Wreath*, focuses on application in which one will find a more in-depth handling of diagnosis, as well as analysis of pressing topics such as suffering and loneliness.

My hope is that these books will not serve to merely inform, but rather will implement God's work of change in those he claims as his own. If you are already a Christian (one personally saved through Jesus' death upon the cross) then this series will advance God's sanctifying work in, and through, you. If you are not yet a believer then this series functions as an apologetic persuasion. The hope is that through this material you will see the unfathomable power of Christ-centered counseling, and in response find new life in him.

Wedding Procession, Gustave Brion, 1873

Ask for the Ancient Paths: From Art to Artifice to Arisen

Chapters

1. The Exordium to Biblical Counseling

2. The Counseling Ambition

3. The Centrality of Scripture in Counseling

4. The Gospel as Inception Point: From Immorality to Immortality

5. Redefining the Pygmalion Effect: Exploring the Image of God in Man

6. Man Before the Face of God: The Imperium of the Psyche

7. The Needs Imperative

8. What Has Jerusalem To Do With Vienna?: The Case Against Psychology

9. Integrationism: The Modern Day Babylonian Captivity

10. The Third-Way of Sanctification: From Abominable to Indomitable

Appendix: A Sanctification Plan

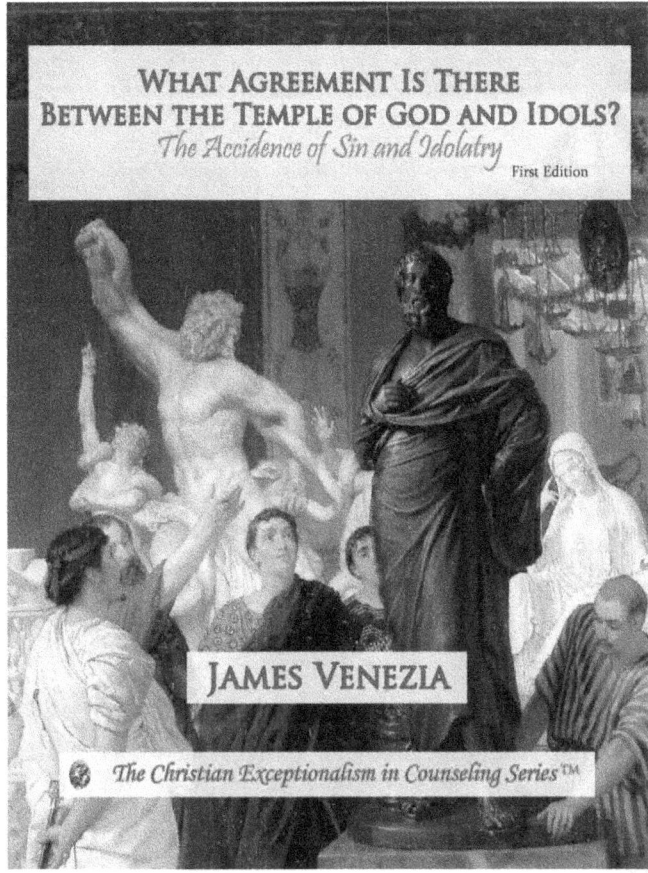

What Agreement Is There Between the Temple of God and Idols?:
The Accidence of Sin and Idolatry

Chapters:

1. Deliver Us from Evil

2. The World, the Flesh, and the Devil: Assessing the Threat Matrix

3. Total Depravity: This Imperiled Arcadia

4. Hamartiology: Sin in All Its Ignobility

5. Metaphors for Sin

6. Uncovering Idols of the Heart: Make Us Gods to Go Before Us

7. The Idolatry Doppler Shift

8. The Search for Eldorado Ends: Repenting of Idols of the Heart

9. Marauding Visigoths: The Autocratic Self

10. A Nouthetic Analysis of Moses

Appendix: The Demon Possession Case Study

The Days of Reckoning Are at Hand: From Fig Leaf to Olive Branch to Laurel Wreath

Chapters:

1. Memories Preserved in Amber: Adopting God's Retrospective

2. Suffering: The Kintsugi Objective

3. The Hobgoblin in the Inglenook: Assessing Loneliness

4. The Umbilicus of Personal Relationship with Christ

5. Navigating the Counseling Fjord: Preliminary Reconnaissance

6. The Basic Plotlines Which Emerge in Counseling

7. Artisanal Counseling: A Foray into Methods

8. Diagnosis: Vanishing Secrets

9. Emerging from the Chrysalis: Issues the Counselor Observes and Seeks to Change

10. Counseling and the Church: Syndicating the Vision

ALSO BY THE AUTHOR

*The Lord Kept Vigil That Night:
An Exposition of the Parable of the Lost
Son*

*Rescue Us from the Present Evil Age:
Array of Hope*

*Hurl All Our Iniquities
into the Depths of the Sea*

Contents

Preface	xix
Acknowledgements	xxv
Introduction	1

1. Memories Preserved in Amber: *Adopting God's Retrospective* — 5

The Lewis Terman Study on Intelligence and Success	5
The Heart's Interpretive Quest	8
The Role of Memory	9
The Memory Palace	12
Universal Truths about the Human Existence	14
Vorlage: The Text Behind Personal History	16
The Wernicke's Syndrome of the Worshipping Heart	18
Hagiography: Contrived and Confabulated Sainthood	21
Personal Revisionist History	23
Case Study: Homosexuality and the Issue of Personal History	28
Assessing Personal History: The Relevance of a Father's Love	31
The Freudian Fatherhood Fable	33
God Stands in Both Continuity with, and in Contradistinction to, Earthly Examples	36
God's Care for the Widow, the Orphan, and the Alien	39
Excursus: The Book of Esther: A Silent and Invisible, Yet Present, God	40
Sanctification as the Adoption of God's "Revisionist" History	42
Rewriting One's Life Story as an Act of Repentance	46
The Memory Palace Festooned in Splendor	47

2. Suffering: *The Kintsugi Objective* — 51

Suffering as a Universal Human Experience	51
The Human Quest to Overcome Finitude	53
The Search for Answers in an Evil World	55
Categorizing Suffering	58
Suffering's Blueprint	62
The Question of Retribution Theology	70
A Biblically-Sound Theodicy	71
Two Poles in the Sinful Response to Suffering	76

"Soft-Suffering"	78
Recipient and Responder	80
When Suffering Arises from One's Own Failing.	81
Suffering and Complaint	83
Case Study: Suicide: Idols in Death Throws	87
Counseling Those Who Suffer	100
God's Objective in Suffering	104
The Christian's Interaction with Suffering	108
The Gospel and Suffering	110
Suffering as Preparation for Judgment	113
Breaking the Suffering Axis	119
The Kintsugi Objective	121
The Counselor's Compassion	122
Case Study: God's *Sui Generis* Love	124
Excursus: Should One Love Himself?	142
Excursus: Faith, Hope, and Love	143
Concluding Thoughts	145

3. THE HOBGOBLIN IN THE INGLENOOK: *Assessing Loneliness*   147

The Historical Trajectory of Loneliness	147
Excursus: The Relational Curse of the Recorded Line	148
The Growth of Loneliness: "Do I Dare Disturb the Universe?"	149
Loneliness as Modern Blight	150
The Advent of Chronic Relational Boredom	153
The Bible's Assessment of Loneliness	155
Various Methods for Dealing with Loneliness	157
Perceived Solutions Which Exacerbate the Problem	164
Case Study: The Invisible Relational Circle	168
The Search for Answers at the Foot of the Cross	173

4. THE UMBILICUS OF PERSONAL RELATIONSHIP WITH CHRIST   181

Introduction	181
The Relational Nature of Biblical Covenant: "The Right Relationship is Everything"	183
The Coming of the Kingdom	185
Personal Knowledge of Christ	186
The Bible's Four Primary Metaphors for Relationship with Jesus	187
If Not Relationship with Christ, Then Relationship with Satan	194
Assessing the Merits of Personal Relationship with Christ	195

The Dangers When Relationship with Christ is Marginalized	199
Excursus: Pastor as Servant	205
Abiding in Christ	206
Case Study: Prayer as Life-Blood of Relationship with Jesus	210
Categories for Prayer	217
A Prayer Outline	220

5. NAVIGATING THE COUNSELING FJORD: *Preliminary Reconnaissance* — 223

From *Urim* and *Thummin* to Incarnational Counseling	223
The Travail of Societal Expectation	224
The Allure of Counseling	228
The Presenting Problem	232
The Temptation of Circumstance	235
Forging Automorphic Alliances	238
The Counseling Exchange: Mitigating the Cobra Effect	240
Constituents and Contours of the Counseling Engagement	242
Excursus: Counseling and the Coming Apocalypse: Renovating Wardenclyffe Tower	245
Excursus: Alien Abduction	251
When the Dust Settles God is There	255

6. THE BASIC PLOTLINES WHICH EMERGE IN COUNSELING — 257

Introduction	257
Why is Classic Literature Still Read Today?	257
Literature as a Conduit into the Heart	259
Competing Stories	260
The Question of Literary Interpretation	263
Excursus: Bible Characters	264
Analyzing the Plot: Narrative, Metanarrative, Subtext	265
The Counselee's Story Commonalities with Literature	269
What is the Difference Between Literature and Psychology?	270
Twenty Basic Plotlines	271
Concluding Thoughts	277

7. ARTISANAL COUNSELING: *A Foray into Methods* — 279

Introduction	279
Artisanal Counseling	280

Biblical Counseling Introduces a Person, Not a Set of Principles	282
The Fractal Method of Counseling	286
Counseling as Incarnational Ministry	287
The Counselor as Prophet, Priest, and King	288
The Counselor's Love: "I Love Mankind – It's People I Can't Stand"	292
The Willingness to Disrupt Harmony	294
Establishing the Terms of Engagement	295
Both Upholding and Vacating the Social Contract	297
Does the Counselor Hold a Measure of Rightful Authority Over the Counseling Interaction?	298
The Judah and Tamar Syndrome	299
Illegitimate Totality Transfer	301
Recording Evidence	303
The Art of Confrontation: Confronting Sin, Not Sinful Confrontation	304
Counseling as Confession	313
Counseling as Evangelism	315
Matters of Sound Practice	316
A Summary of Crucial Truths about Counseling	318
Note to Counselors: Seize the Day!	319

8. DIAGNOSIS: *Vanishing Secrets* — **321**

God Seeks to Thoroughly Cleanse His People	321
Bringing Idols to Justice	323
The Search for Themes and Patterns: Initial Observations	325
The Search for Themes and Patterns: Data Gathering	329
Chipping Away at the Façade	331
Asking Analytical Questions: The Stealth "Truth Serum"	332
"X-Ray Questions" Which Uncover Idols or Faith	334
Case Study: Questions Which Might Uncover the Lust of the Eye	340
Assessing Responses	340
What Christians Often Say and What They Mean	342
Counseling Threats: Stigmas and Stereotypes, Straw Men and Shibboleths	356
Diagnosis: "Tree Diagrams"	362
Case Study: The Ping-Pong Match	370
The Counseling Practicum	372
An Example of the Counseling Practicum	376
Excursus: The Anxiety Game Plan	380
Bible Study: Insights into the Heart from the Book of Philippians	381

9. EMERGING FROM THE CHRYSALIS:
Issues the Counselor Observes and Seeks to Change — **385**

Deuteronomy 6:4-25	385
Issues the Counselor Observes and Seeks to Change	387
Excursus: The Psychology of the Speedometer	412
Conclusion	415

10. COUNSELING AND THE CHURCH:
Syndicating the Vision — **417**

Introduction	417
The Disintegration of Community	418
Defining the Church	421
The Nature of the Church	423
The State of the Modern Church	424
The "Disney-fication" of the Church	427
The Prevalence of False Believers	431
The Danger of Church Hierarchy	435
The Abdication of the Church's Counseling Birthright	439
Impediments to Counsel	442
The Peter Principle Redefined	444
The Church Family: Moving from "Church" as Noun to Verb	446
Those in Christ Possess a Core Competency to Counsel	450
The Victory and Vision of the Counseling Church	453

EPILOGUE — **455**

THE AUTHOR — **459**

Preface

In 1934, in Mons, Belgium an inventor, Paul Otlet (1868–1944), had a conceptual breakthrough. He envisioned a means for categorizing and storing all knowledge. He sketched out plans to create a network in which people from throughout the world could find and share information. Otlet is possibly the true inventor of the concept of a World Wide Web, and even more remarkably, he foresaw a paperless future long before the computer was invented.

Born in 1868, Paul Otlet was kept out of school until age twelve by his wealthy father who believed that education stifled creativity. Hungry for knowledge, the boy became a prolific reader. The first time that he entered a library he was fascinated by the card catalogue. How could so much knowledge be accessible in one place?

In 1895, at age twenty-seven, Otlet and a friend set out to categorize all knowledge. They collected data on every book, article, and photograph ever published, and over the course of forty years produced over 12 million entries. Otlet setup a proto-search engine in which anyone in the world could submit a query via mail or telegraph.

Young Man at His Window
Gustave Caillebotte, 1875

The problem that Otlet faced, however, was how to manage the sheer volume of paper. He first sketched out a "mobile computer" with spoke-wheels that could organize cards on a table. However, Otlet soon recognized that the future was in a paperless system.

In Otlet's 1934 book, *Monde*, he posited the first ever vision for electronic data storage, as well as for a global network for transmitting that data. While the web today uses static links, Otlet's planned network involved dynamic links which facilitate conceptual relationships between documents.

Sadly, Otlet's brilliant endeavor was never realized as his project went bankrupt in the late 1930s, and the Nazis destroyed most of his work when they marched through Belgium in 1939. Otlet died in 1944 broken-hearted.

I introduce the story of Paul Otlet for a few reasons. There is something about this man that stirs my sense of pathos. Otlet is a forgotten soul, seemingly born far before the proper time, in some way impoverished by a lack of conventional education, yet rising to meet an insurmountable challenge through sheer determination, only to have his hopes dashed by a cruel and unrelenting world. This one man, crushed in the gears of history, resembles the ancient Greek tragic hero, one who meets his certain demise through no fault of his own.

There is something noble in Paul Otlet, something endearing, something admirable, something bewildering, something cinematic. I wish that I had had the opportunity to speak with him, to tinker in his workshop, to share his passion for knowledge, to glimpse the workings of his mind, to share with him the gospel of a savior who died to know him.

Despite being little more than an historical footnote, Otlet was not a forgotten soul. He was loved by the God of the universe, a God who longed to make sense of his mad experiment, a God who sought to give him rest from a heavy yoke, a God with a passion to fill him with a treasure far greater than knowledge, a God eager to comfort him in the grip of agonizing defeat, a God who died to save him from himself. This book is written for the "Paul Otlets" of the world, the ones for whom life seems a confusing maze of trials and failures, whose hopes are dashed and lay in a crumpled heap. The objective in this work is not to rehabilitate dysfunctional idols, but to install an entirely new subject of worship, the person of God himself.

Over the past two decades I have grown both enamored and grateful with the way that God works through biblical counseling (formerly "nouthetic counseling") to effect lasting change. This textbook arises from an abiding passion for helping people change through knowing the God who makes change a reality. Like Otlet, I have labored for years to realize a dream, helping to advance the kingdom of God as Jesus seeks to search out, find, and reclaim lost lives for himself. If this book helps even one to find him, or to know him better, I would joyfully repeat this task a thousand times over.

In reading *The Days of Reckoning Are at Hand* please keep the Bible at your side. It is crucial that this text be seen as building upon the foundation of Scripture. The better the reader knows Scripture, and the more closely he reads Scripture in conjunction with this text, the richer and more vivid this counseling model will become.

One may notice frequent sections throughout the book labeled, "case study" and "excursus." What is the difference? A case study is so denoted because, following the natural trajectory of the chapter, it offers an opportunity for deeper study and reflection. An excursus is similar except that it is more tangential. It may be a cultural, historical, literary, artistic, or scientific reference which is fascinating to consider but not as directly relevant. Thus, an excursus offers a rest-stop in which to exercise the imagination.

The New Novel
Winslow Homer, 1877

While I encourage the reader to study all three books in *The Christian Exceptionalism in Counseling Series* ™, each is designed as a stand-alone unit, and most of the constituent chapters are, to some degree, stand-alone. The reason is that each topic is positioned on a tripod of the Bible's creation-fall-redemption paradigm.[1]

Finally, I have included over 400 pieces of classical artwork throughout the entire series. This art is intended to more persuasively marshal the imagination, to offer the mind a reprieve from propositional truths, to extend the delight of magnificent fare. In most instances, the art is simply a creative augmentation to the topic at hand. If a painting helps expand one's grasp of the concept, then it has served this work's purpose.[2] But please don't allow style to overwhelm substance.

> "'What is the use of a book,'" thought Alice, "'without pictures or conversations?'" (*Alice in Wonderland*, Lewis Carroll)

---

[1] This I describe as the fractal method of counseling in chapter 7: "Artisanal Counseling: A Foray into Methods."
[2] Please note that nearly all the artwork included in these books could be classified as "classical." On occasion, classical artwork contains nudity. While that nudity is never gratuitous, where it is conspicuous, it has been discretely covered so as to maintain the book's modesty. This covering is not an attempt to alter the painting, but simply to guard those readers who might otherwise be tempted to sin.

Isaac Newton (1642–1726) humbly stated, "If I have seen farther than others it is because I stand on the shoulders of giants." This presentation stands on the shoulders of the Christian Counseling and Education Foundation (CCEF) in Willow Grove, Pennsylvania. This is my contribution, and I hope, my gift to the biblical counseling movement which serves Jesus Christ so faithfully. In all essentials of the faith my thinking aligns precisely with CCEF, not out of blind compliance, but out of sincere conviction. This work, like theirs, is triumphantly gospel-centered to its core.

Spotlight on the Second Edition

The first edition of *The Christian Exceptionalism in Counseling Series*™ was officially launched on June 20, 2015. Since that time, myriad edits, updates, and additions have been applied. ("…Of writing many books there is no end…"[3]) As stated previously, reading this material is, to the extent that it accords with Scripture, an encounter with the person of Jesus Christ, not just knowledge about him, but to be confronted and searched by him. In this sense, this material is not so much informative as it is formative.

In the course of this work's advance, at crucial junctures, there have been pronounced spiritual attacks. Yet, despite the setbacks, an invisible hand presses this work forward. With each seemingly insurmountable obstacle, an unanticipated breakthrough emerges. The sense of God himself prospering this work, and seeking to bring it to fruitful completion, has invested me with a towering Christ-centered confidence, an indomitable perseverance, and an unspeakable joy in the final result.

As a side note, it has been an intriguing case study to observe reactions to this work over the past several months. It would appear that this material functions like a prism clarifying those who desire to know, and be known, by Christ. I can only surmise that with each turn of the page Jesus' own winnowing fork is at the threshing floor, an axe to the root of the heart, the disentangling of faith from apostasy. May he will and work to further his kingdom in each who encounter this series.

Please contact the author at jamesvenezia@yahoo.com with questions or comments on this series.

Like Sherlock Holmes it is time to don the deerstalker hat and insert the meerschaum pipe to investigate the psyche!

S. D. G.
January 20, 2016

---

[3] Ecclesiastes 12:12

> "To this end I strenuously contend with all the energy Christ so powerfully works in me." (Colossians 1:29)

Acknowledgments

Thank you to my parents, Peter and Jo-Ann, for providing me with the opportunity and encouragement to write. They have read more of my writing than anyone I know and have taught me a great deal about the perseverance and discipline required to complete such a task. My father also proofread a considerable quantity of this text. I am grateful for his assistance.

Thank you to many Christ-centered teachers for their priceless mentoring and instruction. Their voices echo throughout this book series because they echo throughout my faith. They each, in distinctive ways, have continually reintroduced me to Jesus through, not just their formal instruction, but in their daily experience of knowing, and being know by, Jesus. Their collective counsel serves as a perennial corrective, encouragement, and scriptural realignment to my heart.

An Allegory of Fame
Bernardo Strozzi, d. 1644

"Never trust a scholar who won't tell you who his teachers were." (Aristotle)

This book series is a celebration of Jesus Christ's work in and through Westminster Theological Seminary. Westminster set me on the right path early on in life, a path that continues to lead me into ever richer experiences of Christ. With warm gratitude I thank Westminster for its care for my soul and for the abundant harvest it has produced in and through so many.

INTRODUCTION

When I attended Westminster Theological Seminary there was a copy machine just adjacent to the library lobby. Besides accepting coins, the machine received one-dollar and five-dollar bills. If one fed a bill into the machine, the credit was maintained as long as the machine was in active use. However, after about a minute of inactivity the machine spewed out one's change with a clang into a tiny metal receptacle. Upon receiving my copies I had, on occasion, run off forgetting to retrieve my balance.

Once, as I approached this copier, I saw the change slot filled with coins (maybe two dollars' worth). I looked around, but it seemed no one was using the machine. So I promptly removed the coins, placing them on the adjacent table. I assumed that in a minute or two an absentminded student or professor would jog in for his change (as I had at times).

Charity
William-Adolphe Bouguereau, 1878

That pile of change remained on the corner of that table for an entire week, and no one touched it. Hundreds of students and staff members daily pass through, and loiter, in that room and not one touched that money. While to most this may seem like a trivial matter, that event serves as a minor milestone in my faith. I saw that these Christian brothers and sisters, with whom I daily study, interact, and dine, are genuine. This faith in Jesus is so much more than intellectual assent; it is an actuality in the hearts of believers. That two-dollars resting on the corner of a wooden table in a small room in a non-descript building along an inconsequential road, served as a kind of monument to the power of the living Jesus to change hearts.

What is the secret of these orphaned coins? Those in Christ have forsaken perishable wreaths for an imperishable crown.[1] They recognize that this life is not about temporal gain but about preparing to stand before the great tribunal of Christ with the hope of hearing,[2] "Well done, good and faithful servant."[3] There is, for faithful Christians, a consuming focus on the final judgment event, one in which those in Christ will be judged righteous with regard to sin, but tested with fire concerning their works.[4] The Christian recognizes that the kingdom of God is not to be measured in terrestrial terms, that the Christian life is not about building a crumbling Christendom, but about preparing for a cataclysmic encounter with the living God. May this book prepare you, dear reader, for that encounter both now and in eternity.

---

[1] 1 Corinthians 9:25
[2] Preston Graham, Christ Presbyterian Church, New Haven, Connecticut
[3] Matthew 25:21
[4] 1 Corinthians 3:13-15

From Fig Leaf to Olive Branch to Laurel Wreath

- 1 -

MEMORIES PRESERVED IN AMBER:
Adopting God's Retrospective

The Lewis Terman Study on Intelligence and Success

In 1921 Lewis Terman (1877–1956), an educational psychologist at Stanford University, undertook a landmark study. He endeavored to investigate elementary students with the absolute highest IQs. He tested 250,000 students born between 1903 and 1917 selecting the 1,470 most intelligent. These students had IQs over 140, representing the top 0.5% of intelligence. Terman believed that "nothing about an individual is as important as IQ, except possibly his morals."

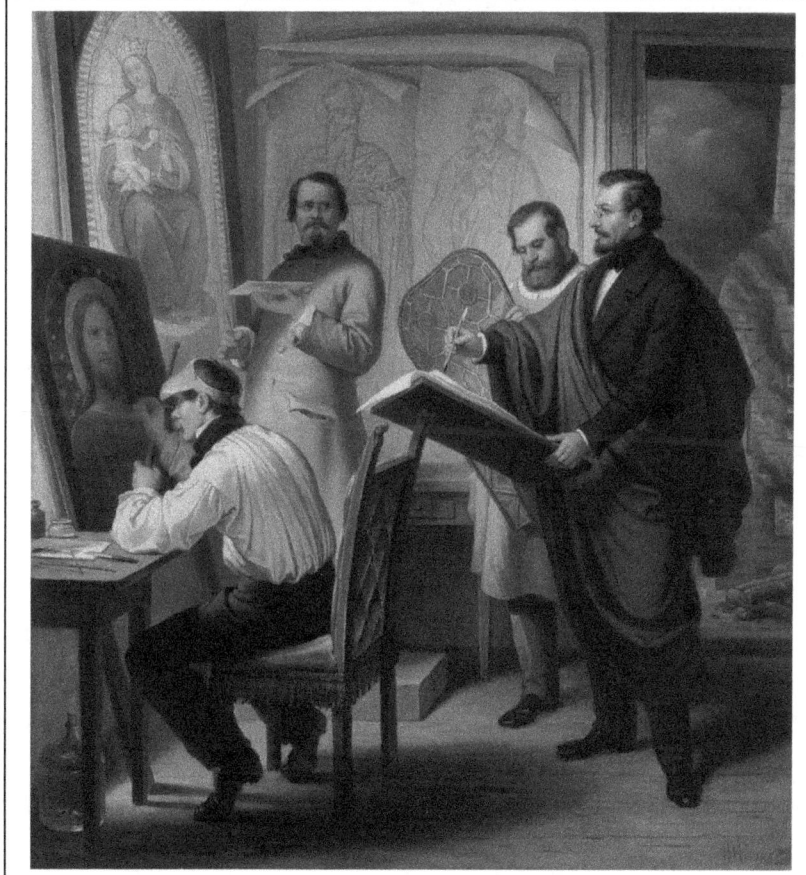

Painting School in Munich
Wilhelm Von Kaulbach, 1853

Terman spent the rest of his life studying these students in the most minute detail, tracking, measuring, and evaluating every aspect of their lives. Throughout high school this group won a preponderance of scholastic awards and scholarships. Terman asked literary critics to compare the group's best writers to renowned authors in their early years. The comparisons revealed strikingly similar ability.

In Terman's estimation, this group was poised for greatness; they would one day achieve "heroic stature." He expected that among these 1,470 subjects several would receive Nobel prizes, become national political leaders, and head major corporations.

Throughout their lives, Terman painstakingly noted the group's career choices, educational achievements, illnesses, job promotions, and marriages. However, after thirty years Terman realized that he had made a grave error. While his subjects sometimes did achieve a measure of greatness, they did not do so in numbers out of proportion with their larger socio-economic group. For example, a few of his subjects published best-selling books, founded successful companies, or became superior court judges. While most of the subjects earned a good income, as a group they earned just marginally above average. None became nationally known figures. In fact, the vast majority pursued ordinary careers, and a significant number were termed "failures" by Terman.

> "I have seen something else under the sun: The race is not to the swift or the battle to the strong, nor does food come to the wise or wealth to the brilliant or favor to the learned; but time and chance happen to them all." (Ecclesiastes 9:11)

Terman adjudged the top 20% of his subjects successes: prestigious professionals with graduate degrees. The next 60% he considered satisfactory achievers: middle-managers, teachers, etc. The lowest 10% he considered failures: clerks, postal workers, etc.

In fact, this once elite group posted almost identical achievements to a randomly selected group from the same socio-economic background. Terman, devastated by his findings, concluded in his *Genetic Studies of Genius* (1959), "We have seen that intellect and achievement are far from perfectly correlated."

So what hindered this group in the top 0.5% of intelligence? Most lacked "practical intelligence": the ability to rightly decide what to say to whom, when to say it, and how to influence others. This is tacit knowledge – know-how that is not gained propositionally (from a book). Analytical intelligence and practical intelligence are "orthogonal." This means that one has no bearing on the other. It is rare to find a person with both abundant analytical and practical intelligence; but those with both achieve tremendous success.

Where does practical intelligence come from? Terman determined that his group's successes and failures were attributable to family background. The successes came from homes in which parents promoted learning as a lifestyle. The failures tended to regress back toward a family proclivity for failure. They therefore lacked models for success. Certain families seem to spur on success and feed it, while others seem to subtly undermine it.

> "The more sand has escaped through the hourglass of our life, the clearer we should see through it." (Jean Paul Sartre)

There is, however, another crucial piece of data. Terman found that the successes were usually born between 1912 and 1917 and the failures between 1903 and 1911. The successes finished college and entered the job market after the worst of the Great Depression, while the earlier group was likely entering the job market at or before the Great Depression. Additionally, when World War II began the older group was likely disrupted from its career path, while the younger group was still young enough to recover after the war ended.

> "For a man to achieve all that is demanded of him he must regard himself as greater than he is." (Johann Wolfgang von Geothe)

In what way is the Lewis Terman study blind to a deeper reality presented in the Bible? In what way does it miss a truth that can never be discerned through unaided human reason but requires the regenerated gaze offered in the Bible? The Terman study misses crucial components such as belief, worldview, moral decisions, a proclivity for certain "worship" addictions, and the subjects' response to pressures applied by associates, spouses, and even rivals.

In the Concert Café
Edouard Manet, 1878

This is a suitable introduction to the issue of personal history. In studying gifted children Terman focused his analysis on intellectual and other circumstantial factors. However, he failed to see a guiding belief system at play either leading one to the proper use of his gifts or else causing those gifts to lay fallow. Additionally, Terman employed a worldly definition of success, equating it with discernable wealth, prestige, and what one might term "macro-achievement." How does God define success? Is God's focus upon macro-achievement or upon a sanctified heart which learns to love and obey him regardless of circumstance? What if success and failure actually have nothing to do with Terman's definition, but rather with humble obedience to God and faithful commitment to family and other responsibilities? What if success is not an outward reality but an inward condition redefined as faith in, and submission to, Jesus Christ?

The Heart's Interpretive Quest

> "And what happens to your two sons, Hophni and Phinehas, will be a sign to you – they will both die on the same day…" (1 Samuel 2:34)

On the morning of March 5, 2002, in the tiny Finnish town of Raahe, two elderly twin brothers rode their bicycles, as they usually did.[1] At 9:30 a.m. one brother was struck and killed by a truck. About two hours later, one mile away on the same highway, the other brother was struck and killed by a different truck.

The deaths were explained in the following ways:

1. A policeman investigating the accident said, "It is hard to believe this could happen just by chance." He looked for a cause, thinking that the second death was really a suicide. But the investigation uncovered that the second man was completely unaware that his brother had died earlier that morning.

2. A nephew said that the deaths were "destiny." Throughout their lives the brothers shared similar experiences such as becoming ill at the same time or feeling pain at the same time. It made sense that they should die at the same time.

3. The men's sister claimed that the chance of this happening purely by accident was impossible. She insisted that there was a plot to murder them, and wondered if terrorists might be involved.

4. A cousin asserted that the brothers died as "martyrs" sending a wakeup call for improved driver safety. These senseless deaths demonstrated how careless Finish drivers had become. The cousin called on the government to enact driver education reforms so that no more innocent lives would be lost.

The fact that the deceased were *brothers* has nothing to do with the events. Two elderly men riding bicycles on a busy highway in a snowstorm could easily be killed in separate traffic accidents.

> In a world of seven billion people events which seem like one-in-a-billion might

---
[1] *The New York Times*, March 7, 2002

> happen seven times a day.

Often where there is limited or confusing information, the mind inserts data that makes sense of the events, giving order to one's world. The psyche is uncomfortable with the unexplainable. However, in many instances an explanation is beyond the limits of human reason. There are some mysteries which cannot be resolved.

> Optical illusions are a good example of interpreting facts as one wants to see them. When viewing a confusing picture, the brain naturally inserts facts into the picture. This is a way to resolve mystery.

The Role of Memory

Historical facts are never neutral; they are always theory-laden. Consider that the Union labeled the Civil War, "The Great War of the Rebellion," while the Confederacy called it, "The War of Northern Aggression." There is something in this labeling process which speaks to the human condition. Mankind characterizes situations and events in drastically different terms than God does. While God might label the human experience "The Great War of the Rebellion," humanity casts it as "The War of Cosmic Aggression." Thus sinners, while blind to their nascent rebellion, display eagle-eyed acuity with regard to God's supposed aggressive focus on changing the heart.

The human nouthetic constitution is composed of three components: memory, reason, and will.[2] Man has a memory to remember what God has done, reason to meditate on and interpret God's work in light of his Word, and a will to commit himself to serving and obeying God. These three aspects are intrinsic to personhood. However, memory is easily distorted, and the reason is damaged on account of sin. The will, while wrongly directed, stands apart as inviolable. This means that one's will cannot be taken over through satanic forces without one's consent.

Memory, on account of sin, is routinely interpreted from a man-centered perspective. The reason is warped into irrational conclusions, and the will pledges itself to false gods. Thus, memory, reason, and will, while created to be pillars of glorious image-bearing, lay damaged and desolate as mankind pursues his rebellious cause.

> Israel principally defined itself in light of three historical events: the Exodus, the Exile, and the rebuilding of the Temple. Likewise, each person tends to define himself, tends to orient his sin around, principal life events. In the context of counseling, those events will likely emerge time and again as a kind of Rosetta Stone offering indications of how the heart has constituted itself. While the particulars of

---

[2] Clair Davis, "Doctrine of Man" class, Westminster Theological Seminary, Philadelphia, Pennsylvania

> those events are not always important, the heart's response to them is.

The Wolf and Fox Hunt, Peter Paul Rubens, c. 1621

Concerning mankind's memory, there is a tendency in the sinner to apply a retrospective slant to his current situation in life. This causes him to see his current plight as the inexorable outworking of his past experiences. A retrospective pressure surfaces time and again in Scripture as God's people continually view their present situation from the perspective of a supposed past in which God failed. Acts 7:39 summarizes this, "But our ancestors refused to obey him. Instead, they rejected him and in their hearts turned back to Egypt."

> "We live and learn, but not the wiser grow." (John Pomfret)

This retrospective slant grows out of a victim mentality and a grievance lifestyle which, while endemic to the sin nature, particularly permeates modern thinking. Today, most (not just the overtly disenfranchised) perceive that they have in some way been unfairly treated. The sinner, whatever his walk of life, sees himself as outside of God's goodness and grace, and therefore an aggrieved party vying against the universe's resident imperialist. This gives rise to a reflexive victim-mentality with regard to besetting sin (whatever the nature of that sin).

> It is fascinating that olfactory-based memories are the most powerful. Just a slight smell can conjure a rush of memory, whether positive or negative. The heart is desperate to live in the past, and to use that past as a makeshift weapon against a God

> who has not delivered that for which the sinner believes himself entitled.

Thus, the counselor who permits the counselee to indulge a reckless revisit of past events runs the risk of dangling the temptation and opportunity to blame-shift. On the other hand, a biblically-driven look at a counselee's past can offer profound benefit for recognizing the covenants into which the counselee has entered, whether idolatrous or God-centered. The counselor must therefore walk a fine line when exploring a counselee's history. He should engage that history only to the extent that it helps him see the counselee's covenant commitments, but should not engage it to the extent that it prompts a tacit invitation to blame-shifting.

> It is clear that mankind's sin problem does not arise from his circumstances, his sufferings, or his experiences in a fallen world. His sin arises from what he brings to those experiences. The emotional scars that one carries are not so much the result of what has happened, but rather are the result of how he has responded to what has happened.[3]

Many television episodes are filmed on Hollywood backlots with buildings made to look like a certain target location. The director simply inserts a few seconds of aerial footage from the intended destination and the viewer assumes that all subsequent action takes place there.[4] This sleight of hand uses the deception of association contrived through spliced images. In a similar fashion, the psyche splices together memory shards to fashion a believable narrative which exonerates present sin. Just as a director inserts aerial footage to craft a setting, and then connects that image with subsequent action, so too, the psyche actively works to generate a "setting" in which sin is rationalized.

> Be assured there is a skeleton in everyone's closet,[5] but it is coiffed and dressed in the event someone opens the door.

It is crucial to recognize that no historical gaze is ever neutral, but is always overlaid with a particular set of interpretive lenses. *Per se*, a retrospective slant (the tendency to look back on one's personal past) is not sinful but serves as a convenient means for temptation. A historical purview when not sanctified by Christ, more often than not, easily becomes a longing lustful gaze. The Christian, however, recognizes that his past was guided by a force majeure, God himself, and is not the whimsical play of a capricious universe. The Christian, therefore, need not dissect the often confusing minutiae, but rather merely praise the architect of the grand plan.

---

[3] David Powlison, Westminster Theological Seminary, Philadelphia, Pennsylvania
[4] This observation from Tobias Iaconis, Hollywood screenwriter
[5] This concept from an unknown source

> "History does not repeat itself, but sometimes it rhymes." (Mark Twain)

While God calls his people to see their past as the work of his mighty hand leading them to salvation, the Bible always draws this past into a present focus on daily obedience, the joy of sanctification, and the comfort of ultimate deliverance. One's personal history serves as a loose point of reference, a means of faithful remembrance and, when rightly interpreted, a form of stability and grounding. However, the Christian recognizes the inherent pitfalls in a long gaze at the past, one which is prone to dally on grievance, to sketch out perceived wrongs or, conversely, to cast a shadow on one's present situation. Ecclesiastes 7:10 even warns against dwelling on the past, "Do not say, 'Why were the old days better than these?' For it is not wise to ask such questions." The Bible understands the heart's affinity for revisionist history, its crouching readiness to warp and warble history for past, or present, self-serving purpose.

> Why is a car's engine compartment open underneath? Noxious fumes are produced by heating an engine's rubber components and liquids. These gases are heavier than air so they fall; the engine compartment is open at the bottom to permit these gases to escape. In the same way, the human psyche is constructed to allow it to forget that which is destructive, carcinogenic, to its existence. Thus, God, in his mercy, causes "falling noxious gases" of memory to flush themselves from the psyche.

The Memory Palace

The memory palace was a mental tool developed by the ancient Greeks to help students remember their teachers' lectures. It involved inserting key facts into imaginary rooms. The rooms' objects were carefully placed to help students recall particular details during an exam. The beauty of this system is that it allows one to "travel" from room to room in any order so that facts can be recalled more quickly. (Other memory systems, for instance using mnemonics, are linear, and therefore facts must be recalled in an exact order.) The memory palace offers a metaphor for the way in which the sinner rummages through the past. He moves from memory to memory with great alacrity when those memories uphold his personal grievance narrative. However, with regard to his guilt before God, the sinner does not display the same facility with memory.

Ecclesiastes 7:10 states, "Do not say, 'Why were the old days better than these?' For it is not wise to ask such questions." Often reminiscing about the "good old days" is cloaked hatred of God, a form of blame-shifting, a distraction from the pangs of a guilty conscience, or even a disguised love of money. This is a longing for a time of better health, freedom from the mounting guilt in one's daily sin, or better economic prospects. This type of reminiscing serves as a psychic anodyne through subtly questioning God's goodness and sovereignty over history. The assumption is that God is not good, that he is withholding gifts, that he is not guiding one "in paths of righteousness for his name's sake,"[6] that his path leads to death.

Crossing of the Red Sea, Nicolas Poussin, 1634

In Numbers 11:5, 6, the people complained that they had no meat. They nurtured fond memories of plentiful Egyptian fish, having lost their appetite for God's daily provision of manna. Again, in Numbers 16:13, the rebellious Levites called Egypt a "land flowing with milk and honey," forgetting the trials and tragedy of Egypt. What the people choose to remember was driven by their sinful desire. Memories were held captive by what they worshipped. They remembered that which accorded with their polarized historical narrative, and readily forgot that which such a narrative filtered out. This selective memory was forged in their deepest beliefs about God and themselves.

> "Nostalgia is a seductive liar." (George Ball)

The Israelites soon forgot the tyrannical persecution and oppressive slavery under the Egyptians. They revised their history to highlight the enjoyment of free food, while overlooking that their food was free because as slaves they likely had no money. They reinterpreted their past to be a situation of receiving gratuitous and bountiful gifts, when in reality they were subject to debilitating forced labor. Regrettably, they

---

[6] Psalm 23:3

would rather return to a position of slavery, to a land of oppression, than enjoy God's daily provision in the desert.

Martin Luther (1483-1546) said, "The greatest obstacle to faith is experience." By this he meant that one's experience, when interpreted through a man-centered set of lenses, does not look like a God-directed reality. Faith is making a conscious decision to trust and follow God, even when one's experience communicates that there is no future in this.

The Israelite's selective memory serves as a window into sin. Sinful man routinely reinterprets his past to read that God is not good, and that the world, the flesh, and the devil are in fact good. Mankind desires to return to his slavery to sin under the misguided notion that sin is a place of fulfillment, satisfaction, and joy. Yet, sinners soon forget the piercing pain, and staggering loss, that sin brings. Without the Bible, each man is nothing more than a prisoner of his own experiences.

> "When times are good, be happy; but when times are bad, consider: God has made the one as well as the other. Therefore, a man cannot discover anything about his future." (Ecclesiastes 7:14)

How does the counselee routinely interpret his past? The first observation is that his memory is highly-selective. The counselee readily filters out the past curse of sin, while inserting blessing where none really existed. The sinner attempts to justify his past sin as somehow leading to an abundant life, an abundance stripped from him by cruel circumstance. He likewise overlooks God's deliverance, goodness, and provision, reinterpreting God as a shadowy figure bent on the sinner's destruction. The memory is deeply rutted with rehearsed sin patterns.

> Voltaire (1694–1778) wrote, "History is nothing more than a tableau of crimes and misfortunes." This statement takes on profound meaning when one considers that the sinner sees God himself as the "criminal," as well as the author of man's misfortunes. The sinner keeps this "tableau of crimes and misfortunes" up-to-date.

Universal Truths about the Human Existence

On July 16, 1945, famed physicist Enrico Fermi (1901-1954) witnessed the Trinity test, the detonation of an atomic bomb in the sands of New Mexico. Located several miles from the blast sight and lacking precision detection equipment, Fermi devised what has come to be known as the "Fermi Method" for estimating a bomb's strength. As the bomb was detonated, it created a stiff breeze. Thinking quickly, Fermi tore a page from his notebook and ripped it into tiny pieces. He then dropped those pieces in the breeze, estimating the distance they traveled until they settled to the ground. From that Fermi calculated the speed of the wind and the force of the blast. His calculation was stunningly accurate.

Just as Fermi successfully estimated the force of an atomic blast from a distance, so too, the wise counselor employs "estimating" devices for uncovering the machinations of the psyche. Fermi did not need to be present at the sight, and he did not need precise equipment. So too, the counselor, knows certain truths about the psyche, based solely on God's Word, without having lived another's life. The counselor can estimate the force of the heart's "breeze" and offer sound and impactful counsel without having to enter the "blast site" (the intricacies of prior life events).

Universal truths about every human existence:

1. Every person has suffered in the face of evil.

2. Every person has been both the helpless victim of, and the perpetrator of, evil to some extent.

3. Every person feels something was taken from him in life.

4. Every person feels that something about life is fundamentally unfair, and that he must overcome some disadvantage which exists through no fault of his own.

5. Every person feels that others have an easier time in life.

6. Every person feels that others cannot possibly understand what has happened to him, or how he feels.

There are various ways in which these truths play out:

1. Some may show a morbid obsession with their past. This can lead to paralyzing scrutiny of past events, so that one cannot focus on present imperatives. Those consumed with their personal history tend to be angry and harbor a trenchant sense of unmet needs.

2. Related to the morbid obsession with one's past, is a plan to project upon one's history one's *current* needs, fears, desires, and emotions, so that history is recast to serve a present perceived need.

3. As postmodern people are increasingly caught up in the here-and-now, a proper view of one's history is easily discarded under the tyranny of the poignant present. The exhilaration of pressing pursuit may render the historical a distant abstraction.

It is hard for history to compete with that which is front and center, and so it is forgotten. Thus, any look upon one's history (including one's sin) can easily be swept up in an incessant chasing.

Spring Morning in a Han Palace, Qiu Ying, 1550

The common thread throughout this discussion of personal history is that in each scenario one seeks to place himself in the position of God, to either reinterpret his past with towering judgment for perceived wrongs sustained, or else to neglect his past so as to overlook his guilt. Thus, obsessive focus on one's past is usually to condemn God and others, while the neglect of one's past is to eschew condemnation from God and others.

> The one who is not present is always considered the guilty party in any matter. Therefore, it is vital that a counselee not to be permitted to disparage one who is absent from a discussion. This is a form of character assassination that both poisons the hearers, and the one speaking the disparaging words.

Vorlage: The Text Behind Personal History

Giacomo Puccini's (1858-1924) opera *Turandot* (1924) is set outside the imperial palace in Peking. A mandarin reads an edict to the crowd: any prince seeking to marry the princess Turandot must answer three riddles. If he fails, he will die. The most recent failed suitor, the Prince of Persia, is to be executed at the moon's rising. The rabble, having previously cried for blood, now greets the rising moon with a fearful silence. As the Prince of Persia is led to his execution, the crowd calls upon the princess to spare him. Turandot appears, and with a contemptuous gesture orders the execution to proceed.

Turandot, although of stunning beauty, is a woman at war with men. She delights in gaining the upper-hand over her suitors, seeming to relish their failure and eventual death. Puccini presents a cruel cold world devoid of love.

Meanwhile, inside the palace, Turandot's three advisors, Ping, Pang, and Pong, lament her bloody reign, praying that love would conquer her heart and restore peace. Turandot enters and describes how her ancestor, Princess Lou-Ling, was abducted and murdered by a conquering prince. In revenge, Turandot has turned against men, determined that none shall ever possess her.

This story reveals something of the way the human heart operates. As with Turandot, the heart misplaces evil upon incidental qualities (appearance, gender, national identity, etc.) refusing to recognize the desperately sinful heart within. Thus, with regard to man, the nexus of evil is not in the external but in the internal, not in the incidental but in the worship headquarters. Sinners often refuse to recognize this because it is easier to designate superficial qualities as the enemy, rather than to recognize one's own errant worship culminating in evil.

In textual criticism a vorlage is a text (or group of texts) that seems to directly influence, or give rise to, another text. For example, the author of First and Second Chronicles likely used Samuel and Kings as a vorlage. In counseling, one might think of a vorlage as the elemental "text" or proto-story out of which a counselee derives his own text or story. A vorlage refers to a historical pre-text giving rise to particular heart worship, the idea that a deliberately cultivated personal history lies behind current worship issues. The challenge is in uncovering this source so that the heart's desires come into clear focus.

Incidentally, the term vorlage could apply to both the individual or to society as a whole. For example, in 1938, "War of the Worlds," a radio program hosted by Orson Welles (1915-1985), was broadcast throughout the United States. The program, a fictional account of an alien invasion, was so realistic that many thought it was truly happening. Some panicked and jumped in their cars to escape an impending attack. Why was the public so fearful of an invasion? In 1938, Adolf Hitler (1889–1945) was gaining power through annexing Eastern Europe. To many Americans it seemed that war was imminent. This latent fear drove some to irrational behavior. The point is that a certain vorlage stood behind the public's extreme reaction to the "War of the Worlds" radio show. How does the wise counselor read society's "text" so as to see its patterns replicated in individual counselees?

Consider Deuteronomy 22:9-11 which commands not to intermingle different seeds, animals, or fabrics. This was a command to keep separate that which is separate in God's ordering of creation. Therefore, wisdom is joining that which God has joined and keeping separate that which God has separated.[7] In terms of one's history, wisdom is focusing on one's history as God sees it, assigning to it the grace and goodness of a sovereign God. Thus, infusing God's truth into one's own personal story, rendering one's story submissive to that truth, produces the proper vorlage for current life events. Conversely, one is careful not to formulate destructive associations which separate God from one's history, an improper vorlage.

Several years ago I spoke to an older gentleman who had just had surgery to remove a cancerous skin growth. He stated that the cancer likely developed when, as a child, he *once* sustained a severe sunburn. That sunburn induced the cancer which lay dormant for decades, until it finally showed itself in life's twilight (or so the theory goes). Since that time I have heard others recount similar stories, such as a senior whose bad back is attributed to heavy lifting as a teenager, the damage again remaining dormant for decades. This is similar to blaming Catherine O'Leary's cow for knocking over the lantern that supposedly ignited the Great Chicago Conflagration of 1871. In other words, I strongly suspect that these alleged precursors are highly-speculative, that no causality can actually be established in these matters.

I wonder if this notion of some distant event which lies dormant only to assail the victim later in life is a vestige of a collective Freudian consciousness in which one must search for some early antecedent to one's current affliction. It is as if a kind of Freudian ethos wends its way into otherwise sound medical practice. The point is that people are haunted by this sense that some latent childhood mistake now visits itself upon them, finally exacting a price. The danger is that people search their past in order to pinpoint that moment in time in which they made one misstep which now haunts them.

I would wager that there is no cancerous precursor, no latent back ailment, nothing which lies in wait to visit judgment. This search for past events may be a misplaced guilt over prior transgressions, the heart's outworking of culpability before a holy God in which one feels he must finally pay for an antecedent offense. (In this sense, something far more profound than the Freudian is operative in the heart.)

The Wernicke's Syndrome of the Worshipping Heart

I recently read an article in which archeologists, excavating an ancient site, discovered a Roman coin dating to 135 B.C. The author confidently declared (based on this and other evidence) that the site could reasonably be dated to about that date. While on the

---
[7] Cornelius Plantinga Jr., *Not the Way It's Supposed to Be: A Breviary of Sin* (New York: William B. Eerdmans Publishing Co., 1996)

surface this seems logical, it conceals a fallacy. Just because a coin dating to 135 B.C. was located does not mean it has been there since 135 B.C. For example, I have a coin collection with one example dating to 1880. The house in which it is stored was built in 1972. The point is that collectors can easily setup an anachronism which misleads archeologists.

A Performance of the Flute Player in the Roman House of Prince Napoleon III
Gustave Clarence Rodolphe Boulanger, 1861

Closely related to the issue of vorlage is Wernicke's syndrome, a condition in which one's thinking is locked in a particular date in history so that he is unable to live past that date. The obsession with living in a particular moment in history might seem to resolve some nagging failure, loss, or rejection. However, this obsession is based in a refusal to focus on the sinful intentions in the middle of one's history, and as such, is marked by a refusal to repent.

Wernicke's syndrome, in a sense, serves as an indicator of the way in which psychology as a whole views the human experience. There was a particular historical event (or events) which shapes, determines, prescribes, and holds captive the psyche. (In fact, Victor Hugo (1802–1885) echoed this sentiment when he wrote, "To reform a man, you must begin with his grandmother.") The Bible, instead, views personal history as incidental to the weightier issue of discerning the machinations of the heart.

Consider Exodus 14:10-14 which states,

> As Pharaoh approached, the Israelites looked up, and there were the Egyptians, marching after them. The Israelites were terrified and cried out to the LORD. They said to Moses, 'Was it because there were no graves in Egypt that you brought us to the desert to die? What have you done to us by

bringing us out of Egypt? Didn't we say to you in Egypt, 'Leave us alone; let us serve the Egyptians'? It would have been better for us to serve the Egyptians than to die in the desert!'

Moses answered the people, 'Do not be afraid. Stand firm and you will see the deliverance the Lord will bring you today. The Egyptians you see today you will never see again. The Lord will fight for you; you need only to be still.'

Terrified, Israel charged both Moses and God with wrong-doing. They interpreted their situation through the prism of the fear of man. This was a seminal episode in Israel's history because it was this moment of apostasy which defined them for the next forty years (and beyond). They would, time and again, fall back into this response of terror and suspicion of God, like a reflexive formulation to nearly every encountered trial. Once that formulation, arising from a heart of worship, gained a strangle hold, the people seemed irretrievably in its grip.

However, while the historical event offers some perspective, it is not the focus of the account. In other words, it was not the event (Pharaoh's approach) which gave rise to Israel's apostasy. The apostasy predated the event and merely surfaced given the right prodding. Thus, the Bible's focus is on the idolatry in the middle of the history, the lust of the flesh afforded an opportunity to display itself.

Remember, collectors can easily setup an anachronism which misleads archeologists. Let's draw an analogy between the discovery of the ancient Roman coin and the heart. The sinful heart is ruled by "pliable idolatry" so as to use historical events to serve its worship.[8] Those events are therefore something of an anachronism transported through time to serve a present agenda. Thus, the biblical counselor never confidently holds up an "artifact" as the key to deciphering the heart. Instead, he sees the "collector mentality" in all sinners, one which delights in misleading would-be excavators of the heart's intentions.

> A paleo-anthropologist searches for fossils and relics. Fossil remains are notoriously difficult to date and study because they are so often uncovered as little more than calcified fragments. A paleo-anthropologist may then reconstruct those fragments as he desires them to appear. However, that reconstruction may or may not reflect the being's actual structure. Drawing an analogy to counseling, the counselor does not seek to become a "paleo-anthropologist" of the soul. He recognizes that the fossil remains of prior events are often little more than calcified fragments. Those fragments can be reconstructed in a host of ways, none of which may fit with the reality in the counselee's heart.

---

[8] The term "pliable idolatry" from Edward Welch, Westminster Theological Seminary, Philadelphia, Pennsylvania

Consider one who is afraid to speak in front of others. When he stands to speak he feels nervous, cannot think, and is consumed by self-doubt. The psychologist might exert great energy and time delving into past events to uncover the source of the fear.

Faulty counsel would offer the following advice:

1. Simply avoid speaking in front of others. (Tell others that this is not one's gift and therefore others should speak.)

2. Redact one's personal history so as to recast past failures; find some past (for example, a cultural arrogance) or current means (for example, superior intellect) to feel self-empowered. (For example, transform fear into a more effective emotion, such as a subtle posture of anger.)

3. Use some manageable method for thinking or acting. (Pretend that the audience is somehow humiliated before oneself.)

4. Shut out the audience so as to remove any perceived threat (such as to close one's eyes in front of an audience).

The loving counselor would, of course, seek to teach another how to be an effective speaker; that is often needed practical counsel. But the counselor never stops there. He delves into uncharted waters of the heart to expose the evils which lurk in their depths, and to bring those depths to glorious light. The counselor recognizes that each of the pragmatic solutions listed above, while often well-intentioned, is Satan's handicraft. Each misses the opportunity to deal with the true problem, dysfunctional worship, raising up people as gods, and refusing to allow the true God to be ruler of one's heart. The right counsel does not find a manageable solution. It exposes the heart's lusts. It zeroes in on the heart's perfectionism, pride, fear of men, and ungodly cravings. The biblical counselor, thus, focuses the lion's share of his time on the desires of the heart, not just in the context of public speaking, but with a full-orbed approach to life.

Hagiography: Contrived and Confabulated Sainthood

Hagiography is the tendency to aggrandize saints of the past so as to invest them with mythic capabilities. Each sinner has a tendency toward hagiography with regard to himself, to exonerate past sins, to see past temptations as an indictment of God himself, and to invest himself with a certain dormant greatness waiting for release.

"Write injuries in dust and benefits in marble."

A wealthy Christian businessman once spoke about his childhood, a time in which his impecunious father was routinely humiliated among neighbors. This businessman saw his father's humiliation as validation for his own present obsession with wealth and success. This man felt justified in lavishing his family with luxuries in order to ensure that such an evil was never visited upon them. This man rightly understands that evil exists in the world, and that it is often attended by horrendous degradation. However, his answer was to find a vanguard in money, to circumvent future attacks with wealth as a supposed shield. One could think of the father's life story as a kind of vorlage, a kind of preamble or prologue, crouching behind his son's life story. The hagiography comes in the father's expanded suffering to the point of becoming a martyr to a cruel world which took advantage of a condition that was beyond his control.

> "Half the work that is done in the world is to make things appear as they are not." (Elias Root Beadle)

The Triumph of Saint Augustine
Claudio Coello, 1664

People in emotional pain have an axe to grind. This means that when people are aggrieved, facing a profound loss, or burdened with their own failing or sin, they are quick to raise the failings of others. When speaking with those who are eager to point out, and even luxuriate in, other's errors, failings, and sin, be aware that their own errors, failings, and sin are at the forefront of their minds. Their own guilt, emotional pain, sense of loss, and search for a succor, find a ready outlet in their rehearsal of other's shortcomings. The stage is set for self-directed hagiography, to aggrandize oneself at the expense of others. Sinners readily engage in a kind of makeshift hagiography with each passing moment.

Often those actively seeking counseling come highly-prepared to rehearse others' sins. They confess others' transgressions as the prelude to self-exoneration. The counselor takes countermeasures for the simple reason that the counselee's strategy conceals a rouse. Rehearsing other's wrongs never led to a repentant and renewed heart. On the contrary, it leads to a more recalcitrant heart, one more deeply invested in its idolatry and more hostile toward God.

> Consider the Greek tragedy *Oedipus Rex* in which Oedipus encountered on his path of escape the very situation he sought to avoid, murdering his father in a fit of rage.[9] Often that which one seeks most to avoid is the very thing one brings down upon himself. This is often the plight of the unregenerate heart. The sinner becomes like that which he worships, and that which he worships may be either what he desires or what he seeks to avoid. Thus, worship is either a direct pursuit, or a pursuit bearing Rorschach characteristics.

Personal Revisionist History

The Bible contains synoptic histories such as Samuel-Kings/Chronicles and Matthew, Mark, and Luke. God teaches something about the nature of history through these presentations. The reader's goal should not be to harmonize various accounts but to understand the authors' intents and tendents, to recognize the distinctive theology which underlies each. Thus, each book employs its own theological slant, including and excluding, so as to advance its distinctive theology.

The Old Testament's presentation of redemptive history is:

1. Selective
2. Emphasized
3. Carefully arranged
4. Theologically interpreted
5. Prone to summary[10]

For example, the post-exilic book of Chronicles offers a competing view of historical events in contrast to the more traditional pre-exilic Samuel-Kings accounts. In this way, Chronicles is more "midrashic," presenting a creative embellishment of events (while in no way compromising its inclusion in the canon as inspired and inerrant). The Kings-Chronicles tension reflects a deeper tendency within the Old Testament toward an unresolved, and often elusive, interpretation of events. This textual tension is viewed as beneficial for theological reflection and growth through interaction with the text.[11]

---

[9] Sophocles, *Oedipus Rex* (5th Century B.C.)
[10] Alan Groves (1952–2007), "Old Testament History and Theology" class, Westminster Theological Seminary, Philadelphia, Pennsylvania
[11] Tremper Longman, "Old Testament History and Theology" class, Westminster Theological Seminary, Philadelphia, Pennsylvania

Likewise, mankind's presentation of his own personal history follows a similar pattern: selective, emphasized, carefully arranged, theologically interpreted, and prone to summary. Just as each Bible author displayed a particular tendent, a certain theological slant on history, so too, each person displays a selected tendent. The major difference being that the Bible's historical presentation is inerrant (even in its synoptic approach), while personal historical presentation is subject to being shaped and shaded by sin.

> "I wouldn't have seen it if I hadn't believed it." (Marshall McLuhan)

Consider "The Parable of the Rich Man and Lazarus," in Luke 16:19-31, which reads,

> There was a rich man who was dressed in purple and fine linen and lived in luxury every day. At his gate was laid a beggar named Lazarus, covered with sores and longing to eat what fell from the rich man's table. Even the dogs came and licked his sores.
>
> The time came when the beggar died and the angels carried him to Abraham's side. The rich man also died and was buried. In Hades, where he was in torment, he looked up and saw Abraham far away, with Lazarus by his side. So he called to him, 'Father Abraham, have pity on me and send Lazarus to dip the tip of his finger in water and cool my tongue, because I am in agony in this fire.'
>
> But Abraham replied, 'Son, remember that in your lifetime you received your good things, while Lazarus received bad things, but now he is comforted here and you are in agony. And besides all this, between us and you a great chasm has been set in place, so that those who want to go from here to you cannot, nor can anyone cross over from there to us.'
>
> He answered, 'Then I beg you, father, send Lazarus to my family, for I have five brothers. Let him warn them, so that they will not also come to this place of torment.'
>
> Abraham replied, 'They have Moses and the Prophets; let them listen to them.'
>
> 'No, father Abraham,' he said, 'but if someone from the dead goes to them, they will repent.'
>
> He said to him, '*If they do not listen to Moses and the Prophets, they will not*

be convinced even if someone rises from the dead.'

In light of this parable, consider the well-known adage, "Those who do not study history are doomed to repeat it."[12] This parable directly refutes such a notion with the admonition, "'If they do not listen to Moses and the Prophets, they will not be convinced even if someone rises from the dead.'" Those who study history (study Moses and the Prophets) time and again repeat their error because they study with faulty lenses, under flawed assumptions, and for fallacious purposes. Thus, avoiding a repeat of history has never been a matter of merely studying it, but a matter of repenting of the idolatrous heart that gave rise to it. In the same way, the wise counselor is careful to direct others to not simply investigate their personal history, but to repent of the erroneous worship at the core of life events. In other words, merely studying history is meaningless unless it results in heart change.

With this in mind, how does one reinterpret…:

1. One's difficulties, losses, and suffering as leading him to faith in God?

2. One's pleasant, happy, and enjoyable experiences as leading him to "taste" God's goodness?

3. The nature of past relationships?

4. The causes of one's current sin patterns?

For the seven of the past eight years I have had no medical insurance. Being without medical insurance suddenly makes one hyper-vigilant to potential health risks. The opportunity to take a ride on a motorbike, to go spelunking, or to pet a stray dog induces reflexive caution in light of potentially expensive injuries. Thus, the extent of one's medical coverage makes one more or less willing to take health risks.

An analogy could be drawn with interpreting one's past. I find that people are as cavalier and reckless in interpreting their past as they feel they can get away with. Thus, if a counselor seems permissive and inviting vis-à-vis recounting the past, the counselee will soon flaunt his personal history in vivid detail, lavishing attention on perceived wrongs sustained and loses endured. On the other hand, a less indulgent counselor will likely not receive such an ostentatious spread.

Revisionist historians are not concerned with what *actually* happened; they focus on what people *thought* happened. It is the story that is important, not the truth, since truth does not exist to this type of historian. For instance, a Marxist view of history

---

[12] Edmund Burke (1729-1797)

would denounce the historical study of presidents (or those in power) as just bourgeoisie propaganda. For the Marxist, history must highlight the plight of the proletariat and draw all discussion of power into the service of the common man. This offers a truncated, and highly-propagandized, form of history for certain socio-political ends.

It is crucial to understand that, like revisionist history, personal history is never a neutral stream of facts. Therefore, each sinner engages in a daily form of propagandized history as he projects a story onto his personal past. Personal history is always interpreted, so that one looks at his past either with eyes of faith in recognition of God's perfect purposes, or else with eyes wired to a grumbling heart.[13] Put another way, a man-centered look at personal history is an incubator for sin, while a God-centered look is an incubator for faith.

The Beatitudes Sermon
James Jacques Joseph Tissot, c. 1890

> Genesis 2:24 states that a man will leave his father and mother and be joined to his wife. This leaving, both physical and emotional, accords with God's design. However, Sigmund Freud (1856-1939) sought to keep this relationship (parent to child) wrongly intact so that the parent would represent an ongoing excuse for the child's moral and social failing long into adulthood.

The Action-Reaction Dynamics of the Psyche

Isaac Newton's (1642–1726) third law of motion states, "For every action there is an equal and opposite reaction."[14] How does this concept apply to the psyche with

---

[13] David Powlison, Westminster Theological Seminary, Philadelphia, Pennsylvania
[14] physicsclassroom.com

regard to sin? The psyche, as an infinite and eternal entity, is never content to let insult, slight, rejection, harassment, neglect, or any other transgression, go unanswered. Any grievance, no matter how slight, will be responded to in one way or another. Being sinned against necessarily results in a sinful response whether at the moment or at a later date, whether toward the perpetrator or toward others, whether outwardly directed or inwardly nurtured. Thus, sin begets sin, so that the one sinned against cultivates an equal and opposite sinful response within himself (defensiveness, competitiveness, hostility, pride, depression, brooding, fear of man, etc.).

> "I suppose it is tempting, if the only tool you have is a hammer, to treat everything as if it were a nail…" (Abraham Maslow)

In this regard, consider the psyche like a Mobius strip, an endless loop from which one can never escape. If assaulted, if slighted, if mocked, if neglected, if rejected, if harassed, that sin will revisit itself upon humanity like an endless loop of vengeful response (in one form or another). The only way to break the Mobius is faith in Jesus Christ. This is the great liberator allowing the offended to not just forgive the transgression, but to relinquish any claim to erecting sinful responses within himself. Then there is no revenge-based backlash, either toward the offender or within the offended. The psyche's action-reaction law is broken in Christ.

As recounted in the book, *Unbroken: A World War II Story of Survival, Resilience, and Redemption* (2010),[15] Louie Zamperini (1917-2014) experienced some of the most heinous atrocities a human being could endure and live to recount. He was daily beaten, starved, humiliated, and under moment by moment threat of violent death while imprisoned in a Japanese POW camp during World War II. Four years after his release, in October, 1949, Zamperini gave his life to Jesus. In that moment, the torturous anger of his past treatment melted from his soul. The ball-and-chain of hatred and lust for revenge was removed and Louie was a free man.

Upon becoming a Christian, Louie reinterpreted his life as God leading him to himself. When Louie's B-24 Liberator crashed into the Pacific Ocean he was trapped inside, held fast by a web of strangling cables. Yet, miraculously he was freed. When, a Japanese bomber strafed him and to two other survivors as they floated on the ocean, riddling their raft with sixty-four bullet holes, miraculously not one of them was hit. Time and again, Zamperini was delivered from death by the hand of a God who longed to draw him to himself. As Louie looked back upon his past with man-centered lenses, seeing only his pain and loss, sin arose like a white-hot flame. When Louie looked upon his past with God-centered lenses, seeing the hand of deliverance, faith arose like a white-hot flame.

---

[15] Laura Hillenbrand, *Unbroken: A World War II Story of Survival, Resilience, and Redemption* (New York: Random House, 2010)

Thus, it is crucial to note that looking into one's past is a dangerous endeavor when it is with eyes of unforgiveness.[16] Just as dredging river sediment can reintroduce toxins into the water, so too, a torrid look at the past can easily reintroduce long forgotten (and hopefully, forgiven) accusation and resentment. A spirit of forgiveness dictates that past wrongs are forgotten and never mentioned again, just as they are from God's perspective for those in Christ.[17] This is one of the reasons that biblical counseling takes a limited and tepid gaze at personal history, recognizing that the heart is so naturally tendentious with regard to the past, that it readily slips into a spirit of shifted culpability for transgression.

> "Endure hardship as discipline; God is treating you as his children. For what children are not disciplined by their father? If you are not disciplined—and everyone undergoes discipline—then you are not legitimate, not true sons and daughters at all. Moreover, we have all had human fathers who disciplined us and we respected them for it. How much more should we submit to the Father of spirits and live! They disciplined us for a little while as they thought best; but God disciplines us for our good, in order that we may share in his holiness. No discipline seems pleasant at the time, but painful. Later on, however, it produces a harvest of righteousness and peace for those who have been trained by it." (Hebrews 12:7-11)

Case Study: Homosexuality and the Issue of Personal History

Myriad psychological studies have been conducted in order to uncover the root for homosexuality. One supposed scientific investigation attempts to link homosexuality with an atrophied pituitary gland. However, this study finally demonstrated that homosexuals produce the same range of hormones as heterosexuals. Another study packed rats into a confined space and found that they soon engaged in homosexual activity. This study suggested that homosexuality is an instinctual response to conditions of overpopulation or perceived crowding (such as in an urban setting).

Some studies have tried to link homosexuality with personal history, asserting that various scenarios such as a domineering mother, a passive father, a mother who coddled her son, or a father who rejected his son, result in homosexual behavior. The truth is that any scenario is equally likely in the homosexual's background.

Other research rejects the parental component altogether seeking instead to demonstrate that when a young person experiences deviant sexual relations he or she associates this with normalcy. The assumption in such studies is that parental

---

[16] For additional discussion of this topic see "The Transformative Power of Forgiveness" in the first book in this series, *Ask for the Ancient Paths: From Art to Artifice to Arisen*, chapter 4: "The Gospel as Inception Point: From Immorality to Immortality"
[17] Hebrews 8:12

behavioral may have little influence; rather, it is early sexual experimentation which is determinative.

At the Beach, Edward Potthast, d. 1927

What one finds is that *any* parental background, or *any* early experience, can lead to *any* outcome, whether homosexual, heterosexually promiscuous, or idolatrously abstinent. Thus, in spite of supposed scientific studies, any outcome can be associated with any background. Personal history, in fact, has nothing to do with the particulars of sexual sin. In other words, personal history is in no way determinative of sin patterns for the simple reason that each continually interprets his personal history, responding to it either in defiance of, or in submission to, Christ.[18]

For instance, a homosexual may just as easily speak of nurturing and encouraging relationships with a father or mother, destructive and fearful relationships with a father or mother, or early childhood experiences and expectations that were either constructive or destructive. This exact same "data" could just as easily lead to heterosexual promiscuity or asceticism. Thus, any personal history can lead to any outcome. Anything that can potentially explain everything in actuality explains nothing.[19]

Psychologists sometimes point to birth order for discerning personality type.

---

[18] David Powlison, Westminster Theological Seminary, Philadelphia, Pennsylvania
[19] David Powlison, Westminster Theological Seminary, Philadelphia, Pennsylvania

> However, in light of psychology's tendency to fabricate theories, birth order, like personal history, reveals little or nothing. Any birth order can result in any set of personality traits. It is a matter of how birth order has been viewed and responded to.[20]

Nearly all homosexuals believe that they were born homosexual, and most assert that they were merely pressured into heterosexual behavior for a time through societal expectation. From the Bible's perspective there is absolutely no way to be born a homosexual since the Bible never associates homosexuality with a design flaw. The Bible sees homosexuality as a moral choice based on idolatrous worship.[21] In mankind's deluded attempt to rationalize his sin, he searches for any plausible means to make senseless acts appear sensible, even commendable.

God is clear that homosexuality is an abomination, one which he condemns in the strongest language. Homosexuality is spun from a heart bent on inventing perverse ways of rebelling against God. It is sexual lust run off the tracks so that the sinner not only sins with "natural" sexuality, but goes further than this. He rends the very fabric of the created order in committing that which is by design abnormal. So while heterosexual sin is heinous, it remains within the confines of God's created order. Homosexuality, however, reinvents sexual sin as an assault upon God's own creative acts. Thus, homosexuality is like a double-edged sword – an attack upon God's moral law (sexuality to be confined to marriage), and an attack upon God's creative fiat (man and woman as rightful partners). Romans 1: 26, 27 states,

> Because of this, God gave them over to shameful lusts. Even their women exchanged natural sexual relations for unnatural ones. In the same way the men also abandoned natural relations with women and were inflamed with lust for one another. Men committed shameful acts with other men, and received in themselves the due penalty for their error.

> There appears to be a strange phenomenon in unbelievers; they expend great energy to avoid the truth.[22] Time and again, those who do not know God seek cloaking mechanisms to deflect the truth from others' notice. Those outside of Christ seem to innately know that they are on the wrong side of reality and, therefore, seek to squelch the truth at every turn.[23] Conversely, those in Christ are not afraid of the truth because they recognize that they are on its side, that the truth only magnifies the reality resident within themselves. Note the way in which those outside of Christ eschew discussions of the gospel, especially its piercing gaze at the heart. At times this avoidance mechanism appears to function like a chronic illness.

---

[20] Edward Welch, Westminster Theological Seminary, Philadelphia, Pennsylvania
[21] Leviticus 18:22
[22] Acts 7:57
[23] John 3:20 offers some insight into this.

Thus, in summary, the counselor rightly shows modest interest in a counselee's personal history.[24] This only to draw a mental image of that person's *Sitz im Leben* ("situation in life"), while recognizing that such a *Sitz im Leben* is not particularly insightful to the heart's machinations. *Sitz im Leben* may offer some clues on where to probe more deeply, but it certainly does not offer definitive answers. Thus, the investigation of personal history only serves to offer a general personality sketch, but little more. The source of one's psychic problem is not in the particular events of one's personal history, but in one's sinful heart-directed response to that history.

> God always describes the sinner's past with an eschatological vision for his future. This means that God's interpretation of one's past is always for the purpose of delivering him to a glorious future in which he himself reigns supreme.

Assessing Personal History: The Relevance of a Father's Love

At the time of Abraham (and his contemporary Job) each head of a household maintained his own worship site. Abraham erected an altar to the Lord;[25] Job daily offered sacrifices on behalf of his children.[26] A problem soon arose as each patriarch turned to gods of his own choosing. Each household claimed its own gods, and fashioned altars to them. For example, Genesis 31:19 records that Rachel stole her father's household gods.

For this reason, the Lord centralized worship in the Tent of Meeting. As Leviticus 17:3 records, the Tent of Meeting was to be the only place in which animals were to be sacrificed. Thus, worshipping the true God as one saw fit, at one's own times, and in one's own ways, was strictly forbidden. The Israelites were to worship God at appointed times, in approved ways, and in accordance with set decrees. (However, exceptions were made for Gideon's,[27] Manoah's,[28] Samuel's,[29] David's,[30] and Elijah's sacrifices.[31])

What is the lesson for biblical counseling? Invested with the position of "priest" (as the Bible defines it), fallen mankind quickly becomes vain in his imagination and offers idols to demons.[32] Mankind is apt to invent idols to advance self-serving purposes and lustful desires, as well as to assuage his nascent fears. Man was designed to be under the authority of God himself, and therefore, in submission to

---

[24] Edward Welch, Westminster Theological Seminary, Philadelphia, Pennsylvania
[25] Genesis 12:8; 22:9
[26] Job 1:5
[27] Judges 6:26
[28] Judges 13:19
[29] 1 Samuel 7:9; 1 Samuel 9:13; 1 Samuel 11:15
[30] 2 Samuel 24:18
[31] 1 Kings 18:23
[32] Matthew Henry Commentary, Bible Study Tools, 2012

Christ. Only the Holy Spirit's work can free man from his self-serving idolatry and destructive worship. Thus, when, for example, the Holy Spirit regenerates a father, as head of his household, he is enabled to rightly serve his family as God intended, to firstly be under authority so as to properly exercise authority.

Antonio Stradivari, Edgar Bundy, 1893

Central to this discussion is the question of whether God's Word, or one's interpretation of his personal experience, is ascendant and formative in one's life. Should personal experience have authority over God's Word, or should God's Word have authority over personal experience? According to psychology, one's interpretation of his experience should dictate his understanding of reality. According to the Bible, God's self-revelation must interpret one's experience so that one sees reality as God sees it. If experience is ascendant, then mankind falls victim to the Freudian calumny. If God's Word is ascendant, then one is free to know and worship God, regardless of personal experience which may indicate the contrary.

"The remedy for injuries is to forget them." (Latin proverb)

For example, a recent article on psychology mentioned that quarrels and arguments are normal in any relationship, whether that of marriage, friendship, siblings, or between parents and children. While this sounds innocent enough, it conceals a trap. Does God ever call quarrels and arguments normal? James 4:1 is clear. "What causes fights and quarrels among you? Don't they come from your desires that battle within you?" While the Christian should expect conflict as a result of living in a depraved world, he is never called to participate in any quarrel, regardless of the situation. He may speak the truth with passion and persuasion, but he stops short of getting into a back-and-forth argument for any reason. Thus, the point is that God's Word directly contradicts the sinful heart's inclinations, inclinations are easily codified as "normal" (normative) through a man-centered system of thought (psychology).

The Freudian Fatherhood Fable[33]

Once as a violinist played in a Boston subway station, passersby nonchalantly tossed loose change into the hat placed in front of him. Few paid much attention as he played for nearly an hour. Parents pulled their children along, businessmen jogged to catch a train, and college students wearing earphones shuffled by without so much as a glance in the man's direction. A few stopped for a moment, almost mesmerized by the music, but glanced at their watches and scurried away.

It turns out that the subway violinist was Joshua Bell, one of the premier violinists in the world. He played the most intricate Bach composition using a $3.5 million violin. Just two nights before he had played the same piece to a sold-out concert with an average ticket price of $100.

This social experiment demonstrates that human perception is driven by environment and expectation. In other words, if incomparable art were found in a pedestrian environment would people still recognize it as such? The idea is that people see what they want to see, or more accurately, what they *expect* to see at any given moment. Context drives perception.[34]

This issue of context driving perception comes into play with the question, "What if one's father did not love him?", a question which haunts and hobbles the modern psyche. There is a trenchant societal belief that children are crucially scarred by the absence of a father's love. However, this very question runs counter to the Bible as it was Sigmund Freud (1856–1939) and Erik Erickson (1902–1994) who taught society to even raise such a question (themselves building on Plato's (427–347 BC) deterministic views of fatherhood).[35] Freud implanted this idea in the modern consciousness, theorizing that people craft their view of God based on their view of their fathers. Freud made normative the portrayal of God as a "bottom to top" portrayal (earthly father to heavenly Father). However, God's own explanation of himself is "top to bottom" (heavenly Father to earthly father).[36] God rebukes the

---

[33] This section is largely a reaction to Sigmund Freud, *Totem and Taboo: Resemblances Between the Mental Lives of Savages and Neurotics* (Beacon Press, 1913)

[34] Mark 6:4

[35] For a more detailed response to Sigmund Freud see "The Gang of Six: Influences on the Growth and Development of Psychology," and "Psychology's Tetrad Sophistry" in the first book in this series, *Ask for the Ancient Paths: From Art to Artifice to Arisen*, chapter 8: "What Has Jerusalem To Do With Vienna?: The Case Against Psychology"

[36] David Powlison, "Is God's Love Unconditional?" *The Journal of Biblical Counseling* (Glenside, Pennsylvania:

sinner's vain imaginings with the truth of who he is.

> "Jesus said to them, 'Very truly I tell you, it is not Moses who has given you the bread from heaven, but it is my Father who gives you the true bread from heaven. For the bread of God is the bread that comes down from heaven and gives life to the world.'" (John 6:32, 33)

Based on Freud's spurious claims, society seeks to interpret and understand God through the lens of its experience with earthly fathers. This is yet another example of mankind holding tenaciously to his experience as accurate and normative in rendering reality and in defining truth. Yet, the Bible is clear that that experience is tainted by the gaze of sin. Thus, mankind's interpretation of his experience is warped and clouded by his own self-serving desire. Mankind readily gravitates toward a distorted view of God because he seeks plausible deniability for his sin. Since man seeks an excuse for why he sins, he must recast God as a vindictive, abusive, negligent, uncaring, tight-fisted God who delights in the suffering of those he created. Thus, mankind must grab for anything it can from this enemy-God, and views himself as justified in seeking to oppose and circumvent this God. (Even those who would never describe God in this way frequently function upon this basis.)

Thus, for fallen mankind, operating under the delusion of psychology, if one's earthly father is deemed controlling and harsh, this is because God himself is controlling and harsh. Therefore, one is justified in defending himself against again being controlled. The sinner, in his devised abstraction for God, legitimates his demand for control over his world against and without God.

> The psychological term "Oedipal anxiety" is the boyhood fear of retribution by an exigent father.

Freud sought to make experience determinative. In this, he conflated the earthly father with the heavenly Father. Just as a child, by placing his fingers near a light, can cast ominous and haunting shadows upon a wall, so too, Freud reduced God to nothing more than shadows cast by an earthly longing. Freud made the earthly determinative of the heavenly, the heavenly being nothing more than a fanciful projection of the earthly.

However, in the Bible's purview there is never lockstep correlation between the sinner's experiences and his view of God. The former is in no way determinative of the latter. Rather, the heart is far more insidious and cunning than that. The sinner fashions his view of God, not so much based on what has happened to him, but in conformity with his idolatrous response to the world. Therefore, there is no causality between one's experience of his earthly father and one's view of God; this is the great Fruedian *non sequitur*.

> "The smallest minds speak about people. Average minds speak about events. The greatest minds speak about ideas." (Eleanor Roosevelt)

For example, the children of deeply caring and godly fathers at times view God with suspicion and enmity. The children of demeaning and destructive fathers sometimes exhibit a penitent, submissive, and devoted relationship with God. Children whose fathers abandoned them, or who never knew their fathers, can still enjoy bountiful love from their true Father in heaven, a Father who lavishes attention on the orphan.[37] From the opposite side, the action or neglect of an earthly father is never a permitted justification for disobedience to the heavenly Father.

The Punishment of Korah and the Stoning of Moses and Aaron
Sandro Botticcelli, 1482

Numbers 16:1, 2, records that Korah, along with Dathan and Abiram, led a rebellion against God.

> Korah son of Izhar, the son of Kohath, the son of Levi, and certain Reubenites—Dathan and Abiram, sons of Eliab, and On son of Peleth—became insolent and rose up against Moses. With them were 250 Israelite men, well-known community leaders who had been appointed members of the council.

---
[37] Psalm 27:10; Isaiah 1:17

Numbers 16:27-33 then records that the households of Korah, Dathan, and Abiram were swallowed by the earth and cast into "the realm of the dead." Later Numbers 26:10 records that Dathan's and Abiram's households indeed perished, yet quite surprisingly, Korah's line did not.[38] The Bible student may infer that Korah's children did not participate in their father's rebellion, and may have even denounced said rebellion.

David eventually employed Korah's posterity as singers in the Temple, hence many psalms are said to be for the sons of Korah. Commentator Matthew Henry (1662–1714) speculates that perhaps the Korah lineage was made to bear their rebellious progenitor's name, rather than the name of any other ancestor, to serve as a warning against future rebellion. Bearing Korah's name may also offer a lesson in the power of God to bring "choice fruits" out of a "bitter root." "The children of families that have been stigmatized should endeavour, by their eminent virtues, to roll away the reproach of their fathers."[39] Thus, while Korah rebelled against God, and in his ensuing death rendered his children orphans, his children were not consigned to their father's false worship. Presumably, Korah's children made worship decisions, in contrast to their father's defiance, which rendered them submissive to God.

> "To be wronged is nothing unless you continue to remember it." (Confucius)

God Stands in Both Continuity with, and in Contradistinction to, Earthly Examples

Every entity in the creation is perfect. Colors match with a flawless aesthetic; proportions are balanced with precision; textures add depth and richness, and scaling is the work of a cosmic measuring line. One could never tire of the seemingly endless variation in nature. God clearly has an aesthetic sense which knows when to blend, when to contrast, when to soften, when to embolden, when to smoothen, when to roughen, when to highlight, when to deemphasize, and how to produce beauty in both form and content.

The same could be said for the way God fashions and directs human life. God is masterful in his work, and therefore must not be doubted with regard to his sovereign will for each life (although he can be respectfully questioned, as Job did). While the counselor grieves with those who grieve and rejoices with those who rejoice, he recognizes that a good and sovereign God stands behind each life, so that there is no forgotten person, no one callously subject to the vagaries of evil. Each life is perfectly planned.

---

[38] Numbers 26:11
[39] Matthew Henry Commentary, Bible Study Tools, 2012

Matthew 7:11 states, "If you, then, though you are evil, know how to give good gifts to your children, how much more will your Father in heaven give good gifts to those who ask him!" God is both distinct from earthly forms and examples, and at the same time displays a certain coherence with earthly forms and examples. The ways in which an earthly father has shown good and loving parenting (and even the worst fathers have at times) reflects God's character and love for his children. Yet, God says his love is even greater than this.

Conversely, the ways in which an earthly father has shown ungodly and neglectful parenting (and even the best fathers have at times) is in no way a reflection of God's character. God says that he is not like this. Deuteronomy 31:6 states, "Be strong and courageous. Do not be afraid or terrified because of them, for the LORD your God goes with you; he will never leave you nor forsake you." This is the antidote to seeing an earthly father as a potentially wounding presence in his children's lives. There is no *determinative* psychic wound inflicted by a father (a wound to which the child is hopelessly subject); any potential wound comes in the child's sinful response to his father (which is never to excuse or marginalize a father's sins against his children[40]). Thus, Jeremiah 31:29, 30 states,

> In those days people will no longer say,
>
> > 'The fathers have eaten sour grapes, and the children's teeth are set on edge.'
>
> Instead, everyone will die for his own sin; whoever eats sour grapes – his own teeth will be set on edge.

> Romans 8:15 states, "The Spirit you received does not make you slaves, so that you live in fear again; rather, the Spirit you received brought about your adoption to sonship. And by him we cry, *'Abba,* Father.'" According to the NIV Bible footnote, "the Greek word for 'adoption to sonship' is a term referring to 'the full legal standing of an adopted male heir in Roman culture.'" Thus, the Father's adopted children are full heirs, highly-honored, and experience the blessing of one exalted in God's household. This is the ultimate antidote to seeing an earthly father's sin as determinative and enslaving.

Therefore, earthly fathers must never be "absolutized." Every father has exhibited a mixture of kindness and cruelty, provision and neglect, discipline and disregard. Each father has, in his interaction with his children, displayed both godly characteristics and ungodly ones. Rarely has a father shown utter contempt and cruelty toward a

---

[40] Ephesians 6:4

child, and rarely has a father offered completely wise counsel and totally other-centered self-sacrifice. The point is that God as Father absolutely distances himself from a father's evil, while drawing a parallel with a father's good, a reflection of God's own good character.

> "Jesus replied, 'Anyone who loves me will obey my teaching. My Father will love them, and we will come to them and make our home with them. Anyone who does not love me will not obey my teaching. These words you hear are not my own; they belong to the Father who sent me. All this I have spoken while still with you. But the Advocate, the Holy Spirit, whom the Father will send in my name, will teach you all things and will remind you of everything I have said to you. Peace I leave with you; my peace I give you. I do not give to you as the world gives. Do not let your hearts be troubled and do not be afraid.'" (John 14:23-27)

The Finding of Moses, Lawrence Alma-Tadema, 1904

Sinners remember selectively, and that non-uniformly. This means that one remembers that which suits his sinful desire and his idolatrous demands. There is, therefore, nothing objective about memory since it is directed by heart worship. So the issue of whether one's father did or did not love one is really a question of selective memory (and selective memory is a quintessentially childish quality). Thus, one father adjudged a "bad" father by one child might be considered a "good" father by another, and vice versa. The unregenerate sinner's heart is actively engaged in interpreting his father for selfish purpose. In this regard, it is crucial to emphasize that any real or perceived parental failing easily slips into a source of excuse-making for a child who is intent on justifying the intentions of his rebellious heart.

> "Never does the human soul appear so strong as when it foregoes revenge and dares to forgive an injury."

The sinful heart wrongly believes that a *person* caused one's problems, and therefore a *person* must fix them. This is the blame-shifting, championed by psychology, which so readily poisons, not only one's heart, but one's interpersonal relationships. In reality a person (God himself) does correct the heart's problem, but this is not the provenance of an earthly person, and the problem corrected is not one of vindicating aggrieved self-pride. Thus, God deliberately describes himself as "Father" because he wants his children to see him as their true heavenly and perfect father, and themselves as his progeny sired in eternal love.

Additionally, one never has a right to think that because his parents did not love him (as he desired to be loved) that he cannot love and serve others (as God desires them to be loved). The entire notion behind this is nothing more than a Freudian lie foisted upon a pagan world. One can, and is expected to, love others regardless of his personal history. There is never an excuse for bitterness, brooding, compulsiveness, greed, cruelty, debauchery, promiscuity, lust, or other manifestations of the worshipping heart. Thus, errant worship is never a father's fault. It arises through defective personal faith commitments which must be conclusively renounced through a personal faith commitment to Jesus.

With daily repentance, God as Father becomes more vivid and alive to the Christian. As the Christian's heart allegiances are less compromised he is enabled to see God as he really is. In this way, the Christian is daily challenged to adopt a new set of lenses so as to view his personal experience as God leading him home to himself.

God's Care for the Widow, the Orphan, and the Alien

Throughout Scripture God is attentive to the plight of the widow, the orphan, and the alien. He commanded the Israelites to take particular note of, and to offer hospitality to, these often forlorn souls. Deuteronomy 10:17, 18 reads,

> For the LORD your God is God of gods and Lord of lords, the great God, mighty and awesome, who shows no partiality and accepts no bribes. He defends the cause of the fatherless and the widow, and loves the foreigner residing among you, giving them food and clothing.

In each of these three states, the vulnerable person is without a "male" (or national) protector, yet God himself steps in to provide for his needs, to care for his safety, and to offer refuge in himself. For this reason, God calls himself "Father" throughout Scripture. He is the quintessential father who can never fail, abuse, neglect, or overlook the lives under his watchful eye. As a reflection of God's own character, he commanded those in a position of authority to trade in the currency of mercy, mercy to the most vulnerable in society. Those without a husband, without a father, and outside of their "fatherland" are, in God's provenance, extended special protection and a unique outpouring of grace.[41]

Isaiah 49:15-18 states,

> Can a mother forget the baby at her breast
>   and have no compassion on the child she has borne?
> Though she may forget,
>   I will not forget you!
> See, I have engraved you on the palms of my hands;
>   your walls are ever before me.
> Your children hasten back,
>   and those who laid you waste depart from you.
> Lift up your eyes and look around;
>   all your children gather and come to you.
> As surely as I live," declares the LORD,
>   "you will wear them all as ornaments;
>   you will put them on, like a bride.'

> "But while he was still a long way off, his father saw him and was filled with compassion for him; he ran to his son, threw his arms around him and kissed him." (Luke 15:20)

Excursus: The Book of Esther: A Silent and Invisible, Yet Present, God[42]

The book of Esther is one of the most perplexing inclusions in the Old Testament canon. It does not mention God and does not mention Israel's temple. There is no concern for Jewish dietary laws. There is no mention of prayer in the entire book. There is no eschatological vision and no miracles. Further, the main character, Esther, exploited her beauty for personal gain and fornicated with an uncircumcised Gentile for her own advancement (a plan promoted by her equally self-promoting uncle, Mordechi). Esther was neither chaste nor faithful to her Jewish heritage, and represents a kind of Israeli anti-hero. In fact, to highlight the ambiguity in Esther's

---

[41] One may find herself without a husband, or outside of her homeland, through her own fault. God often provides for those who, even on account of their own failing, are in a vulnerable state. That is the wonder of the gospel, that God would lavish grace even on those who have been derelict with their own lives.

[42] Most of the following from a lecture by Karen Jobes, "Old Testament History and Theology" class, Westminster Theological Seminary, Philadelphia, Pennsylvania

loyalties, she is the only character in the book with both a Hebrew name and a Persian name.[43]

On its face, the book of Esther appears to be a conspicuously "unreligious" book, one filled with satire, irony, and humor. A subplot is its parody of political bureaucracy, and the expediency attendant in marriage relationships. However, an unexpected transformation happens. Esther moves from manipulation and self-promotion to self-sacrifice for the sake of her people. This is the book's peripety – a sudden change in the course of events. This literary technique reveals the author's worldview, that God is a God of peripety.

> The book of Esther is organized around three Jewish feasts. These feasts, in fact, mirror three Persian feasts. (There is a parody in this.) Additionally, these feasts mark the beginning, middle, and end of the book. At the end, the feast of Purim is the moment of joyous reversal for the Jews, the feared day of mourning has become a day of gladness.[44] The irony in the name "Purim" is that it means "dice." However, as the reader discovers there was nothing by chance in the Jews' deliverance.

The book of Esther speaks volumes about God without ever mentioning his name. God worked through a pagan nation using morally questionable people (Mordecai and Esther) to effect redemptive history for his people. The book reveals God's sovereignty without mentioning miracles or supernatural events. God worked through ordinary events to effect history; even the book's language is completely secular language. In recording ordinary events, and in using secular language, the book is *sui generis* in the Bible canon. The intention is that when God is invisible, participants are called to the greatest faith in recognizing that God is still powerfully present.

> It is fascinating that the Greek redactors of the *Septuagint* (*LXX*) inserted mention of God throughout the book of Esther in exactly the same way that God is mentioned in Daniel, Nehemiah, and Ezra. The redactors chose to interpret Esther for the reader by filling in the conceptual lacunae and textual silences.

This analysis of Esther serves as an apt starting point for a discussion of the issue of personal history. Often counselees, as they look back upon their personal history (possibly a childhood filled with tragic events) feel that God has been silent and distant. They feel that God has not held true to his promise to never leave nor forsake them.[45] The book of Esther serves as a reminder that God is intensely present, even in life's "secular" episodes. God orchestrates events even when it appears that the godless have ultimate power. The book of Esther should serve as a humbling

---
[43] Esther 2:7
[44] Karen Jobes, "Old Testament History and Theology" class, Westminster Theological Seminary, Philadelphia, Pennsylvania
[45] Deuteronomy 31:8; Hebrews 13:5

declaration that there is no ambiguity in God's intimate involvement throughout history.

> "History never looks like history when you're living through it. It always looks messy and confusing when you're living it." (John W. Gardner)

Sanctification as the Adoption of God's "Revisionist" History

Jews Praying in the Synagogue on Yom Kippur
Maurycy Gottlieb, 1878

In Numbers 15:37-41 God commanded the Israelites to fashion tassels on the corners of their garments, with a blue cord on each tassel. They were to look upon these tassels in order to remember the Lord's commands, that they should obey him and not prostitute themselves by chasing after the lusts of their own hearts and eyes. Then they would remember to obey all God's commands and would be consecrated.

The blue cord, *tekheleth* (תְּכֵלֶת:), is best translated "violet cord." This color could either refer to the royal nature of the Jews, a people set apart among the nations, or to a call for their repentance. (Purple has traditionally been the color of royalty, while violet was the color of repentance). Whether a statement of nobility or a call to repentance, the tassels were intended as a symbol of remembrance to the Lord's commands. In Numbers 15:39 the Lord told the Israelites that they would have the tassels "to look at." They were to physically look upon the tassels rather than "going after the lusts of [their] own hearts and eyes."

This issue of remembrance is crucial to the Christian, to remember the right events at the right times, in the right way, and to abjure that which is merely the prattle of the sinful heart. Just as the Pharisees soon exaggerated the length of their tassels in order to appear especially pious, so too, Christians may honor God with their lips while recasting their history to exclude the knowledge of God. Similarly, just as the Pharisees lost the meaning of the tassels, making them into an object of cultic devotion rather than a means to remembrance, so too, Christians are prone to a similar failing. Thus, Ecclesiastes 1:9 warns, "What has been will be again, what has been done will be done again; there is nothing new under the sun."

> "…though I myself have reasons for such confidence. If someone else thinks they have reasons to put confidence in the flesh, I have more: circumcised on the eighth day, of the people of Israel, of the tribe of Benjamin, a Hebrew of Hebrews; in regard to the law, a Pharisee; as for zeal, persecuting the church; as for righteousness based on the law, faultless. But whatever were gains to me I now consider loss for the sake of Christ. What is more, I consider everything a loss because of the surpassing worth of knowing Christ Jesus my Lord, for whose sake I have lost all things. I consider them garbage, that I may gain Christ." (Philippians 3:4-8)

God puts his people into the same situation time and again for two purposes: to either confront idols anew for the purpose of repentance, or to expose a heart of abiding faith. Often God engineers situation to either offer evidence of a heart overrun by idolatry (and thus to ignite a movement toward repentance), or else to offer evidence of the heart's progress in faith. The situation is in some sense immaterial; it is what it reveals that is vital. The situation either offers a window into an ongoing need for change, or else heralds victory over sin.

> While the counselor does not necessarily seek to change the counselee's circumstance (except in the case of imminent danger), circumstance can at times be a reason that sin is not fully embraced or fully developed. Thus, circumstance can function as a hedge against the movement into deeper sin.

Psalm 23:4, 5 states, "Even though I walk through the valley of the shadow of death, I will fear no evil for you are with me…; you prepare a table before me in the presence of my enemies…" Notice that God does not remove the believer from "the valley of the shadow of death," nor does God isolate one from his enemies. Rather, God offers the opportunity to walk by faith so as to experience God himself in the midst of such threats.

> "If the world hates you, keep in mind that it hated me first; …if they persecuted me, they will persecute you also." (John 15:18, 20)

Just as God does not primarily focus on changing circumstances, so too, God does not promise to change one's past. Through Scripture the Christian knows that he lives in a world in which evil exists, not because God is weak or capricious, but because God allows evil to operate as part of his plan to differentiate the righteous from the wicked, to disambiguate idolatry from faith (which are often difficult to disentangle). God does not promise to free Christians from all evil, but to shepherd them through it, to be with them in the midst of it, the goal being to incline their hearts to himself. God does not promise to erase the evil in the Christian's past, but to give him the means to overcome that past, to understand it in a new light. The Christian is empowered to make the past a means to gratitude for the way in which it has prompted relationship with Jesus. God transforms the past into a source of joy for its role in salvation, a means of towering inner strength birthed in the knowledge of a God who delivers, and into a basis of wisdom for counseling others.

> "A wise man can see more from the bottom of a well than a fool can from a mountain top."

However, the Bible is not overly attentive to the Christian's personal history or circumstance,[46] because this easily becomes a source of vigorous defense for sin. The Bible knows that every sinner's past bears a common mark, a sinful interpretation and approach to God, oneself, and the world around. Ephesians 2:1-3 summarizes the sinner's past:

> As for you, you were dead in your transgressions and sins, in which you used to live when you followed the ways of this world and of the ruler of the kingdom of the air, the spirit who is now at work in those who are disobedient. All of us also lived among them at one time, gratifying the cravings of our flesh and following its desires and thoughts. Like the rest, we were by nature deserving of wrath.

The Bible is clear that, regardless of the particulars of one's past, each sinner is bound to certain core characteristics. Each invariably followed the ways of this world, and its chief architect, Satan. Each has spent his life outside of Christ gratifying the cravings of the flesh and following its desires.[47] For this reason, each is rightfully deserving of God's wrath, without caveat and without condition. This is, in a nutshell, the plight of everyone outside of Christ. The particulars of history soon fade as one considers the weightier present, and the pressing imperative to repentance and participation in Christ's suffering.[48]

> For most, a look into one's personal history is a long study on the way in which one was sinned against. For God, a look into one's personal history offers a brief

---

[46] Philippians 3:13
[47] Ephesians 2:3
[48] Philippians 3:10

> reminder of the way in which one has sinned in the midst of being sinned against (while experiencing God's goodness). Since God keeps a flawless record of transgressions against his people (and a promise to reprise each of them),[49] the Christian's focus is rightly upon the way in which he himself sinned in the context of being sinned against.

While the counselor rightly avoids a boilerplate approach to counseling, there is an underlying template to which he is privy, a set of common themes which under-gird each sinner's past. This becomes the wise counselor's focus. The counselor need, in effect, look no farther than the Bible to understand personal history, to uncover that history's cogent elements.

Daniel in the Lion's Den, Peter Paul Rubens, c. 1615

> "We demolish arguments and every pretension that sets itself up against the knowledge of God, and we take captive every thought to make it obedient to Christ." (2 Corinthians 10:5)

In this way, the Bible focuses attention, not on the particulars of one's personal history, but on the sinner in the midst of that history,[50] one in need of a recreated heart to gaze upon his history and circumstance rightly. The Bible delves into the God-ward referent deeply embedded in each personal event, exposing that referent. Consider, for example, the man born blind in John 9:3, "'Neither this man nor his parents sinned,' said Jesus, 'but this happened so that the works of God might be displayed in him.'"

---

[49] Luke 12:7
[50] Paul Tripp, *Instruments in Redeemer's Hands: People in Need of Change Helping People in Need of Change* (Presbyterian and Reformed Publishing Company, 2002)

Sin did not lead to this man's blindness, but his blindness existed so that, when coupled with Jesus' message, sin would be exposed in the man and in those surrounding the event (the disciples, parents, Pharisees, and crowd).

> "We are made wise not by the recollection of our past, but by the responsibility for our future." (George Bernard Shaw)

Rewriting One's Life Story as an Act of Repentance

Adolf Hitler (1889-1945) is rightly thought of as among the worst of humanity; the most craven and vile of men. By God's grace, those one counsels will never commit all that Hitler perpetrated, but each possesses the same evil heart prone to such atrocities; each shares the same selfish ambition,[51] the same abiding murderous intent,[52] the same delusions of grandeur (albeit on a far more limited scale). However, each does not have the means at his disposal to act upon those evil intentions in all their flaunt and fury. Each does not sit in the midst of circumstances (totalitarian control of a populace, military power, economic and technological prowess) to act out all that inhabits his heart. This is God's mercy to mankind, that he does not provide each person the opportunity to live out all that lives within his heart. Thus, God's mercy is often found in mankind's limitations,[53] not in his achievements. God, as part of his common grace, often shields man from the exploits of his heart in making its intentions ponderous and untenable.

First Thessalonians 5:18 admonishes, "…give thanks in all circumstances; for this is God's will for you in Christ Jesus." Thus, for the Christian there is both thankfulness for one's talents and achievements and for one's limitations, losses, and "failures." (This might be called the Christian's "Morton's Fork of gratitude.") The Christian recognizes that limitations, losses, and failures are a gift often keeping him from self-destructive or distracted worship, prompting reliance on a God who overcomes all such particularities.

> "Until further notice: Celebrate everything."[54]

The Christian continually repents of a heart which seeks:

1. To be one's own god
2. One's own comfort above all else
3. To work in one's own strength

---

[51] Consider James 3:16 in this regard.
[52] James 4:2
[53] For example, as with the tower of Babel (Genesis 11:1-9)
[54] This quote from an unknown source

> "Some trust in chariots and some in horses, but we trust in the name of the Lord God." (Psalm 20:7)

    4. To define one's own meaning
    5. To lean on one's own wisdom

> "Trust in the Lord with all your heart and lean not on your own understanding." (Proverbs 3:5)

    6. To chart one's own future
    7. To seek one's own glory

> "You are a mist that appears for a little while and then vanishes." (James 4:14)

While, of course, the Bible is complete and the canon is closed, God's story is not finished. He continues to work in and through history for his eternal purposes. The Bible prods the Christian to enter into God's story, so that he would no longer live out his own story. The Christian is to become a living extension of God's story. What are God's purposes in history? It is that the knowledge of Jesus Christ might fill the world, that his kingdom might reside within believers. Thus, the Christian participates in God's story of creation and redemption through being re-created and redeemed,[55] a living temple who advances in small part God's kingdom building efforts on earth. Thus, in the course of being sanctified, the Christian "bends the arc of history."[56]

> Hurting people, who nourish their pain, hurt others; healed people heal others.[57]

The Memory Palace Festooned in Splendor

Numbers 27: 1-11 offers a look at five orphaned daughters who, instead of bemoaning their plight in life, honored their flawed father as would surrogate "sons." This vignette presents a lavish bouquet of all that God can do in those who see their personal history as he does, who see him as their vanguard and provider. This episode offers a portrait of those who overcome their past with faithful requests to a good and giving Father.

Numbers 27:1 states that the daughters of Zelophehad, of the clan of Manasseh, were Mahlah, Noah, Hoglah, Milcah and Tirzah. It is noteworthy that Zelophehad was not among Korah's followers, and therefore did not disgrace the Lord's honor through open rebellion. However, the name "Zelophehad" (צְלָפְחָד) means "the shadow of fear or dread," which may be related to the mention, in Numbers 27:3, that Zelophehad

---

[55] 2 Corinthians 5:17
[56] "Bend the arc of history" from Barack Obama, inauguration speech, January 20, 2009
[57] This concept from an unknown source

"died in the desert for his own sins and left no sons" (a source of disgrace among ancient Israelites). Yet, Zelophehad's daughters wisely sought propitiation for his sin.

Zelophehad's daughters brought a request before Moses (and the other leaders) in which they asked for property among their father's relatives, that their father's inheritance (due to a son) should be turned over to them (daughters not entitled to realty).[58] These young women showed faith in presenting their case directly before Moses at the entrance to the Tent of Meeting. They did not seek a representative to the council, but felt that the force of their request was sufficient to stand on its own merit. They also showed faith in assuming that the Promised Land would eventually be taken, and that they would one day live in it. They presented their appeal in such a way that it was a forgone conclusion that the land would be acquired, exactly as the Lord had promised. (Incidentally, these five daughters may serve as a prelude to the parable of the ten virgins, five of whom trimmed their lamps and prepared their oil.[59])

His First Birthday, Frederick Morgan, 1899

> It is fascinating that in Numbers 27:1-7 the Hebrew pronouns used to describe the five daughters are all masculine pronouns. Is this merely a textual aberration of no consequence? Could this offer a statement that the daughters were functionally "sons" on account of their faith, and a proleptic indicator of Galatians 3:28 in which

---

[58] Numbers 27:4, 7
[59] Matthew 25:1-13

> there is neither male nor female in Christ?

The meaning of Zelophehad's daughters names:

1. Mahlah (מַחְלָה), "infirmity"
2. Noah (נֹעָה), "wandering"
3. Hoglah (וְחָגְלָה), "turning about or dancing for joy"
4. Milcah (וּמִלְכָּה), "a queen"
5. Tirzah (וְתִרְצָה), "well-pleasing or acceptable"[60]

These five daughters were figuratively born in "the shadow of fear and dread." This captures Hebrews 2:15,

> Since the children have flesh and blood, he too shared in their humanity so that by his death he might break the power of him who holds the power of death — that is, the devil — and free those who all their lives were held in slavery by their fear of death.

These daughters represent, in a symbolic way, the gospel.[61]

1. The oldest daughter, Mahlah, insinuates the infirmity of a soul plagued by sin.

2. The second daughter, Noah, signifies the wandering involved in searching for comfort for the soul.

3. The middle daughter, Hoglah, hints at, in finding Christ, the joy of salvation.

4. The fourth daughter, Milcah, is the Christian's pedigree as a royal priesthood.[62]

5. Finally, the youngest daughter, Tirzah, connotes being presented to Christ holy, blameless and without blemish, well-pleasing to him, and found acceptable through Christ's blood.[63]

The story of Zelophehad and his daughters almost offers a mirror-image of the parable of the Prodigal Son. While the prodigal sinned against the father, in the Numbers account the father sinned against God the Father. In the Lucan parable the father made propitiation for his son, but in the Numbers account the daughters (functioning as sons)

---

[60] Song of Songs 6:4a reads, "You are beautiful, my darling, as Tirzah, lovely as Jerusalem..." It appears that Tirzah was a beautiful location, which would fit with the definition of Tirzah in this section.
[61] Matthew Henry Commentary, Bible Study Tools, 2012
[62] 1 Peter 2:9
[63] Ephesians 5:27

made propitiation for their father. They sought to honor their father despite his transgression.[64]

---

[64] Numbers 27:4

- 2 -

SUFFERING:

The Kintsugi Objective

Ivan the Terrible and His Son, Ilya Repin, 1885

Suffering as a Universal Human Experience

In Giacomo Puccini's (1858-1924) opera *Tosca* (1900) is found the aria "Vissi d'Arte, Vissi d'Amore" in which piercing sorrow and grief is considered a mainstay of this world.

>I lived for my art, I lived for love,
>I never did harm to a living soul!
>With a secret hand
>I relieved as many misfortunes as I knew of.
>Always with true faith
>My prayer rose to the holy shrines.
>Always with true faith.
>
>I gave flowers to the altar.

> In the hour of grief
> Why, why, O Lord,
> Why do you reward me thus?
> I gave jewels for the Madonna's mantle,
> And I gave my song to the stars, to heaven,
> Which smiled with more beauty.
> In the hour of grief
> Why, why, O Lord,
> Ah, why do you reward me thus?

Every person suffers in some way, for some reason, since suffering is as ubiquitous as breathing. It is visited upon the wealthy and the destitute, the educated and the ignorant, the young and the old, and quite enigmatically, the righteous and the wicked. Under the tyranny of a world system in Satan's grip,[1] suffering, of many stripes and colors, is a daily reality. In fact, as the book of Job indicates, Satan engineers suffering so that those under his dominion would curse God and die.[2] However, for those in Christ, those rescued from death and brought to life,[3] suffering induces the opposite response, praise of a God who endured intense pain on behalf of his people and emerged victorious.[4]

As this selection from *Tosca* reveals, suffering is such a thorny topic because most convince themselves that they are inherently good, have essentially acted rightly toward God and others, and therefore deserve a life free from pain. In the unregenerate heart, so much of what passes for piety, charity, and kindness is nothing more than a grand bargain with a reclusive and frightening God, to be free from the volatility and vicissitudes of a daunting world. Thus, much human energy and activity revolves around a scheme to finally be free from suffering.

On account of man's isolation from God, his Faustian pact for peace, and his relentless quest to conquer conflict, suffering becomes a highly-confusing experience. The confusion arises because man does not understand that the focus of the entire universe is upon the human heart, that it would be subdued and sanctified. When one understands God's consuming focus upon exposing and renewing heart worship,[5] stone cold hearts made supple and submissive to God,[6] suffering is transformed from a foreign and torturous prospect into a loving event with an attached promise.[7]

> "For our light and momentary troubles are achieving for us an eternal glory that far

---
[1] 1 John 5:19
[2] John 1:11
[3] Ephesians 2:5; Colossians 2:13
[4] Isaiah 53:5; Philippians 2:9
[5] Consider James 5:10 in this regard.
[6] Ezekiel 36:26
[7] Isaiah 41:13; Jeremiah 30:22

> outweighs them all. So we fix our eyes not on what is seen, but on what is unseen, since what is seen is temporary, but what is unseen is eternal." (2 Corinthians 4:17)

From the get-go it is vital to point out that the Bible never countenances the question, "Why do bad things happening to good people?" In fact, the Bible reverses the logic so as to query, "Why does anything good happen to anyone at all?" Through the Bible's set of lenses, there are no "good people" (some called "righteous" and "saints" on account of faith, but not inherently good) as each rightly deserves God's condemnation and wrath, a commination visited upon Jesus to the benefit of those who would believe in him.[8] Additionally, there are no truly "bad things" when one knows God, recognizing that he carefully calibrates all things to induce, or intensify, faith. Thus, the Bible reverses the entire hermeneutic behind suffering, casting it in an eternal light with a Christ-glorifying objective.[9]

The Lament for Icarus
Herbert James Draper, 1898

> "Consider it pure joy, my brothers, whenever you face trials of many kinds, because you know that the testing of your faith produces perseverance. Let perseverance finish its work so that you may be mature and complete, not lacking anything." (James 1:2-4)

The Human Quest to Overcome Finitude

---

[8] 1 Peter 2:24
[9] Romans 11:36 upholds this concept.

> "I mourn the loss of something I can't quite place." (Leigh Ann Henion)

American author, James Weldon Johnson (1871-1938), described New York City as a witch who perches a man on a giant bubble of fortune. She watches him soar high into the sky where he is dazzled by stelliferous wonders and thrilled with his soaring freedom. The witch then impishly pricks the bubble, observing the man falling to his doom, as she cackles with delight.[10] This seems to characterize, not just New York, but the world in general. How does the Christian understand, and relate to, a good God in the midst of an often confusing and capricious world?

In light of the presence of evil, the sinner may muse, "If God truly loved me…":

1. I would be shielded from attack by a titanium-alloy exoskeleton

2. I would possess a mind and body impervious to decay and disease

3. I would exhibit intelligence far in excess of every possible challenge

4. I would successfully navigate life with an abiding sense of purpose and triumph

5. I would enjoy the full use of my gifts and the complete exercise of my abilities

6. I would be surrounded by a loving family with many well-disciplined children

7. I would pursue a bountiful career offering abundant opportunity for growth and enjoy the fruit of my labor

8. I would luxuriate in loving, exhilarating, and fulfilling friendships

9. I would bask in the frequent praises of men as I age gracefully

Why does it seem that most of these desires do not come to fruition and never will? In fact, quite often the opposite occurs; it appears that life is slanted against these outcomes. This is the flashpoint for most suffering, the realization that life not only does not meet expectations but, quite often, runs directly counter to them. In fact, God deliberately does not permit that which would make life appear satisfying and fulfilling in man's eyes. This is his supreme mercy, so that some would place uncompromised faith in an unseen, yet present, God.

---

[10] James Weldon Johnson, *The Autobiography of an Ex-Colored Man* (New York: Sherman, French and Company, 1912)

Additionally, if God loves his people then why do very reasonable desires go unrequited? The answer is two-fold. God's focus is never on the here-and-now but on the eternal, so that, he passionately pursues one's complete and total heart worship, either to transform that worship or to reveal it as pleasing to him.

> "This life is a blink of an eye compared to eternity."

While here-and-now events seem so pressing and dominant, while the world holds a clinquant allure, God knows that an infinitely more preferable reality awaits. It is, therefore, with a view toward an eternal time horizon that God engineers present events. However, resisting his efforts is a trenchant indolence in the middle of man's sense of reality, an evil that renders the heart tatterdemalion. God is, therefore, on a search-and-destroy mission to rid his people of their dilapidated state. It is because of hearts blighted with evil that God often has no choice but to place his people into a situation of grave disappointment, pressing pain, and stinging loss. God brings his people to temporal defeat, often time and again, without seeming relief until his work in their hearts is finally accomplished. Therefore, on account of a far greater victory to be won, God's greatest mercy is frequently found in what he does *not* give mankind, since God knows exactly what might serve as a ready distraction to relationship with himself.[11] Often God has no choice but to shatter a misshapen heart so that it can be reassembled as an exquisite mosaic.

> "There are some defeats more triumphant than victories." (Michel de Montaigne)

It must be emphasized that the specific nature of one's suffering may not necessarily be directly related to one's own particular sin, but suffering exists in one's life to expose worship commitments, whether sinful or faithful. Where sin is present God vigorously incentivizes the heart to repent and turn; where faith is present the heart's noble commitments are commended and amplified.

The Search for Answers in an Evil World[12]

Before writing this chapter I visited a Holocaust museum. It offered vivid descriptions of the atrocities perpetrated upon the Jews during World War II, each account more heinous than the last. After that visit, for quite some time I was not the same. It is not just that I did not complain as much; it was that complaint did not even enter my mind (as it is want to do). It was as if my life had entered a new dimension in which my "light and momentary troubles" had evaporated before my eyes.[13] Daily endured insults, infractions, frustrations, ailments, losses, and failures seemed almost

---

[11] Deuteronomy 30:17
[12] For further discussion of evil see the second book in this series, *What Agreement Is There Between the Temple of God and Idols?: The Accidence of Sin and Idolatry*, chapter 1: "Deliver Us from Evil"
[13] 2 Corinthians 4:17

comically quaint in comparison what others have had to endure through no fault of their own.

"There was no obvious path for us, no manual with step-by-step directions about how to deal with a blow like this, no teacher telling us what to do." (Marina Krim)

Lamentations over the Death of the First-Born of Egypt
Charles Sprague Pearce, 1877

The study of suffering (such as that witnessed in the Holocaust) is couched in the term "theodicy" which seeks to answer the question, "If God is omniscient, omnipotent, and omnibenevolent, how does one explain the existence of evil with its attendant suffering and injustice?" The following is a common line of reasoning in fallen mankind:

1. If God is omniscient then he knows evil's machinations before they occur.

2. If God is omnipotent then he can prevent evil.

3. If God is omnibenevolent then he would prevent evil.

4. Evil exists; therefore God is either not omniscient, not omnipotent, not omnibenevolent, or some combination of the three.

So how does one rightly reconcile God's character with the presence of evil?

In exploring theodicy, philosopher Gottfried Leibniz (1646-1716) postulated that this is "the best of all possible worlds."[14] Leibniz reasoned that some amount of evil must exist in order to show the extent of God's power and goodness. Additionally, a measure of evil is necessary to draw out human good. So, for example, the presence of evil might afford one the opportunity to experience the generosity of a neighbor; it might forge a war hero, or set up the opportunity to forgive.

Labeled "absurd optimism" by its critics, Leibniz's view asserts that God formulated the perfect admixture of good and evil in order to most reveal his omniscience, omnipotence, and omnibenevolence. So, for God to reduce evil even slightly would impinge upon the incidence of good as well. Therefore, according to Leibniz, God maximized his display of goodness through the optimal balance of intermingled evil. (As Voltaire (1694-1778) pointed out in his work *Candide* (1759), it was the death of some 80,000 in the Lisbon earthquake of 1755 that finally laid to rest the notion of the "best of all possible worlds.")

> "Have nothing to do with godless myths and old wives' tales; rather, train yourself to be godly." (1 Timothy 4:7)

While Leibniz's theodicy builds upon a reasonable, yet fallacious, premise, what might the biblical counselor rightly say about evil?

1. It is perpetrated by a personal being, Satan (and his emissaries).

2. It is active, has a mind, pursues an agenda, and desires to destroy God's work and his people.[15]

3. It seeks to deceive, enslave, humiliate, and obliterate God's self-revelation through his creation.[16]

4. It is so powerful that human beings are not able to resist it.[17]

5. Christians are not under God's wrath so that,[18] for those in Christ, there is never divine vengeance, but loving discipline which reinforces and reinvigorates faith.[19]

---

[14] Gottfied Wilhelm Leibniz, *Essays on the Goodness of God, the Freedom of Man and the Origin of Evil* (1710)
[15] 1 Peter 5:8
[16] John 8:44
[17] Mark 3:27
[18] John 3:36; Ephesians 2:3
[19] Hebrews 12:6

6. The only way evil could be defeated was for God himself, Jesus Christ, to die.[20] Those in Jesus are promised final deliverance from evil.[21]

7. Through his death on the cross, Jesus destroyed evil's power;[22] at the end of time Jesus will completely remove its presence.[23]

> "A bruised reed he will not break, and a smoldering wick he will not snuff out. In faithfulness he will bring forth justice;" (Isaiah 42:3)

Categorizing Suffering

At this point, it may be instructive to introduce seven core conflicts:

1. Man vs. man
2. Man vs. self
3. Man vs. nature (flora and fauna)
4. Man vs. the environment (topography, the elements)
5. Man vs. machine/technology
6. Man vs. the supernatural (angels, demons, apparitions)
7. Man vs. God

These conflicts offer a means by which to more precisely categorize suffering. Suffering arises in the context of each of these categories, some of it under the umbrella of general suffering, in other instances as the result of indirect human agency and, still in others, as the result of direct human agency.

Thus, these seven conflicts can be summarized under three umbrella categories for suffering:

1. General suffering

Some years ago a careening boulder crashed through the windshield of a car as it coursed through a Californian forest, killing the occupants instantly. Imagine a family rusticating with a drive through majestic scenery and in the blink of an eye it is all over. Consider the precision timing required to affect this tragedy, the boulder dislodging at the exact moment, at the precise height and trajectory, to meet a moving vehicle far below in the very manner that would kill its occupants. Often tragedy strikes with seemingly ruthless exactitude for no discernible reason and without fair warning.

---

[20] Colossians 2:15
[21] 1 Corinthians 15:42
[22] Colossians 2:15
[23] 1 Corinthians 15:24-26

> "Or those eighteen who died when the tower in Siloam fell on them—do you think they were more guilty than all the others living in Jerusalem? I tell you, no! But unless you repent, you too will all perish." (Luke 13:4, 5)

While generalized suffering might be seen as an abstraction, it origin is anything but. When Adam fell in the garden he initiated a cascade of evil resulting in varied experiences of suffering.[24] Women were blighted with pain in childbirth and men with toil in working the ground.[25] Thus, a certain clearly defined and measurable suffering has been injected into the human experience. More broadly, evil of all shades and textures is the result of mankind's original transgression. Yet, the related suffering may not be traceable to specific human acts. As a result of the fall, mankind is generally culpable for giving evil (and its concomitant suffering) an unobstructed portal into the created order. Thus, mankind is besieged by conflict, like a Dyson sphere wrapped around his being, the result of the general presence of evil.

Milo of Croton
Joseph-Benoit Suvee, d. 1807

2. Suffering from indirect human agency

Suffering may result from oppressive social structures which keep some subjugated in one form or another. For example, shortsighted government policies may keep some in a chronic state of poverty. Corruption and greed may keep one choking on

---

[24] The term "cascade of evil" from Douglas Green, Westminster Theological Seminary, Philadelphia, Pennsylvania
[25] Genesis 3:16-19

pollution. At the time of this writing there is a newly-minted political theory that global terrorism is an outgrowth of global warming, that because of spreading drought and crop failure throughout the Middle East, some are more easily drawn to terrorist activity. While I reject such a thesis, it would offer a vivid illustration of the suffering that accrues from indirect human agency.

> "I have told you these things, so that in me you may have peace. In this world you will have trouble. But take heart! I have overcome the world." (John 16:33)

3. Suffering from direct human agency

Mankind may deliberately visit physical or psychological torment upon himself or others for various motives, some purely wanton, others based in hard-hearted ignorance.

> As a personal note, my alma mater, Haverford College, like the overwhelming majority of institutions of higher education, is trenchantly liberal, avowedly anti-gospel, and firmly set against the assertion of absolutes. Yet, as a Christian, Haverford was the greatest educational gift I could have received. I thrived both in the classroom and in the social arena, steadily growing into my faith and taking ever greater ownership of it. My senior year I wrote for the school newspaper, championing a Christian worldview, and relishing the ensuing maelstrom. Something about persecution in that milieu didn't feel like persecution at all, but like a cornucopia of refreshing grace. Haverford's intellectual challenge and forum for debate nurtured my spirit, enlivened my mind, and invested me with a passion and daily purpose that I look back on with a sense of nostalgia.
>
> In the intervening years I have taught in several churches and Christian schools. While I cannot emphasize enough how much I have been wonderfully enriched by many faithful Christians, quite remarkably, I have at times experienced fierce, cutting, debilitating persecution at the hands of those who claim to be Christians (likely false believers).[26] I have, at times, been maligned, insulted, lied to and lied about. Some have deliberately sought to destroy my reputation and teaching with cunning and underhanded attacks. There is something about persecution at the hands of supposed Christians which cuts me to the quick, which strips my soul bare, which renders me a burnt-out husk, something ill-defined that confuses and frightens me. (I sense this same pattern in the apostle Paul, as well.)
>
> The point is that persecution, even when very deliberate, is not homogeneous, and likewise, one's response to it may assume varied hues. There is something about

---

[26] For a more comprehensive discussion of this topic see chapter 10, "Counseling and the Church: Syndicating the Vision"

> opposition at the hands of the world which is forthright, honest, expected, and oddly conquerable, while persecution at the hands of the church is chthonian. In the context of the world, persecution emboldens my spirit; in the context of the church, it crushes it.

Core Conflict and Suffering

	Man vs.						
	Man	Self	Nature	Environment	Machine/Technology	The Supernatural	God
General Suffering			✓	✓		✓	✓
Indirect Human Agency	✓	✓	✓	✓	✓		
Direct Human Agency	✓	✓					

General suffering may result from man's conflict with nature, his environment, the supernatural world, or with God himself. Thus, for sinful man, this form of suffering takes on a somewhat abstract quality, the result of living in a capricious world under the dictates of a vengeful faceless God. Suffering which results from indirect human agency may arise

Time Revealing Truth with Envy and Discord
Nicolas Poussin, 1642

from man's struggle with mankind, with his limitations within himself, with his design (nature), with an environment tainted by human activity, or with cold technology, the work of man's hand. Lastly, suffering may result from direct human agency, as man may deliberately and maliciously seek to inflict harm upon himself or others.

Mankind believes that conflict stands behind suffering (which may or may not be true). Therefore, the preponderance of human activity is directed toward either eliminating conflict, or else ensuring that one comes out on its winning side. Rather than resting in the plans of a good God, who has already achieved triumph over conflict in all of its various forms,[27] mankind takes this conflict upon himself in a Promethean quest to finally emerge as his own god.

Suffering's Blueprint

While there is general suffering, that which arises from indirect human agency, and that which is inflicted through direct human agency, the Bible offers some clues (often murky) for discerning suffering's precise source. The following are common questions concerning specific suffering in individual lives:

1. Is this specific suffering Satan's attack, God's punishment for ongoing disobedience, or God's testing to confirm faith?

2. Is this suffering simply part of living in a fallen world (such as the effects of environmental pollution, for example), or is it more directed, deliberate, and personal than that?

3. To what degree does one's suffering arise from his own lust of the flesh, so that, the heart is pierced by its own idols?

4. Why does certain suffering seem to intensify with increased victory for God's kingdom?

While answers to these questions often remain cloaked behind a cosmic shroud (as with Job), the perceptive counselor may discern patterns, pick up clues, and spy something of God's larger purpose to induce ever more purified heart worship.

The following chart offers a blueprint of the specific sources of suffering, with their effect upon believers and unbelievers alike.

---

[27] Colossians 2:15

SUFFERING

	God's Sovereignty			
	Sources of Suffering:			
	The World[28] (general, external)	**The Flesh**[29] (internal)	**The Devil**[30] (specific, external)	**The Hand of God**[31]
The Unbeliever:				
1. The Mocker	The world glorifies the mocker.	The mocker exhibits a seared conscience.	Satan is allied with the mocker.	God opposes, but does not address the mocker directly
2. The Fool	The world loves the fool.	The fool is tormented by his sinful flesh.	Satan cultivates the fool.	God opposes, and actively engages the fool.
3. The Simple	The world mentors the simple.	The simple is confused by the flesh.	Satan entices the simple.	God pursues the simple.
The Believer:				
1. The New Christian	The world hates and discourages the new Christian.	The new Christian exhibits a growing awareness of his need for sanctification.	The new Christian enjoys a protective hedge for a time.	God nurtures the new Christian.
2. The Disobedient Christian	The world hates, yet tolerates, the disobedient Christian.	The disobedient Christian is unstable and tormented by his sin.	Satan largely disregards and ignores the disobedient Christian.	God punishes the disobedient Christian.
3. The Obedient Christian	The world hates and undermines	The obedient Christian is joyful and at	Satan viciously attacks the	God prunes the obedient Christian.

---

[28] For a detailed handling of the concepts, the world, the flesh, and the devil, see the second book in this series, *What Agreement Is There Between the Temple of God and Idols?: The Accidence of Sin and Idolatry*, chapter 2: "The World, The Flesh, and the Devil: Assessing the Threat Matrix"
[29] The flesh refers to man's sin nature.
[30] The category "Satan" includes demons, and unclean spirits.
[31] The category "The Hand of God" includes angels.

| | the obedient Christian. | peace. | obedient Christian. | |

Notes on the chart:

1. **God's sovereignty.** The ancient Manicheans saw God and Satan as equals vying for supremacy in the universe. The outcome of that battle was uncertain, lending an often ill-defined anxiety to life, like a background psychic static. The Bible offers a drastically different perspective. God is sovereign over all events, whether implemented by his own hand, or by Satan's. While God allows Satan to engineer evil, nothing is outside of God's will, and he is always good in all that he ordains. Thus, Satan cannot act unless God permits and, when he does act, he is conscried to God's carefully calibrated limitations.[32]

Joseph's Brothers Welcomed by Pharaoh
James Joseph Jacques Tissot, c. 1903

"You intended to harm me, but God intended it for good to accomplish what is now being done, the saving of many lives." (Genesis 50:20)

"And we know that in all things God works for the good of those who love him, who have been called according to his purpose." (Romans 8:28)

"Do not be anxious about anything, but in every situation, by prayer and petition,

---

[32] Job 1:12; 2:6; 1 Corinthians 10:13

> with thanksgiving, present your requests to God." (Philippians 4:6)

2. **Unbelievers.**[33] The mocker has confirmed his rebellion against God, teaching and encouraging others to do the same.[34] The fool is rebellious, but not to the same degree. While set in his ways, the fool does not actively promote his godlessness. (Yet, as the fool, in time, deepens his God-hatred, he soon grows into a mocker.) The simple is naïve and in need of instruction, not yet having confirmed himself as a fool.

3. **Believers.** The new Christian, having just passed from death to life, is *de novo* exploring the wonder of regeneration. The disobedient Christian is backslidden, living in a state of rebellion, and trampling the Son of God.[35] The obedient Christian walks faithfully with God, and is found pleasing in his sight.[36]

4. **The world.** The world is an instrument for suffering inflicted in a generalized and externalized manner. This includes systems and societal institutions (corporate lust of the flesh) which, while promoting godlessness, oppress Christians in the process.

The world glories in the mocker as he is its salesman, one who makes the world system attractive and workable. The world loves the fool since he has firmly entrenched himself in its delusion. The world mentors the simple as it makes rebellion against God look like a winning proposition, profitable and wise.

> "If you belonged to the world, it would love you as its own. As it is, you do not belong to the world, but I have chosen you out of the world. That is why the world hates you." (John 15:19)

The world despises all Christians, but tends to tailor its hatred to the Christian's spiritual condition. Thus, while the world discourages the new Christian, it largely does not attack him, as the "infant" in Christ does not yet pose a pressing threat.[37] The world tolerates the disobedient Christian because his faith has been neutralized. In fact, the disobedient Christian legitimates the world's rebellion, and might even be called a friend of the world.[38] However, the obedient Christian, walking faithfully with God, poses a grave threat to the world's hegemonic designs. This Christian will be vigorously opposed.[39] (Incidentally, disobedient

---

[33] The types of unbelievers are based on the categories in the book of Proverbs
[34] Mockers include false believers (2 Corinthians 11:26; Galatians 2:4), false prophets (Matthew 7:15), and eschatological persons such as the antichrists (1 John 2:18) and the man of lawlessness (2 Thessalonians 2:3).
[35] Hebrews 10:29
[36] Zechariah 2:8; 1 John 3:22
[37] 1 Corinthians 3:2
[38] James 4:4
[39] John 16:2

Christians may also serve as the world's attack agents,[40] as that which is fake hates, above all else, the genuine article.)

> "At this they covered their ears and, yelling at the top of their voices, they all rushed at [Stephen], dragged him out of the city and began to stone him. Meanwhile, the witnesses laid their coats at the feet of a young man named Saul." (Acts 7:57, 58)
>
> "For we are to God the pleasing aroma of Christ among those who are being saved and those who are perishing. To the one we are the smell of death; to the other, the fragrance of life…" (2 Corinthians 2:15, 16)
>
> "Some faced jeers and flogging, and even chains and imprisonment. They were put to death by stoning; they were sawed in two; they were killed by the sword. They went about in sheepskins and goatskins, destitute, persecuted and mistreated— the world was not worthy of them. They wandered in deserts and mountains, living in caves and in holes in the ground." (Hebrews 11:36-38)

5. **The flesh.** The flesh operates like a double-edged sword. It presents the occasion for internal suffering in the one who perpetrates sin; it is also an instrument to inflict suffering upon others. Thus, the flesh cuts both ways, as a brandished weapon (positioned externally) which causes self-inflicted wounds (internal). Thus, one's idols function as barbs slashing the heart, so that certain suffering is the result of faulty worship. That faulty worship serves as both an attack agent upon others, and as a self-impaling blade.

The mocker's conscience is seared so that he largely does not carry a burden for sin,[41] having convinced himself of his justified and reasonable self-worship. The fool, plagued by a tortured conscience, feels the crushing weight of sin,[42] but is powerless to remove that burden. The simple is confused and conflicted so that his heart bears some burden for sin, but that sin does not yet exert crippling force.

> Acts 26:14b reads, "…'Saul, Saul, why do you persecute me? It is hard for you to kick against the goads.'" This verse indicates that Saul, in persecuting the church, also inflicted pain upon *himself*, that he suffered through his own megalomaniacal designs.

The new Christian's awareness of his need for repentance and change is recently arising. While he may bear regret for past transgression, his spirit is being renewed.[43] The disobedient Christian, double-minded and unstable,[44] is

---
[40] Matthew 16:23
[41] 1 Timothy 4:2 offers an example of this.
[42] Luke 23:30; Revelation 6:16
[43] Ezekiel 36:26

tormented by his sin so that he finds no peace. The shadow of his unfaithfulness follows him like a haunting scepter. The obedient Christian finds joy in all circumstances,[45] and is at peace as he faithfully walks in God's will.

The Victory of Alexander over Porus, Charles-André van Loo, c. 1738

6. **The devil.** Satan is a person with an active will who works with forceful intent to oppose God and, thus, to destroy his creative fiat.[46] Satan inflicts suffering with wanton delight, and in callous disregard for those afflicted.

In the mocker, Satan finds a dedicated ally willing to promote Satan's cause (in whatever form it takes).[47] Satan cultivates the fool so that he would more assiduously take up Satan's mantle and, in time, become a mocker.[48] Satan pursues the simple, enticing him with an attractive masquerade.[49] Yet, despite his delight in those snatched from God, Satan has no love within him, so that he eventually humiliates and desecrates those who are his own.

> "…Therefore, in order to keep me from becoming conceited, I was given a thorn in my flesh, a messenger of Satan, to torment me." (2 Corinthians 12:7)

---

[44] James 1:8
[45] 1 Thessalonians 5:16
[46] Job 1:7
[47] John 8:44
[48] Psalm 73:3
[49] 2 Corinthians 11:14

> "Be alert and of sober mind. Your enemy the devil prowls around like a roaring lion looking for someone to devour." (1 Peter 5:8)
>
> "The beast and the ten horns you saw will hate the prostitute. They will bring her to ruin and leave her naked; they will eat her flesh and burn her with fire." (Revelation 17:16)

Satan is largely unable to attack the new Christian since God maintains a protective hedge around him. (This allows the roots of faith to take hold without disruptive opposition.) For the most part, Satan disregards and ignores the disobedient Christian, since he poses no functional threat (although he poses an existential threat). Satan viciously attacks the obedient Christian since he is an enemy combatant.[50] Yet, Satan attacks only to the extent that God permits, for the Christian's ultimate good.

> "Simon, Simon, Satan has asked to sift all of you as wheat." (Luke 22:31)
>
> "…hand this man over to Satan for the destruction of the flesh, so that his spirit may be saved on the day of the Lord." (2 Corinthians 5:5)

7. **The hand of God.** God may directly inflict suffering (through elements in the creation),[51] never for malicious purpose, but only so as to induce repentance and subsequent growth in holiness. While upon the sinner, God is justifiably wrathful,[52] this is tempered by common grace,[53] which overlooks transgression for a time.[54]

While God opposes the proud,[55] he largely disregards the mocker since he is a confirmed enemy, vitriolic in his God-hatred.[56] God briskly confronts and confounds the fool, seeking to frustrate his efforts lest he inflict ever greater damage.[57] As with Satan, God pursues the simple, that the simple would be turned to faith.[58] Yet, while Satan entices with sweet allurements, God pursues with life-giving sustenance.[59] Thus, with the simple, God works with a gentle hand, as this sinner is somewhat tender-hearted.

---

[50] Job 1:8; Ecclesiastes 8:14
[51] Job 1:16, 19; 2:3
[52] John 3:36
[53] For further discussion of the issue of common grace see "The Nature of Common Grace" in the second book in this series, *What Agreement Is There Between the Temple of God and Idols?: The Accidence of Sin and Idolatry*, chapter 1: "Deliver Us from Evil"
[54] Romans 5:6
[55] Proverbs 3:34
[56] Acts 9:4-6 offers an exception, as Paul breathed murderous threats against God's people (Acts 9:1), yet God addressed him directly, transforming him into Paul.
[57] Genesis 19:11 and Jonah 4:11 offer two examples of this.
[58] Proverbs 19:20; Isaiah 55:1
[59] Proverbs 9:1-6

> "…the magicians said to Pharaoh, 'This is the finger of God.'" (Exodus 8:19)
>
> "Out in the open wisdom calls aloud; she raises her voice in the public square;" (Proverbs 1:20)
>
> "…They perish because they refused to love the truth and so be saved. For this reason God sends them a powerful delusion so that they will believe the lie." (2 Thessalonians 2:10, 11)
>
> "How much more severely do you think a man deserves to be punished who has trampled the Son of God underfoot, who has treated as an unholy thing the blood of the covenant that sanctified him, and who has insulted the Spirit of grace?" (Hebrews 10:29)

God nurtures the new Christian that he would grow in faith without substantial opposition.[60] God punishes the disobedient Christian, not in burning wrath, but with surgical discipline,[61] that he would come to his senses and return to God.[62] God prunes the faithful Christian that he would be even more fruitful.[63] Often this pruning can be spirited,[64] as the greater the yield of fruit the more vigorous the pruning, that that fruit would be cornucopian.

> "He cuts off every branch in me that bears no fruit, while every branch that does bear fruit he prunes so that it will be even more fruitful." (John 15:2)
>
> "For those who eat and drink without discerning the body of Christ eat and drink judgment on themselves. That is why many among you are weak and sick, and a number of you have fallen asleep." (1 Corinthians 11:29, 30)

The objective of this blueprint is to point out that suffering arises from an assortment of sources. It can stem from general affliction at the hands of a corrupt world system, be the result of idols piercing the heart, be the outworking of Satan's tactical movements, or arise from God's direct intervention. Additionally, suffering assumes various purposes, intensities, contours, and textures depending upon one's status with regard to God, whether trenchant unbeliever, faithful believer, or some middle status. While specific suffering may not always be attributable to a definitive source, this chart offers a guideline in the discernment process.

---

[60] 1 Peter 2:2
[61] Hebrews 12:6; Revelation 3:19
[62] Luke 15:17
[63] Matthew 13:12; Luke 12:48
[64] As in the case of Ananias and Sapphira, in Acts 5:1-11, God's punishment was fatal.

The Question of Retribution Theology

The Last Day of Pompeii, Karl Bryullov, 1827

Job's three friends, Eliphaz the Temanite, Bildad the Shuhite, and Zophar the Naamathite, visited him during a time of intense physical and emotional suffering.[65] These friends propound what might be termed "retribution theology," the erroneous teaching that suffering is inextricably linked to specific sin in the one suffering. Wrongly believing that God slavishly operates by means of a *lex talionis* formula ("an eye for an eye"), Job's friends called on Job to repent in order to effect healing. Since Job was clearly a righteous man,[66] the book of Job refutes retribution theology, asserting that physical suffering is often unrelated to specific sin.[67] (Incidentally, if God did deal by means of the *lex talionis*, each person would, immediately upon conception, be pulverized into dust.)

> Ecclesiastes 1:18 informs that "with much wisdom comes much sorrow; the more knowledge, the more grief." Ignorance is one of God's gifts to men, protecting him from searing anxiety and paralyzing fear.

---

[65] Job 2:11
[66] Job 1:22
[67] Deuteronomy 28 offers itemized blessings for obedience and curses for disobedience, which lends the appearance of retribution theology. However, Israel was on the verge of taking the Promised Land and so at that crucial redemptive-historical juncture God offered compelling incentive to remain committed to the task. Thus, while at times the Bible offers what appears to be retribution theology, it has a much more comprehensive and grander perspective than this. Also consider John 9:3 in this regard.

When faced with suffering or loss, many ask, "Why is this happening to me?" Behind such an inquiry is the deeper question, "Why is God doing this to me?" Although it may not always be easy, the Christian trains his heart to see God's gracious hand in all that comes to pass. Romans 8:28 is clear, "And we know that in all things God works for the good of those who love him, who have been called according to his purpose." For the non-Christian, though, there is no such assurance, nor comfort in the midst of life's trials. Thus, the non-Christian implicitly suspects God's motives, denies God's goodness, and furthers the narrative that he is on his own, an adversary of God vying for survival in a hostile world aligned against him. (This is the idea behind the classic protagonist in ancient Greek literature, the tragic hero.) Thus, the non-Christian routinely ignores and denies God's wisdom, power, and goodness in those events which seem fortuitous, while reflexively impugning God for suffering.

> A glaring problem in the modern world is the confusion of sin with the somatic. Much of what the world labels a form of brain chemistry malfunction or "mental illness" the Bible would label "sin." Thus, the modern world often works in the opposite direction of Job's friends. While Job's friends wrongly accused Job of sin, the world wrongly excuses sin. The world readily reduces sin to an issue of purely unwarranted suffering, a physical ailment, some deficiency, a disease, or an emotional imbalance for which one is not culpable. The world, then, wrongly looks to some false somatic or psychic healing to alleviate that which it erroneously labels. In fact, repentance is the cure for much of what the world labels as mental suffering.

A Biblically-Sound Theodicy

> "Ignorance is a necessary condition in life. If we knew everything, we could not endure for a single hour." (Anatole France)

In May of last year, I was introduced to a twenty-eight year old woman named "Julie," who four years prior had been diagnosed with colon cancer. When I first met Julie she was a phantom of her former self, her frame seemingly fashioned from balsa wood, her eyes hollow and encircled by dark rings. Julie's body was riddled with pain, often so acute that just being awake was an excruciating ordeal. Most days she could not eat and so she progressively weakened.

Above Julie's bed hung a large framed photo of her in a wedding gown. After our introductions, I asked her, "When were you married?" She replied that she was never married, but took the photo just after being diagnosed as a reminder of better days ahead. The photo hung as an encouragement to fight, to persevere, to keep pressing on, that a joyful day awaited.

About a year after being diagnosed with cancer, Julie became a Christian, receiving

Christ as her savior. Bed-ridden, she took advantage of large swaths of time to read the Bible and pray. Quite remarkably, she had nothing but praise for God and thankfulness in her heart for being saved. I never heard a single word of complaint. But what moved me was that Julie had made a vow to God that if she were healed, if she ever regained her strength, she would spend the rest of her life traveling from town to town telling people the good news of Jesus Christ. She promised to make the spread of the gospel her life's work, to be sure that everyone heard of his marvelous deliverance, not so much in body, but in spirit.

One night, in late June, I received a message that Julie had come down with a high fever. Fearing that she might expire, I stayed up much of the night in fervent prayer. Julie recovered, but remained weak. Then, in August, tragedy struck as her father died quite suddenly of cancer. I visited Julie soon after and she looked worse than ever, yet, remarkably, she maintained her praise and core joy. In November, we received news that Julie had gone home to the Lord, the bride adorned for her bridegroom.[68]

In Julie's case, her suffering served a glorious purpose; it brought her to faith in Jesus. For this she, and others, praised God. However, her affliction, while it deepened her faith, hung on far too long to make sense. She had committed herself to a lifetime of evangelism. It would seem that at that point she should have recovered, that full-restoration would have been perfectly logical, that a Cinderella story could have crystallized. However, despite all the prayer, Julie progressively worsened, the pain intensified, and she was struck with grief in seeing her unbelieving father pass away.

Julie's life, like that of so many others, did not follow a majestic arc, did not unfurl a fairytale ending. I still struggle to carve out a heartwarming narrative of triumph and ascent. In my limited frame of reference, her story ended with the impression of defeat, with the unsettled sense of lost opportunity, with a numbing feeling of futile prayer, with the cold haunt of weakness, ugliness, and confusion. Often this is the story that God writes, even for those who love him. Sometimes the narrative appears twisted and convoluted, grossly unappealing, as untimely ripped from the universe's womb. But as Julie voiced and lived out, all the Christian can do is call God good and blindly trust in his greater plans. That is God's aeonian frame of reference.

Reasons that God Allows Suffering[69]

Julie's story serves as a prelude to the issue of understanding God's intention in suffering. The following is a list of reasons that God allows suffering.

1. As wrath upon the confirmed wicked

---
[68] John 3:29; Ephesians 5:27
[69] These categories adapted from the New International Version, topical index for "pain"

Sodom and Gomorrah, the twin evil metropolises, came under God's wrath on account of unrelenting and heinous sin. The inhabitants experienced untold suffering as a result of God's fiery judgment.[70]

The Consequences of War, Peter Paul Rubens, 1638

2. To test his people in order to see if they live by faith or are ruled by idolatry

God tested Abraham to see if he would, as had been commanded, indeed sacrifice his promised son, Isaac.[71] Abraham submitted to God's will, reasoning that God could raise Isaac from the dead.[72]

> Recently, I mentioned to a friend the difficulty in discerning true Christians from false believers. My friend's response seems right on the mark. "That is why God will bring intense persecution, because then we will see who the real Christians are." My friend is right. Persecution functions like a prism clarifying faith from unbelief. In fact, the more intense the persecution, the greater the prism's clarifying effect. So that, as persecution rises, one gains ever greater acuity to discern genuine faith.[73]

3. To discipline or punish his people

> "...the Lord disciplines the one he loves, and he chastens everyone he accepts as his

---

[70] Genesis 19:24
[71] Genesis 22:1-10
[72] Hebrews 11:19
[73] Matthew 24:10; Luke 18:8

son." (Hebrews 12:6)

4. To purify his people

"He cuts off every branch in me that bears no fruit, while every branch that does bear fruit he prunes so that it will be even more fruitful." (John 15:2)

5. To make his will known

"It is good for me to be afflicted so that I might learn your decrees." (Psalm 119:71)

6. To advance the gospel

As Saul went from house to house to destroy the church, "those who had been scattered preached the word wherever they went."[74] Thus, Satan's attempts to squash the fledgling church only resulted in the gospel's propagation.

Of the reasons for suffering listed above, only the first conforms to the human conception of the universe's blueprint. According to a man-centered construal of justice, the wicked are supposed to be severely punished, while the innocent escape unscathed (retribution theology). If God's wrath were an easily delineated matter, then suffering would make perfect sense. However, it is the subsequent five categories which frequently confound even the wisest Christian. How does a Christian know whether he is being tested or disciplined, whether he suffers as a result of living faithfully or as part of God's plan to bring submission to his will, whether suffering is from Satan's hand or God's directly? These questions can be difficult to untangle. The Christian may ask for wisdom to understand God's intention, but often that understanding does not appear. Sometimes God's intention clarifies in time, but often it does not.

Many seek out counseling hoping for answers concerning horrific personal tragedies. They may want to understand how God could possibly love them when they have experienced such bitter loss, or have been sinned against so brutally. How can God possibly be omniscient, omnipotent, and omnibenevolent when the world is a quagmire of piercing grief, searing hardship, and torturous defeat? In answering this question there are two dangers, both based in sinful pride. The first is to see all human suffering (even one's own) as the direct result of specific failing and sin.[75] (Some suffering is simply the result of living in a fallen world.) The second is to see suffering as God's fault because he is either unknowing, impotent, or uncaring.[76]

---

[74] Acts 8:3, 4
[75] John 9:2, 3
[76] Andrew Field, "Introduction to Redeemer," p. 6, Westminster Theological Seminary, Philadelphia, Pennsylvania

Fallen man desperately searches for cause-and-effect in an evil world, a hidden cipher to unwind life's mystery. Outside of the parameters of the gospel itself, the Bible does not offer a decisive explanation for evil. Additionally, on account of God's common grace sometimes the wicked prosper, while the righteous, under God's special grace, suffer. While the wise counselor rejects retribution theology (what might be termed "negative causality"), he does not pretend that a positive causality exists when it does not, that on account of being God's child one should be free from the stinging presence of evil.[77]

> "I have seen a wicked and ruthless man flourishing like a luxuriant native tree, but he soon passed away and was no more; though I looked for him, he could not be found." (Psalm 37:35, 36)
>
> "Surely God is good to Israel, to those who are pure in heart. But as for me, my feet had almost slipped; I had nearly lost my foothold. For I envied the arrogant when I saw the prosperity of the wicked." (Psalm 73:1-3)

The counselor cannot:

1. Explain the reason that God allows evil to exist
2. Explain why God allows his children to often acutely experience evil
3. Promise freedom from evil in the future[78]

What can safely be said about suffering:

1. Mankind was never meant to suffer since he was not designed to be subject to evil. Suffering is an unwelcomed intrusion into God's perfect order.

2. God allows suffering for empyrean purpose, and he is always good in the way that suffering takes effect.

3. Mankind brought general suffering upon himself in the fall, but specific suffering may or may not be the result of personal culpability.

4. God has numbered the hairs on the Christian's head,[79] has counted his days,[80] and promises never to leave nor forsake him.[81]

Mankind, in the fall, tragically brought suffering upon himself when he formed an

---

[77] For further discussion of the issue of evil see the second book in this series, *What Agreement Is There Between the Temple of God and Idols?: The Accidence of Sin and Idolatry*, chapter 1: "Deliver Us from Evil"
[78] John 16:33
[79] Luke 12:7a
[80] Psalm 56:8; Luke 12:25
[81] Deuteronomy 31:6

alliance with Satan. However, the reason for specific suffering is often part of a concealed calculus to which mankind is not privy. What the Bible does reveal is that suffering was, and is, a component of a far greater redemptive-historical purpose, the uncovering and transformation of the human heart.

> Second Samuel 18:33 states, "The king was shaken. He went up to the room over the gateway and wept. As he went, he said: 'O my son Absalom! My son, my son Absalom! If only I had died instead of you – O Absalom, my son, my son!'" David was indirectly to blame for Absalom's death, as he failed to discipline his son. Was this retribution from God? No. It would be more accurate to describe this as the wages of sin, that sin always brings unforeseen consequence.
>
> "Nevertheless, when we are judged in this way by the Lord, we are being disciplined so that we will not be finally condemned with the world." (1 Corinthians 11:32)

Two Poles in the Sinful Response to Suffering

The Nightmare, John Henry Fuseli, 1781

Traditionally a tension exists in the methodology behind children's fairytales. *Aesop's Fables* (6th century BC), built upon unbridled fantasy, offers a sanitized and glossed form of moralistic storytelling, one in which the good, wholesome, and pure always prevail. This approach sketches out for children a largely unblemished world in which they could find refuge for a time, unburdened by the life concerns that would invariably visit them later.

At the opposite pole, *Grimm's Fairytales* (1812), the purveyor of shadowy realism, involves often gruesome and unsettling plotlines and images which could easily frighten a child. Antagonists are grotesque, duplicitous, and heartless, and, quite surprisingly, sometimes they vanquish the protagonist. *Grimm's Fairytales* were written to offer children an accurate understanding of reality, one in which evil not only exists, but often prevails for a time. Behind this pedagogy was the hope to adequately prepare children for that which they would undoubtedly face as they ventured further along life's path.[82]

As with this tension in children's fairytales, adults, when faced with suffering, generally exhibit two sinful responses, the Stoic (possibly in the vein of *Grimm's Fairytales*) and the Romanticized (possibly in the vein of *Aesop's Fables*).[83] (These two approaches represent diametric extremes between which exists a spectrum of hybrid responses.)

On one end of the spectrum, Stoicism (apatheia) ignores suffering since suffering is seen to hold no intrinsic value. The idea is to take one's mind off of emotional pain, to deny that it exists. The Stoic ignores pain, buries it, and renounces it, so that he assumes an impassive exterior which closes himself off to God and his work. (It is worth noting that 1 Corinthians 15:58a reads, "Therefore, my dear brothers, stand firm. *Let nothing move you*." Did the apostle Paul advocate stoicism? No. Paul exhibited a vivid and bountiful sense of emotion, one carefully cultivated to accomplish the task for which he was called.)

> "Slight sorrows are loquacious; deep anguish has no voice." (Seneca)

On the other end of the spectrum, Romanticism (a certain form of ataraxia) exalts suffering since suffering is seen as a potent and expeditious expression of the human drama. The sinner often embraces his suffering, relishing pain with a sense of pride in perseverance. The romanticized view of pain celebrates it, reminds the heart daily of it, and builds a case for a tragic-hero narrative, the notion that God is against the sufferer and mankind must fend for himself in a cruel world. Based in pride, both responses, the Stoic and the Romantic, refute the notion that God acts for the good of those who

---

[82] It is possible that the book of Proverbs mediates between these two extremes as it, directed toward a young man, offers both idealized morality and unvarnished graphic realism. Additionally, it is fascinating that Deuteronomy 6 commands fathers to teach the Word of God to their children, but does not limit that teaching. There are myriad sections of Scripture which contain highly-graphic violence and even explicit description of sexual perversity. It would appear that children were not necessarily to be shielded from those sections of Scripture.

[83] These two categories, the Stoic and Romanticized, from Paul Tripp, "Psalm 73: Exalting Pain, Ignoring Pain: What Do We Do with Suffering?," *The Journal of Biblical Counseling* (Glenside, Pennsylvania: The Christian Counseling and Education Foundation)

love him.[84]

> The romanticized view of suffering could be summarized with the statement, "No cross, no crown."[85] If separated from the gospel, this motto transforms Jesus' cross into an existential abstraction so that suffering is elevated and validated as a means for supposedly deserved glory.

Romantic author Percy Shelley (1792-1822) wrote, "Our sweetest songs are those that tell of saddest thought." There is something within fallen humanity which seeks to rehearse past sadness. There is something exonerating, something ennobling, something which spurs on and defends defiance. Past sadness and loss makes one feel that he is justified in his rebellion, that God is not good, cannot be trusted, and that therefore one must wisely become his own god.

> "Faith is to believe what you do not see; the reward of this faith is to see what you believe." (Augustine)

"Soft-Suffering"

> Vincent van Gogh (1853-1890) sold only one painting during his lifetime, and it was to his brother.

The modern mindset about suffering tends to follow the contours of television drama, easily definable "broadcast-able" events. Thus, when people think of suffering they conjure images of Biafran victims, the Columbine massacre, or the events of September 11, 2001, unbridled and brutal physical displays of evil. While these are clearly tragedies involving incalculable human suffering, there is a more subtle, often unnoticed, form of suffering, what might be termed "soft-suffering":[86] plodding anonymity, daily frustration, existential angst, and the loss of meaningful métier or relationship.

> "Misfortunes come on horseback and depart on foot." (French proverb)

In a world in which 38 million people are subject to functional slavery, and 13 million people die each year from malnutrition, how could one justifiably think of any well-fed, clothed, and housed person as suffering? Although one may have his physical needs met, there is nevertheless throbbing pain in being overlooked, rejected, humiliated, shouted down, slandered, unfairly criticized, unjustly accused, seeing one's work end in failure, unable to use one's God-given gifts, sacrificing one's

---

[84] Romans 8:28
[85] The full quote is "No pain, no palm; no thorns, no throne; no gall, no glory; no cross, no crown." (William Penn)
[86] Some might term soft-suffering as "First World suffering."

reputation to serve others, forsaking one's livelihood and future for a just cause, standing for truth and being hated for it, and growing old while forsaking the usual "rewards." (A comprehensive list would encompass just about every human experience in some sense.)

> A friend once joked, "The universe refuses to acknowledge your existence." In some sense this aptly encapsulates my Christian experience. In life's daily commerce, in the world's eyes and in the eyes of worldly people, it is as if I stand behind an ill-defined and haunting shroud of anonymity, the universe sensing that I am not its own, an alien species unwelcomed in this world.[87]

There is often a slow corrosive suffering that garners little attention and is frequently labeled in benign terms. However, many suffer in ways that others never see and cannot understand because that suffering is cloaked. It is the burden of a slow march of days with few punctuating events to break the monotony; it is the sting of continual social alienation for no fault of one's own; it is the searing pain of seeing a lifetime of work eviscerated or rendered inconsequential. It is the agony of seeing those around oneself persist in self-destructive delusion without ears to hear the truth. This soft-suffering is often the most difficult to understand and

Faded Laurels
Edmund Blair Leighton, d. 1922

counsel since it is not demarked by observable assault; there is no flash of light, just a hinterland of varied shades of pain.

---
[87] 1 Peter 2:11

> A young Christian woman recently enrolled in a graduate program in psychology at an elite university. I spoke to her about the poisonous nature of psychology, outlining that her life and faith are being severely damaged, and that she is being taught to harm other's lives as well.[88] This woman's serene comportment unraveled quite suddenly, as she became belligerent and personally attacking. I was shocked that one who calls herself a Christian would display such seething rage, especially toward another Christian offering sound wisdom.
>
> I recount this anecdote to highlight the issue of soft-suffering. Two people suffered in this exchange. The woman suffered as she contemplated her time, money, and effort wasted, the possibility that what she thought to be service for God's kingdom was a fraud. I suffered the sting of hurtful words hurled with the malicious intent to discredit me and my teaching. The cumulative effect of such wounding interactions can be formidable.

As a side note, while the Christian may endure suffering with a profound sense of trust in an unseen God who has only his best in mind, he does not passively allow those he loves to speak or act abusively toward him, when he can prevent them from doing so. The reason is that the one who abuses another heaps a burden of sin and guilt upon himself.[89] Thus, the Christian, when it is within his reasonable power, does not passively allow another to increase his sin in this way.

St. George and the Dragon
Peter Paul Rubens, 1606

Recipient and Responder

Mankind's emotional pain has two components:

---

[88] For a comprehensive response to psychology see the first book in this series, *Ask for the Ancient Paths: From Art to Artifice to Arisen*, chapter 8: "What Has Jerusalem To Do With Vienna?: The Case Against Psychology"
[89] Proverbs 25:22; Romans 12:20

1. Each person has been sinned against. Everyone is a victim of evil in some form.

2. Each, as a sinner, responds to being sinned against, sinfully. In the midst of an evil world, the sinner makes himself into god. Each "plays god" by trying to alleviate his pain, loss, and suffering in a godless manner, for his own self-serving purpose. Thus, while one has been sinned against, he responds sinfully, adopting various tones and textures of revenge (some overt, some covert). While one experiences suffering in being sinned against, that suffering amplifies, taking on distinct contours, as one responds sinfully.

> Roman philosopher Publilius Syrus (1st C. BC) wrote, "The wounds of love can only be healed by the one who made them." In fact, the sinner routinely inflicts his own wounds, wounds that are only healed through submission to God's healing intervention through Jesus Christ.

Thus, the sinner's emotional pain has built within it a two-fold experience – being sinned against, and in response, sinning. Fallen man's pain is often directly related to the degree to which he functionally makes himself into a Pythagorean priest seeking to live out a surrogate form of salvation, one of his own supposed reasonable designs.

When Suffering Arises from One's Own Failing

> "No man is hurt but by himself." (Diogenes)

A young Christian man expressed a fear of having to face an audience. He described every word spoken in front of others as "a painful proposition." Something about this young man's fear brings to mind Matthew 26:75, "Then Peter remembered the word Jesus had spoken: 'Before the rooster crows, you will disown me three times.' And he went outside and wept bitterly." Peter suffered at his own hand, on account of a self-induced fear of man. This young man's fear of his audience contains within it echoes of Peter's disavowal of Christ, a root denial of Jesus's death for him. This man's heart must be exposed in its derelict fear so that he would be brought to repentance in the responsible fear of God. As the fear of people dissipates, and as the fear of God grows, the pain will lift, the suffering will vanish.

> Judges 10:16 states, "Then they got rid of the foreign gods among them and served the LORD. And he could bear Israel's misery no longer." This verse implies that Israel's misery resulted from its idolatry.

The counsel for suffering must distinguish between that which results from living innocently in an evil world (as with Job), and that which results from one's own sinful response to an evil world.[90] While many suffer at the hands of a world permeated with evil (for example, 150 million executed by totalitarian governments in the twentieth century alone), in daily life the greater source of suffering accrues from one's own sinful response to an evil world (or, at times, a just world). Sometimes suffering is the direct result of idols of the heart which skewer the heart like internal shards of glass. First Timothy 6:10b states, "…Some people, eager for money, have wandered from the faith and pierced themselves with many griefs." In light of God's warranted punishment upon sin, the counselor should not ameliorate nor mitigate the effect of God's discipline unless God himself does.

> "…and that in this matter no one should wrong or take advantage of a brother or sister. The Lord will punish all those who commit such sins, as we told you and warned you before." (1 Thessalonians 4:6)

First Peter 4:15 reads, "If you suffer, it should not be as a murderer or thief or any other kind of criminal, or even as a meddler." Suffering frequently arises as a result of the Christian's own doing, the consequence of his own desire, and obsession with, unmet perceived needs. In fact, I find that the vast majority of emotional suffering arises from expectations that go unmet, expectations that may be perfectly reasonable

False Dmitrys Agents Murdering Feodor Godunov and His Mother
Konstantin Makovsky, 1862

but, nevertheless, have taken on idolatrous proportions. In this vein, Isaiah 50:11 states,

---

[90] 1 Peter 4:14-16

> But now, all you who light fires and provide yourselves with flaming torches, go, walk in the light of your fires and of the torches you have set ablaze. This is what you shall receive from my hand: You will lie down in torment.

Sometimes torment results from daily lying on a self-constructed Procrustean bed, a certain weariness of the soul in struggling to live without God and against God. Some even fashion for themselves a narrative of pain as a way to exonerate a guilty heart, gain attention, deflect potential criticism, maintain a ready excuse for failure, or hedge against imminent rejection. The "wounded" narrative is a facile means of gaining what one wants. Some cultivate and augment their wounds so as to gain some real or perceived social advantage. Consider Jesus's words to Saul on the road to Damascus, "…'Saul, Saul, why do you persecute me? It is hard for you to kick against the goads.'"[91] This idea of kicking against the goads is to bring acute physical suffering upon oneself through resisting the truth, through fighting against God himself. Saul was to blame for his own tormented spirit.

> "If a man speaks of his misfortunes there is something in them that is not disagreeable to him." (Samuel Johnson)

The one in pain often seeks, through his own suffering posture, to install himself as a hero. An effective way to do this is to prop up a foil, to designate a scapegoat of one's own imagining. (This is true of both individuals and of cultures, more broadly.) Often those who bring about their own destructive consequences desperately seek someone to blame outside of themselves, or outside of their own subculture. Often a subculture visits evil upon its own members, yet the greater the intensity of the pain, and the more evident that that pain is the subculture's own doing, the more vociferously it searches for external culprits. So pain, when clearly attributable to internal causes and close associates, is blamed on any visible, dominant, and assailable group, especially those who hold significant power or a traditional worldview.

> If counseling does not expose the idols of the heart then it tends to institutionalize those idols through strengthened rationale for them.[92]

Suffering and Complaint

The Bible outlines three types of grace:[93]

1. Common (to all men)

---

[91] Acts 26:14b
[92] Paul Tripp, *Instruments in the Redeemer's Hands: People in Need of Change Helping People in Need of Change* (Presbyterian and Reformed Publishing Company, 2002)
[93] For further discussion of grace see "The Nature of Common Grace" in the second book in this series, *What Agreement Is There Between the Temple of God and Idols?: The Accidence of Sin and Idolatry*, chapter 1: "Deliver Us from Evil"

2. Prevenient (calling sinners to repentance)
3. Special (for those in Christ)

All grace, whether common, prevenient, or special, is the direct emanation from Jesus' death on the cross. All grace is an undeserved gift at the direct expense of Christ. Consider Romans 3:25, "God presented Christ as a sacrifice of atonement, through the shedding of his blood--to be received by faith. He did this to demonstrate his righteousness, because in his forbearance he had left the sins committed beforehand unpunished—." Thus, all of humanity has experienced a cosmic forbearance on sin (to various degrees in times and places).[94] So even the sunshine on the wicked is Christ's gift freely lavished on his enemies.[95]

> "...for he knows how we are formed, he remembers that we are dust" (Psalm 103:14)

A Little Nimrod, James Jacques Joseph Tissot, c. 1882

Numbers 11:1 recounts that "the people complained about their hardships in the hearing of the Lord." God responded with potent chastening discipline. On account of his Son, God most hates grumbling and complaint among his own people, those specifically claimed by Christ. The logic unfolds in this way. If everything is from Christ, through Christ, and for Christ,[96] then all of human history, all events, are ultimately authored to display something of Christ's sacrifice on the cross, to reveal

---
[94] Luke 2:10
[95] Matthew 5:45
[96] Romans 11:36

his glory. The life's plenary experience arises from Christ, so that all life, in its multifarious display, is maintained by the grace Jesus won on the cross.

Now consider that grumbling and complaining are birthed from a distain of events and, in this sense, represent an implicit assault upon the grace gained through Jesus' sacrifice. Thus, the boy who complains about the rain prohibiting his outdoor fun, in essence denies the grace Christ offers in the context of that day, a grace that plans events for eternal purpose. Through complaint, that boy implicitly attacks the God who created the day for his purposes in the hearts of those impacted. If one understands the pervasive nature of Christ's death, then one understands God's burning hatred for complaint, since complaint, regardless of where it is directed, is nothing short of a curse specifically against God's Son.

In other words, that rainy day exists for one purpose - to glorify Jesus. That day was carefully designed to in some way encroach upon the hearts of those living through it, that they would desire Jesus more (in the midst of either disappointment or gain). Such an understanding precludes complaint since complaint arises from a heart of foolishness, blind to Jesus standing at the pivot of all circumstance. Additionally, that day perfectly coincides with the condition of each impacted heart as part of either God's calling (to the non-Christian) or sanctification (in the Christian).

Thus, the boy who forgoes his outdoor fun with a Christ-glorifying heart has learned something more about his need to trust in a good God, has learned something of the imperative to exercise discipline. He has grown in wisdom to see God's hand directing events for eternal purposes, not for temporal ones. He glimpses the joy of praising God in all circumstances.[97] That day, like all others, was perfectly planned for that boy's knowledge of, and growth in, Jesus.

That being said, how does the counselor encourage those he counsels to honestly express their thoughts, to openly share their feelings, and even their doubts, without allowing such expression to descend into complaining? When does sharing one's story crossover into grumbling? How does the counselor guard against exacerbating or tacitly condoning a grievance mentality in the course of the counsel itself? The answer to these questions has a great deal to do with the posture and motive of the discussion. Is the motive to calmly recount facts, or it is to stoke retributive anger for painful wounds?

The one who suffers is invited to air his grievance directly with God (as Job did), but not to lodge a complaint with others (as did the Israelites in the desert). The counselor must be vigilant to maintain the integrity of the interaction, so as to guard God's honor, never allowing a spirit of complaint to permeate the counseling endeavor. The

---
[97] 1 Thessalonians 5:18

counselor may certainly encourage Jobian pondering and query under the aegis of reverent supplication, but he must never allow any trial to descend into a phillipic against God's goodness.

Thus, the wise counselor takes responsibility to gently nudge the counselee toward the gospel in the midst of the counselee's often painful story. As the counselor senses complaint creeping into the narrative, he mobilizes to draw the counselee back to Jesus, his goodness, his faithfulness, his love for those who belong to him. The counselor, sensing the arc of the discussion's trajectory, works proactively to keep the counselee on a single path to know and be known by Jesus.

The Execution of Lady Jane Grey
Paul Delaroch, 1834

It is important to note that, in the face of another's suffering, merely stating platitudes such as, "It could be worse," or "Look on the bright side," accomplish nothing (except to possibly rehabilitate idols). The heart does not reckon its pain in a cosmic balance; it does not set up comparisons with some ethereal standard of tragedy.[98] Thus, stating clichés both aggravates the discomfited heart and leaves its idolatrous core unchallenged. In other words, the wise counselor knows that the assessment of suffering tends to operate outside of the dictates of sound reason. He, therefore, navigates the counselee's complaint as God does - on its worship terms (a return to the gospel and Jesus' purposes in the lives of those who belong to him). At times, when I have personally been in emotional pain, I simply restate the gospel to myself, time and again. The gospel, not merely as a propositional truth but as a re-acquaintance with Jesus himself, is deeply cleansing; it lightens a burden of grief; it girds up the heart to press on.

Idols of the heart operate just as vigorously in suffering as they do in relative contentment. The suffering sinner is not to be relinquished of his responsibility to

---
[98] Job 6:2

repent. However, that being said, the counselor must exercise caution so as not to provoke a grieving heart, unduly burden a fragile conscience, or inadvertently break a bruised reed.[99] Suffering may expose the heart's contours and contents, but the counselor must be wise to know when and how to elucidate that content. To isolate a need (whatever that need seems to be), and deal only with that need, is to leave the individual untouched. In wise ways and at appropriate times, the individual is to be challenged; ambitions are to be studied; the sinful nature is to be addressed, and the fiber of character is to be exposed. To neglect this work is not only to forsake God's intentions in the counselee's life, but to leave the counselee vulnerable to ongoing emotional pain.

> "For with much wisdom comes much sorrow; the more the knowledge, the more grief." (Ecclesiastes 1:18)

Case Study: Suicide: Idols in Death Throws[100]

> Crystals form in a supersaturated solution. Such a solution can sit indefinitely without crystallizing until some small object, a nidus, is dropped into it. Just a single grain of sand can start the process, and once the crystal begins to form the process is irreversible. This is an apt description for understanding people. Many operate in a near "supersaturated solution" of psychic need poised for emotional tragedy. All that is required is a nidus to begin the cascade effect toward debilitating depression.

In Nathaniel Hawthorne's (1804-1864) short-story, "Ethan Brand" (1852), one night a man commits suicide by throwing himself into a blazing limekiln. In the morning, all that was found was his skeleton with his heart turned to lime. Hawthorne seemed to recognize not only the centrality and enduring nature of the human heart, but that in suicide, as with no other act, the heart's worship is decisively exposed. While the previous section explored the question of suffering and complaint, this next section analyzes complaint in its most extreme form – suicide, the final and fatal protest toward the person of God himself. Suicide is complaint cast beyond the pale of hope, without the expectation of response. It is grievance thrust into a cosmic vacuum out of which one expects only bitter cold silence.

Paths to Suicide

People commit suicide, or engage in suicidal ideations, for a host of reasons. The following are some examples:

1. Unrequited or lost love

---
[99] Isaiah 42:3
[100] For some additional analysis of suicide, using an example from the Bible, see the section, "Competing Stories" in chapter 6: "The Basic Plotlines Which Emerge in Counseling"

Giacomo Puccini's opera *Madame Butteryfly* (1904) is set in Japan in the early 20th century. Lieutenant B.F. Pinkerton of the U. S. Navy inspects a house overlooking Nagasaki harbor that he leases from Goro, a marriage broker. The house comes with three servants and a geisha wife, Cio-Cio-San, also known as Madame Butterfly. Butterfly agrees to marry Pinkerton, who departs soon after the wedding. Three years later Pinkerton returns to visit Butterfly with his newest acquisition, an American wife named "Kate." Overcome with grief, Butterfly brandishes a dagger with which her father committed suicide, choosing to die with honor rather than live in shame. In the context of the opera, Butterfly's suicide appears justified and noble, as she is cast as a hapless victim of cruel forlorn love.

Jeremiah
Michelangelo Buonarroti, c. 1512

2. The loss of honor or prestige

Qu Yuan (屈原) was a wise official under Governor Huai of Chu during the Warring States Period (475–221 BC). Rival officials, envious of Qu Yuan, persuaded the governor to exile him. Qu Yuan penned his anguish in the poem, "Leaving the Tumult," and on the fifth day of the fifth month committed suicide by jumping into the Mi Luo River. The locals searched for his body, but it was lost.[101]

> "Where the river is deepest, it makes the least noise." (Italian proverb)

> 'Cursed be the day I was born! May the day my mother bore me not be blessed! Cursed be the man who brought my father the news, who made him very glad, saying, 'A child is born to you—a son!' May that man be like the towns the LORD overthrew without pity. May he hear wailing in the morning, a battle cry at noon. For he did not kill me in the womb, with my mother as my grave, her womb enlarged forever. Why did I ever come out of the womb

---

[101] Ren Xiu Hua, *Classic Legends of Traditional Chinese Culture* (2009) 17-19.

to see trouble and sorrow and to end my days in shame?' (Jeremiah 20:14-18)

3. The avoidance of humiliation or defeat

In December, 2015, the French Foreign Ministry named Benoît Violier (1971-2016) "the world's best chef." His Le Restaurant de l'Hôtel de Ville, in Lausanne, Switzerland, was one of only one hundred restaurants in the world to receive three Michelin stars. Yet, basking in international fame, Violier inexplicably committed suicide on January 31, 2016. His death draws attention to the excruciating perfectionism that goes into haute cuisine. Some describe Violier's craft as daily creating a work of art, watching it disappear, and creating it all over again every evening (like Sisyphus laboring in Hades). And as is common with world-renowned chefs, the prospect of losing a Michelin star induces almost paralyzing fear. For one who had reached the pinnacle of his profession, possibly the thought of falling from that height was a burden too great to bear. Suicide seemed like the most dignified way to avoid the perceived humiliation of potentially slipping to merely "one of the best."

Other examples of the avoidance of humiliation or defeat include:

> Abimelek went to the tower and attacked it. But as he approached the entrance to the tower to set it on fire, a woman dropped an upper millstone on his head and cracked his skull. Hurriedly he called to his armor-bearer, 'Draw your sword and kill me, so that they can't say, 'A woman killed him.' So his servant ran him through, and he died. (Judges 9:52-54)

> Saul said to his armor-bearer, 'Draw your sword and run me through, or these uncircumcised fellows will come and run me through and abuse me.' But his armor-bearer was terrified and would not do it; so Saul took his own sword and fell on it. When the armor-bearer saw that Saul was dead, he too fell on his sword and died with him. So Saul and his three sons and his armor-bearer and all his men died together that same day. (1 Samuel 31:4-6)

> 'How long, Lord? Will you forget me forever? How long will you hide your face from me? How long must I wrestle with my thoughts and day after day have sorrow in my heart? How long will my enemy triumph over me? Look on me and answer, Lord my God. Give light to my eyes, or I will sleep in death, and my enemy will say, 'I have overcome him,' and my foes will rejoice when I fall.' (Psalm 13:1-4)

Matthew 27:5 states, "So Judas threw the money into the temple and left. Then he went away and hanged himself." Judas betrayed God in life, and with his death offered a final exclamation of his refusal to repent.

4. When under extreme duress and paralyzing fear

> Then Jacob tore his clothes, put on sackcloth and mourned for his son many days. All his sons and daughters came to comfort him, but he refused to be comforted. 'No,' he said, 'in the morning I will go down to the grave to my son.' So his father wept for him. (Genesis 37:34, 35)

> Elijah was afraid and ran for his life. When he came to Beersheba in Judah, he left his servant there, while he himself went a day's journey into the wilderness. He came to a broom bush, sat down under it and prayed that he might die. 'I have had enough, LORD,' he said. 'Take my life; I am no better than my ancestors.' (1 Kings 19:3, 4)

> 'Even then you frighten me with dreams and terrify me with visions, so that I prefer strangling and death, rather than this body of mine. I despise my life; I would not live forever. Let me alone; my days have no meaning.' (Job 7:14-16)

Revelation 9:6 bears a warning that in the end times many will suffer. "During those days people will seek death but will not find it; they will long to die, but death will elude them."

5. As a form of defiance or revenge

> Then Samson reached toward the two central pillars on which the temple stood. Bracing himself against them, his right hand on the one and his left hand on the other, Samson said, 'Let me die with the Philistines!' Then he pushed with all his might, and down came the temple on the rulers and all the people in it. Thus he killed many more when he died than while he lived. (Judges 16:29, 30)

> In ancient Rome and in medieval Japan suicide, performed in defiance of perceived or actual tyrants, was seen as an assertion of personal freedom.[102]

> 'Did I [Moses] conceive all these people? Did I give them birth? Why do you tell me to carry them in my arms, as a nurse carries an infant, to the land you promised on oath to their ancestors? Where can I get meat for all these people? They keep wailing to me, 'Give us meat to eat!' I cannot carry all these people by myself; the burden is too heavy for me. If this is how you are going to treat me, please go ahead and kill me—if I have found favor in your

---
[102] Wikipedia article on suicide and legislation

eyes—and do not let me face my own ruin.' (Numbers 11:12-15)

Jonah 4:3, 4 records the prophet's demand, "'Now, Lord, take away my life, for it is better for me to die than to live.' But the Lord replied, 'Is it right for you to be angry?'"

> "Anger: an acid that can do more harm to the vessel in which it is stored than to anything on which it is poured." (Seneca)

The Bible is filled with characters who struggled deeply with the searing pain of life's debilitating disappointment. Throughout the Bible, those who faithfully served God often exhibited a piercing travail of the soul, the quest for deliverance and, at times, even high-handed defiance toward a God who was perceived to have failed. Many begged for death as an act of God's mercy. However, for those in submission to God there was always the recognition that God himself is justly sovereign over life and death. Despite bitter cries, those of faith continued to live in the expectation that God would deliver them in time.

Alenushka
Viktor Vasnetsov, 1881

I [Paul] eagerly expect and hope that I will in no way be ashamed, but will have sufficient courage so that now as always Christ will be exalted in my body, whether by life or by death. For to me, to live is Christ and to die is gain. If I am to go on living in the body, this will mean fruitful labor for me. Yet what shall I choose? I do not know! I am torn between the two: I desire to depart and be with Christ, which is better by far... (Philippians 1:20-23)

Understanding Modern Suicide[103]

---

[103] Much of the data which follows is from the Englewood Hospital and Medical Center (Englewood, New Jersey)

Consider a herd of water buffalo under chase from a pride of lion on the open savannah. Which buffaloes are most likely to be taken? The stragglers, the outliers, will be culled from the herd. The young, the old, the sick, and the wounded are vulnerable, while those which remain within a close pack will go unscathed.

This analogy offers some limited explanation of the way in which suicide affects certain segments of society with greater profundity than others. Those who operate on the fringes, outside of the safety of a tight "herd" (certain cultural institutions and expectations), are most vulnerable.

In the United States who is most likely to commit suicide?

1. Those under age twenty four, often from divorced homes, and usually while abusing drugs or alcohol

2. Those in an abusive relationship, or subject to a turbulent home environment

3. The socially isolated

4. Homosexuals

5. Among blacks, men are most likely to commit suicide as young adults

6. Among those of European descent, men are most likely to commit suicide after age sixty-five

7. The chronically ill

8. Senior citizens, especially those over age eighty

Findings for Further Investigation

1. Prior to about 1960, suicide was largely confined to the aged and infirm, but since that time suicide has risen precipitously among those under age twenty-four, increasing by 300% among young men, and by 100% among young women.

2. Studies indicate that three million American teenagers consider or attempt suicide each year. Women under age twenty-four are twice as likely to attempt suicide (10.9%) as their male counterparts (5.7%), but men are far more likely

---

Behavioral Health "Suicide Facts" seminar notes.

to actually commit suicide.

3. A sizable percentage of what are labeled "accidents" are actually masked suicides. Those contemplating suicide are prone to taking unnecessary risks (such as a high-speed driving) in order to increase the chance of a fatal outcome.

4. Until recently, the state of North Dakota had the highest suicide rate in the United States. Those familiar with North Dakota know that it is particularly cold, desolate, and wholly devoid of typical cultural trappings.[104]

5. Smokers and coffee drinkers tend to have a lower rate of suicide than the general population.

It is perplexing that as the standard of living has increased dramatically in modern times so has the incidence of suicide. Young people today enjoy never before imagined access to wealth, technology, entertainment, travel, healthcare, education, and employment. Yet, suicide is exploding among the young.[105] How does the Bible both shed light on this phenomenon and offer meaningful solutions?

> A dark horse lurks in suicide data, something of which few seem to be aware. The incidence of suicide among young people is, I believe, closely tied to a general loss of innocence, especially with regard to sexuality. Sexual immorality brings with it caustic burning and crippling burden. I have never seen young people so distraught, so forlorn, so lost and afraid as when they are in the clutches of sexual sin. Psychologists and psychiatrists are blind to the consequence of immoral sexuality (and all sin for that matter) because there is no God in their investigative matrix. Thus, psychologists view sexuality (of any type) as natural and healthy. For this reason, they are chronically blind to a central driver in modern depression and suicidal ideation among the young.

Idols in Crisis

A person cannot exist without a suitable object of worship, either worshipping the true God or false gods. As the idolater strikes alliances with idols, he seeks a dividend of blessing, meaning, and power. However, idolatry always delivers cursing, purposelessness, and weakness. When idol after idol has been tried and proven a failure, there comes a crisis point, a juncture at which hope is abandoned in the

---

[104] In culturally vibrant areas, such as cities, people are kept preoccupied with a steady stream of distraction so that the guilt of sin is continually muted and suppressed. In a place like North Dakota, with few cultural diversions, existential angst finds no deflectors. Thus, in the normal course of life, as one's sin is exposed, one either turns to God in repentance, or descends into depression since there are few cultural trappings in which to find existential shelter.

[105] As society enjoys a higher standard of living the pressure to maintain that standard increases disproportionately. Large segments of the population feel that they cannot maintain the "herd's" speed and so seem to drop back, making them vulnerable to the predatory attack of perceived failure and rejection.

idolatry swap and grab. When every presumed source of hope has been exhausted there are only two choices, either repent and believe in the true God, or end one's life. When false gods have failed time and again, and one refuses repentance, suicide appears to be the only viable option. Thus, suicidal ideations are closely tied to debilitating idolatry.

Shipwreck in the Desert, Carl Haag, d. 1915

When his worshipped gods have proven to be nothing but cruel taskmasters leading him into greater deception and pain, the suicidal person finds himself at an existential crossroads. He can either turn to the true God in repentance and find life, or persist in his prideful attempt to define life in his own way, for his own purposes. He either humbly admits that what he previously called god was worthless or, in his impudence, asserts that he would rather curse God and die. At his core, the suicidal person is eminently proud, choosing to be his own ruler in death than God's servant in life.

> People display a curious trait. They often build themselves up only to tear themselves down. Through words, appearance, associations, and possessions, people are often self-infatuated. They then use the very same means to debase themselves. Why? The sinner is fundamentally "schizophrenic" as a result of sin. This means that he lives in a fantasy world in which he seeks to function as a god, while continually abutting with the reality that he is not. As each lives out his deluded god fantasy he also denigrates himself, and others, in self-loathing and disgust.

The various groups listed above (those abusing drugs or alcohol, homosexuals, octogenarians, the chronically ill, North Dakotans, etc.) may be prone to suicidal ideations because their idolatry is more easily exposed and assailed. Their hearts are possibly more vulnerable to unmasking as they largely function without buttressed social ramparts. These groups may live in a world in which it proves difficult to keep their idolatry consistently or uniformly shielded and functional. They may either be less adept at swapping out idols, or the loss of community support structures may leave them more susceptible to existential exposure. Thus, these groups, may find themselves as something of societal stragglers (either within society as a whole, or within their socio-economic or cultural subdivision). In this way, they may tend toward hypersensitivity with regard to real or perceived deficiencies, and may be easily disillusioned with scarified idols.

> Malcolm Gladwell, in his work *The Tipping Point: How Little Things Can Make a Big Difference* (2000),[106] speaks about a chilling phenomenon. Within the span of about two years in the 1990s, Micronesia developed the highest suicide rate in the world. The Micronesian epidemic, which seemed to arise overnight, was almost exclusively limited to adolescent boys (some as young as eight years-old). What was so bizarre was that these suicides occurred in highly-mimetic fashion under shockingly similar circumstances. Suicide developed into a kind of fad among Micronesian boys, a way to express social shame and angst, "a kind of proxy for language."

Defenseless Before the Face of God

As one remains blind to his sin, ensconced in a supposedly propitious life pursuit, he is contented and seemingly fulfilled. In the midst of the cavorting herd, safely concealed from marauding predators, one is quite content to continue on. It is when one struggles to keep up, slowly slips to the fringe, that one is at risk. It is when exposed to the vulnerabilities and vicissitudes of life, when sin and its consequence are palpable, that thoughts of suicide find fertile ground.

> To one with little to live for, and nothing to die for, suicide seems like a welcomed option.

Murder, whether of another or of oneself, is a blatant attempt to usurp God's position. Those who seek suicide, as with all murder, functionally install themselves over God's throne in order to exercise authority over his earthly jurisdiction. They seek to grab the reins of life so as to halt its course for their own purposes. However, the righteous, despite their occasional consternation, recognize that God himself holds sole discretionary power over human life and death.

> "No temptation has overtaken you except what is common to mankind. And God is

---

[106] Malcolm Gladwell, *The Tipping Point: How Little Things Can Make a Big Difference* (New York: Little Brown, 2000)

> faithful; he will not let you be tempted beyond what you can bear. But when you are tempted, he will also provide a way out so that you can endure it." (1 Corinthians 10:13)

Numbers 17:12, 13, recounts that the Israelites, after witnessing the budding of Aaron's staff, said to Moses that in their lost state they desired death. In calling for their own deaths, the Israelites implicitly denied God's goodness, and his ability to deliver them. In fact, the people's fear at approaching God's tabernacle in Numbers 17:13, was neither innocent nor reverent. Their words revealed a profound distrust of God, and a suspicion of his motives. The people's final question, "Are we going to die?", was an assertion that God is fickle and capricious in meting out justice. Later, in Numbers 20:3, "They quarreled with Moses and said, 'If only we had died when our brothers fell dead before the Lord!'"

The desire to die when faced with daunting, confusing, or seemingly insurmountable odds is generally based in a strong-willed, heavy-handed rebellion against God, against his goodness, against his plans for salvation, and ultimately against his glory. Whenever the Israelites assumed a hostile posture toward God, a willful denial of his goodness, they longed to die. This is essentially the inner condition of every suicidal person, a root hatred of God's design and plans, and his supposed inability to deliver one from seemingly humiliating circumstances.

The First Mourning, William-Adolphe Bouguereau, 1888

> "The Lord is a refuge for the oppressed, a stronghold in times of trouble." (Psalm 9:9)

While the counselor is rightly sensitive to the flailing travail of the soul, he does not allow the agony of those he counsels to blind him to reality. The counselor recognizes suicidal ideations as more than a mere flight of existential angst, but rather as a smoldering anger specifically directed toward a God who has not met demands. In this sense, suicide is a profoundly with-regard-to-God action. It, like all sin, does not arise in a vacuum, nor does it arise out of the workings of mere societal agency. Suicide is perpetrated against the person of God himself.

> While the Christian propositionally asserts God's sovereignty and goodness (the two pillars of relationship), he often fails to reconcile this with his suffering and trials. Thus, he sees himself as caught in an intractable dilemma. He simply cannot square his life situation with his belief system. It is exactly this confusion which drives many to depression, and in the extreme, suicide.

Suicide, like no other act, reveals the *coram Deo* concept in Romans 1,[107] that each lives before the face of a holy God responding to him moment-by-moment either in rebellion or in faith. The sinner, with each breath, suppresses the truth in unrighteousness, denying God's self-revealed existence. Suicide is the conclusive act of suppression, the final attempt to silence God's voice within one's own conscience. It is in suicide that denial of God, and his will, is decisively exercised beyond all shadow of doubt.

> Every sunset displays the goodness of God. Witnessing God's goodness (whether in a sunset or in any element of the creation) should result in continual repentance. Thus, God's self-revelation should quell man's rebellion in both form and content. God's revealed glory should function as a definitive silencing agent to one's internal maelstrom, an implicit rebuke of one's lust to play God.

Suicide at Its Root Is Based in Unrelenting Pride

Although some may recoil at the thought, there is no existential difference between Cain's murder of his brother Able and one's murder of himself.[108] All murder is based in anger toward a holy God who has presumably rejected one's "sacrificial offering" (one's prideful demand for acceptance on one's own terms).[109] And just as Cain refused to repent, instead choosing to be "a restless wanderer on the earth,"[110] one

---

[107] For additional development of the *coram Deo* concept see the first book in this series, *Ask for the Ancient Paths: From Art to Artifice to Arisen*, chapter 6: "Man Before the Face of God: The Imperium of the Psyche"
[108] Genesis 4:8
[109] Genesis 4:5
[110] Genesis 4:14

ruled by fear rather than by faith, so too, those who refuse to repent find themselves under the same curse. Why would one choose suicide rather than repentance and submission to a God who promises never to forsake his children,[111] a God who guarantees to prosper those who belong to him? Why would one choose suicide over relationship with a God who did not spare his only Son on one's behalf? The answer is not always straightforward, except to say that one refuses God because one would rather be his own god. One spurns repentance, seeking instead mastery over his own life through ending it.

Suicidal ideation does not arise out of a low self-opinion. Quite the opposite, it percolates out of a high self-opinion. It is the result of demanding one's own way, and when that way is refused, willfully denying God his rightful place in one's life. Suicidal ideations develop over a lifetime of distain for God and his will, and are not the product of a momentary aberration in a life otherwise marked by obedience and faith. Suicidal thoughts are cultivated day-by-day, year-after-year, as one continues to serve and bow to idols of the heart, continues to feed the narrative that God is malicious and set against one's highest good. At a crisis point, when all plausible idols have seemingly failed, when one is alone on a windswept plain of hopelessness, self-destruction soon becomes a very serviceable option.

> Many of those I have counseled (as well as personal friends) reveal that they have, at some point in their lives, harbored suicidal thoughts. This leads me to believe that such thoughts are pervasive, so that most counselees will at some time entertain them. It would appear that at a crisis point, where suicide seems like a viable alternative, this is a crucial (possibly once-in-a-lifetime) opportunity to present the gospel with bountiful cogency and unbounded potential.

Ravishing the Temple

What does the suicidal person seek to accomplish in death? God created each person to be his temple on earth, the sacred receptacle for his Holy Spirit.[112] Suicide destroys God's intended earthly dwelling. Murdering oneself is the supreme act of revenge toward a God who failed to meet one's perceived needs in one's own way. Thus, one refuses to allow God to dwell within himself, razing the temple rather than offering it to be sanctified.

Instead of being thankful for one's life, the suicidal person wields his life as the ultimate weapon against God, destroying the very body that God intended as a manifestation of his glory. The suicidal person in effect dares God to send him to hell. Just as he prefers bodily death to life, so too, he prefers spiritual death to eternal life.

---

[111] Hebrews 13:5
[112] 2 Corinthians 3:16

There is a strong-armed contempt for God that seeks ultimate and final separation from all marks and signs of his goodness. To separate oneself from the world God has designed is to seek to finally and fatally insulate oneself from all evidence of God. (Put very simply, suicidal ideations grew from a spoiled brat mentality, placing demands upon God which, if unmet, result in a kind of temper tantrum of the spirit.)

> Consider the growing practice of scrawling tattoos on the human body. This is graffiti on the temple that God raised to honor himself. The one who defaces God's temple expresses hatred of God's work.[113]

Suicide is part of a broader objective to blot out the evidence of God in creation. This is why mankind routinely desecrates the environment, replacing it with cities. Cities are essentially an attempt to gain covering from the knowledge of God. They, to some extent, obliterate the external evidence of God so that his truth is easier to suppress.[114] Thus, mankind "borrows from God that which serves his self-interest, but suppresses that which challenges his supposed autonomy or reveals his rebellion."[115] Suicide furthers this objective of suppressing the knowledge of God within oneself. If one can obliterate God's self-revelation within, then one has furthered the delusion that one can become his own god.

> There is something deeply therapeutic in plunging one's hands into soil, beholding a spectacular sunrise, letting the gurgling of a mountain stream tickle one's ear. The creation reveals God's sovereignty and goodness with every sight, sound, and tactile experience. There is a continual reminder that each was created for a purpose, by a purposeful God. Each experience of the natural world is a new confrontation with the truth, and that truth is designed to offer healing, hope, refreshment, revitalization, and an invitation to know the God who authored it all. To be separated from God's creation is to be severed from this humbling knowledge, denied this daily source of renewal, and to be cut off from the whispered invitation to repentance and relationship with God.

Taking One at His Word

How should the counselor deal with a suicidal counselee? Firstly, take the counselee at his word. Suicidal statements are never to be taken lightly. Talk of suicide is the overflow of a heart that seeks to terrorize itself, and often those voicing strong words act upon them. Secondly, it is vital that the counselor incarnate a God who is desperate to save hurting people. This means the counselor, more so than ever, must reflect the character, goodness, love, kindness, and gentleness of a God who weeps with the loss of just one sinner. The hope is to offer the suicidal counselee a glimpse

---

[113] Leviticus 19:28
[114] Romans 1:18
[115] Cornelius Van Til, *Christian Apologetics* (Presbyterian and Reformed Publishing, 2003)

into a God who longs for his worship, and is eminently worthy of it. The hope is that in stable and sober moments, when the rush and rage of suicidal thought has passed, the counselee will engage in a meaningful and productive conversation about the ravaged condition of his heart and his desperate need for a revitalizing God who can, and will, make all things new for those who place their trust in him.

The Day of the Dead
William-Adolphe Bouguereau, 1859

The danger is to merely seek to diffuse suicidal talk with words of empty praise and futile hope, to merely seek to make one feel better for the moment without the substantive presence of God himself. Most suicidal people see through fluff and flattery; Panglossian visions of the future only induce more bitterness. Such attempts, while they may force-feed hungry idols for a moment, only further enrage those who resent perceived patronizing or placating efforts. Additionally, empty praise and palliative hope wrongly resuscitate idols already on life-support, and do not summon the power and persuasion of God.

Let menacing idols die so that God can finally live in a hurting person. Reveal the Bible's truth in all its glory; share the gospel with all its compunction. To one who has been ravished by war and decidedly needs peace with God, do not extend a fig leaf but an olive branch. Hold forth the laurel wreath with which God longs to crown those who place their trust in him. The counselor is therefore simultaneously confrontational and conciliatory: inviting abandonment, surrender, and the opportunity for renewal.

> "A person should hear a little music, read a little poetry, and see a fine picture every day in order that worldly cares may not obliterate the sense of the beautiful which God has implanted in the human soul." (Johann von Goethe)

Counseling Those Who Suffer

> "And we know that in all things God works for the good of those who love him, who have been called according to his purpose." (Romans 8:28)

Sigmund Freud (1856-1939) said, "Life is a tiny island of pain floating on a sea of indifference." Job 6:15-17, echoes something of this same sentiment,

> Anyone who withholds kindness from a friend
>   forsakes the fear of the Almighty.
> But my brothers are as undependable as intermittent streams,
>   as the streams that overflow
> when darkened by thawing ice
>   and swollen with melting snow,
> but that stop flowing in the dry season,
>   and in the heat vanish from their channels.

In contradistinction to Job's counselors, the biblical counselor is never indifferent to pain and, in effect, functions as a trustworthy refuge from the world's indifference. The counselor acknowledges pain, grieves with those who grieve,[116] comes alongside those who suffer, and comforts the afflicted, while never losing sight of the larger objective to free the sinner from his true affliction: besetting sin in the midst of suffering.

> "For he has not despised or disdained the suffering of the afflicted one; he has not hidden his face from him but has listened to his cry for help." (Psalm 22:24)

The face of one who has suffered bears a certain hollow empty quality. There is a heaviness about the eyes, a defeat about the mouth. There is a stillness in a sufferer's gaze, as if his mind labors to decipher a befuddling cosmic code, trying to reckon the why and wherefore of a painful world that offers precious few clues. How does the counselor rightly offer a word to sustain the weary?[117] The wrong answer is to follow the world's path of merely offering a vacuous humanistic message of well-being, seeking to impart an abstract sense of pragmatic purpose. The counselor must turn to God's Word for answers, and to God directly for the needed wisdom.

> "These were all commended for their faith, yet none of them received what had been promised. God had planned something better for us so that only together with us would they be made perfect." (Hebrews 11:39, 40)

Deuteronomy 8:2 states, "Remember how the LORD your God led you all the way in the wilderness these forty years, to humble and test you in order to know what was in

---

[116] Romans 12:15
[117] Isaiah 50:4

your heart, whether or not you would keep his commands." God's people suffer so that he might expose worship commitments, and then cleanse the heart of wayward devotion. But it is crucial to be clear that the Christian is never under God's vengeful wrath. There is no curse, no condemnation, and no final judgment visited upon those in Jesus.[118] It is absolutely essential to reinforce this for those who suffer. God never seeks retribution against a Christian; he never redresses an offense. Jesus already satisfied that once-for-all. Jesus took God's wrath, curse, and condemnation upon himself in the most spectacular display of love which any mind could ever conceive. Thus, all suffering, in its myriad forms and in its full-array, is incorporated into God's design so as to bring about his people's eternal betterment and permanent holiness. God often tests his people to see where their loyalties lie and, when necessary, he punishes his people, not to satisfy the penalty for a transgression, but in loving discipline. While God allows one to be tempted to expose the heart's worship,[119] and while he opposes the proud,[120] God never visits vengeance upon those in Christ.

> Those who suffer often build a protective fortress around themselves. If Jesus is one's fortress, then one does not need to raise his own ramparts. The one who suffers can rest in the safety of a God who cares for him and is able to make all things new.[121]

Shipwreck, Claude Joseph Vernet, 1759

The world rarely sees value in suffering and, in fact, for those outside of Christ, who

---

[118] Romans 8:1
[119] 1 Corinthians 10:13
[120] James 4:6
[121] Revelation 21:5

remain outside of Christ, suffering holds no promise and no hope. Trials, suffering, and pain are just the flotsam and jetsam of a capricious universe. As such, the world views struggle and conflict as an unmitigated blight upon humanity, and seeks to decisively eliminate it. Christians, on the other hand, should not seek to blindly eradicate all measure of suffering if there is work God seeks to do through it. In seeking to remove gauged suffering, or purposed trials, too quickly, one will invariably miss the larger intent, setting the stage for the same or similar trials to resurface until God's work is done. The Christian rests in a promise that for those in Christ there is an assured future deliverance from evil, already ascertained, but not yet fully in effect. That is the empyrean schematic from which God operates.

> The counselor can assert two truths with confidence: that God is sovereign in all things, and that God promises to bring good from all things for those who belong to him.[122]

The biblical counselor does not merely fill lacunae in the counselee's self-understanding.[123] He does not blindly seek to alleviate pain (although this may be entirely appropriate). The counselor does not simply make the counselee feel better about his life; he endeavors to impart a justifiable reason for hope, the opportunity for repentance (if that is warranted), and a perspective which highlights God's purposed work in, and through, believers to effect sanctification.

> "Those who sow in tears will reap with songs of joy. He who goes out weeping, carrying seed to sow, will return with songs of joy, carrying sheaves with him." (Psalm 126:5, 6)

Leviticus 3:22, 23 states, "Because of the LORD's great love we are not consumed, for his compassions never fail. They are new every morning; great is your faithfulness." God's mercies are new every morning. While this statement often makes for a warmhearted Hallmark® sympathy card, it holds a profound and poignant implication for counseling. In light of this promise of renewal with the dawn, the counselor needs wisdom to know which emotional pains to chase down and which to leave alone, which to actively counsel, and which to let the mercies of the morning heal.[124] Some light daily angst is not necessarily based in trenchant tight-fisted idolatry, but rather is the temporary suspension of trust in a good all-powerful and holy God. Sometimes, wisdom dictates just leaving the heart's tremors alone, so that by morning they have dampened out. Many cares evaporate with the rising sun (a kind of "reboot" for the soul, if you will).[125]

---

[122] Romans 8:28
[123] Paul Tripp, *Instruments in the Redeemer's Hands: People in Need of Change Helping People in Need of Change* (Presbyterian and Reformed Publishing Company, 2002)
[124] Lamentations 3:22, 23
[125] It is worth noting that physicians traditionally recommended, "Take two aspirin and call me in the morning." There is, in God's common grace, a kind of mercy about the morning, a certain renewal and revitalization from the

> "Most things get better by themselves. In fact, most ailments are better by morning."
> (Lewis Thomas)

God's Objective in Suffering

> "What are the thoughts of a piece of canvas on which a masterpiece is being created? 'I am being soiled, brutally treated, and concealed from view.'" (Jean Cocteau)

A young woman acted with a measure of belligerence at a church meeting. I respectfully, but firmly, confronted her unacceptable behavior with a call for repentance. Another woman in the group jumped to her defense, "You do not know how much she has suffered!" This anecdote drives straight to the heart of a sinful handling of suffering. Real or perceived suffering becomes a ready excuse for moral depravity and contempt toward God himself. In fact, suffering seems to justify just about any human failing. That is why most are so quick to recount their suffering, since in their minds this exonerates, defusing any possible confrontation of the heart. Thus, for many, suffering is a facile device for maintaining a heart of errant worship. The flawed logic is often that the one who most suffers most deserves impunity.

A Music Party, Arthur Hughes, 1861

Throughout the Bible, God prioritizes growth in holiness over physical or emotional

---

ravages of the night to which even unbelieving physicians seem privy.

SUFFERING

wellbeing.[126] Often the purpose of physical ailments or limitations is to place deeper trust in God, to witness his provision in the midst of loss, to experience his power in the context of weakness,[127] to bask in his grace in the face of defeat, to luxuriate in his healing in the sting of injury. Consider 2 Corinthians 12:7-10,

> …Therefore, in order to keep me from becoming conceited, I was given a thorn in my flesh, a messenger of Satan, to torment me. Three times I pleaded with the Lord to take it away from me. But he said to me, 'My grace is sufficient for you, for my power is made perfect in weakness.' Therefore I will boast all the more gladly about my weaknesses, so that Christ's power may rest on me. That is why, for Christ's sake, I delight in weaknesses, in insults, in hardships, in persecutions, in difficulties. For when I am weak, then I am strong.

While a humanistic social justice movement prioritizes temporal condition, God works in the opposite direction, cultivating faith, not the mere alleviation of limitations (whether real or perceived). Therefore, the Bible does not prioritize the physical or emotional over the nouthetic (heart/mind/soul/will), the worshipping center. The Bible's all-consuming drive is to effect proper worship. If one does not understand this, he will always find himself at cross-purposes with God, always confused, always flailing in the dark with little sense of direction. Consider that, when struck with a plague of blood which rendered the Nile non-potable, the Egyptians "dug along the Nile to get drinking water."[128] Instead of repenting, they sought to circumvent the plague in their own effort, by their own means. (Similarly, much of man's effort is an attempt to merely avoid God.) Yet, God refused to remove the Egyptian's suffering until his intended work was completed.

> "As he went along, he saw a man blind from birth. His disciples asked him, 'Rabbi, who sinned, this man or his parents, that he was born blind?' 'Neither this man nor his parents sinned,' said Jesus, 'but this happened so that the works of God might be displayed in him.'" (John 9:1-3)

A few years ago I attended a New Year's Eve church service in which the congregation sang, "All Things Are Possible."[129] After the song, participants were invited to step forward to share what God had made possible in their lives that year. One offered thanks for being admitted to medical school, another for finding a job, and a third for a loved one's healing. All of this is indeed worthy of praise but, as participant after participant stepped forward, I did not hear one person thank God for a changed heart, for ongoing deliverance from sin, or for freedom from himself. I heard

---

[126] 2 Corinthians 4:16
[127] 1 Corinthians 1:27, 28; 2 Corinthians 12:9
[128] Exodus 7:24
[129] "All Things Are Possible" by John Popper and Chan Kinchla

no thanks for another year of bearing fruit for Christ or for growth in wisdom. I heard nothing about increased desire and love for Jesus, and certainly no thanks for the suffering that might produce such love. What was designed to offer praise to God sounded more like a well-concealed litany of successes in the world's eyes, a catalogue of humanly-defined blessing: thankfulness for that job promotion, for that new house, for a marriage engagement. Every focus of gratitude was upon some temporal or situational gain, upon some perceived deliverance from circumstance.

That night I struggled to feel joy. Something about the evening felt stilted, like I was standing on the edge of enemy territory without a map. As I made my way through the jovial crowd, I was conflicted, grateful for successes sustained in the lives of dear friends but sorrowful that something had been neglected. Certainly, God deserves praise in all things,[130] for all gifts and gains. However I felt that an opportunity had passed to spy the real treasure that is Christ himself working in the midst of hearts often besieged by weakness, failing, loss, setback, and groaning, yet migrating toward him with a plodding and yearning to drink from the living water, to partake of the bread of life, to step into the light of life. When one understands that to be the paragon of all life pursuits, one finally unlocks the enigma of suffering, so that suffering is not the towering enemy to receiving perceived gifts, not the trenchant obstacle to experiencing abundant life, not the stealthy assassin of joy, but quite the opposite, a cloaked gift, a dormant seed, a catalyst to holiness. The secret of suffering is to know and be known by Jesus as never before, to taste eternal relationship with one's God with greater clarity, profundity, and passion.

> "Knowledge is a process of piling up facts; wisdom lies in their simplification." (Martin H. Fischer)

In light of the New Year's Eve nocturne "All Things Are Possible," what did Paul mean by, "I can do everything through him who gives me strength."?[131] What was "the secret of being content in any and every situation"?[132] The secret is the knowledge that Jesus was Paul's only need, that through Jesus, Paul was strengthened to accomplish the impossible, namely to experience a transformed heart capable of loving God and others.

God's towering intention is to know you, to be with you, to relate to you. This is why he seeks to make you holy, that you would desire him. In this pursuit, God spares nothing, no material possession, no relationship, no experience, no achievement. Once one understands God's zealous pursuit of perfection in his people (the eradication of their sin and their growth in holiness),[133] and his all-consuming desire to know them

---

[130] 1 Thessalonians 5:18
[131] Philippians 4:13
[132] Philippians 4:12
[133] Jude 24

personally, one begins to understand the reason for his works.

> Marcel Proust (1871–1922) stated, "Happiness is beneficial to the body, but it is grief that develops the powers of the mind." There is, in fact, something in suffering, under God's direction and for his glory, which focuses the mind and heart. The one who has suffered (with godly attention) has forged for himself a cartographer's drafting tools to rightly assess space and time.

Consider Exodus 9:34, "When Pharaoh saw that the rain and hail and thunder had stopped, he sinned again. He and his officials hardened their hearts." As was the case with Pharaoh, the heart may temporarily submit to God so long as it is harassed by clear and present threats. However, once those threats are lifted it often returns to its hostile defiance.[134] In his wrath upon them, God loved Pharaoh and the Egyptians, the purpose of that wrath being to induce their repentance. However, they put on the mere pretense of repentance only so long as the threat remained, soon reverting back to their pilgarlic.

In light of Exodus 9:34, consider the purpose of a fever. A fever, while painful, exists to incinerate invading pathogens, pathogens which, if left unchecked, would kill their host. The fever's intensity and duration are carefully calibrated to match the threat, so that that fever might break the pathogen's "will." Once the pathogen has been rendered effete, once the invasion has been thwarted, the fever lifts to allow the body to return to normalcy. In the same way, God often brings the "fever" of suffering,

The Drowsy One
Friedrich Von Amerling, d. 1887

that something of the heart's will would be broken, that sin would be defeated. The intensity and duration of that suffering is carefully calculated to soften the heart's

---

[134] It is fascinating to consider that Job 1:11 takes the opposite tact. "But stretch out your hand and strike everything [Job] has, and he will surely curse you to your face." Satan reckoned that Job only obeyed God because of a hedge of protection and prosperity (Job 1:10).

obduracy. If that calculation is accurate, the heart is freed from its besetting sin to enjoy newly-minted fellowship with God. However, if the suffering lifts too quickly, like a dog returning to its vomit, often the heart reverts into its recalcitrant folly.[135]

As rain, hail, and thunder brought calamity upon Egypt, they served as a "fever" upon Pharaoh's heart. Likewise, anything that induces God's chastening work can be used to prompt repentance. And, just as Egypt lost nearly everything (even its firstborn sons),[136] anything that comes between the Christian and his God will be sacrificed. God will not spare one's health, one's wealth, one's career, one's home, one's pleasures, one's reputation, or one's relationships (although, of course, marriage is a covenantal relationship that was never intended to be willfully broken). God is willing to sacrifice anything in the Christian's life that he would find a bounty in his God. In this sense, God is not pragmatic; he is passionate. He is not efficient; he is eternally-minded. While God often leaves the unbeliever to his own devices, the Christian is carefully disciplined and directed,[137] febrile for a time that a glorious normalcy might ensue.

> When I was about seven years-old my mother allowed me to ride my bicycle to the end of our street, but no farther. I also had to check-in each hour. This was a firm rule not open to negotiation. Once I road farther than I was allowed and returned later than I was supposed to. I impertinently snapped at my mother, "The other kids don't have to hold to these rules! Why should I?" My mother's reply, "The other kids are their mothers' concerns. You are mine."
>
> This is how God views his people. Those who are in Christ are his concern, while the world is largely not. God sanctifies his people, but he does not sanctify the world. God disciplines his people, but he does not discipline the world.[138] My mother established protective rules because she loves me. Likewise, God disciplines me because he loves me. Therefore, as I see the world prosper while I struggle, this is not because God is weak or callous. Quite the opposite, God shows me, time and again, that he has a far greater purpose in store for me, to be like his Son, Jesus.

The Christian's Interaction with Suffering

Shakespearean irony is a literary device in which an unsuspecting victim falls into circumstance he had foolishly overlooked or specifically sought to avoid. The plot crystallizes around this ironic nucleus as characters are unwittingly driven by unforeseen circumstances. There are times when life feels like a Shakespearean tragedy, when there seems a besetting cosmic mockery. But this is nothing more than

---

[135] Proverbs 26:11
[136] Exodus 7:14-11:10
[137] Hebrews 12:6
[138] John 3:36 states that the world is under God's wrath.

an illusion ducking within Satan's shifting shadows. God has never been, and will never be, wanton or capricious. His plans for each life are good and worthy of praise.[139]

When faced with suffering, the Christian may spontaneously ask about the action to take, "What do you want me to do, Lord?" or "How do you want me to respond?"[140] But the correct biblical understanding will produce the question, "How is this an opportunity to experience deeper faith and growth in holiness?" So the Christian, when faced with suffering, rightly asks, "How do you want me to change, Lord?"

> "He says, 'Be still, and know that I am God;
>   I will be exalted among the nations,
>   I will be exalted in the earth.'" (Psalm 46:10)

Consider that much Christian suffering is intimately tied to the gospel. For example:

1. "Now if we are children, then we are heirs – heirs of God and co-heirs with Christ, if indeed we share in his sufferings in order that we may also share in his glory." (Romans 8:17)

2. "Have you suffered so much for nothing – if it really was for nothing?" (Galatians 3:4)

3. "Dear friends, do not be surprised at the fiery ordeal that has come on you to test you, as though something strange were happening to you. (1 Peter 4:12)

Thus, the Christian rightly expects to suffer as part of his participation in Christ's suffering.

Work Interrupted
William-Adolphe Bouguereau, 1891

---

[139] James 1:17
[140] David and Sharon Covington, "Introduction to Biblical Counseling" notes, 2004

This is the will of a good God in the lives of those he cherishes as his own special inheritance. In this regard, consider John 15:2, "He cuts off every branch in me that bears no fruit, while every branch that does bear fruit he prunes so that it will be even more fruitful." The faithful Christian, the committed disciple, the believer who desires Christ, should expect to be pruned most vigorously so as to produce ever more abundant fruit. Thus, the Christian life, with regard to suffering, is under the dictates of a "reverse hermeneutic," not that faith should produce freedom from suffering, but that suffering often results from greater faith, so that the faithful would overflow with lush fruit in Christ.

Of course, in the midst of intense suffering an instinctive trust in God's goodness may seem somewhat strained. For example, in Job 3:3, Job said, "May the day of my birth perish, and the night that said, 'A boy is conceived!'" Again in Job 21:4, Job voiced his grievance. "Is my complaint directed to a human being? Why should I not be impatient?" (However, the Bible tells us that Job did not sin in this because in his heart he never denied God's goodness or sovereignty.[141]) Like Job, the Christian may at times question God's intent, but always with a spirit of reverence and submission, so that he rightly asks, "What is God doing *in and through* me?", rather than, "Why is this happening *to* me?" Again, the principle reason for suffering is that the heart's dross would be burned away. God often forges the heart in the fires of searing loss, frustrating delay, and deferred hope, so that it would be purged of impure motives or shown to be basking in pure ones.[142]

> One's time on earth is not a ponderous and plodding succession of futile days but a portrait conceived by a master artist.

The Gospel and Suffering[143]

In writing this chapter I had an epiphany: the entire Bible is about suffering, stories of people either suffering (a present event), moving toward suffering (a future event), or being delivered from suffering (a past event). In the Bible, the epicenter of suffering is the book of Lamentations, a flight of burning misery beyond all comprehension. Lamentations, like the rest of the Bible, orbits around suffering because it orbits around Jesus, the suffering servant,[144] the savior born to die,[145] the one who stretched out his hands with no one to comfort him.[146] Jesus' life was the most profound entering into suffering that could ever be conceived, so that all biblical accounts of suffering are portraits of Jesus himself.

---

[141] Job 1:22
[142] Proverbs 25:4; Ezekiel 36:25; 1 Peter 1:7
[143] For additional discussion of this topic see the first book in this series, *Ask for the Ancient Paths: From Art to Artifice to Arisen*, chapter 4: "The Gospel as Inception Point: From Immorality to Immortality"
[144] Isaiah 52:13-53:12
[145] Hebrews 10:5-7 indicates that Jesus knew he was brought into the earth to die.
[146] Lamentations 1:17

> "He is not a mere mortal like me that I might answer him,
>   that we might confront each other in court.
> If only there were someone to mediate between us,
>   someone to bring us together,
> someone to remove God's rod from me,
>   so that his terror would frighten me no more.
> Then I would speak up without fear of him,
>   but as it now stands with me, I cannot." (Job 9:32-35)

No human being ever suffered as much as Jesus Christ. To understand this, one must consider that there are two time horizons for Jesus' suffering - one historical, the other ongoing. Concerning the historical, while others had been crucified, Jesus sustained something no one else had, the fire of hell while still alive. Jesus withstood excruciating separation from his Father as he hung on the cross.[147] Thus, while Jesus suffered unimaginably in his body, he suffered infinitely more in his spirit. This casts human suffering in an entirely new light. God himself personally endured suffering to the greatest extent imaginable and remained sinless throughout. God entered into the worst of human degradation and perdition, emerging from it victorious.

The Martyrdom of St. Bartholomew
Giovanni Battista Piazzetta, 1723

> "The Lord will fight for you; you need only to be still." (Exodus 14:4)

Verses which speak of Jesus' suffering:

1. "He was despised and rejected by men, a man of sorrows, and familiar with suffering. Like one from whom men hide their faces he was despised, and we

---
[147] Matthew 27:46

esteemed him not." (Isaiah 53:3)

2. "He was pierced for our transgressions, he was crushed for our iniquities; the punishment that brought us peace was upon him, and by his wounds we are healed." (Isaiah 53:5)

3. "About the ninth hour Jesus cried out in a loud voice, '*Eloi, Eloi, lama sabachthani*?' which means, 'My God, my God, why have you forsaken me?'" (Matthew 27:46)

4. Colossians 1:24 states, "Now I rejoice in what I am suffering for you, and I fill up in my flesh what is still lacking in regard to Christ's afflictions, for the sake of his body, which is the church." Jesus Christ suffered inexorably, not just to share his people's suffering, but more importantly, that his people might share his.[148]

In light of the torment Jesus endured on the cross, the Christian continually reorients his view of suffering so as to align it with the cross, so as to intertwine it with Christ's suffering. Thus, suffering takes on new meaning as it leads one to faith in Christ, to participate in his anguish and subsequent victory. Jesus' crucifixion forever changed the human perspective on suffering, so that suffering, for the Christian, is no longer a silent scream into a cosmic vacuum, but a purposed entering into the cross' triumph.

> To the liberal theologian, Jesus' crucifixion is a senseless historical distraction because to liberalism there is no need for salvation from sin. Thus, according to liberal theology, Jesus was, in his death, crushed in the gears of history as he mishandled, and imprudently interfered with, the lethal political machinery buzzing and whirring around him.

This brings us to the second, often forgotten, aspect to Jesus' suffering - his ongoing suffering. Hebrews 6:6 reads, "...and who have fallen away, to be brought back to repentance. To their loss they are crucifying the Son of God *all over again* and subjecting him to public disgrace." According to this verse, those Christians who defy Jesus, turning to false gods for salvation, figuratively re-crucify him. Additionally, Ephesians 4:30 reads, "And do not grieve the Holy Spirit of God, with whom you were sealed for the day of redemption." The Holy Spirit experiences ongoing grief as believers persist in sin. The Christian, in taking on Christ's concerns, also grieves for sin, shuttering at the thought of re-crucifying Christ. It is for this reason that the Christian, abhorring the sin within himself and others, commits himself to sin's complete eradication.

It is crucial to understand that, while the counselor empathizes with those who suffer,

---

[148] David and Sharon Covington, "Introduction to Biblical Counseling" notes, 2004; 2 Corinthians 1:5

he never sees suffering as a driver for sinful behavior. The lusts of the heart alone animate sin; suffering merely offers the opportunity, exposes that which *already* resides in the heart. (Consider, for example, the contrast between the two crucified thieves; one hurled insults and the other pled for mercy, while in the exact same situation.[149]) Just as Jesus' heart was impervious to sin in the context of intense suffering, so too, those in Christ can experience this same freedom. Jesus died to change the heart so that when tempted, on account of suffering, that suffering would have no effect. This is not a call to Stoicism, but the hope of deliverance from futility, the recognition that suffering is weighed in a cosmic balance for God's eternal glory.[150]

> "Now if we are children, then we are heirs—heirs of God and co-heirs with Christ, if indeed we share in his sufferings in order that we may also share in his glory." (Romans 8:17)

Suffering as Preparation for Judgment

Years ago I met a middle-aged Christian man, "Donald," who, ten years prior, had been diagnosed with Multiple Sclerosis. Donald lost feeling in his legs, suffered with facial distortions, felt chronically fatigued, and had little ability to concentrate. He had an active mind but trouble forming words. Donald easily lost things, could not maintain a train of thought, and felt that his life was out of control, especially since he could no longer work. As he daily watched his body deteriorate, he slowly lost his dignity as a father and husband. Just getting up in the morning was a towering act of faith, knowing that each day would invariably bring more pain than the last. Somewhat naïvely, I asked Donald what God had taught him through this experience. With a flash of anger, he snapped, "Nothing!" I felt a sting of sorrow.

As incredible as it may sound, a Christian would never wish to turn back the hands of time to avoid suffering. He would never trade a day of suffering for one of empty happiness, recognizing that as painful as any day may be, it was created by God for eternal purpose.[151] Thus, with a hidden and often muted sense of joy, the Christian trades suffering for a little more knowledge of, and praise for, his God, praise that grows from understanding that he is given an unfathomable gift in sanctification. This leads to the issue at hand, "How does one gain a firmer handle on suffering from God's perspective?"

In answering this question, one must begin with this fact - at the end of time two judgments await. The first is judgment on sin,[152] the second, a judgment on the

---

[149] Luke 23:39-42
[150] Consider James 1:12 in this regard.
[151] Psalm 118:24
[152] Luke 13:28; John 3:18

Christian's works.[153] The Christian will most assuredly pass through the first judgment since he is in Christ, shielded from God's wrath on account of Jesus' payment for his sin. The non-Christian, however, will not survive this judgment,[154] and as such, is destined for hell's fury.[155] Yet, while the Christian will pass through the first judgment unscathed, a second judgment awaits in which his life and work will be judged as either conforming to Christ or in defiance of him. It is at this juncture that God winnows out those who are merely saved from those who are committed disciples.[156] Consider 1 Corinthians 3:12-15,

> If anyone builds on this foundation using gold, silver, costly stones, wood, hay or straw, their work will be shown for what it is, because the Day will bring it to light. It will be revealed with fire, and the fire will test the quality of each person's work. If what has been built survives, the builder will receive a reward. If it is burned up, the builder will suffer loss but yet will be saved—even though only as one escaping through the flames.

Titans and Other Giants Imprisoned in Hell (Dante's *Divine Comedy*, Inferno - Plate 65 (Canto XXXI)), Gustave Dore, d. 1883

The Christian, while saved, will suffer loss if he builds on any foundation other than Christ. First Corinthians 11:29-32 expands upon this theme,

---

[153] 1 Corinthians 3:15
[154] John 3:36
[155] Revelation 21:8
[156] Matthew 3:12

For those who eat and drink without discerning the body of Christ eat and drink judgment on themselves. That is why many among you are weak and sick, and a number of you have fallen asleep. But if we were more discerning with regard to ourselves, we would not come under such judgment. Nevertheless, when we are judged in this way by the Lord, we are being disciplined so that we will not be finally condemned with the world.

> "If you suffer, it should not be as a murderer or thief or any other kind of criminal, or even as a meddler." (1 Peter 4:15)

Consider that all earthly suffering is preparation for these final cataclysmic events - the two last day judgments. The non-Christian's suffering is intended to induce his repentance that he might be justified, saved from his sin, so as to survive the first judgment. First Thessalonians 5:9 states, "For God did not appoint us to suffer wrath but to receive salvation through our Lord Jesus Christ." The Christian's suffering is intended to induce his sanctification, growth in holiness, so as to be rewarded in the second judgment. First John 4:17 states, "This is how love is made complete among us so *that we will have confidence on the day of judgment*: In this world we are like Jesus."

Present suffering is, in effect, an entering into these judgments, so that the one who suffers is given a foretaste of what is to come, that he might seek Jesus, escape the damning fires and pass through the purging fires, and be fitted with crowns of glory. This is why Romans 8:30 informs the Christian that he is *already* glorified, since he already operates in an eternal frame of reference. Present suffering is part of that already obtained glory. In suffering, the non-Christian receives a warning to repent and believe; in suffering, the Christian receives a gift that he would "have confidence on the day of judgment," a confidence which grows from becoming "like Jesus."[157]

> Hebrews 11:35b reads, "...Others were tortured and refused to be released, so that they might gain a better resurrection." Some Christians allowed torture to continue that they might be more fully conformed to Christ on the last day.

Thus, for the Christian, present suffering is a "pre-testing," that he would turn from sin and grow in faith. In this way, when the final test comes one's heart has already been cleansed. Consider Matthew 13:41-43,

> The Son of Man will send out his angels, and they will weed out of his kingdom everything that causes sin and all who do evil. They will throw them into the blazing furnace, where there will be weeping and gnashing of teeth. Then the righteous will shine like the sun in the kingdom of their Father.

---
[157] 1 John 4:17

Whoever has ears, let them hear.

Present suffering offers a foretaste of the "weeping and gnashing of teeth" that awaits the unbeliever, and implements shining "like the sin in the kingdom of their Father" in the righteous. As mentioned previously, through her affliction, Julie found faith in Christ (justification), and subsequently grew in holiness (sanctification). Her searing pain, bitter disappointment, and daily humiliation served to remedy the first judgment and prepare her for the second.

> Consider an intriguing analogy. No one would ever willingly consume moldy bread, fruit, or meat, as such food would likely make one sick. However, inexplicably, moldy cheese such as Bleu d'Auvergne, Gorgonzola, and Roquefort are considered culinary treasures, often commanding a high price. Mold that would induce illness in one form is a gastronomic delight in another. (In fact, some types of bleu cheese are created using the same streptococcus bacteria that is a common illness.) A similar analogy could be made with suffering. Suffering which would induce revulsion in the world, to the Christian could be a source of delight as he considers the eternal joy that it brings.

A Man-centered Cosmology:

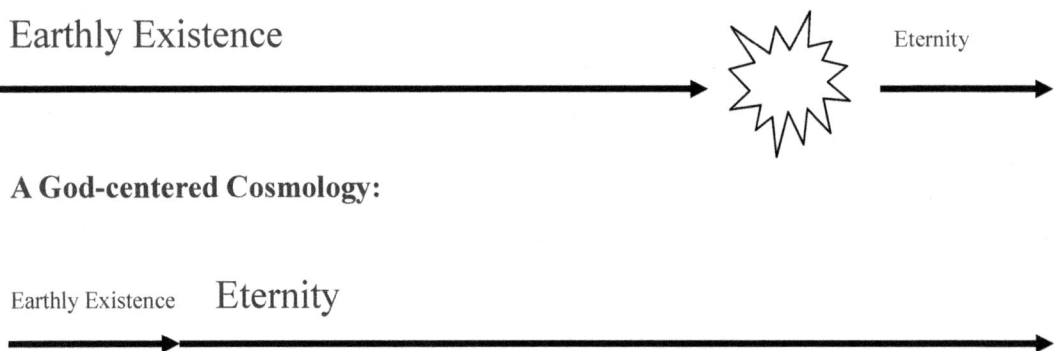

A God-centered Cosmology:

In a man-centered cosmology, earthly existence predominates and the aeonian is a distant mythical abstraction. The sinner builds his kingdom in the here-and-now, seeing little or no continuity between his earthly existence and eternity (as eternity is nothing more than a mysterious unknowable state). However, in a God-centered cosmology, the eternal predominates so that the earthly is merely the prelude to what comes next. There is also an organic connection between the temporal (the phenomenal) and the eternal (the noumenal), so that the eternal is a direct extension of the temporal.[158] Thus, each person, in effect, already lives in the eternal. God uses suffering to prepare the sufferer to enter into that eternity "successfully": as a wakeup call to a gathering judgment upon sin, or as a refining process ahead of a second

---
[158] 1 Timothy 6:12 alludes to this.

judgment upon the Christian's heart.

In other words, God works on an eternal timeline, by means of the chiming of a cosmic clock.[159] Out of his mercy, he leverages suffering to resuscitate those under his wrath, that they would pass from death to life. Likewise, those already brought to life are being prepared to pass through the second judgment with pure materials set to withstand the fires of holiness. In 1 Corinthians 9:27b, Paul refers to not being "disqualified for the prize." For the Christian a prize awaits, that prize, the result of being presented to Jesus as a pristine bride,[160] is a thoroughly transformed heart.

Second Corinthians 5:10 states, "For we must all appear before the judgment seat of Christ, so that each of us may receive what is due us for the things done while in the body, whether good or bad." Thus, present suffering fits into an empyrean mosaic. It is part of God's master schema to ensure that his people, when they stand before Christ's judgment seat, are not disqualified for the prize. God burns away the dross now, that it would not be a source of regret later. Thus, God forges the heart in fire,[161] that an unadulterated faith would emerge, a gift "without stain or wrinkle or any other blemish, but holy and blameless" to be presented to Christ on the last day.[162] Hebrews 11:40 reads, "God planned something better for us so that only together with us would they be made *perfect*." Present suffering is part of this purifying and perfecting objective in the one who is already saved by faith.[163] Thus, the old saying, "Great art is produced by great suffering," takes on new meaning as one considers that Jesus is in the process of creating masterpieces, redeemed men and women thoroughly transformed into his likeness.

> "What are the thoughts of a piece of canvas on which a masterpiece is being created? 'I am being soiled, brutally treated, and concealed from view.'" (Jean Cocteau)

Acts 5:41 reads, "The apostles left the Sanhedrin, rejoicing because they had been counted worthy of suffering disgrace for the Name." Picking up on this idea is James 1:2-4,

> Consider it pure joy, my brothers and sisters, whenever you face trials of many kinds, because you know that the testing of your faith produces perseverance. Let perseverance finish its work so that you may be mature and complete, not lacking anything.

---

[159] John 11:25b, 26a reads, "...He who believes in me will live, even though he dies; and whoever lives and believes in me will never die..." Jesus, here, seemed to infer a continuity between the earthly and the eternal, similar to the God-centered cosmology diagramed above.
[160] Ephesians 5:27
[161] Matthew 3:11b
[162] Ephesians 5:27
[163] It is crucial to understand that nothing one does can every save him. Thus, suffering is never a means for salvation, but a means for growth in holiness for the one who is already saved.

Perseus and Andromeda, Charles André van Loo, c. 1740

The Christian's trials are part of an aeonian strategy that he would "not lack anything," and "might gain an even better resurrection,"[164] in having been thoroughly conformed to Christ. Listen to the words of Shadrach, Meshach and Abednego,

> If we are thrown into the blazing furnace, the God we serve is able to deliver us from it, and he will deliver us from Your Majesty's hand. But even if he does not, we want you to know, Your Majesty, that we will not serve your gods or worship the image of gold you have set up. (Daniel 3:17, 18)

Few passages more succinctly encapsulate the Christian's rightful response to suffering at the hands of the world. The Christian anticipates the deliverance of his God, but even if God allows suffering and death, the Christian still unwaveringly trusts in his God's good purposes.[165] Regardless of the supposed temporal benefits, the steadfast Christian refuses to turn to false gods for deliverance. In this way, the Christian abides in a God-centered cosmology.

Finally, the Christian finds great comfort in Hebrews 2:11, 12,

---

[164] Hebrews 11:35
[165] Hebrews 11:17-19 offers another fitting example in which, despite Abraham's confusion, he was willing sacrifice his son Isaac, reasoning that God could raise him from the dead. Thus, Abraham humbly submitted to God's plan, trusting in unseen means for final deliverance.

Both the one who makes men holy and those who are made holy are of the same family. So Jesus is not ashamed to call them brothers. He says,

> 'I will declare your name to my brothers;
> In the presence of the congregation I will sing your praises.'

As the Christian suffers, he is purified; as he is purified, there is more for Jesus to praise. Thus, burning away the dross of sin and idolatry invokes in Jesus greater rejoicing for his people.

> "Great occasions do not make heroes or cowards; they simply unveil them to the eyes of men. Silently and unnoticed, as we wake or sleep, we grow strong or weak; and at last some crisis shows what we have become." (Brooke Foss Westcott)

While, of course, the Christian can, and should, act and pray to alleviate suffering wherever he finds it,[166] he recognizes that suffering now is inextricably linked to judgment later, that the non-Christian would be saved, that the Christian would be sanctified. As one views suffering through this prism, one sees it in a clarifying light, no longer a confusing, threatening, and ugly proposition, but a liberating, merciful, and glorifying eternal treasure.[167]

> "Dear friends, do not be surprised at the fiery ordeal that has come on you to test you, as though something strange were happening to you. But rejoice inasmuch as you participate in the sufferings of Christ, so that you may be overjoyed when his glory is revealed. If you are insulted because of the name of Christ, you are blessed, for the Spirit of glory and of God rests on you. If you suffer, it should not be as a murderer or thief or any other kind of criminal, or even as a meddler. However, if you suffer as a Christian, do not be ashamed, but praise God that you bear that name. For it is time for judgment to begin with God's household; and if it begins with us, what will the outcome be for those who do not obey the gospel of God?" (1 Peter 4:12-17)

Breaking the Suffering Axis

Thus, the gospel serves as a master cipher to decode the suffering enigma, to break the suffering axis. In other words, the light of the gospel dispels both previously mentioned errors, the Romantic and the Stoic, so that one neither exalts suffering to a position of personal identity, nor dismisses it as a worthless experience. Suffering is not ignored, nor is it afforded a privileged status. Instead, in recognition of Jesus' suffering, the Christian sees his own suffering metamorphosed into a means by which

---

[166] James 5:14 gives an example.
[167] James 5:11 offers some assurance of a coming reward for those who persevere.

to become more like Christ. So, suffering serves a role in building (although there is a risk of destroying) one's faith and, in this way, serves as a means to a greater, more glorious, end.

> "The apostles left the Sanhedrin, rejoicing because they had been counted worthy of suffering disgrace for the Name." (Acts 5:41)

C.S. Lewis (1898-1963) described pain as a "megaphone," a clarion call for the sufferer to turn his attention to God.[168] Suffering's value comes in the context of relationship with a God who leverages pain to intensify longing for himself. While suffering is a concealed gift to the Christian,[169] it is one that God alone sovereignly administers. Thus, the Christian neither obsessively avoids suffering, nor actively seeks it out. The Christian never deliberately brings suffering upon himself or others (as a means of inducing sanctification),[170] and never sees suffering as adding to his salvation (a once-for-all work accomplished solely through Jesus' death on the cross).[171]

Chrysanthemums in a Chinese Vase
Camille Pissarro, d. 1903

Suffering fits into an eternal plan devised for the good of those who know and love God.[172] In this way, it serves a vital purpose in revealing the content of the heart. God alone permits suffering to expose the heart, to manifest with stunning clarity its contents, whether of faith (tested to be of pure gold) or of sin (dross to be burned

---

[168] C. S. Lewis, *The Problem of Pain* (HarperOne, 2009)
[169] James 1:2
[170] However, Hebrews 11:35b offers an intriguing counterexample. It reads, "...Others were tortured and refused to be released, so that they might gain a better resurrection." Some Christians allowed torture to continue that they might be more fully conformed to Christ on the last day.
[171] In 1 Corinthians 9:27, Paul spoke about beating his body to make it his slave. Paul neither advocated masochism nor saw his suffering as a salvific event. He refers to self-control.
[172] Romans 8:28

away).

Proverbs 27:21 reads, "The crucible for silver and the furnace for gold, but a man is tested by the praise he receives." The Bible views suffering through the lens of testing, exposing, repentance, and faith so that, in itself, suffering is neither ignored nor afforded a privileged status. Suffering, while not God's direct doing, does serve a specific purpose in his economy. It reveals either a faithful heart or an idolatrous one. When suffering's lessons are learned, when its intended sanctification is effected, it bears no additional purpose.

Thus, for the Christian, suffering is not embraced as a means for supposed nobility, nor as inducement for revenge, nor as an excuse for self-righteous anger, nor as a source of existential purpose and identity, nor as a twisted means to cause God to love one more. For the Christian, suffering is not a tightly gripped weapon brandished in the face of God, but the catalyst and context for quiet praise as God works in the heart to effect holiness. Suffering reveals hearts, and for that the Christian is eminently thankful.

> "Then Job answered the Lord:
> 'I am unworthy—how can I reply to you?
>   I put my hand over my mouth.
> I spoke once, but I have no answer—
>   twice, but I will say no more.'" (Job 40:3-5)

The Kintsugi Objective

Kintsugi is a style of Japanese pottery in which a shattered vessel (whether shattered deliberately or accidentally) is reconstructed using golden joinery. In other words, each shard is meticulously put back in place using a gold compound as glue. In this way, the reconstructed vessel (with gold veins running through it) becomes both more aesthetically pleasing, and more valuable. In fact, this shattering effect is a treasured art form in itself, as each Kintsugi vessel is one-of-a-kind.

One observes with Kintsugi that each broken piece is fully surrounded by gold, on its inner and outer surfaces and along the break-line. Thus, the break is "bathed" in gold so that nothing of the fractured surface remains exposed. Additionally, the greater the number and density of breaks the more gold that is applied, so that at the point of impact, where the breaks are most pronounced, the gold joinery is most abundant. Thus, that which might otherwise be rendered worthless has been redeemed, so that it is far more prized than ever before.

The concept of Kintsugi, in some way, captures the nature of the Christian's life with regard to suffering. The Christian suffers, often intensely, so that his life may at times feel shattered. Yet, God is at work reconstructing the vessel by means of a "golden compound," Jesus himself. In the midst of an evil world, God does not necessarily save a vessel from being shattered, but rather promises to reconstruct it using pure elements. The Christian trusts that God's reassembly will render him far more treasured and unique (sanctified) in God's sight. Thus, for the Christian, suffering, when under God's direct provenance, produces something vastly greater than what was lost.[173] Additionally, where the wreckage is greatest God's grace is most pronounced,[174] and that grace is all-encompassing so that no aspect of the break-site is left exposed. God redeems fractured lives so that they take on the golden glory of Christ, elevated to that which is of incomparable esteem in his sight. This is God's "Kintsugi Objective."

> God makes the imperfect perfect.[175]

Exploring the Kintsugi metaphor further, from the Bible's perspective there is value in suffering when seen through a theocentric lens. There is something in the timing and extent of suffering which accomplishes an often unseen, but eternal, purpose. Suffering should never be passively overlooked since there is always a hidden treasure nestled within it, an advancement of the sanctification ambition. While the world sees little benefit to suffering, the Christian knows that suffering is part of God's redemptive purposes. To a certain extent, and in constructive ways, God-ordained suffering should be seen as a gift, one which God does not ostensibly author, yet allows for good.

> "Those who go out weeping, carrying seed to sow, will return with songs of joy, carrying sheaves with them." (Psalm 126:6)
>
> "For just as we share abundantly in the sufferings of Christ, so also our comfort abounds through Christ." (2 Corinthians 1:5)

The Counselor's Compassion[176]

> "The Sovereign LORD has given me a well-instructed tongue, to know the word that sustains the weary. He wakens me morning by morning, wakens my ear to listen like one being instructed." (Isaiah 50:4)
>
> "I saw the tears of the oppressed and they have no comforter; power was on the side

---

[173] Romans 8:28
[174] 2 Corinthians 12:9
[175] Jeremiah 18:3, 4 captures this concept.
[176] For additional discussion of this topic see "The Counselor's Love: 'I Love Mankind – It's People I Can't Stand'" in chapter 7: "Artisanal Counseling: A Foray into Methods"

of their oppressors and they have no comforter." (Ecclesiastes 4:1)

The Raising of Lazarus (detail)
Joachim Uytewael, c. 1610

Sympathy is feelings "that are similar in kind to those that affect another person." Sympathy "is general and can apply to small annoyances or setbacks." Empathy, however, "denotes a deep emotional understanding of another's feelings or problems." "Empathy means a mental or affective projection into the feelings or state of mind of another person." [177] Counseling involves more than mere sympathy; it involves empathy. Empathetic counselors feel pain when others suffer, anger when others have experienced injustice, and regret when others have dissipated their life in sin.

"...so that there should be no division in the body, but that its parts should have equal concern for each other. If one part suffers, every part suffers with it; if one part is honored, every part rejoices with it." (1 Corinthians 12:25, 26)

John 11:35 states "Jesus wept." Jesus grieved the tragedy of death, recognizing that this was not part of the original design but rather an encroachment from the heart and hand of evil. Jesus did not just sympathize with those grieving, he empathized.

In Leviticus 10:17-20, God commanded Aaron to daily eat the people's sin offering. However, on the day that his two sons, Nadab and Abihu, were killed, Aaron refused to eat the offering. Aaron felt that abstaining was justifiable in light of his grief. Moses was satisfied with Aaron's reasoning. This passage indicates that painful circumstances often call for a measure of merciful latitude. God does not blindly uphold his directives (such as Sabbath rest, for example) but sees, and cares for, the entire person and his every need.

---

[177] Thesaurus.com

The counselor is compassionate with those who suffer, first because God himself is compassionate, and secondly, because the counselor himself has been shown compassion.[178] The counselor's display of compassion must closely follow God's own unique display of compassion. Just as the Bible's explanation of God's love can easily be corrupted into a secular concept (such as reducing love to a mere emotion, or love as falsely unconditional), so too, compassion is susceptible to the same perversion. Misguided compassion, like its cousin, unconditional love, strips the person of God from the equation. Compassion is not a mere sentimental exchange, nor a display of permissiveness with regard to the human plight. True compassion, as God expresses it, mourns with those who mourn,[179] binds up the broken hearted,[180] and quenches the longing of those who hunger and thirst for righteousness,[181] all based in relationship with the person of God himself.

> "Keep your lives free from the love of money and be content with what you have, because God has said, 'Never will I leave you, never will I forsake you.'" (Hebrews 13:5)

Compassion is active, at work, and in motion, to discern faith and eradicate sin. It has vision; it hates evil; it fights with and against the sinner (often in subtle ways). There are, of course, times when compassion listens silently,[182] manifesting the presence of a God who is attentive. However, compassion, when fully applied, does much more than merely offer muted grief; it seeks to instill hope in a renewed and reinvigorated heart which has been given a glimpse into its own worship intentions.

> "The Lord is good to all; he has compassion on all he has made. The eyes of all look to you, and you give them their food at the proper time. You open your hand and satisfy the desires of every living thing. The Lord is righteous in all his ways and faithful in all he does." (Psalm 145:9, 15-17)

Case Study: God's *Sui Generis* Love[183]

> "The supreme happiness in life is the knowledge that we are loved." (Victor Hugo)

Observe people carefully and one finds a solitary all-consuming passion, the desire to be

---

[178] 1 John 4:19
[179] Romans 12:15
[180] Psalm 147:3; Isaiah 61:1
[181] Matthew 5:6
[182] James 1:19
[183] Many of the concepts in this section from David Powlison, "Is God's Love Unconditional?" *The Journal of Biblical Counseling* (Glenside, Pennsylvania: The Christian Counseling and Education Foundation). For further discussion of God's love see, "Excursus: First Corinthians 13:1-12" in the first book in this series, *Ask for the Ancient Paths: From Art to Artifice to Arisen*, chapter 10: "The Third-Way of Sanctification: From Abominable to Indominable." For a discussion on speaking to others about God's love see "How Does the Christian Rightly Tell Others of God's Love?" in the second book in this series, *What Agreement Is There Between the Temple of God and Idols?: The Accidence of Sin and Idolatry*, chapter 9: "Marauding Visigoths: The Autocratic Self"

loved and to in turn love another. People seem obsessed with wanting to know that they are loved by someone. When that love seems to be present, it is like a taste of heaven, the fulfillment of the human *raison d'etre*. When that love seems absent, the fires of hell seem favorable by comparison. This fixation with finding, and keeping, love is often slavery to meeting perceived needs, and frequently a denial of the incomparable love of a heavenly Father who longs to lavish love upon those who seek him. How does one rightly characterize God's love? What are its distinctive attributes, attributes which stand in sharp contradistinction to a human construal of love?

The Return of the Prodigal Son, Illustration from the Holman Bible (Caber), 1890

Any philosophical description of God necessarily makes him into an abstraction. This means that God loses his personhood and becomes a mere concept of human design (more akin to Greek god than to God of the Bible). While Christians know God as person (a person to whom they can relate), they often make his *qualities* into abstractions to suit their purposes. They may call him by name, but they reduce his characteristics to humanly-derived musings. In other words, the sinful heart tends to typify God's qualities based on concepts that it finds attractive, such as mercy, grace, and love, while denuding those concepts of their God-ward referent. In actuality these concepts are intimately tied to God's personhood and, therefore, inextricably bound up with his justice and wrath. In stripping God's love from his personhood, in reducing it to a palatable human concept, the sinner suits the machinations of a guilt-ridden heart. The point is that God's love must not be seen in abstraction, but in highly-concrete terms commensurate with both his personhood and his plenary self-revelation.

Observe parents and one finds that most are generally confused on how to rightly love their children. They often think that giving the child what he wants, indulging him, and building self-esteem, are the highest goals. This is the curse of unconditional love, a form of love that does not see the need for change. Rather, it assumes that the human heart is fundamentally good, and will pursue that which is right on its own. In reality, most modern parenting merely feeds a heart that in time invents more persuasive ways

Vladimir and Rogneda
Anton Losenko, 1770

to sin. The child does not need self-esteem; he needs discipline. He needs a heart impacted by a holy God whom he fears to disobey and delights to obey. Under most circumstances, the child needs to be protected from the sin within himself much more so than from the dangers outside of himself. Yet, tragically, most parents reverse the threat matrix to the detriment of their children and themselves. (The idea is that as the child is reformed from within he soon makes sound choices which guard him from much of the evil without.)

Whether exhibited through parenting or in other contexts, the most pervasive modern expectation of love is that it ought to be unconditional. The concept of unconditional love grows from Rogerian psychology masterminded by humanistic psychologist Carl Rogers (1902-1987). Rogers was a pastor who renounced the ministry for psychology, thinking that he could better serve the church in this way. Rogerian psychology is built upon the concept of "unconditional positive regard." The philosophy behind this is that the counselor should impose no values and offer no moral judgments. Rogers envisioned the counselor's function as simply to make the counselee feel affirmed and understood, that this would serve as the source of existential healing.

Why has the concept of unconditional love become a cultural cornerstone, a seeming axiomatic truth of both the world and the church? The concept of unconditional love seems to serve as a proxy for solving a host of relational problems. For example, it appears to counter certain relational threats such as:

1. Conditional love
2. Love as impatient
3. Love as manipulative
4. Relational acceptance predicated on change

However, unconditional love easily slides to the opposite extreme so that it becomes:

1. Detached
2. Non-directive
3. Holding no expectations
4. General
5. Impersonal
6. Imposing no values
7. Neutral
8. Smoothing over differences, seeing no distinctions

The term "unconditional" falls into what might be termed the "antithesis trap," a defining of the concept in contrast to what it is not. Where love is often capricious the answer is not to dispense with expectations. Where love is bossy or controlling, the answer is not to fashion a kind of non-directive love. In this sense, unconditional love misses the far richer scriptural metaphors for love.

Additionally, there is a common logical fallacy with regard to unconditional love; it is often confused with forgiveness. Yet, these are wholly distinct concepts. For example, Matthew 18:21, 22 reads,

> Then Peter came to Jesus and asked, 'Lord, how many times shall I forgive my brother or sister who sins against me? Up to seven times?' Jesus answered, 'I tell you, not seven times, but seventy-seven times.'

Jesus' command is that his followers would exhibit unlimited forgiveness. However, this never implies unlimited acceptance, or even the slightest acceptance, of sin. There is an immense difference between forgiving another's transgressions (which is the secret to "mental health") and turning a blind-eye to those transgressions. The form of forgiveness that Jesus commanded was to render his followers cognizant of the forgiveness they have first received, but never to render them blind to sin.

While Rogerian psychology appears eminently altruistic, genuinely caring, and supremely sensitive, in reality it is an emissary of Satan to destroy the recognition of sin, to further, and make more comfortable, slavery to a depraved heart.[184] While Rogerian psychology appears values-neutral and morally non-directive, it is the exact opposite. In reality, it advances and imposes a set of values and offers a definitive moral direction. It is itself an agenda with a deeply opinionated directive. That directive is that the counselee is fundamentally good, and in no way in need of repentance and change. This is the resurrected Pythagorean priest in his purest and most insidious form.

> Unconditional love finally spawns the same social blight as that of an entitlement state. (An entitlement state forges co-dependency between citizens and government, so that each views himself as a victimized subject in need of a handout.) The concept of unconditional love is the handmaiden of entitlement thinking.

To many Christians the concept of unconditional love sounds like a biblical concept. In fact, most Christian literature asserts that God's love is decisively unconditional. What such Christians do not understand is that they have blindly accepted a psychological term fraught with lethal assumptions and implications. They have allowed a Trojan horse of error to enter the Christian *Weltanschauung*, wrongly assuming that they have received a conceptual gift.

Careful study of Scripture reveals that God's love is not unconditional. It is far richer and deeper than unconditional love ever could be. It is a love that searches, chastens, pursues, and pleads with. It is a love that holds a vision of what people can be and has the courage to pursue that vision, to step out in the realization that change is possible and will be accomplished.[185]

No person has ever met God's demands for acceptance except Jesus, who met them at the cross where divine justice was executed and the Father's wrath was quelled. Thus, God's conditions for salvation, and his love for his people, stand upon the perfect obedience and blood sacrifice of Jesus. In this way, relationship with God is wholly without condition, not because God imposes no conditions, but because Jesus met them flawlessly.[186]

The Bible is clear that the good news of salvation through the shed blood of Jesus Christ is a free invitation, not predicated on meeting a standard of performance. God invites all who desire to be saved to receive Christ, through whom, and by whom,

---

[184] Jeremiah 23:17 captures something of this concept, false prophets who proclaim peace from the mouth of the Lord, when in reality there is no peace.
[185] David Powlison, "Is God's Love Unconditional?" *The Journal of Biblical Counseling* (Glenside, Pennsylvania: The Christian Counseling and Education Foundation)
[186] Matthew 5:17

The Elevation of the Cross
Peter Paul Rubens, c. 1611

each becomes the recipient of unmitigated and undeserved grace. Thus, Christians hold out the gospel without condition, inviting all to drink living water and partake of the bread of life without cost.[187] So the gospel's invitation is, in this sense, an unconditional invitation since the call to salvation is free and without condition. However, the work of sanctification (the change process that God initiates and directs in each Christian) is marked by a form of God's love which is far greater than unconditional love ever could be. It is in the context of sanctification that the "unconditional" nomenclature breaks down, as it presents a crucial departure from the Bible.

> The Bible describes God using the title "Father," and Jesus using the title "Son." God, thus, refers to himself in masculine terms. Yet, in Mark 14:36, Romans 8:15, and Galatians 4:6, God is described with the Aramaic term "*Abba*." Some point out that this term is not masculine but neuter. The intent in this interpretation is often to subtly promote a feminist agenda, to depreciate God as a Father in order to render him somewhat androgynous (and, therefore, presumably less threatening and more accessible). Thus, the purpose is not to submit to God by means of his own self-description, but to remold him into a being which affords women equality on their own terms. (It is with this same refusal to submit to God's Word that most introduce the concept of unconditional love.)

God desires to restore his people, to retrofit them for friendship with himself. To this end, when one becomes a Christian God's sanctifying work begins in earnest. God

---
[187] Isaiah 55:1

orchestrates a lifelong plan of comprehensive rehabilitation in which he works in each moment to amplify and extend faith, while seeking to expunge the curse of indwelling sin. Thus, God's agenda is not unconditional positive regard, but rather the rebuilding of broken and lost lives in himself. God's goal is not that the real "you" would emerge but, rather, that the real "him" would emerge in you.[188] Thus, the concept of unconditional love is a direct affront to God's sanctifying work. The unconditional concept cannot be explained away or redefined to avoid this inevitable collision of concepts.

> As the modern church is increasingly infiltrated by secular thought, the Christian view of God undergoes a stunning metamorphosis. In the Christian consciousness, God is emerging from his authoritative and judgmental cocoon into a brilliant and fluttering God who is only unctuous and compliant. In the process, God's Word has been whittled down to Rockwellian pietistic piffle. While often the objective is to make Christianity palatable to an increasingly pagan world, falsehood always backfires as the world increasingly dismisses Christianity as a feckless and flaccid faith.

While one man-centered concept is dangerous (conditional love), its opposite is equally dangerous (unconditional love). Disrupting human reason's faulty dialectic (the logic that the opposite of error corrects the error), God deals in "third-ways." Thus, the gospel intrudes into, and transcends, the dialectic, so that, on account of Jesus, God's love is neither conditional nor unconditional. It is a wholly other form of love, a third option that one may label "contra-conditional."[189] By this is meant that God's love is above the concept of conditional or unconditional. It is an entirely different concept, based upon, and conveying a wholly unique locution.

> "Batter My Heart, Three-Personed God"[190]   (John Donne)
>
> Batter my heart, three-personed God, for you
> As yet but knock, breathe, shine, and seek to mend;
> That I may rise and stand, overthrow me, and bend
> Your force to break, blow, burn, and make me new.
> I, like an usurped town to another due,
> Labor to admit you, but oh, to no end;
> Reason, your viceroy in me, me should defend,
> But is captived, and proves weak or untrue.
> Yet dearly I love you, and would be loved fain,
> But am betrothed unto your enemy;

---

[188] John 3:30
[189] This term from David Powlison, Westminster Theological Seminary, Philadelphia, Pennsylvania
[190] Some words in John Donne's (1572–1631) "Batter My Heart, Three-Personed God" have been modernized to accommodate readers who may not be familiar with Elizabethan English.

> Divorce me, untie or break that knot again,
> Take me to you, imprison me, for I,
> Except you enthrall me, never shall be free,
> Nor ever chaste, except you ravish me.

The Nature of Love

> It is impossible to know how to love until one has first received God's forgiveness. Once forgiven, one is delivered from evil. This is the first step in knowing what it means to love another.

Love is seeking the highest good of another.[191]

Mother and Children
Friedrich Von Amerling, d. 1887

1. Love "seeks" because it is active, has an agenda, has vision.

2. By "highest" is meant that it operates on an ultimate and aeonian vista. It is not concerned with temporal objectives, but desires change that will stand for an eternity.

3. It is "good" because it knows the goodness of God, a goodness that is utterly other than man's understanding of goodness. It knows that God's goodness is to impart holiness, and it seeks to induce this in fallen people.

4. It is "of another" because it is not self-seeking, and in fact, forgets about oneself. It is entirely focused on concern for others, and helping them know God, without any regard for oneself.

---

[191] This definition of love from Mark Potter, Greentree Campus Ministries, Atglen, Pennsylvania

John 3:16[192]	
For God	the greatest lover
so loved	to the greatest degree
the world	the greatest number
that He gave	the greatest act
His only begotten Son	the greatest gift
that who ever	the greatest invitation
believes	the greatest simplicity
in Him	the greatest person
should not perish	the greatest deliverance
but	the greatest difference
have	the greatest certainty
everlasting life	the greatest possession

> "And let us consider how we may spur one another on toward love and good deeds, not giving up meeting together, as some are in the habit of doing, but encouraging one another—and all the more as you see the Day approaching." (Hebrews 10:24, 25)
>
> "Dear friends, let us love one another, for love comes from God. Everyone who loves has been born of God and knows God. Whoever does not love does not know God, because God is love. This is how God showed his love among us: He sent his one and only Son into the world that we might live through him. This is love: not that we loved God, but that he loved us and sent his Son as an atoning sacrifice for our sins. Dear friends, since God so loved us, we also ought to love one another. No one has ever seen God; but if we love one another, God lives in us and his love is made complete in us." (1 John 4:7-12)

God's Love:

> "Are not two sparrows sold for a penny? Yet not one of them will fall to the ground outside your Father's care. And even the very hairs of your head are all numbered." (Matthew 10:29, 30)

1. Is active

God's love moves; it has force; it is not tame. It goes to wild extreme in its mission to claim souls and reclaim lives.

> "Suppose one of you has a hundred sheep and loses one of them. Doesn't he leave

---

[192] This development of John 3:16 borrowed from an unknown source

> the ninety-nine in the open country and go after the lost sheep until he finds it? And when he finds it, he joyfully puts it on his shoulders and goes home. Then he calls his friends and neighbors together and says, 'Rejoice with me; I have found my lost sheep.' I tell you that in the same way there will be more rejoicing in heaven over one sinner who repents than over ninety-nine righteous persons who do not need to repent." (Luke 15:4-7)

2. Has an agenda to change

> "Yet you desired faithfulness even in the womb; you taught me wisdom in that secret place. Let me hear joy and gladness; let the bones you have crushed rejoice. Create in me a pure heart, O God, and renew a steadfast spirit within me." (Psalm 51:6, 8, 10)
>
> "We are God's workmanship created in Christ Jesus to do good works which God prepared in advance for us to do." (Ephesians 2:10)

God's love is an act of "re-creation." Tantamount to his creation of the universe, God labors to display himself in people. As stated previously, God does not seek the real "you," but the real "him" in you.

> Consider the concept of "drafting" in auto-racing. Drafting is getting as close as possible to the car in front so as to benefit from a vacuum created behind it. The lead car plows the air aside forming a pocket or vacuum which envelops the car behind. The car behind is then drawn forward effortlessly. This is a fitting metaphor for the Christian's relationship with God. As he draws closer to God, the Christian is pulled forward by God's Spirit. The closer one is to God the greater the suction drawing one forward. However, as one falls farther from God, he is suddenly working in his own strength and finds that the change process is impossible as he labors but achieves nothing.[193]

3. Cares

> "Shout for joy, Oh heavens. Rejoice Oh earth; burst into song, Oh mountains. For the Lord comforts his people and will have compassion on his afflicted ones. See I have engraved you on the palms of my hands." (Isaiah 49:13)
>
> "I knew that you are a gracious and compassionate God, slow to anger and abounding in love, a God who relents from sending calamity." (Jonah 4:2)

---

[193] This analogy borrowed from an unknown source

Home from the Sea, Arthur Hughes, 1862

4. Is complex

> "As the heavens are higher than the earth, so are my ways higher than your ways and my thoughts than your thoughts." (Isaiah 55:9)

5. Confronts

> "Who is this that darkens my counsel with words without knowledge?" (Job 38:2)

Jesus spoke to the Pharisees in harsh confrontational tones; he bluntly stated the truth and departed. However, to the broken in spirit Jesus spoke in gentle and instructive ways, came alongside, comforted, and taught. Unconditional love would never capture this distinction because it whitewashes the heart. In other words, under the aegis of unconditional love, the Pharisees might just have needed to be better understood and encouraged.[194] The point is that God understands that there is something desperately wrong with the sinner, and so he steps forward to free him from it. God's love seeks the sinner's emancipation, his liberation from himself, and often that liberation comes through godly confrontation.

6. Is creative

---

[194] David Powlison, Westminster Theological Seminary, Philadelphia, Pennsylvania

> "'Come now, let us reason together,' says the LORD. 'Though your sins are like scarlet, they shall be as white as snow; though they are red as crimson, they shall be like wool.'" (Isaiah 1:18)

God's love invents new ways of reaching sinners with his message of salvation; he finds imaginative ways of attracting people to himself.

7. Defends

> "Therefore, say to the Israelites: 'I am the LORD, and I will bring you out from under the yoke of the Egyptians. I will free you from being slaves to them, and I will redeem you with an outstretched arm and with mighty acts of judgment. I will take you as my own people, and I will be your God. Then you will know that I am the LORD your God, who brought you out from under the yoke of the Egyptians. And I will bring you to the land I swore with uplifted hand to give to Abraham, to Isaac and to Jacob. I will give it to you as a possession. I am the LORD.'" (Exodus 6:6-8)
>
> "Do not be afraid, little flock, for your Father has been pleased to give you the kingdom." (Luke 12:32)
>
> "Who shall separate us from the love of Christ? Shall trouble or hardship or persecution or famine or nakedness or danger or sword? ...nor anything else in creation will be able to separate us from the love of God that is in Christ Jesus our Lord." (Romans 8:35, 39)

8. Disciplines

> "...because the Lord disciplines those he loves, and he punishes everyone he accepts as a son. Endure hardship as discipline; God is treating you as sons." (Hebrews 12:6, 7)

9. Is energetic

> "'What do you think? If a man owns a hundred sheep, and one of them wanders away, will he not leave the ninety-nine on the hills and go to look for the one that wandered off? And if he finds it, truly I tell you, he is happier about that one sheep than about the ninety-nine that did not wander off. In the same way your Father in heaven is not willing that any of these little ones should perish.'" (Matthew 18:12-14)
>
> "But while he was still a long way off, his father saw him and was filled with

compassion for him; he ran to his son, threw his arms around him and kissed him." (Luke 15:20)

10. Fights for you

"The LORD said to Joshua, 'Do not be afraid of them; I have given them into your hand. Not one of them will be able to withstand you.'" (Joshua 10:8)

11. Fights with you

"So I declared on oath in my anger, 'They shall never enter my rest.'" (Psalm 95:11)

"Come let us return to the Lord. He has torn us to pieces but he will heal us; he has injured us but he will bind up our wounds." (Hosea 6:1)

"Therefore I cut you in pieces with my prophets, I killed you with the words of my mouth; my judgments flash like lightning upon you." (Hosea 6:5)

Jacob Wrestling with an Angel
Eugene Delacroix, 1861

12. Hates (evil, sin, the world's rebellion)

"My anger burns against the shepherds, and I will punish the leaders; for the LORD Almighty will care for his flock, the people of Judah, and make them like a proud horse in battle." (Zechariah 10:3)

God's love hates evil, the world's rebellion, sin committed by his people, and sin committed against his people. God's love does not rest until it has finally vanquished the presence of sin in those image-bearers which he has claimed as his earthly temples.[195]

13. Intrudes

---

[195] 1 Corinthians 3:16

> "I know the plans I have for you, plans to prosper you, to give you hope and a future." (Jeremiah 29:11)
>
> "As Jesus was walking beside the Sea of Galilee, he saw two brothers, Simon called Peter and his brother Andrew. They were casting a net into the lake, for they were fishermen. 'Come, follow me,' Jesus said, 'and I will send you out to fish for men.' At once they left their nets and followed him." (Mathew 4:18-20)

14. Is jealous

> "Do not worship any other god, for the Lord, whose name is Jealous, is a jealous God." (Exodus 34:14)
>
> "God is a consuming fire, a jealous God." (Deuteronomy 4:24)

15. Judges

> "Return, Israel, to the LORD your God. Your sins have been your downfall!" (Hosea 14:1)
>
> "The spiritual man makes judgments about all things, but he himself is not subject to any man's judgment." (1 Corinthians 2:15)
>
> "Do not love the world or anything in the world. If anyone loves the world, the love of the Father is not in him." (1 John 2:15)

16. Is passionate

> "Jerusalem, Jerusalem, you who kill the prophets and stone those sent to you, how often I have longed to gather your children together, as a hen gathers her chicks under her wings, and you were not willing." (Matthew 23:37)

17. Perseveres

> "The Lord is not slow in keeping his promise, as some understand slowness. He is patient with you, not wanting anyone to perish, but everyone to come to repentance." (2 Peter 3:9)

18. Is personal

> Numbers 1:2 states, "Take a census of the whole Israelite community by their clans

and families, listing every man by name, one by one." God listed each of his people, an image of the book of life, as each is precious to him.

"Before I formed you in the womb I knew you, before you were born I set you apart; I appointed you as a prophet to the nations." (Jeremiah 1:5)

The Sacrifice of Isaac, Giambattista Pittoni, 1720

19. Pursues

"When Israel was a child, I loved him and out of Egypt I called my son; but the more I called Israel the further they went from me." (Hosea 11:1, 2)

"The Lord sent a great wind on the sea, and such a violent storm arose that the ship threatened to break up. The Lord provided a great fish to swallow Jonah…" (Jonah 1:4, 17)

20. Brings repentance

"Produce fruit in keeping with repentance." (Matthew 3:8)

"The tax collector stood at a distance and said, 'God have mercy on me, a sinner.'" (Luke 18:13)

21. Shares

"For everyone who asks receives; the one who seeks finds; and to the one who knocks, the door will be opened. Which of you, if your son asks for bread, will give him a stone? Or if he asks for a fish, will give him a snake? If you, then, though you are evil, know how to give good gifts to your children, how much more will your Father in heaven give good gifts to those who ask him!'" (Matthew 7:8-11)

"Our fathers disciplined us for a little while as they thought best; but God disciplines us for our good, that we may share his holiness." (Hebrews 12:10)

22. Is specific

"At that time Michael, the great prince who protects your people, will arise. There will be a time of distress such as has not happened from the beginning of nations until then. But at that time your people--*everyone whose name is found written in the book*--will be delivered." (Daniel 12:1, emphasis added)

"And I saw the dead, great and small, standing before the throne, and books were opened. Another book was opened, which is the book of life. The dead were judged according to what they had done as recorded in the books." (Revelation 20:12)

23. Suffers

"Greater love has no man than this, that he lay down his life for his friends" (John 15:13)

24. Watches

"The Lord watches over you. The Lord is your shade at your right hand; the sun will not harm you by day, nor the moon by night. The Lord will keep you from all harm. He will watch over your life." (Psalm 121:5-7)

"Son of man, I have made you a watchman for the house of Israel; so hear the word I speak and give them warning from me." (Ezekiel 3:17)

Unconditional Love	God's Love (Contra-conditional Love)
■ Unconditional positive regard	● Comprehensive lifelong rehabilitation[196]
■ Offers blanket non-detailed	● Acceptance not based upon who one

---
[196] Philippians 1:6; 1 Thessalonians 5:24

<ul><li>acceptance</li><li>Holds forth a good-feeling superficial love</li></ul>	<ul><li>is, but upon who Christ is</li><li>Watches, cares, has intensity, complexity, and a personal quality[197]</li><li>Pursues each person by name[198]</li></ul>
<ul><li>Blindly tolerant</li><li>Imposes no beliefs nor values</li><li>Has a passive quality</li></ul>	<ul><li>Intolerant of sin and evil[199]</li><li>Asserts a belief system and values[200]</li><li>Has an active, pursuing, yet patient, guarding quality[201]</li><li>Involved in another's life</li><li>Not passive and detached, recognizing that God is jealous for those who belong to him[202]</li></ul>
<ul><li>Foolishly affirming, benign</li><li>Asserts that everyone is "okay"</li><li>Just wants to make others feel happy</li><li>No response needed</li></ul>	<ul><li>Aware of deeply-seated problems that need to be addressed[203]</li><li>Asserts that one is not "okay"</li><li>Focuses on growth in holiness, as "the Lord chose us to be blameless in his sight"[204]</li><li>Warrants a response[205]</li></ul>
<ul><li>Imposes no expectations</li><li>The real self is good enough, even to be celebrated</li></ul>	<ul><li>Sees change as crucial[206]</li><li>Sets expectations for growth in faith[207]</li></ul>
<ul><li>Wants peace where peace is not to be found[208]</li></ul>	<ul><li>Necessarily involves some struggle</li><li>God fighting for you, God fighting with you</li><li>Seeks real and lasting peace found through growth in Christ[209]</li><li>Brings lasting freedom[210]</li></ul>
<ul><li>No repentance needed</li></ul>	<ul><li>Repentance needed</li><li>Sees that one's problem, not as his finiteness, but as his sinfulness</li><li>Will not let one rest in his sin</li></ul>

---

[197] Psalm 27:10; Isaiah 49:15
[198] Isaiah 43:1
[199] Matthew 3:12
[200] James 3:15
[201] James 5:19, 20; Jude 1:23
[202] Psalm 121:5-8; Hosea 11:1-7
[203] Jeremiah 8:11
[204] Ephesians 1:4
[205] Job 38:4
[206] James 4:10
[207] 1 Timothy 4:16; Hebrews 5:12
[208] Jeremiah 8:11
[209] John 14:27
[210] Ephesians 2:14-17

SUFFERING

	• Confronts in love[211]
■ Seeks to fill another with a vacuous euphoria and a vapid self-confidence ■ Meets perceived needs	• Does not seek to meet perceived needs[212] • Seeks growth in holiness • Enacts discipline[213]
■ Deceptive, flattering	• Truthful, genuine; not deceptive, forthcoming[214]
■ Never deals with pride, fear of man, lust for success, superiority, selfish ambition, or self-absorption	• Hates sin and evil[215] • Opposes pride[216] • Seeks to increase the fear of God[217] • Puts life's successes and failures into proper perspective[218]

> First Peter 4:8 states, "Above all keep your love for one another fervent, because love covers a multitude of sins." This certainly sounds like unconditional love, like the one who loves is expected to overlook sin. However, interpreting this verse in light of the corpus of Scripture, one understands that God does not overlook sin in his people and, in turn, his people are not to overlook sin when love would dictate helping others to be free from it. Thus, while this verse speaks about one's relationship with others, one's ability to overlook an offense upon oneself, it does not imply turning a blind-eye toward sin. One must remember that First Peter was written to severely persecuted Christians, so that it serves as a blueprint for confronting evil. Peter's message is that when one is sinned against, even grievously, he can respond in love.

With a jeweler's loupe God peers into the recesses of a heart he longs to bring to himself, probing to the subterranean reaches of the soul. God works in highly-specific ways to zero-in on the rogue regions of the heart, to bring them to justice. He haunts those he loves, hunting them with a reckless pursuit. Consider God's implication of David through the prophet Samuel as David was caught square between the eyes with, "You are the man."[219] In this way, God does not let go of those he loves,[220] and does not surrender them to the flames. He approaches, lingers, persuades, and reaches into the sinner's life with an intention and intensity that it beyond human comprehension. God's love is forged in the very fires of his being, and that love is refined to a smooth sheen.

---

[211] Hosea 14:1-3
[212] John 6:15
[213] Proverbs 3:12; Hebrews 12:6; Revelation 3:19
[214] James 1:17
[215] Psalm 5:5, 6
[216] James 4:6
[217] Psalm 111:10; Proverbs 9:10
[218] Mark 8:36
[219] 2 Samuel 12:7
[220] John 10:28

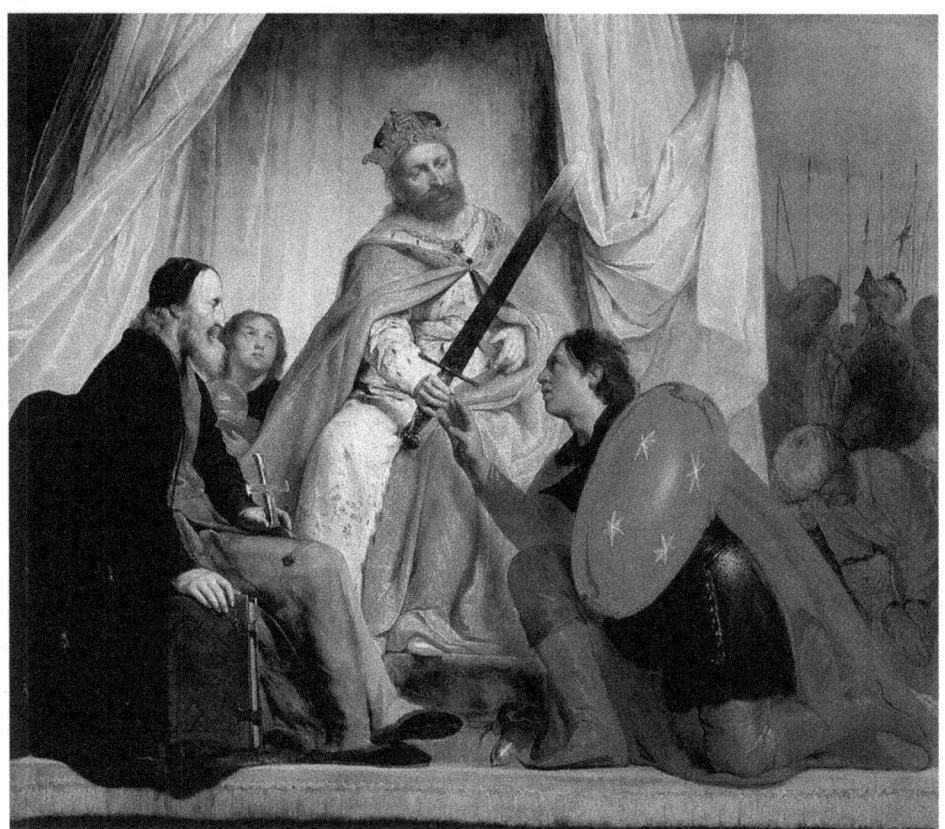

The Legend of the Haarlem Shield, Pieter de Grebber, d. 1653

Excursus: Should One Love Himself?[221]

A church sign read, "To love others, first love yourself."

> 'The most important one,' answered Jesus, 'is this: 'Hear, O Israel: The Lord our God, the Lord is one. Love the Lord your God with all your heart and with all your soul and with all your mind and with all your strength.' The second is this: 'Love your neighbor as yourself.' There is no commandment greater than these.' (Mark 12:29-31)

Mark 12:31 is one of the most misunderstood verses in the Bible, as many wrongly suppose Jesus to state that one should first love himself, so as to subsequently be capable of loving others. This erroneous interpretation comes directly from the Adler-Maslow pyramid of needs, and is far from Jesus' intent. Jesus here states that one should endeavor to love others as one already sinfully loves himself. Jesus correctly recognizes that fallen mankind invariably loves himself. Therefore, Jesus reverses the equation as a directive to love others in the way that one already sinfully loves himself. This does not affirm self-love, nor does it see self-love as a prerequisite

---

[221] For further discussion of the issue of self-love see the second book in this series, *What Agreement Is There Between the Temple of God and Idols?: The Accidence of Sin and Idolatry*, chapter 9: "Marauding Visigoths: The Autocratic Self"

to loving others.[222] Jesus' intent is to affect a seismic shift in the sinner's view of love.

Excursus: Faith, Hope, and Love

> "And now these three remain: faith, hope and love. But the greatest of these is love." (1 Corinthians 13:13)

The context of 1 Corinthians 13:13 is crucial for understanding its meaning. Chapter 13 addresses the manifestation of faith and hope – love. Paul's point is that love manifests invisible realities (faith and hope) so that they become evident. It is through displaying love that one proves that the invisible qualities live within him. Therefore, love is elevated to the highest position because of its ability to make faith and hope evident. Paul, here, is not speaking soteriologically (with regard to the means of salvation), but rather about the role that love plays in manifesting invisible qualities within the Christian.

This chapter uses *agape* (ἀγάπη) love, "worship love," extensively. So Paul explores a love that first worships God. The thrust of Paul's argument is, "Love that first worships God is patient and kind." This is why the love spoken about is of such a dramatically different nature than that displayed by the world. This love has its life-blood in faith. Thus, *agape* love grows out of faith and reveals the essence of that faith.

Paul's formulation:

1. Faith initiates relationship with God.
2. Hope is an extension of that faith.
3. Love is the completion of that faith.

Thus, faith is the foundation; hope is the structure; but love is the crown.[223] Love shows that faith is truly alive because love manifests God's work within believers to perfect their faith. Love is like the proof of faith, and evidences the character (likeness) of God within believers. Love, therefore, gives motion to faith so that it acts and displays itself.

Hebrews 11:1 states, "Now faith is being sure of what we hope for and certain of what we do not see." Thus, faith and hope are invisible. Yet, they are made visible through love which acts and moves with purpose. Thus, love gives proof that faith and hope exist within the believer.

---

[222] Jay Adams, *The Biblical View of Self-Esteem, Self-Love, Self-Image* (Harvest House Publishers, 1986)
[223] Adam Clarke Commentary, Bible Study Tools, 2012

Spring (*Apple Blossoms*), John Everett Millais, 1859

Consider another analogy. This triad of faith, hope, and love could be thought of as a spreading tree:

1. The roots, the tree's source of life, are faith.
2. The trunk and branches, which give it strength and structure, are hope.
3. The fruit, which provides nourishment and propagates the tree, is love.

The tree exists to produce its fruit, as the fruit is the tree's climax and glory. Similarly, faith gives life; hope transfers that life; and the fruit is the outward manifestation of that life, the proof that faith and hope exist. It is faith which draws life from God, and love which imparts that life to others.[224]

The Faith-to-Fruit Formulation

There exists a striking similarity between 1 Corinthians 13:13 and Galatians 5:22, 23. The similarity lies in the linchpin of love in each. While 1 Corinthians speaks of faith giving rise to hope which culminates in love, the Galatians formulation works from the opposite direction. It begins with love which manifests itself in joy and peace. Like faith and hope, joy and peace are inner invisible qualities. Those qualities evidence the believer's love specifically toward God. Joy then manifests itself in kindness, goodness, and faithfulness – each directed toward one's neighbor. And peace manifests itself in patience, gentleness, and self-control. So the invisible (that

---

[224] Adam Clarke Commentary, Bible Study Tools, 2012

which is directed toward God) becomes visible (that which is directed toward others). Thus, the Galatians 5 architecture builds upon, and explicates that of 1 Corinthians 13.

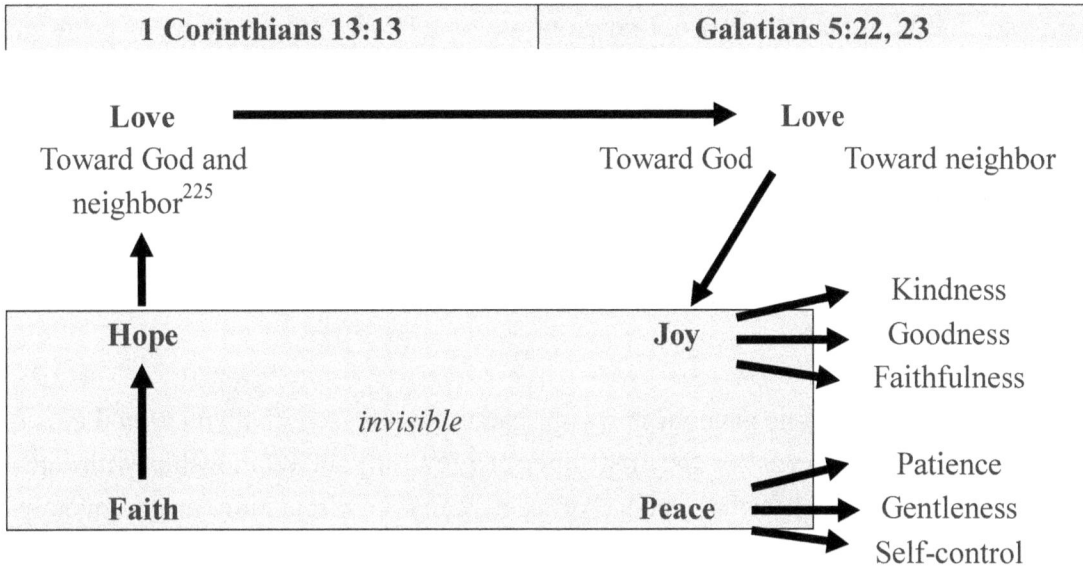

"By their fruit you will recognize them. Do people pick grapes from thornbushes, or figs from thistles? Likewise, every good tree bears good fruit, but a bad tree bears bad fruit. A good tree cannot bear bad fruit, and a bad tree cannot bear good fruit." (Matthew 7:16-18)

Concluding Thoughts

"Teach us to number our days, that we may gain a heart of wisdom." (Psalm 90:12)

Maybe you stumbled upon this material out of casual curiosity, or possibly you deliberately sought it out in the midst of a horrendous ordeal. You might be searching for answers to intense suffering, suffering which feels like a burden too great to bear. Possibly you feel trapped in a life of incessant pain. You may be subject to daily nagging frustrations, or enduring grave injustice and life-threatening persecution. Maybe you were betrayed by a loved one, or carry the shame of failure.

Whatever you face at this moment, whatever the cross you bear, know that a good God sees your plight, hears your pleas, feels your every throbbing emotion, and longs to offer you rest.[226] Jesus died to give you newness of life, that your concerns would become his, that your burdens would be transferred to him, that in the context of any trial you would find blazing hope. Nothing you experience is by accident, nor is your life under the auspices of reckless forces. Jesus is present and perceptive; he desires to

---
[225] Mark 12:30, 31
[226] Matthew 11:28

take hold of you in the midst of the wreckage, to never leave nor forsake you.[227] He is a very present help in time of trouble.[228] Your circumstance is not by accident, as Acts 17:27 states, "God did this so that they would seek him and perhaps reach out for him and find him, though he is not far from any one of us." God may seem far from you, but he is not. Reach out for him.

Romans 8:32 offers a profound assurance, "He who did not spare his own Son, but gave him up for us all--how will he not also, along with him, graciously give us all things?" Jesus died on the cross for you because he loves you. Your life is not a meaningless plodding of numbing experiences; it was carefully planned by a loving God for regal purposes.

I believe that God put this material into your hands for a reason, that you would either encounter the living Jesus for the first time, or grew in your relationship with him. Please take comfort that the readers of each copy in circulation are frequently remembered in prayer. May the Lord bless you and keep you.

> "Now to him who is able to do immeasurably more than all we ask or imagine, according to his power that is at work within us…" (Ephesians 3:20)

---

[227] Deuteronomy 31:6; Hebrews 13:5
[228] Psalm 46:1

- 3 -

THE HOBGOBLIN IN THE INGLENOOK:
Assessing Loneliness

Diogenes, Jean-Léon Gérôme, 1860

The Historical Trajectory of Loneliness

The problem of loneliness, as a society-wide phenomenon, seems to have arisen with the advent of the Industrial Revolution, a time in which families and relationships were often sacrificed in the pursuit of manufacturing and commerce. The opening of the Slater factory on December 20, 1790, in Pawtucket, Rhode Island marked the birth of the American Industrial Revolution and a fundamental shift away from an agrarian economy. The growth of factories altered work habits. Previously, Americans cultivated cottage industries in and around their homes. Entire families labored together, so work and family life were a single integrated experience. Artisans passed on their trade under an apprenticeship system and, in so doing, maintained clear standards for fair business practice. However, the growth of the factory system forever changed society because for the first time parents worked outside of the home, limiting and straining family life.[1] Production became mechanized, impersonal, and individualized, dissolving the previous mentor-apprentice system which had fostered healthy pride and sound business practice.

Factory organizers soon built not only mills, but entire communities around their factories. Northerners, known for their self-reliance and determination, now experienced increasing division of labor with grave social consequence. As farmers, the seasons and weather governed the workday, but now "the rhythm of nature was replaced by the tolling of the factory bell." Time became a commodity strictly controlled and purchased by employers. In this way, time also became an enemy, imprisoning workers to their duties without the flexibility to care for family, health, or life events. Artisan skill was soon lost in the hum and drone of cold machinery. Work was now less a matter of personal pride and more a faceless means of existence.

Excursus: The Relational Curse of the Recorded Line

Until about the year 2000, customer service representatives seemed at ease communicating with phone customers. Often both parties could chat in the midst of conducting business so as to create a kind of cathartic social interaction, the welcomed momentary connection with another human being.

After about the year 2000, customer service was conducted on recorded lines, meaning that conversations could become a source of regret to either party if one seemed to deviate from a prescribed standard. While some may extol the growth in professionalism as a result of the recorded line, there has been a concomitant loss of meaningful interaction. Such conversations are often like speaking to an automaton reading from a script, attended by fear in deviating from that script. Thus, there is no meaningful interaction, only excessively polite but distant commerce. This may be a concealed but powerful contributor to a sense of social isolation.

Additionally, consider this ancillary fact. The telephone was invented in 1886 but did not reach 75% of American households until 1957. Thus, for many Americans (presumably those in more rural settings), even well into the 20th century, social interaction was conducted in person. Today, there is little meaningful person-to-person contact (and even the telephone is used infrequently). Most interaction is veiled behind social media. Thus, the regression in social interaction has been a movement from face-to-face contact, to auditory-but-faceless contact (via telephone), to entirely artificial contact (via social media).

---

[1] Nancy Pearcey, *Total Truth: Liberating Christianity from Its Cultural Captivity* (Crossway Books, 2008)

The Growth of Loneliness: "Do I Dare Disturb the Universe?"[2]

Astronomer Copernicus, Conversation with God, Jan Matejko, 1872

Ask people what they fear most and one will probably hear "loneliness," or some variation on that theme (public speaking, poverty, or death). Listen to and observe people carefully, and indeed they are horribly afraid of being alone. Each person fears being irrelevant, forgotten, excluded, overlooked, abandoned, or anonymous. Children want to know that someone is watching over them, and are anxious when someone is not. Young adults search for romance, the desire for someone to pay attention to their wishes. Husbands and wives crave companionship. The elderly want assurance that their children will not abandon them. Even those about to pass away want to know that their names will be remembered. So much of human behavior can be explained by the piercing dread of being alone or forgotten.

> "Also, if two lie down together, they will keep warm. But how can one keep warm alone?" (Ecclesiastes 4:11)

Despite advances in telecommunications and travel, modern people feel increasingly lonely. Loneliness is attributed to the dearth of meaningful friendships, fractured families, and a highly-transient and money-driven world which often prioritizes material trappings over relationships. A peculiar phenomenon is that loneliness is increasingly prevalent while in the company of others. Often this experience is the most painful because one feels that loneliness should be alleviated through proximity

---
[2] T.S. Eliot (1888–1965)

to people.

> "There is nothing emptier than an empty mailbox." (Charles Schultz)

With the modern growth of self-centeredness there has been a concomitant rise in a particularly excruciating form of loneliness, that which occurs in the midst of others. To be physically alone is one thing; to be in the midst of people and alone, is bitter. This experience of loneliness-despite-proximity is a direct outgrowth of heightened self-love. As people more deeply love themselves others simply find little purpose or fulfillment in being around them. Narcissists may at times be entertaining, but there is a hollow quality to interaction with them. Additionally, as people become brasher, and more relationally brutal, it is not emotionally safe to be around them. It is simply too painful and disappointing to be around self-centered people. For this reason, in modern times social interaction has been reduced to meeting perceived needs, often of a sexual nature. This is a driver for the explosion of homosexuality, especially among women.

> The modern phenomenon of materialism causes the world to focus with sharper acuity with regard to products, but with far less acuity with regard to people – the "micro-fication" of products and purchasing, the "macro-fication" of relationships. In other words, people today are far more astute and perceptive with regard to products than they are with regard to the condition of a friend or family member's heart. This is part of the larger curse upon self-centeredness which shows itself in the worship of that which is material.

A principle driver of modern loneliness is the precipitous loss of trust in society. Today, people overwhelmingly state that they feel little trust in others. This is most acute in urban environments where the population is generally highly-transient and largely anonymous. Twenty-five percent of Americans state that they have no close friends, a partial outgrowth of this erosion of trust.

> City highways function as a "wall" dividing communities, and high-rise buildings tend to isolate residents from the street below. Thus, city life is often the most isolating of any existence, all the while producing the sting of expectation for social interaction on account of the high-concentration of people.

Loneliness as Modern Blight

Until the mid-twentieth century city buildings were constructed so as to be viewed by pedestrians. For this reason, buildings were bejeweled with artistic features like gargoyles or statues. However, with the growth of highways, people soon traversed cities at rapid speeds so modern buildings were streamlined, shear and sleek from a distance and at highway speeds. This serves as a fitting analogy for the nature of modern relationships, once bejeweled with meaningful social intricacies, but now shear and sleek from a distance.

Relationally, modern people seem desperate to break through the hiding, concealing, and social covering which increasingly makes life a superficial experience. What causes this hiding, concealing, and covering? A great deal can be explained by the modern obsession with self-love, a social epidemic which drives a wedge between people. Interaction is hobbled by rampant self-obsession, so that people are unable to enter into others' lives, unable to listen carefully, and unwilling to offer any succor to life's vagary. People today rarely offer meaningful counsel in the midst of life's vicissitudes.

> One of the most pronounced shifts in modern film is the loss of meaningful characters and dialogue. The modern trend is toward mind-numbing extravaganza with little focus on developing meaningful memorable characters. This is often why modern moviegoers feel so existentially empty and lost in their viewing experience; there has been no connection with their deeper human existence. Moviegoers now feel as though they have received a momentary thrill, but have not dealt with, nor wrestled with, the hidden recesses of the human dilemma. Modern movies are less about the human, the organic, and the meaningfully natural, so consequently, as people feed on an artificial technology-saturated diet they are left emotionally starved and longing for the nourishment of human connection.

There is something in loneliness that feels like hell itself, as hell is the quintessence of loneliness, eternal separation from God. However, by God's grace, in loneliness one's conscience can capture his attention. Thus, for the sinner, loneliness is a fearful proposition because his conscience reminds him of impending judgment before a holy God. To be alone with oneself, to be trapped in the prison of one's own thoughts can offer a taste of hell where for eternity one will live in continual separation from God. Thus, there is something in loneliness which gives the sinner a glimpse into his eternal perdition, a prescient warning of that which awaits those outside of Christ. That is why people are often so terrified of loneliness.

> "Turn to me and be gracious to me, for I am lonely and afflicted." (Psalm 25:16)

Postmodern people could each be thought of as planets orbiting a sun. Those planets travel at different speeds and on various planes. Sometimes the planets synchronize so that they traverse space in alignment. At other times they are far from one other, on opposite ends of their solar system. People today function as individual planets, each traveling at his own speed on his own path. Sometimes those planets align with meaningful interaction, life-shaping friendship, or true "cure of souls." But such syzygy is rare, as people are generally lone planets pursuing self-directed goals with little sense or ability to enter into another's world.

Narcissus
Michelangelo Caravaggio, c. 1596

A classic example of self-serving conversation is that involving two friends who meet and the first says, "I just returned from a great vacation." The other responds, "So did I."[3]

When loneliness is based in pride or fear, there is a direct relationship between the degree of one's self-focus and one's degree of loneliness. Consider that the Greek hunter Narcissus was transfixed by his reflection in a pool of water. In his love for his own beauty he was alone and eventually died in his loneliness. Conversely, those who forget themselves and enter into others' lives, while forsaking their own, experience meaningful relationship. Yet, loneliness is at its worst when one longs for something he cannot get. It seems that unmet desires spark lonely feelings, a craving, a love, a seeking after something other than God himself. This is usually the source of loneliness.

People want to be associated with greatness and, at the same time, to express themselves as individuals. The former seems to alleviate one's deepest fears; the latter strokes pride. People want to know that their lives are connected to something significant, glorious, even timeless. Additionally, they want to assert their own personality, to be uniquely set apart from the crowd. This creates continuity (connectedness) and discontinuity (isolation) with the surrounding world, injecting tension into human interaction. Employers, marketers, politicians, and entertainers adroitly leverage, and often exploit, these competing drives.

There is something painful in being around self-centered people. They rob one of his inner-peace while offering nothing of the interaction for which people were designed. Self-centered people may at times offer glimmers of indulgent entertainment, intriguing stories, a dash of charm, or intellectual stimulation, but they finally leave

---

[3] The idea for this anecdote from the Larry Crabb conference on biblical counseling, Wayne, Pennsylvania

their audience empty, devoid of life-giving counsel. On the other hand, there is something so thrilling about being around those who genuinely enter into others' lives with a sense of God's own purpose. They offer a treasure which reminds one of God's own passion to enter into lives with revitalizing friendship.

> "In the country of the blind, the one-eyed man is king." (Erasmus)

The Advent of Chronic Relational Boredom

Pandas are actually carnivores in the bear family (*ursidae*). For some bizarre reason during their history they stopped hunting and simply grazed on bamboo. Their digestive system is not designed to breakdown fiber, so they only extract twenty-percent of the nutrients from what they consume. For this reason, they spend nearly all their waking hours eating, and sleep a great deal to conserve energy. The panda's paw has developed a pseudo-opposable thumb which allows it to grab, pull, and hold bamboo shoots. Pandas spend most of their twenty-five year lifespan completely alone in a forest. They are also remarkably choosy when finding a mate. These peculiar traits make the panda appear oblivious to the concept of survival-of-the-fittest. Is something in this description redolent of the human condition, one in which mankind's design as image-bearer was forsaken for a sinful approach to life, one in which mankind settles for a pail and desolate existence?

There is a shift from Genesis 1:25 to Genesis 1:31. Genesis 1:25 says that God's creation is "good," while in Genesis 1:31, with the creation of mankind, the creation is "very good." People, as "very good" creations, are of a different order than the general "good" creation. Thus, it is axiomatic that God never created a boring person; he created image-bears to witness to his majesty and character. Psalm 139:14 states, "I praise you because I am fearfully and wonderfully made; your works are wonderful, I know that full well." Each person was designed to be a meaning-maker, to display power, and to bring blessing. Each person, as the zenith of God's creation, was designed to actuate something of God's own will and character within the creation. People therefore, by their very design, are inherently exciting. Why, then, are so many relationships boring?

Boring people are not that way by design, but rather as a result of sin. When people seek covering from one another, seek to hide and conceal their inner being, they become boring. It is quite fascinating that generally the more one seeks to ornament and beautify his exterior, the more he seeks to conceal his interior. That appears to be the focus in modern society – attention to the exterior and concealment of that which is worthwhile in the interior. Concealing one's true self generates distance, isolation, and tedious relational monotony.

> Largely driven by a Hollywood-ized distortion, many young women view themselves as "museum pieces under glass," that which is to be viewed from a distance and admired. There is little nurturing interaction as a result; there is voyeurism and fantasy, but little salubrious relationship.

Human relationships were designed to move with purpose. Each was designed to enter into others' lives in a way that is productive for eternal purposes. Relationships exist to help others change and to, in turn, be changed. That gives them meaning and a sense of excitement. People are, in fact, desperate for deep human connection, a connection that offers some healing.[4] One was meant to experience this human connection, not in the fulfillment of a psychological need, but as a gift from a God with whom one was first to experience an eternal connection. Thus, relationships were not to be about the mere exchange of information or emotional thrills; they were intended to be life-shaping, redirecting, and curative.[5]

Portrait of Dr. Gachet
Vincent Willem van Gogh, 1890

> "Laugh, and the world laughs with you; weep, and you weep alone." (Ella Wheeler Wilcox)
>
> "With some people solitariness is an escape not from others but from themselves. For they see in the eyes of others only a reflection of themselves." (Eric Hoffer)

> Have you noticed that when a storm hits, and the power goes out, people seem to huddle with an odd jittery excitement? This is the propinquity effect as people bond together to weather a perceived threat. Similarly, camping seems to evoke a similar connectivity between people as they vie to overcome the real or perceived perils of

---
[4] Proverbs 12:18
[5] Proverbs 27:5, 6

> the outdoors, or face the cold dark night together. It is fascinating that people secretly crave a power outage or a camping trip so as to feel that they have overcome, conquered, and emerged victorious. Is this a way to feel as though for a moment one is not culpable for his sin before a holy God, that in the rush and tumble to overcome, attention has been diverted from one's sinful state?
>
> Additionally, there is an inverse relationship between the pace of one's life and the amount of meaningful friendship one experiences. Any event which slows life offers a rare opportunity to experience relationship, and thus, is a welcomed reprieve from a frenetic world.

The Bible's Assessment of Loneliness

How does the Bible address the issue of loneliness? A good starting point is to understand the Bible's view of relationship. God is triune, three persons, Father, Son and Holy Spirit (the Trinity), eternally in relationship with one another. God is never alone because he enjoys relationship within himself. Each person of the Trinity exhibits a singular focus – to glorify the other two persons. Thus, the Father only seeks to glorify the Son and Holy Spirit. The Son seeks to glorify the Father and Holy Spirit, and the Holy Spirit, to glorify the Father and Son.

> "After Jesus said this, he looked toward heaven and prayed: 'Father, the time has come. Glorify your Son, that your Son may glorify you.'" (John 17:1)

The first man, Adam, fashioned as an analogue of God, bore certain characteristics of all three persons of the Trinity.[6] Yet, Adam was one person, and so, there was no relationship within himself. While Adam enjoyed direct fellowship with God, something was lacking in Adam's experience. God's first concern, expressed in Genesis 2:18, is that it was not good for Adam to be alone.[7] Thus, God created Eve as a helpmate, someone like Adam ("bone of my bones, flesh of my flesh"[8]) who could relate to him. While Adam and God related as creature (finite) to Creator (infinite), Adam and Eve related as creature to creature. This offered Adam a new dimension on relationship (while not to be seen as a substitute for relationship with God), the opportunity to love another as an outworking of loving God himself. Thus, in untainted form, Adam's love for Eve would serve as a derivative of, and kind of non-idolatrous proxy for, loving God. Additionally, Adam and Eve in relationship

---

[6] For additional discussion of this topic see "The Image of God: Man as Analogue" in the first book in this series, *Ask for the Ancient Paths: From Art to Artifice to Arisen*, chapter 5: "Redefining the Pygmalion Effect: Exploring the Image of God in Man"
[7] This should not be understood as a statement of psychic need to be met by another person. God's statement that it was not good for Adam to be alone concerned the superiority of having a helpmate to work the garden, one who would offer companionship in the midst of bountiful relationship with God. God's statement does not imply that relationship with God himself was inadequate for Adam's plenary fulfillment.
[8] Genesis 2:23

more fully glorified God than each separately. There was something in this first human relationship which brought with it the abundant life with which God longed to fill the earth.

Adam was made for relationship, firstly with God, secondly with Eve. Yet, after the fall those relationships went horribly awry. Adam and God became enemies, and Adam and Eve became estranged. The first husband and wife no longer enjoyed self-sacrificial relationship, but rather one marked by shame, covering, and blame-shifting.[9] This same problem carries through to modern man, who finds himself increasingly severed from relationship with God and others. Like Adam, each was created to experience fellowship with both God (the primary relationship) and with others (a means to manifest the relationship with God), but tragically that fellowship now lies shattered. The fall produced oppressive loneliness, and ever since mankind has been desperate to retake his garden paradise.

Sacrifice of Isaac, Giovanni Tiepolo, c. 1726

This brings us to the next major biblical concept with regard to loneliness – the land. The land connected the nation of Israel to its God, as well as offered a social identity, and a relational cohesive. Thus, in the Israelite mindset, to be outside the land was to be in a state of death. In ancient Israel abundant life was defined in three ways:

1. To be in the Promised Land

---
[9] Genesis 3:12

2. To be a part of one's people
3. To have offspring

Likewise, death was defined as being:

1. Outside the Promised Land
2. Excluded from one's people
3. Childless[10]

For an ancient Israelite to be physically isolated, socially disconnected, and without offspring to remember his name, was a terror tantamount to death. That is why widows, orphans, outcasts, and foreigners faced such dire straits; they were the most vulnerable, the most forlorn, the most forgotten. Regardless of historical milieu, mankind seems plagued by this same fear of disconnection from land, society, and offspring. People long to be part of a community, to be included among a social group, and to know that offspring will carry on their identity. For example, 1 Samuel 1:7-20 recounts Hannah's anguish as she earnestly prayed for a son. The story recounts that childless, Hannah wept, refused to eat, was bitter, experienced misery, was deeply-troubled, was in grief, and was downcast.

> It is fascinating that the Old Testament theme of land finds its fulfillment in Jesus Christ who is the fruit-bearing land *par excellence*, the nation's refuge, home, and identity. It is in Christ as "land" that Christians are connected to one another, and receive an eternal inheritance.

This theme of the land offers some insight into modern life, as land is still a means of social cohesion in agrarian societies. As individuals work their land they remain in, committed to, and providing something of value to, community. There is a wholesome sense of permanence as one is connected to land. Conversely, those dissociated from the land (predominantly transient urban dwellers) exhibit little sense of community. With no connection to something of permanence society suffers loss.

> "The farther we get away from the land, the greater our insecurity." (Henry Ford)

Various Methods for Dealing with Loneliness

Why do horses race? One theory is that, when in a herd, each horse seeks to be in the lead position as this represents the greatest assurance of not ending up at the rear. The herd's rearmost position is perilous, because likely the straggler will be taken down by a predator. Thus, it would appear that in the equine world one never wants to be the

---

[10] Douglas Green, "Old Testament History and Theology" class, Westminster Theological Seminary, Philadelphia, Pennsylvania

lone-horse back.

On account of the fall (the fact that each is "in Adam"),[11] each person carries within himself a similar dread of being "the lone-horse back." From the moment of birth, each actively pursues any means to alleviate his unease through the manipulation of all that surrounds him. In time, the sinner learns to effectively machinate his surroundings, to more masterfully grab for that which he believes will guard him from his haunting disquietude. While mankind's methods are vastly more sophisticated than that of galloping horses, his objective may be very similar. Each pursues a self-serving means, be it physical, intellectual, or social, to make himself immune to loneliness. Each seeks to ensure that he is not the relational straggler, as being the straggler brings with it a sense of impending doom, as if a predator is closing-in. (Yet, as each vies for a way to ensure that he will never be alone, his connivance leaves him increasingly accursed.)

The following are some means routinely employed to seek alleviation from the fear of loneliness.

1. Companionship

"Second Life®" is a virtual community in which users interact with one another through avatars, virtual persons. Participants can speak, text message, socialize, form groups, and even buy and sell virtual goods, services, and properties. The community now has over one million participants.

The Second Life® community has no stated objective. There are no set rules, and there is nothing to win. It is simply a virtual society in which "residents" create, explore, and interact as they desire. These types of communities are exploding in popularity as people feel increasingly isolated and longing. Participants hide behind their avatars, while at the same time participating in what they hope will be meaningful interaction.

Although God created Eve as a helpmate for Adam,[12] people today often turn to a companion as a substitute for God himself, one to function as a kind of savior delivering him from his deepest fears. Adam and Eve were not meant to worship one another, but to worship God alone and to work together for his purposes. However, after the fall, shame, distrust, and blame-shifting entered Adam and Eve's relationship so that they were no longer companions walking in lockstep, but rivals seeking to justify themselves in light of their sin.[13]

---

[11] 1 Corinthians 15:22
[12] Genesis 2:18
[13] Genesis 3:7, 12

Adam and Eve sought to remove God as the object of worship and to install themselves as gods. This misplaced worship always results in isolation, bitterness, and ultimately hatred. (It is fascinating that Narcissus, while consumed with self-worship, loathed those who idolized him.) While companionship (in the form of either friendship or marriage) is part of God's common grace to mankind, it can become a ready escape from God, a way to assuage the fear of loneliness without God.

> "I'm one bad relationship away from having thirty cats."

Marriage à la Mode, The Tete à Tete, William Hogarth, 1743

2. Busyness

Until the 1950s it was fashionable for a gentleman to carry a pocket watch (most have a cover which flips open and snaps shut). The noise of the cover opening and closing often disrupted plays and movies the way that ringing mobile phones do today. This serves as a fitting metaphor for the near constant distraction that plagues modern life, driving a wedge into relationship. Busyness has become a modern drug which keeps mankind chasing but never arriving, wanting but never satisfied, and searching but never finding meaning.[14] Busyness functions as an existential shield keeping one from thinking deeply about life, so while one swirls and swoops to and from events, he never has time to consider the poverty, the depravity, the vacuity within.

---

[14] Daniel 12:4b offers a prophetic glimpse of this phenomenon.

Ecclesiastes 1:14 states, "I have seen all the things that are done under the sun; all of them are meaningless, a chasing after the wind." Busyness can often look noble and other-centered, but in reality it is generally a self-serving desire to keep God at a distance in a maelstrom of frivolity.

> On account of the fear of rejection, one often chooses the path of least resistance, a life of incessant hurry, perpetual motion, restless impatience, and nagging fatigue. This kind of existence may feel familiar and safe, a way to manage life without feeling embarrassed or risking rejection. A hurried life offers a sustainable excuse for loneliness (much in the way that procrastination offers a ready excuse for failure). One needlessly pays a tragic price in a futile attempt to avoid the fear of rejection.

3. Being needed

Some engineer events so that others are always dependent upon them. As long as one keeps others dependent there appears to be no threat of abandonment. While the Bible speaks about children as a blessing, the inordinate desire for children may be a camouflaged fear of loneliness, a desire to secure one who is dependent upon one's provision. Likewise, an employer may keep employees beholden to the company. Teachers may withhold crucial lessons from students. The desire to be needed is a subtle, but often effective, strategy to enslave others. Regardless of the form, keeping others dependent requires a well-oiled propaganda machine which seeks to inculcate a sense of need in something other than God, an atmosphere of searching for life outside of God himself.

4. Image

Some look to beauty as a means of guarding against loneliness. If one can either be beautiful, or be associated with beauty, this appears to be an effective means of ensuring that one is the center of attention, the object of desire, that one will not be overlooked. Beauty, as an aspect of God's own being and creative acts, is not sinful in itself. The problem is that it quickly metamorphoses into ugly pride when it becomes the purpose and substance of interaction. Because of the fall, beauty is a dying proposition; it lasts for a moment and is gone.[15] Those who invest themselves in beauty as a means of guarding against loneliness find their fear rising day-by-day. As the source of one's hope, the bedrock of one's future, slowly slips away one is plunged into stinging angst.

> "Your heart became proud on account of your beauty, and you corrupted your wisdom because of your splendor. So I threw you to the earth; I made a spectacle of you before kings." (Ezekiel 28:17)

---

[15] James 1:10

> "The marriage of reason and nightmare which has dominated the 20th century has given birth to an ever more ambiguous world. Across the communications landscape move the specters of sinister technologies and the dreams that money can buy. Thermonuclear weapons systems and soft drink commercials coexist in an overlit realm ruled by advertising and pseudoevents, science and pornography. Over our lives preside the great twin leitmotifs of the 20th century—sex and paranoia." (J.G. Ballard)

Education (center), Louis Comfort Tiffany, 1890

5. Wealth

Wealth looks like the perfect antidote to loneliness because the world eagerly seeks out and panders to spenders. Money seems like a savior, like the answer to every loss experienced through the fall. Those with money believe that they will find companionship, respect from peers, and a place of honor among family members.[16] However, what they do not consider is that wealth often brings superficial frivolous experiences and friendships. The wealthy are often lonely, caged in a world of purchased relationships that last only until another thrill comes along. While accumulating wealth, in itself, is not wrong, the pursuit of wealth is often just a veiled fear of loneliness, simply another way to cast for oneself a surrogate god who will serve one's bidding, namely to ensure that others will not abandon him.

> When people feel financially anxious the only activity that increases is television

---

[16] James 2:1-3 outlines this scenario.

> watching. All other forms of social engagement decrease. People today spend 700% more time watching television than involved in community activities outside the home.

> "Do not wear yourself out to get rich; have the wisdom to show restraint." (Proverbs 23:4)
>
> "There was a man all alone; he had neither son nor brother. There was no end to his toil, yet his eyes were not content with his wealth. 'For whom am I toiling,' he asked, 'and why am I depriving myself of enjoyment?' This too is meaningless—a miserable business!" (Ecclesiastes 4:8)

6. Intellect

Some seek to keep others transfixed through knowledge. The intellect offers the promise of soaring and stirring conversation, answers which suggest power over one's world, and the ability to command through eloquence. The intellectual believes that as long as he has all the answers he will remain relevant, sought after, and noted. However, in the postmodern world knowledge lies splintered and fractured so that the intellectual often finds himself a suspected and neglected resource.

> "For it is written: 'I will destroy the wisdom of the wise; the intelligence of the intelligent I will frustrate.'" (1 Corinthians 1:19)

7. Anger[17]

An Irish proverb states, "Better be quarrelling than lonesome." Anger can be an effective tool for keeping others' attention. Anger keeps others focused, vigilant, engaged, and attuned. It is a way to ensure that one is not forgotten, overlooked, or taken for granted. Some deliberately create conflict, stir up dissension, and conjure anger as a way to guarantee that they are in the spotlight. (Many resort to this method when one of the other methods listed above does not work.) Anger can be a convenient fallback position, a kind of relational "fast food," which quickly draws one back into relevance and the center of attention. Anger also brings with it a handy trapdoor. When one finds himself ostracized, or at least on the outside, anger is a convenient excuse for why people are distant. One offers himself a twisted rationale for separation from others, that rationale being that separation is not because of one's inherent selfishness, but because of others' provocation.

---

[17] For additional development of the topic of anger see the case study "Anger: Shedding Light on the Heat" in the first book in this series, *Ask for the Ancient Paths: From Art to Artifice to Arisen*, chapter 6: "Man Before the Face of God: The Imperium of the Psyche"; also in *Ask for the Ancient Paths: From Art to Artifice to Arisen* see "The Peril of Moralism" in chapter 10: "The Third-Way of Sanctification: From Abominable to Indominable"

> "…for man's anger does not bring about the righteous life that God desires." (James 1:20)

On the opposite side of the coin, keeping others angry is often a manipulative strategy for ensuring that they remain attentive to the object of their anger. Anger focuses, directs, and moves with purpose. One who desperately fears loneliness may seek to make others angry as a way to ensure that they will focus, direct, and move with purpose in the relationship. For lonely people there can be something so deceptively soothing about knowing that another is angry because that means that the other is still emotionally invested in the relationship, still cares enough to expend energy.[18]

> "Passionate hatred can give meaning and purpose to an empty life." (Eric Hoffer)

8. Suffering[19]

A Friend in Suspense
Louis Prang, c. 1897

Years ago my family had a wonderful collie named "Sybil." As a shepherding dog, Sybil loved to gambol. Once Sybil returned home limping; she had twisted her right wrist (ankle). Of course, we each lavished attention on her, rubbing the wrist with salve, and generally making a fuss about her condition. Within a couple of days the leg had healed, but Sybil continued limping. Sometimes she limped on the wrong paw (as she forgot which one was hurt). Her objective was to maintain the wounded-animal routine as this ensured others remained attentive.

Everyone (whether human or animal) is subject to suffering of one form or another and the counselor never minimizes the sting of painful experiences, no matter how seemingly trivial. The counselor is rightly slow to speak in these matters for fear of becoming Job's Counselors, those who pretend to decisively know something about

---

[18] Conversely, those who fear loneliness may seek to placate others at all costs. They may try to keep others happy, avoiding any possibility of making them angry. Thus, lonely people may assume that anger, whether in themselves or in others, begets isolation.
[19] For a more detailed exploration of the topic of suffering see chapter 2: "Suffering: The Kintsugi Objective"

which they are not privy. However, there can be a sinister side to some of what is often labeled as suffering. Often one who is desperate to be the center of attention accentuates and highlights suffering as a way to ensure that others pay attention. The one who suffers often garners an outpouring of support, sympathy, and kindness. To augment the suffering, tears, emotional pain, and a victim mentality can often work wonders in both declawing the opposition and making one look noble and unjustly wronged. The inordinate focus on one's suffering is often another clever disguise for the fear of loneliness, a way to manipulate others to meet a perceived need.

> Cultivating and maintaining a victim status is empowering. Those who cast themselves as victims feel ennobled, entitled, and most importantly, exonerated from their sin. There is a feeling of immunity from life's usual failings, as if one ought to receive a "free pass" in life.

A young Christian woman often spoke at length about her emotional pain. She made sure that everyone knew that she had suffered in her childhood. But what her listeners did not realize was that her pain had become her god, a way to gain power, meaning, and blessing through rehearsing and nurturing her grievances. Rather than releasing her disappointments, rejections, wounds, and sustained abuses to God, she held tightly to them as a source of power over people, as a way to ensure that she would be a focal point of attention, that she would be remembered. (As an ancillary issue, the focus on her suffering worked wonders in diverting attention away from her heart idols so that well-intentioned counselors were continually distracted from pursuing sin issues. Anyone who dared to confront her idolatry was branded an insensitive aggressor.)

God promises to repay all transgressions, to bind up the brokenhearted,[20] to one day bring justice to bear upon every wrong.[21] This is why the Christian can forget, because God promises to remember. We can entrust God with our past; we can live in God's enduring love, provision, and watchfulness, so that our experiences do not shape nor define us as Christians. The believer can live in a God-centered story, in a God-directed reality, rather than in a man-centered interpretation which makes experience determinative. This young woman made her suffering her identity, a way to continually keep others focused on solving her problems, healing her hurts, feeding her need for assurance, and ultimately ensuring their perpetual attentiveness to her self-serving drama.

Perceived Solutions Which Exacerbate the Problem

The Tacoma Narrows Bridge in Tacoma, Washington, when it was completed in 1940, was the third-longest suspension bridge in the world. It was heralded as the forerunner

---
[20] Psalm 147:3; Isaiah 61:1
[21] Romans 12:19

of sleek modern bridge design, a triumphant harbinger of the future. But from its opening, the bridge's roadway swayed and undulated in the wind. Four months after its completion the bridge broke apart in high winds and collapsed. (Engineers today look back on the foibles of its design, one which never countenanced the threat of aerodynamic forces.)

The Tacoma Narrows Bridge collapse offers a chilling reminder of the dangers posed by modernism. When plans are implemented, without a thorough understanding of all that is involved, there is eventual failure and ruin. It serves as an emblematic warning of blindly looking to technology as our savior. Technology, without the proper God-centered design and implementation, is destined to fail miserably.

Miranda - The Tempest, John William Waterhouse, 1916

I raise the Tacoma Narrows Bridge collapse as a metaphor for man-made solutions to loneliness (such as social media which is turned to as an accidental societal savior). In fact, mankind's efforts to abrogate its loneliness (such as with social media) are proving to be a social sarcophagus.[22] Just as that which was intended to serve travelers with state-of-the-art design ended up in Icarus-like perdition, so too, mankind in seeking solutions outside of the person of God, finds himself increasingly stranded in a relational hinterland.

---

[22] A sarcophagus, literally "flesh-eating," stores remains above ground and serves a decorative purpose.

> There is a sense in which technology cannibalizes itself. People do not just want to enjoy technology they want a savior from the futility and vacuity of their lives. For this reason, as technology advances, it reverses its "poles," or characteristics, time and again. The age of automation invariably sews the seeds of its own demise by spawning a resurgence of the age of handicrafts. Because people ultimately want a savior, they clamor for some way to stand out, to achieve superiority, and to appear noble. (adapted from Marshall McLuhan)

As a curse of the fall, that which we believe guards us against loneliness actually sows the seeds of our future loneliness (a kind of gravedigger thesis). For example, the man who pursues wealth in the hope of ensuring he is respected, included, and needed, will find himself lonely and estranged from friends and family. At the moment he believes that he has secured his future, he finds it slipping away into an abyss of infinite need. Thus, any attempt to find life outside of God always ends in emptiness, fear, pain, and loss. As we seek, day-by-day, to wrest from God his rightful place in our lives we find ourselves increasingly faced with a Gordian knot which cannot be severed, a futile fleeing from certain loneliness.

> "Then he said to them all: 'Whoever wants to be my disciple must deny themselves and take up their cross daily and follow me. For whoever wants to save their life will lose it, but whoever loses their life for me will save it. What good is it for someone to gain the whole world, and yet lose or forfeit their very self?'" (Luke 9:23-25)

> The modern world, at every turn, dehumanizes people. City life, consumer culture, advertising, and social media all reduce people to nameless faceless commodities to be bought and sold to the highest bidder. This is often why modern people are so desperate for purposed interaction (and often pay dearly to get it).

The digital age generally fosters disconnection and loneliness as people interact in virtual worlds with little meaningful friendship.[23] Modern people are more alone than ever because their interaction is more superficial and self-gratifying than ever. In a cold technologized world there is a quest for an eminently spiritual experience, to peer into the mysterious, to be in the presence of the supernatural, to touch the otherworldly. Ecclesiastical ritual maintains its appeal because it serves as a mystical counterweight to the oppressive burdens of science, technology, artificiality, commercialism, ostentation, and media. As modern man longs for the noumenal, churches which offer displays of power, emotionalism, and a sense of connection to the spirit world often thrive.

Additionally, as the world continually surges forward, it progressively leaves its least

---

[23] For further discussion of this issue see the case study "Technology as a Form of Covering" in the second book in this series, *What Agreement Is There Between the Temple of God and Idols?: The Accidence of Sin and Idolatry*, chapter 5: "Metaphors for Sin"

adapted members behind. In a technology saturated world the aged are progressively pushed to the sidelines, because often they are least able to reacclimate to technology. Consider for a moment what life was like before the advent of high-technology. In a world based on ancient sources of knowledge, the aged were society's treasures, the locus of sought expertise and insight. Before modern technology, society's most senior members were looked to for sagacious guidance. However, this has been reversed, as seniors are now largely viewed as a quaint nostalgia, one which is easily overlooked. This increasing sense of abandoning the aged, plants a seed of anxiety in *everyone*, because each marches toward the same fate. There is a nagging sense that life is slowly ebbing away, that the world slants toward one's eventual irrelevance, and that in the final scene one will weep alone, forsaken by a society that long ago moved on.

Ophelia
John William Waterhouse, 1894

One fallacy is the assumption that loneliness is cured through marriage. Conventional wisdom says that single people are lonely and marriage is the solution. The good news is that marriage, based on abiding God-centered relationship, does experience an almost surreal immunity from loneliness, while those marriages which are fundamentally estranged from God are invariably beset by bitter loneliness. Thus, it is not that the institution of marriage is flawed, but rather those who participate in it. Often married couples are lonely because they find themselves in the quagmire of a "logistical marriage," one which reduces relationship to pragmatic concerns. A logistical marriage usually arises from unmet desires, the need for more of something other than God himself. Thus, marriage devolves into a mutual chasing rather than a relational resting.

Ironically, urban dwellers, those daily surrounded by people, often report the deepest feelings of loneliness. Isaiah 5:8 states, "Woe to you who add house to house and join field to field till no space is left and you live *alone* in the land." (Quite remarkably, this verse intimates that an urban environment renders its inhabitants alone.) Those who live and work in a highly-concentrated metropolis may seldom experience meaningful social interaction. When interaction does occur it is often of a hurried and superficial nature, marked by matters of convenience, and with little enduring purpose. This phenomenon is exaggerated by social media which promises connectedness, while delivering only the illusion of connectedness.

> A fascinating study might be how media-arbitrated contact has affected professions which necessarily entail face-to-face contact (such as dentistry). In a world in which people are desperate for meaningful human contact, do they actually seek out "hands-on" professionals such as chiropractors, optometrists, cosmetologists, or personal trainers? Those professions which are impossible to practice through a virtual media may thrive long into the future.

As a tangent, the sport of baseball maintains a surprisingly high level of popularity even though the game is slow, and for long stretches lacks much action. Spectators still flock to baseball games, often four-hour events, because they crave a certain reconnection with a community of spectators. They enjoy reading player's faces and deciphering a certain muted human drama unfolding on the field. In this way, baseball is an eminently "human" sport in which one glimpses emotions, and the matching of wits ("the thinking man's game"). Spectators relish the smells and sounds of the park, the freshly cut grass, the popcorn, and the cheer of the crowd. There is something about baseball that offers a counterbalance to a virtual artificial contrived world, something that seems to appeal to psychologized technologized isolated people.

Yet, whether at a baseball game or elsewhere, there is something so painful about being surrounded by people while feeling no connection with them. Job was attended by friends who neither understood his situation, nor offered nourishing counsel. Their words extended no assurance, no assistance, and only furthered Job's pain. Thus, sometimes it is better to be alone than in bad company.

> "I never sat in the company of revelers, never made merry with them; I sat alone because your hand was on me and you had filled me with indignation." (Jeremiah 15:17)

Case Study: The Invisible Relational Circle[24]

The invisible relational circle is an imaginary line on which one wants others to remain (relationally, not necessarily physically). On the one hand, one wants others far enough away so that they will not see one's sin and reject him. On the other, he wants them close enough to luxuriate in his gifts,[25] to behold the glory of his image-bearing. However, there is a vexing problem - others are never on the circle, always too far away (so that they cannot witness one's splendor) or too close (so that

---

[24] The concept of the invisible relational circle borrowed from the Larry Crabb conference on biblical counseling (Wayne, Pennsylvania)
[25] This concept from Dan Allender, Biblical Counselor

they are able to peer into one's sinful heart). Since others are never on the circle, there is continual manipulation to get them there. To those who seem too distant, one beckons them closer. To those who seem too close, one tacitly admonishes them to stay away.

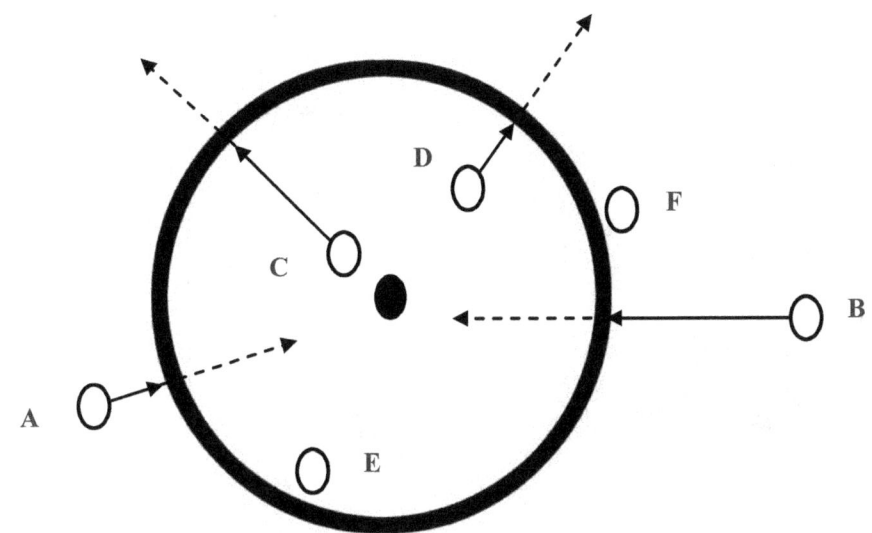

Position	The Relational Dynamics	The Complication
1. A	Considerably outside the circle, being coaxed forward	Continues to move inward, breaching the circle at a slow rate
2. B	Acutely distant, being aggressively drawn forward	Continues to move inward, breaching the circle at a rapid rate
3. C	Dangerously close, being aggressively repelled	Continues to move outward, overshooting the circle at a rapid rate
4. D	Moderately inside the circle, being nudged away	Continues to move outward, slowly slipping past the circle
5. E	For a fleeting moment this person is nearly on the circle (but never perfectly).	At a discrete moment, being fractionally inside the circle, there is anxiety that this person may venture closer (or else develop wanderlust).
6. F	For a fleeting moment this person is nearly on the circle (but never perfectly).	At a discrete moment, being fractionally outside the circle, there is anxiety that this person may drift away (or else dare to step closer).

The sinner's objective is that people remain on the invisible relational circle. However, there are two nagging frustrations:

1. The first is that people are never static. They are continually in motion, either moving forward in relationship or drawing back in isolation. Since no one is ever on the relational circle, one continually draws others forward or pushes them back

with a vexing feeling of desperation.

2. The second frustration is that relational tensile strength can be low. This means that as one manipulates others he finds that those relationships are strained, and grow weaker, until they finally break all together.

Lady Hamilton in a Straw Hat
George Romney, 1785

Each person draws a different diameter relational circle, for some a small diameter (those who tend to be relationally needy), and for others a large diameter (those with a penchant for covering). Additionally, the circle's diameter may change in various contexts. Around those whom one likes, and with whom one identifies, the circle assumes a small diameter.[26] With those whom one dislikes, and with whom one does not identify, the circle will likely expand. Further, one's relative love for his own sin will likely dictate diameter. The more one loves his sin, the more he seeks to keep others at bay (those who might see that sin and label it as such). Those who are likely to challenge an idolatrous heart will be vociferously repelled.

> It is vital to understand that one should not be equally transparent with every person. One must be wise in terms of how forthcoming he is, based on the purposes of each relationship. When a stranger asks, "How are you today?" that will receive a very different response than when one's best friend, pastor, or mother asks the same question. Each receives a response tailored to the dictates of that particular relationship, and with an eye toward God's purposes to further the gospel in that person's life.

---

[26] Esther 4:11; 5:2, 3 offers a glimpse into this phenomenon.

The invisible relational circle is propelled by both fear and pride, often two sides of the same relational coin. The following analysis draws this out.

Large Diameter Tactics (keeping others away)

1. Act preoccupied, serious, hardworking, and focused (for example, a man with an intent look dangling a cigarette).

2. Act hostilely to keep others afraid and at a distance; anger is effective at creating distance, while maintaining a sense of control over others.

3. Act aggressively to maintain a level of control over others.

4. Act detached, distracted, confused, or flustered as a way to keep others off-balance and unable to enter into conversation (for example: a woman engrossed in her cell phone).

5. Act strangely to keep others away. This is driven by fear that if others get too close they will see and reject one; therefore, one hides behind deviant or disconcerting behavior. (Sometimes those who dress strangely, or put forward a distracting demeanor, seek to keep others at a distance, either out of self-pride and superiority, or else out of fear of rejection.)

6. Assume an intellectual façade so as to keep others in awe, confused, or silent.

Small Diameter Tactics (drawing others closer)

1. Flaunt humble or provocative dress[27]

2. Resort to flattery

3. Use humor as a means to maintain the center of attention

4. Feigned ignorance can become a tactic for drawing others closer. If one always needs others help this can keep people focused on one's needs. Making sure that one is incapable or ignorant is a way to keep others attentive.

5. Oddly, anger can be used as a "come closer" tactic, as it can keep people engaged and attentive to the aggrieved party. Anger can be a cleverly disguised way to get

---

[27] A fascinating study found that men are more likely to speak to a woman wearing high-heels. The reason being, she seems to send a message that she wants to interact with men.

needs met, and forces a measure of relationship (albeit on uncomfortable terms). The goal of anger may be to remain the center of attention.

> Some are so addicted to getting their perceived needs met that they resort to any tactic, no matter how seemingly devastating or illogical.

Resolving the Invisible Relational Circle

	Small diameter	**Large diameter**	**Answer in Christ**
Fear-based	Fear of rejection	Fear of judgment	Eternal acceptance;[28] no fear of condemnation[29]
Pride-based	Desire for others to bask in one's greatness	Condescension, desire for isolation	Humility in a repentant heart[30]
Christ-based	Allow others to get close enough to offer counsel and to be counseled, to both confront sin and to encourage faith; allow others to see Christ's work in one's life.	One must be wise to recognize other's motives; there is also a call to remain separate from the world; the Christian is careful not to "cast pearls before swine."[31]	That Christ would impart wisdom so that the believer would neither draw others forward, nor keep them at a distance, but simply love them with Christ as the only focus

While these various large diameter ("stay away") and small diameter ("come closer") tactics are directed toward others, one acts in exactly the same way toward God. Thus, one's dealings with others offer a glimpse into one's dealings with God himself. When relationship with God takes center stage, and when that relationship is vibrant and growing, the tactics end. Thus, abiding in Christ replaces manipulation with honest and loving dealings, either appropriately transparent or distant based on the dictates of love for others and wisdom with regard to motives. One can allow others to get close without fear of what they might see, and one can release others from one's relational tractor beam, resting in a God who is both near and is glorified in one's life.[32] The *coup de grâce* for the invisible relational circle is relationship with Jesus Christ. In Christ the manipulation, the scheming, the maneuvering, and the anxiety end, so that, maybe for the first time, one is truly able to see and love others as God would desire.

---

[28] Hebrews 6:19
[29] Romans 8:1
[30] James 4:10
[31] Matthew 7:6
[32] James 4:8

The Search for Answers at the Foot of the Cross

> "What a lovely surprise to finally discover how unlonely being alone can be." (Ellen Burstyn)

The Flower Picker
John William Waterhouse, 1900

Where does one look for hope in a lonely world? Is one relegated to a life of futile searching, with scattered and fleeting glimmers of relief from fear? The answer to the loneliness problem is simultaneously simple and profound. The answer is found in relationship with Jesus Christ. Isaiah 53:3 reveals that Jesus was a man of sorrows, deeply acquainted with grief. He acutely experienced the pain and isolation that one daily experiences. First Timothy 5:5 states, "The widow who is really in need and left all alone puts her hope in God and continues night and day to pray and to ask God for help." There is a certain blessing in loneliness when it leads one to deeper reliance on God.

> "Instead he went out and began to talk freely, spreading the news. As a result, Jesus could no longer enter a town openly but stayed outside in lonely places. Yet the people still came to him from everywhere." (Mark 1:45)
>
> "But Jesus often withdrew to lonely places and prayed." (Luke 5:16)

Imagine John the Baptist's loneliness as he sat in a dank prison perplexed by the nature of Jesus' deliverance of his people.[33] John was alone for no reason except that he opposed Herod's unlawful marriage to Herodias.[34] He could have easily recanted, and would have likely enjoyed a seat of honor in the king's banquet. However, John chose to remain a forsaken soul rather than to forsake his God. Such is often the plight of those who stand for truth, of those who uncompromisingly stand with Jesus. They will often find themselves alone in a world that will not tolerate the gospel. Of course, such a plight visited Jesus himself as, at the moment of his agonizing torture, Jesus was forsaken by his most trusted friends.[35] While he was mocked and beaten, Jesus stood alone. He carried his cross to Golgotha as one who would face a horrifying death surrounded by insults and jeers, and isolated from all relationship (both human and spiritual).

> "I have trodden the winepress alone; from the nations no one was with me. I trampled them in my anger and trod them down in my wrath; their blood spattered my garments, and I stained all my clothing. It was for me the day of vengeance; the year for me to redeem had come. I looked, but there was no one to help, I was appalled that no one gave support; so my own arm achieved salvation for me, and my own wrath sustained me." (Isaiah 63:3-5)

Far worse than all of this, as Jesus hung on the cross he was abandoned by his Father so that he cried out, "My God, my God, why have you forsaken me?"[36] Jesus experienced pain beyond all imagining in his separation from his Father. For all of eternity Jesus and his Father had been in relationship; yet now, in a taste of hell itself, Jesus was abandoned, accursed, and utterly forlorn in a universe designed for his glory, but suddenly the setting of his greatest torment. Jesus freely accepted this separation on our behalf, so that as our intercessor, we would never need to be separated from God again.

> It is fascinating to consider Genesis 1:2, the original state of loneliness. "Now the earth was formless and empty, darkness was over the surface of the deep, and the Spirit of God was hovering over the waters." Notice three defining conditions: formless, empty, and dark. The Spirit of God gave form to the formlessness, filled the emptiness, and lit the darkness. This could serve as a metaphor for the Christian life. In Christ, the believer's life is given form, filled, and lit. This is the basis for the Christian's assertion that he is not alone.

One does not just look to Jesus as an example of how to deal with loneliness. He seeks relationship with Jesus so that Jesus can redefine his loneliness. Relationship with Jesus reinterprets one's life, so that regardless of circumstance (whether alone or

---

[33] Matthew 11:3
[34] Matthew 14:4
[35] Matthew 26:56
[36] Matthew 27:46

among others) there is refreshing rest in Jesus. Hebrews 6:19 says, "We have this hope as an anchor for the soul, firm and secure." Those in Christ are eternally anchored to him. Hebrews 13:5b further assures, "...God has said, 'Never will I leave you; never will I forsake you.'"

> There is a difference between solitude and loneliness. Solitude is simply being alone, while loneliness is one's interpretation of his situation. Loneliness can occur in solitude or in a crowd. One can be in solitude but not feel lonely. Solitude is a valued state for concentration, honing skills, and for communing with God. Often solitude is required for cultivating godly character. For those who make God their only desire, there is a certain surreal ability to be alone while experiencing a kind of immunity from loneliness. Those in Christ can feel joy, even in the midst of solitude.

Those suffering from loneliness have hope and help in Jesus, one who drank deeply from loneliness on our behalf. In the loneliness Jesus endured, one is offered abiding immutable indestructible relationship with God, relationship that can never be severed. Therefore, the answer to loneliness is not in a change of situation (marriage, children, wealth, beauty, intelligence, etc.) but in a change of worship. When one finds his home in God, finds his hope and future in God, there is a certain blindness to situation, a sense that regardless of what one faces the Father is close at hand. In fact, John 16:7, 8 says that when one grieves, the Holy Spirit draws close as a comforter, one who shoulders the griever's pain.

Just as John the Baptist sent his followers "to the Lord to ask, 'Are you the one who was to come, or should we expect someone else?'",[37] so too, when faced with long periods of solitude, one may question God's intentions. One may wonder why, as victor in Christ, he so often experiences such searing emotional pain. He may wonder if God, in his management of the cosmos, is merely a Potemkin potentate, having forsaken those who belong to him, or simply unable to improve upon their situation in his battle with evil. However, the Bible is clear that God never forgets his people, having engraved their names on the palms of his hands.[38]

Loneliness may or may not be punishment for sin; that can be hard to determine. However, the Christian can rest assured that God is sovereign over all events, and cannot be thwarted.[39] The *mirabile dictu* is that God sees, understands, and is eminently good, in the context of one's loneliness. God has not forgotten; he is not vengeful, and is fully in control of every situation. Thus, for the Christian loneliness takes on a glorious hue. It is part of an eternal plan to sanctify those who belong to Christ. It is part of a divine objective to help those in Christ see their loneliness in the context of the cross, that in Christ one is never truly alone. So a Christian may

---

[37] Luke 7:19
[38] Isaiah 49:16
[39] Colossians 2:10

experience solitude as the crucial setting for rich fellowship with his God, thankful for the discipline that loneliness can offer, and for the repentance it may at times foster.

As mentioned previously, usually loneliness arises from either pride or fear. Pride may breed separation as one sees himself as superior to others. Fear may drive one away from others because of the scepter of rejection. However, for those in Christ solitude may grow out of godly obedience. Thus, sometimes solitude is by God's own design. As previously noted, 1 Timothy 5:5 says, "The widow who is really in need and left all alone puts her hope in God and continues night and day to pray and to ask God for help." There is a gift in being alone when one knows God. Solitude is an opportunity to commune with God himself, to experience his fellowship, to enter into his story. There is an incomparable blessing in allowing God to have one's complete attention, in shutting out the cares of the world and the voices of those who clamor for one's attention, so that one may experience the grander cosmic *coup de foudre* of redemption through Christ.

Sweet Solitude
Edmund Blair Leighton, d. 1922

When one walks in humble obedience with God he should expect a measure of solitude. The following verses support this assertion:

1. "Blessed are you when men hate you, when they *exclude* you and insult you and reject your name as evil, because of the Son of Man." (Luke 6:22, emphasis added)

2. "If the world hates you, keep in mind that it hated me first. If you belonged to the world, it would love you as its own. As it is, you do not belong to the world, but I have chosen you out of the world. That is why the world hates you." (John 15:18, 19)

3. "This is the verdict: Light has come into the world, but people loved darkness

instead of light because their deeds were evil. Everyone who does evil hates the light, and will not come into the light for fear that their deeds will be exposed. But whoever lives by the truth comes into the light, so that it may be seen plainly that what they have done has been done in the sight of God." (John 3:19-21)

4. "May I never boast except in the cross of our Lord Jesus Christ, through which the world has been crucified to me, and I to the world." (Galatians 6:14)

5. "You adulterous people, don't you know that friendship with the world means enmity against God? Therefore, anyone who chooses to be a friend of the world becomes an enemy of God." (James 4:4)

6. First Peter 2:11 states, "Dear friends, I urge you, as aliens and strangers in the world, to abstain from sinful desires, which war against your soul." The Christian is reminded that this is not his home. He is an "alien" and "stranger" in this world, and Hebrews 11:38 reminds that the "world is not worthy" of those in Christ.

Luke 6:22 warns that those in Christ will be hated, excluded, insulted, rejected, and considered evil on account of Christ. Therefore, Christians should be leery of being loved, included, praised, accepted, and considered good by the world. While not always, this may be a sign that they are friends *of* the world and enemies of God (instead of rightly being friends *to* the world).[40] It may seem odd that Luke 6:22 describes those who are hated on account of Christ as "blessed." What is there in being hated which is a blessing? The blessing comes in participating in Christ's suffering, to experience something of what he himself experienced, and to persevere in the midst of persecution. There is eternal glory in being persecuted for Christ.

This serves as a warning to Christians to expect to be alone in certain circumstances, to expect to be overlooked, forgotten, ignored, abandoned, and irrelevant to the world. While the world may mock and ridicule Christians, even more painfully, it often overlooks and forgets them. Being forgotten can inflict as much hurt as being ridiculed, because as God's image-bearers we were designed to be relevant. Consider that many of the prophets were lonely, disregarded, or abandoned. Abraham, alone, pled for Sodom and Gomorrah.[41] Job, alone, grieved his losses, while his friends condemned him, and his wife tempted him to curse God.[42] Isaiah, alone, was sent to Israel to warn of impending doom. Jeremiah, alone, wept over Jerusalem. Jonah, alone, was called to preach to Nineveh.

> "Most of the world's great souls have been lonely. Loneliness seems to be one price the saint must pay for his saintliness. The pain of loneliness arises from the

---

[40] James 4:4
[41] Genesis 18:16-33
[42] Job 2:9

> constitution of our nature. God made us for each other. The desire for human companionship is completely natural and right. The loneliness of the Christian results from his walk with God in an ungodly world, a walk that must often take him away from the fellowship of good Christians as well as from that of the unregenerate world. Why is it easier to talk about revival than to experience it? It is because the followers of Christ must become personally and vitally involved in the death and resurrection of Christ. And this requires repentance, prayer, watchfulness, self-denial, detachment from the world, humility, obedience and cross-carrying!" (A. W. Tozer)[43]

Massacre of the Innocents, François-Joseph Navez, 1824

When one commits himself to personal happiness, loneliness is an enemy. When one commits himself to growing in holiness, solitude is a gift. If God's purpose is to make his people happy then loneliness (or any emotional pain for that matter) makes absolutely no sense. Life becomes nothing more than a series of confounding experiences. However, if God's purpose is to enact greater holiness for those who belong to Christ, then life begins to make sense. In this way, the Christian sees life as God himself sees it, as part of an eternal glorious plan.

---

[43] Thank you to Pei Ling Lin for drawing my attention to this A.W. Tozer (1897–1963) quote.

> "But as for me, my feet had almost slipped;
>   I had nearly lost my foothold.
> For I envied the arrogant
>   when I saw the prosperity of the wicked." (Psalm 73:2, 3)
>
> "Surely in vain I have kept my heart pure
>   and have washed my hands in innocence.
> All day long I have been afflicted,
>   and every morning brings new punishments." (Psalm 73: 13, 14)
>
> "But as for me, it is good to be near God.
>   I have made the Sovereign Lord my refuge;
> I will tell of all your deeds." (Psalm 73: 28)

In the Christian's life loneliness does not have the last word. There is towering hope for those in Christ where relationships, both "horizontal" (with people) and "vertical" (with God), are redefined and renewed. In Christ, one is able to enjoy meaningful interaction, enter into another's story, listen without thinking of oneself, and offer a depth of friendship rarely seen in the postmodern world. Those in Christ will find their relationships enlivened as they love without regard for self, serve without expecting anything in return, are beautiful or intelligent without viewing that as a means of control, express emotion without using it as a relational weapon, and suffer while resting in a God who counts every tear. So as one forgets about himself, and enters into Jesus' story, he soon finds that the problem of loneliness evaporates. One discovers that being alone need not feel painful because in Christ's one has never actually been alone.

> "The one who sent me is with me; he has not left me alone, for I always do what pleases him." (John 8:29)
>
> "For none of us lives for himself alone, and none of us dies for himself alone." (Romans 14:7)

- 4 -

THE UMBILICUS OF PERSONAL RELATIONSHIP WITH CHRIST

Introduction

Recently I spent a weekend teaching a biblical counseling seminar. As I observed the audience, and as I interacted with individual participants, I witnessed stunning theater taking shape. Participants seemed to mimic a constellation of characters found within Scripture itself. Among the group were genuine disciples of Christ eager for heart change. There were some who had received salvation, but appeared to want little more to do with Jesus. A cabal, cowering in the corner, cast aspersions like modern day Pharisees. There was a type of young rich ruler unwilling to part with a treasured idol,[1] and even a "Martha" scrambling to prepare the group's repast while a "Mary" opted to follow the lesson.[2] It was as if Scripture was replaying before my eyes like a film reel; a Manchurian Candidate-like dreamscape was unfolding.

Jesus Walking on the Water, Amedee Varin, c. 1860

Just as biblical accounts reveal that, when confronted with the living Jesus, people exhibited a host of responses in keeping with their heart commitments, so too, in the modern day, as Jesus himself is held up, as his gospel draws or repels, one sees an identical panoply of responses emerge. Two millennia ago people interacted with a

---
[1] Mark 10:17-27
[2] Luke 10:38-42

flesh-and-blood person, Jesus himself. Invariably, people still interact with this same person (albeit not in bodily form).[3]

Diana and Endymion, Nicolas Poussin, 1630

This leads to the issue at hand. Does Scripture call the Christian to direct personal relationship with Jesus Christ? How does the Christian actually relate to Jesus? Is this solely through God's Word, or is there intimate interaction, an abiding in the person of God? How does this issue of personal relationship relate to the Christian's prayer? Is prayer directed to Jesus himself, and does Jesus personally hear prayer?

Look around. The entire creation is personal and relational. Every element of the universe separately, and in aggregate, reveals the character and qualities of a holy eternal God.[4] Who is that God? Is he knowable like a person, and if so, how does one know him? Is he relational, and if so, how does one relate to him?

> In imperial China, one's distance from the emperor's throne (its location varied over time) determined one's relative importance in the civilization, the closer one's proximity to the throne the more important he was. In a certain sense, this captures something of the Christian's need to be close to the "throne," Jesus Christ himself. Yet, the wonder is that that throne is equally accessible to every believer regardless

---

[3] Romans 1:18-21 offers the idea that each person necessarily lives before the face of a holy God (called the *coram Deo* concept), responding to that God in sin or by means of faith.
[4] Psalm 19:1

of his social position or degree of past transgression.

The Relational Nature of Biblical Covenant:[5] "The Right Relationship is Everything"[6]

The term *deus ex machina*, or "god out of the machine," derives from ancient Greek theater. This is an element of a play's plot in which a seemingly intractable dilemma is suddenly resolved with the contrived and unexpected intrusion of a Greek god, or an event he orchestrates. The term developed because a god would appear on stage via a pulley system that seemed to lower him from the sky. However, for the Greeks the term *deus ex machina* was used to criticize a play. It was seen as a convenient and unimaginative way for a playwright to bridge a plot impasse without holding to the play's own internal logic (equivalent to cutting the Gordian knot).

For the Christian, the *deus ex machina* is the actual entrance of the God of the universe onto the human stage.[7] This is not, as with the Greeks, an unwelcomed and awkward intrusion into the human drama, but the conclusive resolution of that drama. The creation was conceived, and is sustained, by a holy God. Thus, it exists to glorify God in his own right, but even more so, it exists that mankind, the pinnacle of creation,[8] might recognize God himself. The creation was birthed that mankind would turn to God in grateful worship.

Man was created in God's triadic image, so that mankind can think (prophet), feel (priest) and will (king).[9] These aspects each carry equal import as man interfaces with God, in the way that God's own being dictates. In other words, man relates to God as prophet, priest, and king, since all are aspects of God's being. Man was made to think about God, to be emotionally involved with God, and to act upon God's will and desires. Any understanding that elevates one aspect of man's design (mind over emotion, for example) at the expense of another aspect results in sinful error and diminished relationship.

Further, mankind was created "very good" in each of his design components so that there is no inherent flaw within man.[10] Yet, as a result of willful rebellion, man became subject to sin, damaged in his ability to interface with God and, thus, isolated from God. However, God did not abandon mankind to his self-imposed peril and perdition but, instead, purely out of mercy, offered a means of redemption, a promised glorious future for those in Christ.

---

[5] David Covington, Biblical Counselor, drew my attention to this concept.
[6] This phrase is a registered trademark of The Chase Manhattan Corporation, New York
[7] Galatians 4:4
[8] Genesis 1:27-31
[9] David Covington, Biblical Counselor
[10] Genesis 1:31

On account of the fact that man is designed in God's image, God initiated covenant relationship with mankind. That covenant is monergistic in nature, meaning that it is sustained solely through God's performance, not through man's.[11] This covenantal relationship, secured in God's own being, and maintained by God himself, is the heart and marrow of the believer's life. Thus, the believer's entire existence is a resting in, and a working out of, this relationship. The nature of God's covenant is so personal that it is embodied in a person, Jesus Christ.[12] The covenant became incarnate, imminent, and intimate in Christ, and is maintained through the indwelling Holy Spirit, resident in believers,[13] as Jesus sits at his Father's right hand.[14] Thus, the Christian's future is not a place, but a person.[15]

> Jesus is the Word of God (prophet),[16] the image of God (priest),[17] the presence and power of God (king).[18]

Consider the following verses concerning relationship with God:

1. "Jesus replied, 'Anyone who loves me will obey my teaching. My Father will love him, and we will come to him and *make our home with him.*'" (John 14:23, emphasis added)

2. Second Corinthians 10:7 states, "You are judging by appearances. If anyone is confident that they belong to Christ, they should consider again that *we belong to Christ* just as much as they do." The Christian is in Christ, belonging to him.

3. James 1:5 reads, "If any of you lacks wisdom, you should *ask God*, who gives generously to all without finding fault, and it will be given to you." James exhorts the Christian to engage in direct communication with God himself.

> "God designed the human machine to run on himself. He himself is the fuel our spirits were designed to burn, or the food our spirits were designed to feed on. There is no other." (C.S. Lewis)

4. Revelation 3:20 states, "Here I am! I stand at the door and knock. If anyone hears my voice and opens the door, *I will come in and eat with that person*, and they with me." Jesus, here, makes specific reference to a covenant meal, as that shared between Moses, Aaron, and the elders on Mount Sinai in the Lord's presence.[19]

---

[11] Genesis 15:17, 18; Hebrews 6:13, 16
[12] Isaiah 42:6; David Covington, Biblical Counselor
[13] Ephesians 1:13, 14
[14] Mark 16:19; Hebrews 12:2
[15] Most biblical allusions to the gates of heaven are allusions to Jesus himself (Psalm 118:19; Isaiah 60:11).
[16] John 1:1
[17] 2 Corinthians 4:6
[18] This idea from David Covington, Biblical Counselor
[19] Exodus 24:11; David Covington, Biblical Counselor, alerted me to this idea

The Coming of the Kingdom

The Magi Journeying, James Jacques Joseph Tissot, c. 1894

Jesus spoke extensively of the coming of the kingdom. What did he mean? He spoke about a time when God would do the unimaginable - live within believers. God himself would dwell with his people, not in a cold stone temple,[20] but within their very spirits.[21] Thus, the coming of the kingdom is not primarily an external event which changes mankind's internal state;[22] rather, it is an internal event which transforms the external. The internal event is repentance and faith, so that the believer becomes the vector for God's kingdom,[23] the living ark in which God's kingdom comes to fruition.

Jesus' death on the cross initiated the kingdom; his Second Coming will fully manifest it. Thus, the salvation won through his death takes up residence within believers, both individually and corporately, overflowing into an external transformation of all human relationships and institutions. Mark 1:15 reads, "'The time has come,' he said. 'The kingdom of God has come near. Repent and believe the good news!'" Luke 10:9 reads, "Heal the sick who are there and tell them, 'The kingdom of God has come near to you.'" Luke 17: 20, 21 states,

---

[20] Ezekiel 11:19
[21] John 4:23, 24
[22] John 18:36
[23] 1 Corinthians 6:19

> Once, on being asked by the Pharisees when the kingdom of God would come, Jesus replied, 'The coming of the kingdom of God is not something that can be observed, nor will people say, 'Here it is,' or 'There it is,' because the kingdom of God is in your midst.'

It is fascinating that even though Jesus was clear that the kingdom is not an observable event, he nevertheless described it in spatial terms ("has come near to you," "is in your midst"). Thus, the kingdom living within believers functions as would a physical force, a realm which operates like a material entity sweeping over humanity, and by extension the entire creation ("a huge mountain [that] filled the whole earth," as Daniel 2:35 augured). That which comes near is Jesus himself entering hearts.

> Consider that there is a future promised land for God's people, a "better country,"[24] a "city which is to come,"[25] a Sabbath rest in the Kingdom of Jesus Christ.[26] Thus, for the Christian, Jesus is his "city" and "nation." Yet, Satan perverts and distorts this reference through Sodom and Egypt, diabolical decrepit city and tyrannical enslaving nation. Revelation 11:8 reads, "Their bodies will lie in the street of the great city, which is figuratively called Sodom and Egypt, where also their Lord was crucified." This highlights Satan's imitation and perversion of the concepts of city and nation, images meant to embody the believer and Christ.

Personal Knowledge of Christ

Relationship with Jesus does not refer to relating to a historical figure, an idea, a cause, an iconic image, a psychological crutch, a theoretical construct, a fantasy, an abstraction, a literary trope, the power of positive thinking, or a distant mystical being. The Bible's teaching is that this relationship is with a living, involved, directed, indwelling, and dynamic person, God himself.

> "For God, who said, 'Let light shine out of darkness,' made his light shine in our hearts to give us the light of the knowledge of the glory of God in the face of Christ." (2 Corinthians 4:6)

Without personal relationship with God, one ends up seeking the gift over the giver, the blessing over the blesser, the principle over the person. Where relationship is absent the giver soon exists only to bestow the gift, and seeking the gift becomes one's highest priority. The giver, in effect, becomes a distant abstraction, no longer a person with whom one can, or should, interact. When personal relationship with God is absent, God becomes nothing more than a "cosmic vending machine" which one

---

[24] Hebrews 11:16
[25] Hebrews 13:14
[26] Hebrews 4:9; John Piper Christmas sermon

manipulates to dispense the object of his desire.[27]

In this regard, Matthew 7:22, 23, reads, "Many will say to me on that day, 'Lord, Lord, did we not prophesy in your name, and in your name drive out demons and perform many miracles?' Then I will tell them plainly, 'I never *knew* you. Away from me, you evildoers!'" "Knew," here, is *gnosko* (γινώσκω), in the active tense, meaning to learn to know, come to know, have knowledge of, to feel, to understand, to perceive, or to become acquainted with (as person to person). Matthew 25:10-13, again, captures this idea:

> But while they were on their way to buy the oil, the bridegroom arrived. The virgins who were ready went in with him to the wedding banquet. And the door was shut. Later the others also came. 'Lord, Lord,' they said, 'open the door for us!' But he replied, 'Truly I tell you, I don't *know* you.' Therefore keep watch, because you do not know the day or the hour.

Personal relationship with Jesus is not merely an appropriation of the benefits that Christ made available by his historical death, burial, and resurrection. Likewise, there is a danger in objectifying the relationship between the Christian and Christ in a forensic or juridical framework which postures that relationship as only justification before a cosmic Judge. Thus, relationship with God can wrongly be viewed as a static reconciliation, no more personal than reconciling one's financial records.[28] In this regard, Hebrews 7:25 reads, "Therefore he is able to *save completely* those who come to God through him, because he always lives to intercede for them." This idea of "saving completely" is more than just a judicial concept, but one's entire life in its most intricate detail. Thus, when Jesus saves it is so that he may enter into the believer's life.

The Bible's Four Primary Metaphors for Relationship with Christ[29]

The Bible describes the relationship between the believer and Jesus with vivid metaphor, each offering another window on sanctification. Thus, each metaphor functions to draw out and clarify that relationship, as well as to elucidate another facet of the covenant Jesus established between God and his people.

Jesus as Capstone or Cornerstone (Keystone)

---

[27] This metaphor from Paul Tripp, Westminster Theological Seminary, Philadelphia, Pennsylvania; for additional discussion of this topic see "Sin as Seeking the Gift Over the Giver" in the second book in this series, *What Agreement Is There Between the Temple of God and Idols?: The Accidence of Sin and Idolatry*, chapter 5: "Metaphors for Sin"

[28] Some ideas in this paragraph from the Adam Clark commentary

[29] For additional discussion of this topic of union with Christ, see "The Sanctification Pentagon'" in the first book in this series, *Ask for the Ancient Paths: From Art to Artifice to Arisen*, chapter 10: "The Third-Way of Sanctification: From Abominable to Indomitable"

> The question posed by Scripture: What is one's guide or standard?

1. "Your Majesty looked, and there before you stood a large statue—an enormous, dazzling statue, awesome in appearance. The head of the statue was made of pure gold, its chest and arms of silver, its belly and thighs of bronze, its legs of iron, its feet partly of iron and partly of baked clay. While you were watching, a rock was cut out, but not by human hands. It struck the statue on its feet of iron and clay and smashed them. Then the iron, the clay, the bronze, the silver and the gold were all broken to pieces and became like chaff on a threshing floor in the summer. The wind swept them away without leaving a trace. But the rock that struck the statue became a huge mountain and filled the whole earth." (Daniel 2:31-35)

   The Transportation of Marble at Carrara
   Nikolai Ge, 1868

2. "In the time of those kings, the God of heaven will set up a kingdom that will never be destroyed, nor will it be left to another people. It will crush all those kingdoms and bring them to an end, but it will itself endure forever. This is the meaning of the vision of the rock cut out of a mountain, but not by human hands — a rock that broke the iron, the bronze, the clay, the silver and the gold to pieces." (Daniel 2:44, 45)

3. "The stone the builders rejected has become the cornerstone; the LORD has done this, and it is marvelous in our eyes." (Psalm 118:22, 23)

4. "But Jesus looked at them and said, 'What then is this that is written: 'The stone which the builders rejected, this became the capstone'? Everyone who falls on that stone will be broken to pieces; but on whomever it falls, it will scatter him like dust.'" (Luke 20:17, 18)

5. "By the grace God has given me, I laid a foundation as an expert builder, and someone else is building on it. But each one should be careful how he builds. For no one can lay any foundation other than the one already laid, which is Jesus Christ." (1 Corinthians 3:10, 11)

6. "Don't you know that you yourselves are God's temple and that God's Spirit lives in you?" (1 Corinthians 3:16)

7. "...built on the foundation of the apostles and prophets, with Christ Jesus himself as the chief cornerstone." (Ephesians 2:20)

8. "As you come to him, the living Stone—rejected by humans but chosen by God and precious to him—you also, like living stones, are being built into a spiritual house to be a holy priesthood, offering spiritual sacrifices acceptable to God through Jesus Christ." (1 Peter 2:4, 5)

Jesus as cornerstone is an architectural metaphor connoting immovability, perfection, permanence, structure, strength, and standard of evaluation. However, the Greek *kephalan gonias* (κεφαλὴν γωνίας), traditionally rendered "capstone" or "cornerstone," is correctly translated "keystone" (of an arch). While a cornerstone serves as the measuring standard for the entire building, the keystone does not just serve as a standard (with perfectly straight and flush surfaces), it receives the arch's entire weight. Thus, the keystone must withstand tremendous adductive structural pressure. Capturing this notion of applied pressure, Jesus stated that his purpose was to break the heart to pieces, lest the keystone fall on it with crushing effect.[30]

> In AD 70 (the year that the Romans sacked Jerusalem and razed the Temple), construction on the Roman Coliseum began. The structure is four-stories tall with massive monoliths once held in place by enormous iron staples. (During World War I those staples were removed as the military scrounged metal for the war effort.) Remarkably, to this day the Coliseum remains intact. It retains its shape because of a skeleton of poured concrete tunnels beneath its seating area. Roman structures, such as the Coliseum, have endured for more than 2,000 years because of a simple construction technique. Roman masons substituted volcanic ash for fluvial sand in their mortar. (Fluvial sand is rounded while volcanic ash is elongated shards.) This causes Roman mortar to exhibit exceptional strength, most notably under seismic

---
[30] Luke 20:18

> stress.
>
> There is something in this historical toast point that might serve as a metaphor for the Christian life. The Christian is held together with a "mortar," not composed of the rounded sand of lenience, but of piercing shards of ash. One could think of such shards as emblematic of Christ pierced for his people.[31]

Jesus as Head of the Church

> The question posed by Scripture: Under whose authority will one place himself?

Jesus as head is an anatomical metaphor highlighting neurological processes. Jesus is the executive function to which the church, as body, responds. This connotes authority, connectedness, direction, hierarchy, obedience, support, and wisdom.

The Coliseum
Sir Lawrence Alma-Tadema, 1896

1. Romans 8:9 states, "You, however, are not in the realm of the flesh but are in the realm of the Spirit, if indeed the *Spirit of God lives in you*. And if anyone does not have the Spirit of Christ, they do not belong to Christ." The indwelling Holy Spirit is Jesus within Christians, to enliven and "re-realm" them.

2. "Instead, speaking the truth in love, we will grow to become in every respect the mature body of him who is the head, that is, Christ. From him the whole body, joined and held together by every supporting ligament, grows and builds itself up in love, as each part does its work." (Ephesians 4:15, 16)

---

[31] Isaiah 53:5

3. "For the husband is the head of the wife as Christ is the head of the church, his body, of which he is the Savior." (Ephesians 5:23)

4. "Do not let anyone who delights in false humility and the worship of angels disqualify you. Such a person also goes into great detail about what they have seen; they are puffed up with idle notions by their unspiritual mind. They have lost connection with the head, from whom the whole body, supported and held together by its ligaments and sinews, grows as God causes it to grow." (Colossians 2:18, 19)

Jesus as the Church's Bridegroom

> The question posed by Scripture: To whom will one wed himself?

Ephesians 5:25-27 reads,

> Husbands, love your wives, just as Christ loved the church and gave himself up for her to make her holy, cleansing her by the washing with water through the word, and to present her to himself as a radiant church, without stain or wrinkle or any other blemish, but holy and blameless.

Here, Paul points to the most intimate interpersonal relationship, marriage, as the highest earthly analogy for the relationship between Christ and the Christian. Marriage involves caring for another, allowing another to care for oneself, passion, purity, self-sacrifice, submission, and vigilant love. It is the profoundest display of unity that can be experienced and, thus, necessitates an experiential oneness, a union, a commonality of identity, an emotional and worshipping intimacy. (Incidentally, those Christians who have never married can, nevertheless, comprehend this analogy just as well as married Christians.)

Leviticus 21:7-15 details the type of bride a priest was to take:

Quality	Meaning	In Christ
1. Undefiled by prostitution (21:7, 14)	Holy	The church is no longer conscripted to sin and idolatry, no longer a metaphorical harlot chasing false gods.
2. Not divorced (21:7, 14)	Not covenantally treasonous	The church is to marry one husband, Christ, and remains loyal to him.
3. Must be a virgin from the priest's own	Pure, without blemish or wrinkle	The one in Christ has become a pure virgin as the stain of sin has

people (21:13, 14)		been blotted out.[32]
4. Must not be a widow (21:14)	Remarriage establishes a second covenant	The church is not to be one mourning a prior death. Rather, it is to be given entirely to a solitary bridegroom – Christ.

All of that being said, the Christian's relationship with Christ, in being marital, becomes familial. Hebrew 2:11, 12 states,

> Both the one who makes people holy and those who are made holy are of the same family. So Jesus is not ashamed to call them *brothers*. He says,
>
> 'I will declare your name to my brothers;
> in the assembly I will sing your praises.'

The word "brother" here is the Greek, *adelphos* (ἀδελφός), meaning a near sibling or children in the same family; it denotes being of the same "blood."

The Vintage at Chateau Lagrange, Jules Breton, 1864

In light of this wine (marriage) and blood (sibling) relationship with Christ, 1 Peter 1:22 states, "Now that you have purified yourselves by obeying the truth so that you have sincere love for each other, love one another deeply, from the heart." This passage builds upon the untainted love between Christ and believers as literally "unfeigned" love which overflows in genuine love for others. Thus, there is causality between one's relationship with Christ and one's relationship with others. If one is

---
[32] Psalm 51:1

cold and distant toward Christ, one will be cold and distant in all interpersonal relationships (whether familial, marital, or otherwise). Thus, the tenor of relationship with Christ directs, and is reflected in, all human relationships.

Jesus as Vine

> The question posed by Scripture: Where does one find life, and how does one bear fruit?

John 15:5 reads, "I am the vine; you are the branches. If you remain in me and I in you, you will bear much fruit; apart from me you can do nothing." Jesus as the life-giving vine and believers as branches, form an agricultural metaphor, one which connotes maintaining organic connection, being fed, growing, and flourishing so as to bear fruit.[33]

Cultivating a vineyard requires intense labor. Grapevines have a tendency to run along the ground where they are easily covered with dust inhibiting photosynthesis in the leaves. Thus, one of the functions of a vinedresser is to lift and wash leaves so as to keep them fully receptive to sunlight. An analogy could be made to the Christian life in which Christ himself "lifts and washes" his people so that they are prepared to fully receive him as daily "sunlight."[34]

Consider Leviticus 25:3, 4,

> For six years sow your fields, and for six years prune your vineyards and gather their crops. But in the seventh year the land is to have a Sabbath of rest, a Sabbath to the Lord. Do not sow your fields or prune your vineyards.

The Lord commanded that a vineyard was to lie fallow in the seventh year. This was a reminder to the Israelites of several important truths:

1. God himself promised to provide for them during the cessation of their own labor. The sixth year would produce a triple harvest so that Israel would enjoy an abundance until the ninth year, when the land was again productive.[35]

2. God's intention was to offer Israel a vision of a time, before the fall, when Adam reaped what he did not sow,[36] when he was at ease, sheltered from work's toil and

---
[33] Luke 20:16 alludes to this.
[34] Bruce Wilkinson, *Secrets of the Vine: Breaking Through to Abundance* (Sisters, Oregon: Multnomah Publishers, 2001)
[35] Leviticus 25:20-22
[36] John 4:38 mention that those in Christ will also enjoy such a situation.

frustration. (The land's Sabbath rest was also reminiscent of Noah's vineyards,[37] the land's fruitful harvest after a time of unimaginable devastation.)

3. The land itself was to experience a period of rest, a time of rejuvenation.

4. Those who were typically in need – servants, aliens, and wild animals, would experience a serendipitous provision.[38]

5. The Sabbath rest would serve as a poignant reminder that Israel must be charitable and not love wealth. A year of rest offered a realignment for their souls, a time to no longer pursue gain, but rather to be spent in both the study of God's Word and in prayer. Thus, the seventh year served as an antidote for greed.

Each of these points offers a distinctive elaboration upon the notion of Jesus as vine and the believer as branch. It is worth noting that the vine does not produce fruit directly. That fruit blossoms from the branch as it remains connected to the vine. Thus, the believer, as he remains in Christ, rests in Christ, and trusts in Christ, yields much fruit.[39] One is reminded of Galatians 2:20, which reads, "I have been crucified with Christ and I no longer live, but *Christ lives in me*. The life I now live in the body, I live by faith in the Son of God, who loved me and gave himself for me."

> It is noteworthy that of the four metaphors for relationship with Christ (cornerstone and building, head and body, bridegroom and bride, and vine and branches) the first and the last are directed toward individual believers, while the middle two are directed toward the church. This interplay of the individual and the corporate highlights the nature of relationship with Christ, one in which the individual and the corporate are intertwined. While the believer will be judged individually,[40] he is, nevertheless, called to join with a body of believers which is evaluated corporately.[41]

If Not Relationship with Christ, Then Relationship with Satan

Ephesians 2:1 states, "As for you, you were dead in your transgressions and sins." This verse alludes to a central truth of the human existence; those disconnected from Christ are in a state of spiritual death, while those connected to Christ have been delivered to life. Thus, one is either dead or alive, in relationship with Satan or Jesus. There is no other choice, no neutral position. The Christian is called to maintain intimate relationship with Jesus, while unregenerate mankind is implicitly in intrapersonal and interpersonal relationship with Satan (albeit not labeling it as such).

---

[37] Genesis 5:29
[38] Leviticus 25:6, 7
[39] John 15:5
[40] 1 Corinthians 3:12-15
[41] Galatians 3:1; Revelation 2, 3

Consider the following verses:

1. "'You belong to your father, the devil, and you want to carry out your father's desires. He was a murderer from the beginning, not holding to the truth, for there is no truth in him. When he lies, he speaks his native language, for he is a liar and the father of lies.'" (John 8:44)

2. "But whoever is united with the Lord is one with him in spirit." (1 Corinthians 6:17)

3. "...and that they will come to their senses and escape from the trap of the devil, who has taken them captive to do his will." (2 Timothy 2:26)

Church Interior
Wilhelm Schubert van Ehrenberg, 1665

4. "This is how we know who the children of God are and who the children of the devil are: Anyone who does not do what is right is not God's child, nor is anyone who does not love their brother and sister." (1 John 3:10)

The unbeliever has no choice but to relate to Satan; the believer makes a choice as to whom he will relate. Yet, Hebrews 4:15 offers this assurance, "For we do not have a high priest who is unable to empathize with our weaknesses, but we have one who has been tempted in every way, just as we are—yet he did not sin." This organic connectivity between Christ and his people results in empathy for their earthly plight, and in the ability to sustain them throughout it.

Assessing the Merits of Personal Relationship with Christ

Completed in 1436, the Cattedrale di Santa Maria del Fiore in Florence, Italy supports a massive octagonal dome. The architect, Filippo Brunelleschi (1377-1446), feared that the structure, built on a quagmire, was in danger of being compromised. In order to determine if the cathedral had shifted, he fashioned a small portal in the dome which allowed a thin ray of light to fall perfectly on a brass plate every June 21st. If the light fails to pinpoint the plate, the building has shifted.[42]

Unlike the Cattedrale di Santa Maria del Fiore, the Christian life is not built on the quagmire of shifting sentiment, but on the solid rock of Christ which lends the Christian an ethereal stability,[43] an ataractic permanence in the midst of a swirling chaotic world. ("Jesus Christ is the same yesterday and today and forever." (Hebrews 13:8)) Yet, like the annual assessment built into the Florence cathedral, the Christian is also called to assess himself in order to determine if he has perilously shifted with regard to his own heart allegiance. Second Corinthians 13:5 reads, "Examine yourselves to see whether you are in the faith; test yourselves. Do you not realize that Christ Jesus is in you--unless, of course, you fail the test?" The Christian's means of assessment is firstly through on-going relationship with Christ, so that Christ's light shines into his heart moment-by-moment. In this way, the Christian is searched by Christ to determine if his foundation has shifted.[44]

The argument is sometimes made that believers may not be mature enough, or do not know Scripture well enough, to enter into relationship with Jesus directly. The reasoning goes that such relationship could easily be used as an interpersonal weapon, or divisive tactic, to assert Gnostic principles (personal knowledge of God's will). The fear is that immature believers could easily defy God's clear directives in Scripture under the guise of misguided personal revelation.

There is a profound difference between experiencing personal relationship with God and receiving personal revelation from God. Personal relationship brings submission to Christ, as Christ himself intervenes and works in the believer's heart. Claiming personal revelation, however, breeds defiance to Christ as one asserts exclusive knowledge of God's will, outside of his revealed will in the Bible. Thus, for example, the Ephesians 5:22 command for a wife to submit to her husband is God's revealed will. Yet, this command is only plausible, and can only bear fruit, as a wife and husband are both first in submission to Christ himself. It is that personal relationship with Christ which gives regenerate mankind the ability to follow the command. Without intimate relationship with Christ, one is left with Pythagoreanism or Confucianism, a wife submitting to her husband out of family piety, fear, or societal obligation, but not out of heart change, nor out of love for Jesus (her first husband).

While it is vital to recognize potential abuses, the answer is not to eliminate

---

[42] Kevin McFarland, *Incredible! But True* (New York: Bell Publishing Company, 1976) 28
[43] Matthew 16:18
[44] Psalm 139:23; 1 Corinthians 3:11; 1 Corinthians 11:31

relationship with God. Rather, the solution is to address the sin and idolatry that clouds and twists relationship. As relationship with Jesus deepens, as sin is brought to continual repentance, there is invariably growth, heart change, increased joy, and renewed interpersonal relationship. Relationship with Jesus is never to be feared because the indwelling Holy Spirit always brings forth good fruit.[45] Tragically, a Christian who shuns relationship with Jesus actively cultivates relationship with Satan (despite his vehement denial).[46] Thus, the great threat in the church is not those who experience relationship with Jesus, but those who do not.

> "Personal" puts God in charge; principles (even a so-called principle of the Word) put man in charge. (David Covington)

Believers principally grow through interacting directly with Christ, a revitalizing relationship which intensifies with the study of Scripture and through a vibrant community of believers.[47] Thus, the denial of the towering need for relationship with Christ is the greatest tragedy in the Christian faith. This strips the believer of his life-blood, his power, and his existential purpose. Denying relationship falls into the trap set by the Pharisees who sought outward compliance without inward submission.[48]

As with the Pharisees, when relationship with God is marginalized the reason is invariably a desire by those in church leadership to maintain control, even a tendency toward cult-like manipulation. To strip a believer of relationship with Christ is to keep him in a puerile condition, to perpetuate a state of debilitating sin, to promote an insular church oligarchy in a way that Christ condemned,[49] and ultimately to invite the presence and peril of Satan.

The following chart offers a summary:

The Pharisaical Approach: Manipulation	God's Approach: Heart Change
1. Establish man-made laws and decrees which eliminate the need for relationship with God[50]	Initiate worship-driven relationship with God through directly receiving Jesus as savior
2. Seek outward compliance that is based on conformity to a man-made standard[51]	Heart change brings inner conformity to God's likeness,[52] which overflows in outward displays

---

[45] Galatians 5:22, 23
[46] Matthew 16:23
[47] Hebrews 10:25
[48] Matthew 23:23-28
[49] Matthew 16:6; Luke 12:1
[50] Matthew 23:15
[51] Matthew 15:9

3. Overlook sin and idolatry because these categories have largely been externalized so as to maintain a particular form of godliness[53]	In love, and for the purpose of restoration to God, show the sinner his sin and the idolater his idolatry.
4. Renounce the need for repentance through cold and distant conformity in one's own strength[54]	Encourage repentance which leads to purposed fellowship with God and others (as sin and idolatry are regularly exposed and renounced)[55]
5. Neglect sanctification because there is no need, nor mechanism, for changing the heart	Effect sanctification through abiding in Jesus, study of his Word, and in giving and receiving counsel within the church

Mary Magdalene's Box of Very Precious Ointment
James Jacques Joseph Tissot, c. 1896

One of the marks of a false church is that it renders God impersonal (metaphorically a movement from Mount Zion back to Mount Sinai). This invariably makes God wrathful, capricious, selfish, and untrustworthy. It makes God unapproachable, so that others are stripped of his mercy, compassion, and means for growth in holiness. As God is cast in an impersonal hue, there is no concept of a God of grace and mercy, a

---

[52] 2 Corinthians 3:18
[53] Matthew 23:5
[54] Matthew 23:13
[55] Matthew 3:8

God who sees and moves with purpose to effect needed change. Such an impersonal God becomes a terrifying idol that must, through some ritual or moral act, be appeased.[56]

> **The Words of One Seeking Relationship with Christ**
>
> "I am very grateful to have this opportunity to be present at your lesson. The message you presented set me free. For a long time I doubted the value of building relationship with the Lord, even though I have been baptized for more than seven years. I thought it was more important to just gain literal knowledge of the Bible and God. Now I know I was just avoiding repentance, and not dealing with the problem of my idols. I am always afraid of failure, failing others, and making others dissatisfied with me. I suffered with this a lot, and became proud so as not to surrender to God. Now I can praise God freely. I recognize my idols and I am very joyful to build relationship with God.
>
> Thank you very much for giving us this lecture, and thank God for giving me this opportunity to know something about biblical counseling. I hope that I can help someone else when I know more."

The Dangers When Relationship with Christ is Marginalized

1. Balaam's error

In the book of Jude, Balaam is spoken of in association with the murderer Cain and the rebel Korah.[57] While Balaam could not curse the Israelites, he eventually induced them to curse themselves through sexual immorality and idolatry. This could be applied to the modern church which curses itself through errant teaching which leads to immorality. As relationship with Christ is marginalized, the body of believers becomes increasingly immoral (which may show itself in many forms, not just sexual). As the indwelling Christ is progressively removed, the church degenerates into an outwardly compliant, but inwardly depraved and dark, body.

> "Woe to them! They have taken the way of Cain; they have rushed for profit into Balaam's error; they have been destroyed in Korah's rebellion. These men are blemishes at your love feasts, eating with you without the slightest qualm – shepherds who feed only themselves. They are clouds without rain, blown along by the wind; autumn trees, without fruit and uprooted – twice dead. They are wild waves of the sea, foaming up their shame; wandering stars, for whom blackest darkness has been reserved forever." (Jude 11-13)

---

[56] Matthew 23:16 alludes to this.
[57] Jude 11-13

> "They have left the straight way and wandered off to follow the way of Balaam son of Beor, who loved the wages of wickedness. But he was rebuked for his wrongdoing by a donkey – a beast without speech – who spoke with a man's voice and restrained the prophet's madness. These men are springs without water and mists driven by a storm. Blackest darkness is reserved for them. For they mouth empty, boastful words and, by appealing to the lustful desires of sinful human nature, they entice people who are just escaping from those who live in error." (2 Peter 2:15-17)

2. The Bible as a weapon for domination

I recently spoke to a student who had attended my Bible study for a year. While she is not yet a Christian, she told me that she is eager to get back to our study. I, of course, was ecstatic and asked her if she was interested in having a relationship with God. She responded, "I am interested in the Bible, but I am not interested in God." My joy turned to sorrow. I explained to her that without relationship with God the Bible has no meaning and no purpose. My student's blunt response reveals a very common problem, however; many study the Bible with no interest in the God who wrote it.

As the Bible is stripped of its purpose (to make Jesus known and to build ongoing relationship with him),[58] it becomes little more than a weapon for maintaining power and a means to manipulate others. The Bible is meant to bring freedom, not a return to enslavement to sin.[59] This means enacting worship of Christ, to empower, rebuke, edify, and embolden believers in the context of Christ-centered relationship.[60]

> "Woe to you, teachers of the law and Pharisees, you hypocrites! You travel over land and sea to win a single convert, and when he becomes one, you make him twice as much a son of hell as you are." (Matthew 23:15)

3. Coercive control

In circumventing relationship with Christ, church leaders may merely want to maintain control over others, so that the leader is always seen as the authority, the dispenser of truth. The objective is that others are kept in a dependent and subservient role. Anyone who threatens the leader's control is reflexively labeled "rebellious," "seditious," or "unteachable" (although these may be true in their own right). Direct relationship with God must be encouraged and enacted in each believer, or church leaders invariably fill the relational vacuum by placing themselves in the position of God himself.

---

[58] Luke 24:44
[59] Galatians 5:1
[60] 2 Timothy 3:16

> "For there is one God and one mediator between God and men, the man Christ Jesus" (1 Timothy 2:5)

If a pastor insists on maintaining control he keeps his flock in a state of slavery to himself. Yet, God always frees slaves in time.[61] Thus, an oppressive pastor will soon find himself removed, unless he willingly repents of his desire to control a church over which he is meant to be a faithful shepherd, and not a subversive. The church does not belong to a pastor. It belongs to Christ and, therefore, the pastor is merely a servant protecting and guiding those for whom Christ died. As soon as the pastor views the church as his own, he has taken the place of Christ and then functions as a cult leader and de facto emissary of Satan.

Jesus Unrolls Book in Synagogue
James Jacques Joseph Tissot, c. 1894

4. Dead faith

Faith without heart change, without renewed worship, is dead. Believers do not grow in Christ when there is no connection, no corrective, and no personal indwelling to make that growth viable. Without connection to Christ, faith is dead.[62]

5. Moralism[63]

Without relationship with God the Christian message degenerates into moralism.

---

[61] Luke 4:18
[62] John 15:5; Colossians 2:18, 19; James 2:26
[63] For additional discussion of the dangers of moralism see the section "The Third-Way of Sanctification" in the first book in this series, *Ask for the Ancient Paths: From Art to Artifice to Arisen*, chapter 10: "The Third-Way of Sanctification: From Abominable to Indomitable"

The moralistic model is "horizontal" in that it sees man's own effort as affecting change. The Christian-relational model is "vertical" in that it confronts the heart with God himself and with ongoing surrender to Christ. In so doing, the sin nature is crucified,[64] so that, one more willingly takes upon himself the cause of Christ's kingdom. Without Christ there is only forced behavioral conformity;[65] with Christ there is right worship from which actions naturally flow.

6. Pharisaism

The Pharisees put on a form of godliness but denied the power therein.[66] For example, a Pharisaical form of prayer is ultimately directed toward winning praise from men as there is no interaction with God.[67]

> 'Woe to you Pharisees, because you give God a tenth of your mint, rue and all other kinds of garden herbs, but you neglect justice and the love of God. You should have practiced the latter without leaving the former undone. Woe to you Pharisees, because you love the most important seats in the synagogues and respectful greetings in the marketplaces. Woe to you, because you are like unmarked graves, which people walk over without knowing it.' One of the experts in the law answered him, 'Teacher, when you say these things, you insult us also.' Jesus replied, 'And you experts in the law, woe to you, because you load people down with burdens they can hardly carry, and you yourselves will not lift one finger to help them.' (Luke 11:42-46)

Jesus' statement about loading people down with burdens was a reference to the inescapable consequence of moralism, a burden birthed through denying the need for relationship with Jesus himself.

7. The sin of the Nicolaitans[68]

Consider Revelation 2:14-16,

> 'Nevertheless, I have a few things against you: You have people there who hold to the teaching of Balaam, who taught Balak to entice the Israelites to sin by eating food sacrificed to idols and by committing sexual immorality. Likewise you also have those who hold to the teaching of the Nicolaitans. Repent therefore! Otherwise, I will soon come to you and will fight against them with the sword of my mouth.'

---

[64] Galatians 2:20
[65] Colossians 2:23
[66] 2 Timothy 3:5
[67] Luke 18:11
[68] For additional discussion of this topic see "The Danger of Church Hierarchy" in chapter 10: "Counseling and the Church: Syndicating the Vision"

What was the "teaching of the Nicolaitans"? The name "Nicolaitan" is a compound of two Greek words: *nikos* (νίκος), meaning "victory" or "conquest," and *laos* (λαός), meaning "people." Thus, Nicolaitan is literally "victory over the people." This group established a dictatorial hierarchy to dominate the church. Thus, autocrats maintained power and pressed the laity into submission. First Peter 5:1-3 warns those in church authority not to function as lords over those in their care, exhorting elders not to wantonly seek power for their own personal aggrandizement. Peter recognized the temptation to division and envy when a church oligarchy forms. Man-centered hierarchy poisons the church's vitality as members are kept in a state of subservience, disempowered to serve as God gifts them.

Churches are centralized with regard to Christ (the only head of the church),[69] and radically decentralized with regard to man (each using his gifts to serve others).[70] Each member is called to function as part of one body under Christ's own authority. Thus, the church is the antithesis of a monarchy and, yet, is neither democratic nor communistic. The church, under Christ, submits itself to no human authority (although it cooperates with earthly authorities).[71] On account of being under Christ directly, the Bible admonishes believers to "submit to one another out of reverence for Christ."[72]

The biblical directive for the church is not the centralization of authority, but the exact opposite, the delegation of responsibility "downward." In short, the biblical pattern of church polity and ministry is decentralized and representative.[73] As relationship with Christ is encouraged and enlivened, church members handle responsibilities as mature, trustworthy, wise, and sincere servants. Thus, placing responsibility with church members is no longer a threatening proposition but a joyous one, to see Christ working through those he has called and sanctified.[74]

8. A patronizing view of women, children, and servants (anyone traditionally outside of the authority structure)[75]

In a church which emphasizes and condones controlling leadership over direct relationship with Christ, woman are often reduced to a low position, patronized, and condescended to. Yet, Galatians 3:28 states, "There is neither Jew nor Gentile, neither slave nor free, nor is there male and female, for you are all one in Christ Jesus." Female believers are clearly equals in Christ and, therefore, never to be seen as

---

[69] Colossians 1:18
[70] 1 Peter 4:10
[71] Romans 13:1
[72] Ephesians 5:21
[73] Douglas Wilson, *Recovering the Lost Tools of Learning: An Approach to Distinctively Christian Education* (Wheaton, Illinois: Crossway Books, 1991) 102.
[74] Acts 4:32
[75] Based on the categories established in Ephesians 5:22-6:9

holding a lesser identity. Vis-à-vis men, women occupy a complementary position of final parity.

With regard to relationship with Christ, men and women enjoy an eternal equality which tempers, shapes, and directs the earthly authority structure so that it reflects Christ himself. Thus, when in relationship with Christ, those in submission to authority do so gladly out of surrender to Jesus, and those in authority govern humbly as an act of self-sacrificial love. However, in the absence of direct relationship with Jesus, these positions quickly degenerate, becoming a source of conflict poisoning the entire congregation. Arrogance quickly takes hold of those in authority so that there is no longer self-sacrificial service, only lust for domination over wives, children, and servants.[76]

In the Rice Fields
Angelo Morbelli, 1901

As per Ephesians 5:21 – 6:9, to remove relationship with Jesus from the husband-wife, parent-child, master-servant equation is to flatten all human roles into the mere exercise of earthly duty. Thus, a submissive wife and a self-sacrificial husband are reduced to pragmatists living out a moral code. When relationship with Christ is at the heart of this dynamic, the equation becomes three-dimensional so that it involves the work of another (Jesus), directly intervening, and superintending the submission and self-sacrifice. Thus, the relationship between husband and wife, for example, is continually renewed, reinvigorated, and transformed into a profound act of worship as

---

[76] See Ephesians 5:21 – 6:9

Christ himself is the motive, the means, the outcome, and the glory of the marital relationship.

Submission to human authority, for its own sake, is functionally Confucianism. The biblical concept of submission, on the other hand, is never toward human authority as the final referent, but has relationship with God as the ultimate objective. A biblical understanding of proper submission to human authority must emphasize and uphold the final intent of submission to God himself.

Excursus: Pastor as Servant

Some years ago, I was invited to present a counseling seminar. The pastor hosting the event asked for advice counseling a couple in his church. My thought was to first discuss their need for relationship with Jesus, that that relationship, when implemented for the first time, or strengthened, would work wonders in their marriage. The pastor's affect changed. He looked visibly angry as he told me that this is a dangerous teaching. He elaborated that he never wants his congregants to see themselves as in *personal* relationship with Jesus. In his words, this breeds pride, factions, dissention, marital strife, and selfishness. He fears his church becoming a group of Gnostics, each personally seeking a word from God, and feels that if Christians see themselves as personally related to Christ, they will not seek to be under church teaching and discipline.

I was aghast. How could one who calls himself a minister of Christ denounce personal relationship with Christ? If not for this relationship, then what is the point of our faith? In probing further, I soon discovered that this pastor teaches that the Word of God *is* Jesus himself that, in knowing the Bible, one knows Jesus not as person to person, but as person to word. ("Many deceivers, who do not acknowledge Jesus Christ *as coming in the flesh*, have gone out into the world. Any such person is the deceiver and the antichrist." (2 John 1:7))

I strongly suspect that this man's deeper motive is one of control. He wants to be God's presence, the dispenser of truth and, thus, discourages believers from going to God directly for wisdom because this undermines his tight grip on power.[77] He wants the flock going to him for their spiritual needs so that he would be praised. (Incidentally, in hearing this pastor pray, I could not help but wonder, "To whom is he praying?" Without relationship with Jesus prayer is just empty words tossed into a cosmic vacuum.[78])

As this vignette indicates, pastors can easily be tempted to compromise. The reason is

---

[77] James 1:5
[78] Matthew 6:5; Mark 12:40

that they traffic in invisible realities (justification and sanctification), yet continually seek to quantify that reality in worldly terms (church growth, attendance records, decisions for Christ), when the two are largely in compatible. The pastorate, more so than any other profession, trades almost exclusively in intangibles, in invisible faith,[79] in otherworldly ideas. However, when they merely serve out of selfish ambition,[80] pastors must, beyond all other interests, maintain control over hearts and minds in order to keep others craving the invisible "product" they peddle (a product which is really nothing more than their own subjective will). Derelict pastors present God as a mere idea, a principle, or a way of life, but not as a person. This error is by design as it keeps the pastor as the "person" with whom others must relate.

To the unregenerate heart, just a taste of power is an instantly addictive drug. Case in point, the Pharisees' lust for power seemed to know no bounds. Jesus posed a pressing threat because he implicitly undermined their every objective. Like the Pharisees, church pastors (or others in leadership) often stealthily pursue self-serving power.[81] Like any who worships false idols, a power-hungry pastor is deeply insecure, paranoid, and anxious about losing control over his congregation. With haunting consistency, many pastors fear outsiders being praised or given any measure of authority. They frequently seek any means possible to make sure that attention remains squarely upon themselves, while keeping up the appearance of humility, servanthood, and other-centeredness.

The pastor must never see himself as the arbiter or dispensary of God's grace, but merely as the ensign tending the lighthouse. He is not an exclusive channel, but a submissive instrument through which God, as person, presents himself to people. The channel is not the focus but, rather, the focus is on the one who conveys himself through that channel.

If a pastor views his role as introducing the congregation to a person then the fear, anxiety, and manipulative tactics soon dissipate. He no longer views outsiders as a threat, because his "product" is not invested in himself. When a personal holy God manifests himself, the pastor no longer sees himself as the end product. Therefore, the faithful pastor, himself in repentance-based relationship with God, does not see himself as an exclusive conduit to Christ, but as a fading servant.[82] This is the key to maintaining sound church governance.

Abiding in Christ

"No wise man ever wished to be younger." (Jonathan Swift)

---

[79] Hebrews 11:1
[80] Philippians 1:17
[81] Philippians 2:3
[82] Philippians 2:17

One could think of the Bible as a skyscraper with a sturdy steel frame which bends slightly in the wind. The Bible speaks with towering authority, but at the same time offers a certain subtle flexibility. Thus, the Bible holds forth a unified infallible message and, simultaneously, allows for some degree of individual choice (often referred to as adiaphora).[83] God's declarative will (as stated in the Bible) is ironclad but God, through ongoing relationship, also seeks to know and work with his people's desires.[84] This is the nature of the Father-child relationship; it is an amalgam of elements, some structural (God's declared will), and others arising through relational extemporization.[85]

Morning
William Holman Hunt, 1866

According to John 3:1-6, regeneration and new birth are the basis for relationship with the living Christ. Against this backdrop John 15:4-7 states,

> 'Remain in me, as I also remain in you. No branch can bear fruit by itself; it must remain in the vine. Neither can you bear fruit unless you remain in me. I am the vine; you are the branches. If you remain in me and I in you, you will bear much fruit; apart from me you can do nothing. If you do not remain in me, you are like a branch that is thrown away and withers; such branches are picked up, thrown into the fire and burned. If you remain in me and my words remain in you, ask whatever you wish, and it will be done for you.'

These verses offer a summary of the interplay between God's eternal declared will (the Bible) and the indwelling personal Christ within believers. The believer is

---

[83] For additional discussion of the proper understanding of Scripture see the first book in this series, *Ask for the Ancient Paths: From Art to Artifice to Arisen*, chapter 3: "The Centrality of Scripture in Counseling"
[84] Exodus 32:14; 2 Chronicles 7:14; Matthew 18:18; Luke 12:32; John 15:7
[85] Matthew 18:18; Luke 12:32; John 14:12; 15:4-7

exhorted to both remain in Jesus personally, and to keep Jesus' words (the Bible) within himself. Thus, there is an organic quality to the Bible since, as it indwells believers, it is "electrified" with Christ himself. Additionally, there is a clear distinction between direct relationship with Jesus (being "in him") and his Word. Simply knowing Jesus' Word does not cause one to be in him. One must deliberately and actively enter into that relationship.[86] (Remember that the Pharisees had memorized most of the Hebrew Bible, yet did not know God.)

> A Christian is a person in whom one can see another person at work. (David Powlison)

The Christian actually participates in the life of Jesus himself, not just as an intellectual assent to his lordship, but in a daily interaction with, and in, him. Consider the following verses:

1. Romans 8:17 states, "Now if we are children, then we are heirs—heirs of God and co-heirs with Christ, if indeed we share in his sufferings in order that we may also share in his glory." The Christian suffers with Christ, and is united with Christ, through Christ's blood which covers him. This is not an abstraction but a direct connection which results in shared suffering,[87] the mark of an intimate, living relationship.[88]

2. "Therefore, since we have such a hope, we are very bold. We are not like Moses, who would put a veil over his face to prevent the Israelites from seeing the end of what was passing away. But their minds were made dull, for to this day the same veil remains when the old covenant is read. It has not been removed, because only in Christ is it taken away. Even to this day when Moses is read, a veil covers their hearts. But whenever anyone turns to the Lord, the veil is taken away. Now the Lord is the Spirit, and where the Spirit of the Lord is, there is freedom. And we all, who with unveiled faces contemplate the Lord's glory, are being transformed into his image with ever-increasing glory, which comes from the Lord, who is the Spirit." (2 Corinthians 3:12-18)

3. "Therefore, if anyone is *in Christ*, the new creation has come: The old has gone, the new is here!" (2 Corinthians 5:17, emphasis added)

4. "Examine yourselves to see whether you are in the faith; test yourselves. Do you not realize that *Christ Jesus is in you*—unless, of course, you fail the test?" (2 Corinthians 13:5, emphasis added)

---

[86] Luke 24:45
[87] For additional discussion of this topic see, "The Gospel and Suffering" in chapter 2: "Suffering, The Kintsugi Objective"
[88] 1 Peter 2:21

5. "And God raised us up with Christ and seated us *with him* in the heavenly realms in Christ Jesus…" (Ephesians 2:6, emphasis added)

6. "Consequently, you are no longer foreigners and strangers, but fellow citizens with God's people and also members of his household, built on the foundation of the apostles and prophets, with Christ Jesus himself as the chief cornerstone. In him the whole building is joined together and rises to become a holy temple in the Lord. And *in him* you too are being built together to become a dwelling in which God lives by his Spirit." (Ephesians 2:19-22, emphasis added)

7. "…and to put on the new self, created to be like God in true righteousness and holiness." (Ephesians 4:24)

8. "To them God has chosen to make known among the Gentiles the glorious riches of this mystery, which is *Christ in you*, the hope of glory." (Colossians 1:27, emphasis added)

Dawn (Aurora Triumphans), Evelyn de Morgan, 1886

9. "When Christ, *who is your life*, appears, then you also will appear with him in glory." (Colossians 3:4, emphasis added)

10. "Do not lie to each other, since you have taken off your old self with its practices and have *put on the new self*, which is being renewed in knowledge in the image

of its Creator." (Colossians 3:9, 10, emphasis added)

> The Puritans were said to have an implanted "moral gyroscope" so that, regardless of society's orientation, they knew and followed God's direction. The Puritans showed a stunning sense of inner fortitude, an unflappable and indefatigable sense of moral direction. This inner moral gyroscope was the direct result of abiding in Christ, cultivating daily personal relationship with him, so that he invested in them an innate, almost visceral, submission to his Spirit.

To enjoy personal relationship with Christ, the sinner invites him into his life. He asks Jesus to forgive him, to usher him from rebellion to redemption, to draw him from death to life. When one honestly repents and seeks to know Jesus, Jesus will find him and bestow the gift of faith.[89] Faith bears fruit for eternity, beginning the process of sanctification so that one is not what he used to be and far from what he will be.

Case Study: Prayer as Life-Blood of Relationship with Jesus

Prayer as a Paradigm Shift

A young woman asked for advice on a personal problem. I queried, "Would you like to study what God has to say about your life?" She parried, "I'm not interested in fantasy; I only deal in reality." This is precisely the posture of a heart ruled by sin. Sin inverts reality and fantasy. It makes that which is reality, God himself, into a fanciful flight of the imagination. To the sinful heart, that which is seen becomes reality,[90] and that which is actuality is reduced to a quaint and trite escape for the weak, the incapable, and the unfulfilled. God's Word, coupled with repentance and faith, reverses the error, removing enslaving fantasy and restoring reality to its rightful place.[91]

Prayer in Jesus' name continually effectuates repentance and faith so that, through prayer, one is confronted with reality anew, brought face-to-face with the truth, and prompted to renounce foolish chimera. Prayer is entrance into the core truth that God is sovereign and good, and that mankind, as creation, is not God, neither sovereign nor good. General Robert E. Lee (1807-1870), Southern commander during the United States Civil War, when informed that his Army chaplains prayed for him, welled up with tears of gratitude. "I sincerely thank you for that, and I can only say that I am a poor sinner, trusting in Christ alone, and that I need all the prayers you can offer for me."

> "'Remember, Lord, how I have walked before you faithfully and with wholehearted

---

[89] Jeremiah 29:13
[90] John 7:24
[91] 1 Peter 1:13

> devotion and have done what is good in your eyes.' And Hezekiah wept bitterly." (2 Kings 20:3)
>
> "I have been driven many times to humble prayer because I had nowhere else to go. My own wisdom, and that of everyone around me, seemed insufficient for the day." (Abraham Lincoln)

Everything about the world is geared for display and recognition from people, to enjoy social status. In this sense, the world hates even the concept of Christian prayer, that which is directed purely toward an all-knowing relational God, offering no ostensible personal aggrandizement. The world cannot countenance any act which does not overtly laud the self, does not garner the praises of men, or does not demonstrably advance one's prospects for the future. In this sense, Spirit-led prayer is the ultimate "anti-world" act, an utterly God-focused self-denial, begetting a lifestyle of disciplined self-denial.

> "Prayer is where the action is." (John Wesley)

The world often co-opts the concept of prayer, making it into a human-generated exercise beneficial for health or personal well-being,[92] or a mere statement of goodwill toward one's fellow citizen. From the world's perspective, prayer is principally a quaint show of solidarity between citizens or family members (while still permitting festering enmity and contempt for God). When the world prays it prays only to itself, and prayer to oneself is actually prayer to Satan.

The Pharisees prayed eloquently, but they prayed in their own strength, for their own glory, and ultimately Jesus charged them with praying to the devil. Mathew 6:5-8 states,

> 'And when you pray, do not be like the hypocrites, for they love to pray standing in the synagogues and on the street corners to be seen by others. Truly I tell you, they have received their reward in full. But when you pray, go into your room, close the door and pray to your Father, who is unseen. Then your Father, who sees what is done in secret, will reward you. And when you pray, do not keep on babbling like pagans, for they think they will be heard because of their many words. Do not be like them, for your Father knows what you need before you ask him.'

> "You belong to your father, the devil, and you want to carry out your father's desire. He was a murderer from the beginning, not holding to the truth, for there is no truth in him. When he lies, he speaks his native language, for he is a liar and the father of

---
[92] In Exodus 8:8 and 10:17, Pharaoh asked Moses for prayer. However, Pharaoh was disingenuous.

> lies." (John 8:44)

Stories of the Life and Passion of Jesus, Gaudenzio Ferrari, 1513

In summary, Christ-centered prayer affects a paradigm shift from self-centeredness to God-centeredness, the renunciation of a man-centered story, while entering into a God-centered story. In this way, prayer is itself an act of repentance. Believers pray to be delivered from temptation that they would not sin against God,[93] but the very act of asking is itself a turning from sin.

> "He who prays as he ought will endeavor to live as he prays." (John Owen)

Throughout Jesus' life each of those around him sought to change him, to pull him off of the center point of his Father's will. However, as Jesus' life demonstrated, truth is like a giant wheel with Jesus himself as its hub. Those who surrounded Jesus functioned as the wheel's spokes. Each sought to pull Jesus off of his center point, to cause him to deny a crucial aspect of his identity and mission.[94] While Jesus was centered on an axis of eternal truth, nearly every interpersonal interaction was an attempt to displace this axis. Satan tempted Jesus to throw himself down from the temple.[95] The Pharisees demanded a sign from heaven.[96] The crowds tried to seize Jesus in an attempt to make him king.[97] Disciples argued as to who would be the greatest in the kingdom.[98] Peter rebuked Jesus upon hearing of his intended suffering and death.[99]

---

[93] Matthew 6:13
[94] This wheel and hub concept from Jack Dean Kingsbury, *Matthew as Story* (Augsburg: Fortress Press, 1988)
[95] Matthew 4:6
[96] Mark 8:11
[97] John 6:15
[98] Luke 9:46
[99] Matthew 16:22

Most of those who interacted with Jesus sought to hijack him for their own wills and agendas, agendas scripted by sin-filled hearts. One could think of those sinful agendas as centrifugal forces (outwardly-directed, scattering) seeking to pull Jesus off his center point of relationship with his Father. (From classical mechanics one knows that centrifugal forces do not exist; they are an illusion arising from centripetal forces (inwardly-directed, focusing).) Try as they may, the various figures surrounding Jesus could not distract him from his ultimate plan to enact salvation. Jesus' life goal could not be thwarted because he remained perfectly centered on his Father's will.[100]

Prayer as Centripetal Force[101]

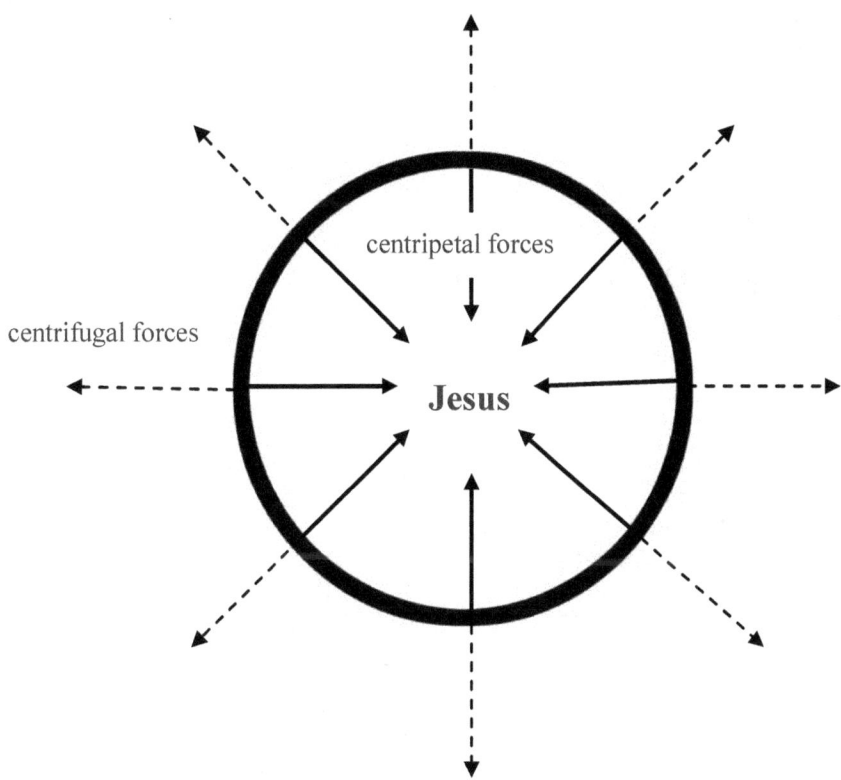

"In prayer it is better to have a heart without words than words without a heart." (John Bunyan)

Jesus' life, under the direction of his Father, could be thought of as being led by the Holy Spirit's "centripetal forces," a pull toward the center point of God's will.[102] Yet, as Jesus remained perfectly in his Father's will, he found himself in conflict with anyone lacking a strong and submissive faith. Those who lacked this faith advanced an agenda for Jesus that contrasted with, and often implicitly attacked, his Father's

---

[100] John 6:38
[101] For further discussion of the nature of Jesus' interaction with others see the excursus, "Bible Characters" in chapter 6: "The Basic Plotlines which Emerge in Counseling"
[102] Luke 22:42

will. Therefore, in contact with Jesus, one either repented and placed his faith in him, or else hardened his heart and turned to the world for answers.

> "Therefore confess your sins to each other and pray for each other so that you may be healed. The prayer of a righteous person is powerful and effective." (James 5:16)

The Presentation of Jesus in the Temple
Simon Vouet, 1641

This leads to a deeper understanding of prayer's import. Jesus taught his followers to pray that God's will would be done, not their own.[103] Prayer is less about changing God, and more about changing the one praying. In this regard, prayer is a realignment of worship, a submission to God's will as one no longer seeks to tug "centrifugally" but allows himself to be lead "centripetally." Prayer seeks to draw the believer to that center hub of Christ, no longer pulled off axis by the world (allure), the flesh (desire), and the devil (liar). Prayer is about entering into a conversation with God in which one is still,[104] sits at his feet, listens to his Word, learns from him, and finally worships him.

> "In prayer we shift the center of living from self-consciousness to self-surrender." (Abraham Joshua Heschel)

Prayer as Lifestyle

---
[103] Matthew 6:10
[104] Psalm 46:10

> "Is prayer your steering wheel or your spare tire?" (Corrie Ten Boom)

W. H. Auden (1907-1973) said, "Pray as though everything depended on God. Work as though everything depended on you." While this is an often quoted adage, it is fundamentally at odds with the Bible's perspective. The Bible recognizes that the believer's work and prayer are not opposing pursuits, but tandem acts of faith. The Christian both works and prays in full recognition of God's sovereignty. Prayer invites God into the believer's life so that his work conforms to God's will. In this way, prayer hammers one's will and work into the mold of Romans 11:36, "For from him and through him and for him are all things. To him be the glory forever! Amen."

> "In her deep anguish Hannah prayed to the Lord, weeping bitterly. And she made a vow, saying, 'Lord Almighty, if you will only look on your servant's misery and remember me, and not forget your servant but give her a son, then I will give him to the Lord for all the days of his life, and no razor will ever be used on his head.'" (1 Samuel 1: 10, 11)
>
> "Jabez cried out to the God of Israel, 'Oh, that you would bless me and enlarge my territory! Let your hand be with me, and keep me from harm so that I will be free from pain.' And God granted his request." (1 Chronicles 4:10)

John 15:7 states, "If you remain in me and my words remain in you, ask whatever you wish, and it will be given you." Jesus posed two conditions, "if you remain in me" and "my words remain in you." This means that as one basks in God himself, and feeds upon his Word, then what one wishes changes. The one who prays in the Spirit's power does not ask for things of the world, the engineering of events, or a change of situation. He asks for growth in holiness, repentance, wisdom, to rightly know how to love, and to desire that which God desires. Prayer should result in sanctification, a turning to God for greater holiness. If prayer does not result in change, it is self-serving and destructive.

> "Hurry is the death of prayer."(Samuel Chadwick)

Second Chronicles 7:14 states, "If my people, which are called by my name, shall humble themselves, and pray, and seek my face, and turn from their wicked ways; then will I hear from heaven, and will forgive their sin, and will heal their land." As the Christian prays he sparks an uprising against Satan's kingdom, launches a revolution that ushers in a heavenly regime on earth,[105] a regime in which God rules, his goodness reigns, and his desire is manifest. Thus, an inner revolution (that within hearts) sparks an outer revolution (that within the world).

---

[105] Hebrews 11:33

> "History belongs to the intercessors." (Henry Wink)

As an example of this inner-to-outer revolution, George Lewis (1769-1829), George Washington's (1732-1799) nephew, recounted that he witnessed "Washington's private devotions in his library both morning and evening; that on those occasions he had seen him in a kneeling position with a Bible open before him and that he believed such to have been his daily practice." During the Revolutionary War, General Robert Porterfield (1751-1843) stated he "found Washington on his knees, engaged in his morning's devotions." Alexander Hamilton (1755-1804) corroborated Porterfield's account, stating "such was [Washington's] most constant habit." A visiting French citizen who consorted with Washington stated, "Every day of the year, he rises at five in the morning; as soon as he is up, he dresses, then prays reverently to God."[106]

> Billy Graham stated that his greatest regret in life is that did not pray more.[107]

> Have mercy on me, O God,
>   according to your unfailing love;
> according to your great compassion
>   blot out my transgressions.
> Wash away all my iniquity
>   and cleanse me from my sin.
> For I know my transgressions,
>   and my sin is always before me.
> Against you, you only, have I sinned
>   and done what is evil in your sight;
> so you are right in your verdict
>   and justified when you judge.
> Surely I was sinful at birth,
>   sinful from the time my mother conceived me.
> Yet you desired faithfulness even in the womb;
>   you taught me wisdom in that secret place.
> Cleanse me with hyssop, and I will be clean;
>   wash me, and I will be whiter than snow.
> Let me hear joy and gladness;
>   let the bones you have crushed rejoice.
> Hide your face from my sins
>   and blot out all my iniquity.
> Create in me a pure heart, O God,
>   and renew a steadfast spirit within me.

---

[106] Jared Sparks, *Correspondence of the American Revolution; being Letters of Eminent Men to George Washington, from the Time of his taking Command of the Army to the End of his Presidency*, 4 volumes (1853)
[107] Billy Graham, *Just as I Am: The Autobiography of Billy Graham* (Harper One, 1999)

Do not cast me from your presence
 or take your Holy Spirit from me.
Restore to me the joy of your salvation
 and grant me a willing spirit, to sustain me.
Then I will teach transgressors your ways,
 so that sinners will turn back to you.
Deliver me from the guilt of bloodshed, O God,
 you who are God my Savior,
 and my tongue will sing of your righteousness.
Open my lips, Lord,
 and my mouth will declare your praise.
You do not delight in sacrifice, or I would bring it;
 you do not take pleasure in burnt offerings.
My sacrifice, O God, is a broken spirit;
 a broken and contrite heart
 you, God, will not despise.
May it please you to prosper Zion,
 to build up the walls of Jerusalem.
Then you will delight in the sacrifices of the righteous,
 in burnt offerings offered whole;
 then bulls will be offered on your altar. (Psalm 51)

The Merciful Knight
Sir Edward Burne-Jones, 1863

Categories for Prayer

> Romans 8:26 states, "In the same way, the Spirit helps us in our weakness. We do not know what we ought to pray for, but the Spirit himself intercedes for us with groans that words cannot express." Even if the Christian's prayers are inadequate and poorly articulated, the Holy Spirit himself intercedes to apply those prayers correctly.

1. Thanksgiving[108]

> "And pray in the Spirit on all occasions with all kinds of prayers and requests. With this in mind, be alert and always keep on praying for all the Lord's people. (Ephesians 6:18)

2. Salvation

> "Simon, Simon, Satan has asked to sift all of you as wheat. But I have prayed for you, Simon, that your faith may not fail. And when you have turned back, strengthen your brothers." (Luke 22:31)

3. Intercession

> "The men turned away and went toward Sodom, but Abraham remained standing before the Lord. Then Abraham approached him and said: 'Will you sweep away the righteous with the wicked?'" (Genesis 18:22, 23)
>
> "As long as Moses held up his hands, the Israelites were winning, but whenever he lowered his hands, the Amalekites were winning. When Moses' hands grew tired, they took a stone and put it under him and he sat on it. Aaron and Hur held his hands up—one on one side, one on the other—so that his hands remained steady till sunset. So Joshua overcame the Amalekite army with the sword." (Exodus 17:11-13)
>
> "But Moses sought the favor of the Lord his God. 'Lord,' he said, 'why should your anger burn against your people, whom you brought out of Egypt with great power and a mighty hand? Why should the Egyptians say, 'It was with evil intent that he brought them out, to kill them in the mountains and to wipe them off the face of the earth'? Turn from your fierce anger; relent and do not bring disaster on your people.'" (Exodus 32:11, 12)
>
> "When a period of feasting had run its course, Job would make arrangements for them to be purified. Early in the morning he would sacrifice a burnt offering for each of them, thinking, 'Perhaps my children have sinned and cursed God in their hearts.' This was Job's regular custom." (Job 1:5)
>
> "Then Queen Esther answered, 'If I have found favor with you, Your Majesty, and if it pleases you, grant me my life—this is my petition. And spare my people—this is my request.'" (Esther 7:3)

---

[108] For additional discussion of thanksgiving see "Incentivized Repentance: Gratitude Reversal" in the second book in this series, *What Agreement Is There Between the Temple of God and Idols?: The Accidence of Sin and Idolatry*, chapter 8: "The Search for Eldorado Ends: Repenting of Idols of the Heart"

> "I thank my God every time I remember you. In all my prayers for all of you, I always pray with joy because of your partnership in the gospel from the first day until now," (Philippians 1:3-5)

4. Imprecatory

The Death of Samson, Gustave Dore, d. 1883

> "Then Samson prayed to the LORD, 'O Sovereign LORD, remember me. O God, please strengthen me just once more, and let me with one blow get revenge on the Philistines for my two eyes.'" (Judges 16:28)

> "May the LORD judge between you and me. And may the LORD avenge the wrongs you have done to me, but my hand will not touch you." (1 Samuel 24:12)

5. Personal Concerns

> "So God said to him, 'Since you have asked for this and not for long life or wealth for yourself, nor have asked for the death of your enemies but for discernment in administering justice, I will do what you have asked. I will give you a wise and discerning heart, so that there will never have been anyone like you, nor will there ever be.'" (1 Kings 3:11, 12)
>
> "'Woe to me!' I cried. 'I am ruined! For I am a man of unclean lips, and I live among a people of unclean lips, and my eyes have seen the King, the Lord Almighty.'" (Isaiah 6:5)
>
> "Do not be anxious about anything, but in every situation, by prayer and petition, with thanksgiving, present your requests to God." (Philippians 4:6)

A Prayer Outline

Thanksgiving and Praise	Scripture
1. For the wonder of the creation	Psalm 8:1
2. For investing God's own image into mankind	Psalm 139:14
3. That the earth's environment was perfectly designed, manifesting God's character	Isaiah 55:12
4. For sending Jesus to die for sinners	Romans 5:8
5. For renewing believers in Christ	1 Corinthians 1:2
6. For glorifying God's people on account of Jesus	Romans 8:30

The Church	Scripture
1. That the church would reflect Christ, preach the gospel faithfully, and be free from doctrinal error	1 Corinthians 1:7, 8 1 Timothy 4:16 2 Peter 1:16
2. That God would uphold his church as salt and light to a dying world	Matthew 5:13-16
3. That false believers and false teachers would not be allowed to destroy the church's witness and vitality	2 Corinthians 11:26 2 Peter 2:1
4. That Jesus' return would be swift and certain	Hebrews 10:25

The World	Scripture
1. For the spread of faith in Jesus throughout the world, and for an outpouring of his Spirit	Psalm 48:10 Matthew 2:9, 10
2. That the Jews would find faith in Jesus, and be used to spread the gospel to the world	Romans 11:1

3. For an end to the persecution of Christians throughout the world, especially in Islamic states	Micah 2:1 Hebrews 11:37
4. For peace throughout the world, and the rebuilding of war-torn and shattered lives	Romans 16:20
5. For stability and abundance in food and water supplies	Luke 12:27
6. For protection of the environment, and the elimination of threats to all living creatures	Hosea 4:2, 3; Matthew 10:29
7. That evil would be decisively eliminated along with its architect, Satan	Revelation 20:1-3

Society	Scripture
1. For a transformative Christian influence on society	Acts 17:2–4
2. That political leaders would be faithful Christians who govern with equity for all	1 Timothy 2:1-2
3. For an end to legalized abortion, and all murder and injustice throughout the world	Jeremiah 1:5
4. For a renunciation of the lies of evolution, humanism, and psychology	Colossians 2:8
5. For an end to damaging cultural influences such as sexualized attire, hip-hop and rap music, pornography, and television	1 John 5:21
6. For an end to deception, the love of money, and obsession with the praises of men	Matthew 6:19
7. That education would present the truth	Romans 1:19, 20, 28
8. That Christians would uphold honest business practice, and pay taxes responsibly	Mark 12:17
9. That society would be free from violence	Matthew 6:13
10. That Christians would be bold to oppose evil regardless of the personal cost	Daniel 3:17, 18

Individuals	Scripture
1. For parents, siblings, and relatives to receive Christ	Joshua 24:15
2. For friends and coworkers to receive Christ	Acts 2:47
3. For acquaintances and strangers to be impacted by believers' witness for Christ	Ephesians 5:15, 16
4. That each Christian would seek forgiveness from those he has wronged, and that he would in turn offer forgiveness	Matthew 18:21, 22
5. To be prepared to share God's Word "in season and out of season"	2 Timothy 4:2

Personal	Scripture
1. That Christians would live a life of humility and simplicity in a perverse world	Acts 4:32-35
2. That Christians would be faithful to Jesus in all things	2 Corinthians 11:24-29
3. That Christians would do violence to their sin and idolatry, forsaking all things that impede complete obedience to Christ	Matthew 18:9
4. For daily Scripture study which stores God's Word within the heart	Psalm 119:11
5. For protection from the world's sights and sounds; that Christians would look upon no unholy thing, and renounce the things of the world	Romans 16:19 Ephesians 5:12, 13
6. For changed hearts from which flow wholesome and edifying words	Colossians 4:6
7. That Christians would more deeply love even their enemies	Matthew 5:44

- 5 -

NAVIGATING THE COUNSELING FJORD:
Preliminary Reconnaissance

Chalk Cliffs on Rugen, Caspar David Friedrich, c. 1818

From *Urim* and *Thummin* to Incarnational Counseling

The ancient Israelite priests consulted the *Urim* and *Thummim* to determine God's answer to binary questions.[1] While this method served an integral purpose in God's redemptive-historical plans, it has been replaced by the living Jesus in the hearts of believers. However, despite the towering gift of Jesus

---
[1] Exodus 28:30

(God with us),[2] many Christians seek counseling which offers a mere *Urim* and *Thummim* approach. Treating counseling like a form of divination - the counselee's search for a cold "yes" or "no" - is a faithless means of dealing with life questions. This approach merely seeks God's affirmation or denial without relationship with God, and as such, is an abuse of the Holy Spirit's work, a manipulation of God for self-serving purpose. The Holy Spirit communicates through ever-deepening relationship, in the context of God's Word, and in the fellowship of a body of believers, not through miracle, sign, or lifeless answer.

In tune with the *Urim* and *Thummim* approach to counseling, people either want God to fit neatly into their stories, or else to remove him entirely. However, while the sinner seeks a midrashic approach in his quest for his own exoneration, the Bible alone interprets man's sinful state, the burden of his incessant guilt and the siren call to repentance. Incarnational counseling works to draw the counselee into the wonder, peace, power, and blessing of relationship with this holy God. To this end, it endeavors to revolutionize sinners with God's own story.

God does not seek mere subservient automatons. He instead longs to include regenerate repentant sinners into his eternal plans for the universe. God makes his people privy to himself and his designs, sons and daughters who are treasured allies in a climactic mission. John 15:15 states, "I no longer call you servants, because a servant does not know his master's business. Instead, I have called you friends, for everything that I learned from my Father I have made known to you." It is the objective of incarnational counseling to maintain this point on the horizon and to navigate toward it, wholly redeemed believers fully participating in God's redemptive-historical plans as glorified saints.

> "These people come near to me with their mouth and honor me with their lips, but their hearts are far from me. Their worship of me is made up only of rules taught by men. Therefore once more I will astound these people with wonder upon wonder; the wisdom of the wise will perish, the intelligence of the intelligent will vanish." (Isaiah 29:13)

The Travail of Societal Expectation

> "Those who laugh on Friday will cry on Sunday."

A cruising airplane is stable as long as it propels itself forward. Yet, as soon as its engines stall, it falls like a rock.[3] A train runs smoothly as long as it remains on its

---

[2] Isaiah 7:14
[3] Based on Bernoulli's principle this statement is technically incorrect. An airplane does not necessarily fall when its engines stall but rather when its wings lose lift. However, for the purposes of this section the analogy has been simplified.

track. Once it leaves that track it is a mangled wreck. The same is often true of people. As long as they are propelled forward and remain on track, they seem to generally function well. They appear balanced, happy, and often prosperous. As long as each meets his personal expectations, fulfills his goals, and achieves a standard set by society, he usually remains content and self-satisfied. As life measures up to expectations people feel no need for God or his offer of salvation.[4] Such people see little purpose for Jesus except as either a quaint model of moral rectitude, or as a Shroud of Turin museum piece to be admired from a distance. Here are some examples:

1. Often ambitious and progressively-minded, college students are optimistic that once they earn a degree they will enjoy numerous prospects for success.

2. "Twenty-somethings" focus on launching a career, finding a spouse, and starting a family.

3. Those in their thirties and forties expect to be thriving in a career, to have raised well-behaved children, and to enjoy leisure time with successful friends.

> In about 1980, 38% of Americans said that a "good life" involved making a lot of money. Today, 63% hold this view. Of those Americans in their thirties, nearly 50% say that making a great deal of money is very important to them, and 75% say that fulfilling their personal dreams is very important.

4. Those in their fifties and sixties expect to reap the fruit of a rewarding career, now that they have reached the pinnacle of their profession. The marks of success are a large house, admirable adult children, and enjoying the company (or soon to) of grandchildren. They look forward to retirement, and its abundant leisure time.

> "In youth the days are short and the years are long; in old age the years are short and the days long." (Nikita Panin)

For most people life is essentially a giant chess match of maneuvering within this life trapezoid (the four stages outlined above). This match seems to follow a set pattern: marry; have children; own a large home; exude an image of ease, prestige, and luxury; and finally, retire at the top of one's game in comfort, surrounded by loving family, and with the world as one's oyster. Those who seem to garner the game-pieces earlier, and more effectively, are seen as more skilled players of "life," the triumphant conquerors. While those who seem to struggle in assembling the pieces, are seen as less skilled. Thus, those who appear to be better at playing the game are labeled "successful," while those who seem to miss crucial pieces are, to some degree, labeled

---

[4] Deuteronomy 8:11-14

"failed."

> The concept "relative deprivation" means that people judge their success or failure based on comparison with their *immediate* peers, not based on the world as a whole. Thus, an average student at a top university may be far more capable than a top student at a lower-level college. However, the average student at the top college often adjudges himself unfit for certain studies (medical school, for example), while the top student at the lower-level college considers himself highly-capable in a host of fields.

As with Adam and Eve, mankind continues to seek mastery of his own destiny, to determine his own future, for his own glory. This is the center point of man's sin, the desire for autonomy vis-à-vis a holy God. Where there is no true God, life events (milestones) become the only motivator, the lode stone of the moral compass. With little other guiding passion, life quickly devolves into a grand vaudeville stage show.

> "Adversity makes men, and prosperity makes monsters." (Victor Hugo)

The Gare Montparnasse, Paris
1895

As long as people stay on the track society has lain down, life is bucolic, happily progressing according to the personal kingdom-building blueprints. However, something unexpected always happens on the path to earthly paradise. At some point, in God's mercy, the engines stall and the airplane plummets; the track buckles, and the train derails, so that one's plans and dreams are imperiled. When people fail to maintain that socially expected "altitude," when they fail to remain on track, they feel vulnerable, lost, afraid, depressed, and angry. They soon search for answers.

> "A heart can ache beneath diamond jewelry, or dance beneath tattered clothing." (Edwin Hubbel Chapin)

The college student who cannot find a boyfriend, the twenty-something who cannot find a suitable job, those in their thirties who are unable to conceive a child, those in their fifties who do not wear the chevron of material success, the retiree who cannot afford to travel the world, these are the ones whose lives have in some way veered off track (as the world reckons). The engine has stalled, and they perceive themselves to be in freefall, hurdling toward the earth with Icarian peril.

One day a man wakes up to discover that everything he has achieved leaves him unfulfilled. A housewife feels trapped in a cold and distant marriage. A retiree worries about not having enough savings and the humiliation associated with continuing to work while his friends traverse the globe. Those who cannot garner all the game pieces (or even some of them) often seek consolation prizes. The young woman who cannot find a suitable husband might pour herself into her work and seek financial accolades. The one who cannot retire in comfort may seek ways to appear noble and altruistic – working late into life or volunteering as an excuse for not enjoying the lifestyle of his peers.

One day each person finds himself at an existential crossroads, a moment when his life fails to measure up to expectations. When life no longer measures up it begins to unravel; it swirls like a constellation of confusing points of light with no guiding pattern. This is when some get involved in an extramarital affair, embezzle from an employer, spend long nights drinking at a bar, fall into fits of rage, or resort to other grievous sins. It is at this crossroads that God posses the question, "Will one seek Jesus and receive him by faith, or will one, in searing angst, begin a downward spiral into oblivion?"

> "There is a crack in everything; this is how the light gets in." (Leonard Cohen)

From a man-centered vantage point, these people's lives are not working. From the wise counselor's vantage point, there is an entirely different understanding; idols are flailing, failing, and being exposed as frauds. This is God's master plan to reach sinners with the gospel's soul-healing balm. It is those who are in freefall, those who are careening off the tracks, who are, in some regard, most prepared to receive Jesus Christ as savior. It is generally those who have lost hope in the things of the world who are most willing to search for hope in a God who offers rescue in the wreckage. Thus, if God is merciful he, sooner or later, wills every sinful pursuit to fail, every human effort at kingdom-building to crumble.

> In the Bible the cistern is synonymous with stagnant festering diseased waters. Thus, Jeremiah 2:13 admonishes those who "hew out cisterns for themselves," those who refuse to tap into the flowing waters of the fountain of life, God himself. Diseased water is the inevitable drink of those seeking life goals to the exclusion of God. For those who build their kingdoms on this earth, life invariably becomes a drawing from a stagnant cistern.

The Allure of Counseling[5]

When life lies in shambles, and dreams are dashed upon the rocks, people seek counseling (whether formal or informal). They look for someone to help them get on track again, help in resuscitating their idols. They seek assistance to become that which they most desire – happy, wealthy, respected, and comfortable (as the counselee defines these concepts). To the counselee, the counselor merely serves as handmaiden to a larger strategy for getting what the counselee most desires. The counselee, to the extent that he loves his sin, does not want to know God in the midst of life's vagary and vicissitude. He simply wants the counselor to "fix" life's presumed brokenness.

> "Religion is regarded by the common people as true, by the wise as false, and by the rulers as useful." (Seneca)

In this pursuit of getting life back on track, people frequently form surrogate therapy sessions (an impromptu social club, a coffee klatch, a smoking clique, etc.) in order to receive counseling. Men playing chess on the street have formed an impromptu counseling session with their own standards of right and wrong, good and bad, and their own "gospel of salvation." Likewise, housewives chatting over tea, offer and receive counseling with their own code of morality and message of salvation. Counseling takes place in every human interaction, and in wildly diverse settings, but the question is, "What type of counseling is it, and for what purpose?"

> "Some people have abundance, but do not live an abundant life."[6]

One seeks counseling (in various forms and venues) looking for a formula for happiness. The wise counselor circumvents this agenda in order to direct the counselee toward seeking greater holiness. Thus, the counselee and counselor are fundamentally at cross-purposes. (That is to be expected, and is frequently a necessary component of the counseling enterprise.) The counselee craves a life that works, while the wise counselor offers a vision of life that submits and obeys. This strikes up against one of the greatest challenges of counseling: how to help others recognize that

---

[5] For additional discussion of the issue of pragmatism in counseling see "The Allure of Caring Pragmatism: 'Solutions Are Not the Answer'" in the first book in this series, *Ask for the Ancient Paths: From Art to Artifice to Arisen*, chapter 10: "The Third-Way of Sanctification: From Abominable to Indomitable"
[6] Statement from Luke Wang

they need help of a very specific type, help that they do not know they need.

> "God takes our twisted insane perspective and makes it sane and rightly aligned." (David Powlison)

The counselor does not merely respond to problems as they arise. He sees the trajectory of one's life and goes on the offensive. He seeks to divert a speeding train on the wrong track before it becomes a mangled wreck. Thus, the counselor continually seeks small but significant confrontations of the counselee's worshipping core.[7] Just as water in time cuts through stone, so too, slight daily realignments with the gospel, in time, have a profound affect (a kind of butterfly effect which regard to heart worship).

I Am Half Sick of Shadows
John William Waterhouse, 1915

Let's be clear about a crucial point. Every life, no matter how seemingly stable and secure, when outside of Christ, is in peril. Every person, when neither indwelled by Christ nor in obedience to him, is in danger of making potentially life-altering decisions. If not for God's restraining grace, every life is one misstep away from disaster. Seemingly inconsequential and innocuous, sin has the potential to overrun and devastate any life. This is why the wise counselor does not focus on social trappings or dwell on behavior. He spies evidence of heart worship as this is the only true predictor of the trajectory of one's life.

> Thomas Edison (1847–1931) was almost completely deaf but listened through his

---

[7] Paul Tripp, *Instruments in the Redeemer's Hands: People in Need of Change Helping People in Need of Change* (Presbyterian and Reformed Publishing, 2002)

> teeth. He could perfectly tune a piano by biting down on its edge and feeling the vibration of the notes.[8] As with Edison, while pragmatism permits life to function, it offers no guidance on what to listen to, or what the point is of listening in the first place. The wise counselor does not merely seek to help the spiritually deaf to hear by other means, but redefines hearing altogether.

An unbelieving single mother is raising her adopted daughter. She keeps her daughter well-dressed and teaches her to be polite. The daughter diligently cleans her room and helps her mother with chores. While to the outside world this mother is held up as a crowning example of model parenting, there are far deeper issues which a wise counselor discerns. The mother has made her daughter into an idol. She meticulously monitors the daughter's activities, never letting her out of her sight (commonly referred to as "helicopter parenting"). This mother makes sure that she and her daughter are emotionally enmeshed. The mother even makes her daughter into her personal counselor and confidant. While this casts the daughter as a trusted friend, it results in the neglect of needed discipline. The mother makes her daughter into the playmate she never had, into the emotional support she longs for in a spouse, and into her daily support group.

While on the surface this appears to be an exemplary mother-daughter relationship, there are relational fissures which will grow with time. As the mother continues to make her daughter her god, she slowly squeezes life from her. Like an abyss of need that is never filled, the mother seeks greater emotional affirmation from her daughter, all the while forsaking the larger mission that her daughter would be disciplined (so as to lay the foundation for future submission to God). To the outside world this is a train firmly on its track; to the wise counselor this train is one misaligned rail away from a wreck. It may be that a measure of teenage independence, moving away to college, or eventually getting married will prove to be that misaligned rail (or the crisis point may come much sooner).

> "My people come to you, as they usually do, and sit before you to listen to your words, but they do not put them into practice. With their mouths they express devotion, but their hearts are greedy for unjust gain. Indeed, to them you are nothing more than one who sings love songs with a beautiful voice and plays an instrument well, for they hear your words but do not put them into practice." (Ezekiel 33:31, 32)

The counselee will never understand his life as long as he operates out of a fallacious set of assumptions and pursues pseudo-triumphant goals. When he relinquishes his quest for happiness, and takes up the cause of holiness in Christ, life begins. When aligned with holiness, life starts to make sense, relationships are rightly ordered, and decisions bring prosperity. The hope is that in time the counselee will abandon his

---

[8] Neil Baldwin, *Edison: Inventing the Century* (New York: Hyperion Books, 1996)

sinful agenda so that Christ will ascend (with the counselor as servant, advocate, and catalyst).

The South Sea Bubble, Edward Matthew Ward, 1846

To those who suffer from dysfunctional idols, feckless Christianity often appears to be a safe haven, a refuge for those who seek to be loved, extended grace, and shown mercy. Some, thus, search for a message that will both shield those idols and advance their self-serving cause. While the counselor rightly loves and cares for people, he affords idols no safe harbor in Christ. Regardless of the perception, God's love, grace, and mercy are neither man-centered nor man-exonerating, and are never to be construed as a tacit sanctuary for sin. While unrepentant mankind seeks an unconditional love which leaves his core rebellion untouched, his root idolatries unchallenged, the Bible seeks the death of the self with its treasonous allegiances.[9] Thus, the Bible stops at nothing less than the resurrection of a new self through faith in Jesus Christ. The Bible casts God's love, grace, and mercy in utterly gospel-centered terms to, in effect, crucify the self and allow Jesus to reign.

> The counselor mirrors God's love which carries with it hatred for sin, jealously when separated from his people, and a desire to fight for, and with, those he loves. The

---
[9] Galatians 2:20

> counselor rightly reflects the entire spectrum of God's love, so that the fullness of God may be manifest to the counselee.[10]

The counselor must recognize that the counselee's idols are operative even while counseling occurs.[11] Idols sprawl and sprattle for protection in the midst of being confronted, wrapping their tentacles around any seemingly unassailable object (anything, be it false piety, blame-shifting, or threats of reprisal, that appears to repel the extraction effort). Thus, the sinner harbors a singular intention, to guard his idols at all costs. To this end, idols adopt highly-sophisticated mimetic devices, taking on the appearance of good and noble character. And while a counselee may generally manipulate others for his own ends, he cannot escape the gospel's glaring light and blaring siren. The gospel is a clarion call to those under the wrath of a holy God to repent, renounce their false gods, and turn to Jesus in faith. This message is highly-resistant to being finessed or finagled. It is either entirely accepted or entirely rejected. It either takes root in the heart with explosive power, or else is trampled underfoot.

Never does anyone seek counseling to remove idols from the heart. With overwhelming uniformity people seek counseling to fundamentally feel better and to find relief for (not from) besieged idols. They seek a means to make their idols work so as to regain lost self-confidence, or as the warrant for life lived without God. The counselor, if he is faithful to his calling, does not seek to make life merely "work" for the counselee. He does not offer mere pragmatic means for coping with, or managing, missed milestones in the lifecycle. In fact, he does quite the opposite; he draws the counselee from pragmatic solutions toward that which most impacts the heart.

> To be effective in impacting the world, Christians must demonstrate that the Bible understands people far better than psychology does, that the Bible makes sense of and gives answers to the human dilemma with far greater persuasion than anything the world can possibly offer. If Christians, under the Holy Spirit's guidance, can convince people that the Bible understands them with stunning clarity that will go a long way toward winning the world to Christ.

The Presenting Problem

On February 25, 1942, an infamous UFO sighting occurred in Los Angeles, California, when, for twenty minutes, the U.S. Army fired at a blazing object in the sky. Without warning the object disappeared. In the process, the Army had battered cars and homes throughout the city causing millions of dollars in property damage. (This incident became derisively known as "The Battle of Los Angeles," and is cited as an

---

[10] For a more complete discussion of God's love please see the case study "God's *Sui Generis* Love" in chapter 2: "Suffering: The Kintsugi Objective."
[11] Paul Tripp, Westminster Theological Seminary, Philadelphia, Pennsylvania

example of the absurdity in thinking that UFOs exist.) This serves as a fitting introduction to the topic of the presenting problem, or diversionary tactics, in counseling. Often the counselor chases "bright objects in the sky" thinking they are the enemy but, when the dust settles, it is revealed that he has only done more harm than good.

Idols of the heart never openly reveal themselves and, in fact, are highly-adept at concealing themselves. They lurk behind a host of experiences, woven into those experiences and navigating them for self-serving purpose. Idols may even lie dormant for a time only showing themselves when a trigger temptation arises. Dysfunctional idols, thus, must be ferreted out of these various experiences. In this way, any experience or life event, when correctly parsed, potentially serves as an entrance point for counseling. The key issue is, "Is that event tied to idolatry? In what way does it offer a window into an idolatrous heart?" It is not the severity or gravity of the event, but what it reveals, that is of importance to the counselor.

> Second Timothy 2:16 states, "Avoid godless chatter, because those who indulge in it will become more and more ungodly." When people speak, listen carefully. Each conversation is a referendum on the speaker's inherent goodness, injustices endured, plights overcome, and his manifest superiority. Most conversation contains a subtext that is cunningly self-centered, self-aggrandizing, and highly-suspicious of God. Every statement, every act, and every thought either advances the cause of God's work in one's life or else vitiates against it. There is nothing neutral with regard to the human experience and psyche. Even what appears as idle chatter, of seemingly no consequence, more deeply embeds godlessness into one's worshipping core.

The presenting problem may include any of the following experiences:

1. Past abuse and emotional pain
2. A pattern of broken relationships
3. A persistent lack of discipline, contempt for authority
4. Chronic financial woes
5. Sought after escapes
6. Seeking to be accepted and encouraged

Think of the counselee as a diamond with facets; any facet can be a window into the diamond's core. Likewise, any presenting problem, no matter how seemingly trivial, can serve as an entrance point into the heart.

> Restaurant menus are carefully designed so that the highest profit items are given prominence while lower profit items are "hidden" somewhere in the middle. This, in many ways, captures the issue of the presenting problem in counseling. Counselees

> carefully conceal idols, obscuring them with circumstantial issues. The key is not to take the bait, not to run after issues at face value, but rather to search for the submerged desires which cower below camouflage.

The Sword of Damocles, Richard Westall, 1812

While the counselor never lacks compassion for hurting people, the counselee's presenting problem is rarely the problem that the counselor should address.[12] The presenting problem is either:

1. A deliberate obfuscation, a carefully designed smokescreen keeping the counselor from the real issue.

2. A distracting superficiality, an attempt to deal with pragmatic issues while neglecting the heart.

> The sinner is vigilant in guarding his own reputation, and quick to defend himself, when he perceives himself to be wronged. Yet, he is slow to guard others'

---

[12] John Bettler, Westminster Theological Seminary, Philadelphia, Pennsylvania

> reputations, and easily overlooks an offense against another, often explaining it away.

Examples:

The Presenting Problem	What Counselee Wants to Hear	What the Biblical Counselor Focuses on
1. The boss criticized counselee's work	The boss is the problem; methods for managing the boss; confidence-building techniques	The counselee has made the boss' acceptance into his idol; repentance for seeking any person's approval over God's
2. The counselee's wife never listens	The wife fails to submit; methods for managing the wife; strategies for getting the wife to comply and show respect	The counselee craves his wife's attention; repentance of inordinately desiring respect
3. The counselee is wasteful with money	Techniques for how to manage money; financial strategies	Wrongly desiring the things of the world; being easily led astray by the lusts of the flesh

The presenting problem is a collection of facts which are necessarily theory-laden. Factual data is always presented in a theoretical framework, and that data is never objective or neutral. The facts that are chosen, and their presentation, always arise out of an interpretive framework of sin or faith. One sees what his paradigm allows him to see.[13] As sinners prioritize circumstance, they are blinded to themselves and others, and most especially, to God and his work. This blinding causes sinners to be darkened with regard to the rhythms and tides of their hearts, making them susceptible to ever greater deception.[14]

> "Experience" is just a euphemism for one's mistakes. (adapted from Oscar Wilde)

The Temptation of Circumstance

> "By radically changing his circumstances the poet [Johann Wolfgang von Goethe (1749-1832)] hopes to get closer once more to the meaning of his own existence and to be able to return again 'reborn.'"[15]

---

[13] David Powlison, Westminster Theological Seminary, Philadelphia, Pennsylvania
[14] 2 Corinthians 4:4
[15] Letter written about Johann Wolfgang von Goethe as he traveled in Umbria, Italy

Adam and Eve rationalized their sin by means of their situation. Genesis 3:12, 13 states, "The man said, 'The woman you put here with me—she gave me some fruit from the tree, and I ate it.' Then the Lord God said to the woman, 'What is this you have done?' The woman said, 'The serpent deceived me, and I ate.'" Sin's counterfeit explanation is that behavior arises from situation, not from the heart.

Indwelling sin changes God-centered questions into man-centered ones:[16]

A God-centered Question…	…Becomes a Man-centered Question	The God-centered Answer
1. Why do I do what I do?	Why is this happening to me?	Heart commitments
2. What should I be like?	What do I want? *To be happy*	Jesus
3. What is wrong with me?	Becomes simply, what is wrong? *Circumstances*	False worship, misdirected glory
4. How do I change?	What would make things alright? *A change in circumstances would fix everything (including me).*	Come to Christ — repent, be changed, pursue his righteousness

People act from their hearts, never from their situation,[17] and regardless of the circumstance, the heart always operates in the exact same manner. If one merely changes the circumstances, the heart continues to bear the same fruit (whether good or bad). Thus, God places each person (whether Christian or non-Christian) in various situations to reveal the truth in, and to, that person.

> "In all chaos there is a cosmos, in all disorder a secret order." (Carl Jung)

In writing this book I experienced recurring fear of inadvertently losing large sections of text, thus possibly negating days of tedious work. I initially sought various approaches to the problem, all of them pragmatic. I could save the contents daily, or make certain that I was the only user on my computer. However, these solutions missed the heart issues. The problem was that at times, and in certain ways, this book had become my idol, a desire to have something to show for my years of study and ministry. This, also, was at times a well-crafted cover for the idol of seeking to be respected by others.

In time it occurred to me that God himself would protect this book to extent he desired. It is his project, his work in and through me, to will and to work for his

---
[16] David and Sharon Covington, "Introduction to Biblical Counseling" notes, 2004
[17] David and Sharon Covington, "Introduction to Biblical Counseling" notes, 2004; also see Matthew 15:10, 17-20

eternal purpose.[18] If certain sections were inadvertently deleted, then either God did not want those sections included, or else he would reconstruct them. But that was all secondary to a far more pressing issue. Seeing God as merely meeting the perceived pragmatic need appeared faithful, but in fact, it was not.

Vanitas Still Life with Thinking Young Man, Samuel Dirksz van Hoogstraten, c. 1645

My heart was fearful of a particular circumstance (the loss of text) so it merely sought to recognize God as sovereign over the circumstance (which he is), while leaving the heart which gave rise to the fear untouched. I superficially defined faith as handing over to God a potentially fearful circumstance, while failing to address the idols which mediate the significance of the circumstance and, thus, stand behind the fear. In order to keep my idolatry well-guarded, I merely sought to mitigate the circumstance's threat with a God who would guard me from its potential consequence. This I defined as "faith," so that faith became submission to God solely within the bounds of the circumstance. Had I not more deeply plumbed my motive, I would have declared myself as having exhibited faith, when in fact the recessed idol remained unaccosted.

At issue was surrendering this project to God as an act of worship, to recognize that this book does not belong to me, was not created by me (from God's perspective), and therefore must be relinquished to God. The book itself (regardless of its final outcome)

---

[18] Philippians 2:13

became a leitmotif for seeking the praises of men. It was, in fact, this idol from which I needed deliverance, not the circumstance. In simply surrendering the circumstance to God, I had left unchecked the idol which characterized the circumstance in my heart. God therefore used the circumstance to prompt repentance of the underlying idolatry; that was his intent all along. Thus, it was through ongoing confrontation of my own heart, and continued restoration of my relationship with God, that God orchestrated much needed change within me.

> "Above all else, guard your heart for it is the wellspring of life." (Proverbs 4:23)

The Elements of Circumstance (using the example presented above)

A Tree Analogy	Element Revealed	Meaning
1. Branches and leaves	A pragmatic need seeking resolution	"I need a way to protect my text."
2. Trunk	Trusting God to meet the pragmatic need	"God himself will protect my text."
3. Roots	Surrendering the notion of pragmatic need so as to focus on idolatry	"God wills and works to affect sanctification regardless of the state of the text."

The sinful heart, while appearing faith-driven, summons God to merely abrogate the pragmatic need, so that faith is defined as trusting God to meet that need. However, this is actually a cunning charade, as God operates in an entirely different dimension. God leverages the pragmatic to expose heart idols. Thus, God effects sanctification regardless of the outcome of the perceived need, mobilizing to expunge idols so that sincere worship would rein. Thus, God's intention is always to go after the root of sin. This means transcending the very concept of the pragmatic (the pragmatic merely addressing the presenting problem).

Forging Automorphic Alliances

A fundamental counseling issue is to recognize that the counselee passionately pursues allies in his sin. He seeks those who will help make his sin work, friends who will not expose his idols, but rather offer tactics by which those idols may function unassailed. The sinner seeks associates who comfort him in his rebellion, who aid and abet his defiance against God, all the while appearing noble. The counselee surrounds himself with any means of support so that the nagging pain of his sin is mitigated.

Those who are particularly fearful are quick to form automorphic alliances, alliances patterned after the idolater's own devious desire. The automorphic alliance is designed to appear mutually altruistic and outwardly loving so as to advance the narrative that one is innocent in his sin. Such associations are actually friendships of convenience, only maintained until the perceived threat is neutralized. The wise counselor keeps an eye out for such pacts of convenience, seeking to expose them if they merely function as a shield for idolatry.

The counselee's desire for an ally in his rebellion is usually the reason he comes for counseling in the first place. He wants the counselor to moralize the gospel, and in so doing, to trivialize his sin. The counselee wants the counselor to reassure him that he can ultimately win in his conflict with God (or, if not, at least minimize the hazards in that conflict), while concocting a false repentance built upon his own prideful effort. The wise counselor sees through such artful tactics. He short-circuits the process, refusing to acquiesce, or to be an accessory to the plan. Instead, the counselor exposes the entire enterprise so as to induce repentance before the living God.

The counselee's quest for allies often hijacks, strong-arms, and coerces the counseling endeavor in the hope that idolatry would produce abundant life. Thus, one of the gravest threats in counseling is the danger of producing false fruit. False fruit can assume many mimetic forms depending on the exigencies of the moment, and it is so deceptive because it can be accompanied by false peace and false confidence. However, the counselor is tipped off to false fruit when the underlying heart idols have never been challenged, have never been confronted in the name of Christ. When idols remain unharassed, the fruit which arises is always fake.

In a world swirling with self-absorbed and barren relationships, the very act of listening to a counselee, showing concern and offering advice, is in itself a comforting experience for most (hence the attraction of Rogerian psychology). However, the counselor must guard the integrity of the counseling engagement, and the God at work in its midst. He must not let the felt demands of the moment override the larger eternal objective. In this way, the counselor must be vigilant to guard the counselee from the false fruit of mock repentance and its perfidious pseudo-sanctification.

> Philosopher Laozi (6th C. BC) wrote "A good traveler leaves no track." Likewise a wise counselor leaves upon the counselee no mark of his own subjective opinion or sin patterns, but rather only that of God's Word and the blessing of abiding relationship with Jesus Christ.

Often if the counselee leaves the counseling interaction with a definitive answer and merely feeling better, both the counselee and the counselor brand the counseling a success. However, a "closed counseling loop" (a tightly-wrapped package of counsel), and a euphoric feeling, may be counterproductive to God's intent. The counselor may have done nothing more than resuscitate dysfunctional idols, or he may have inadvertently exchanged a functional idol for a malfunctioning one. The counselor, as he resorts to pragmatic solutions, often unwittingly dangles before the counselee little more than viable idols made to look like renewed faith.

> Proverbs 13:15 states, "…the way of the transgressor (or treacherous) is hard." The sinner's life is not supposed to work; in some sense it should be miserable.[19]

Wise counsel brings the right measure of confrontation, teaching, and encouragement, so as to effect repentance as God desires it. The ultimate goal is always restored (or initiated) relationship with Christ. The right counsel sets the stage for Jesus to steadily lift a weight of sin, ushering in a deeply-seated joy, not just the rush of momentary happiness. Momentary happiness can be the reflective reaction of a heart freed from its prison, but ongoing repentance and restoration offer a bounty of joy.

The Counseling Exchange: Mitigating the Cobra Effect

The cobra effect occurs when a supposed solution is implemented which actually intensifies the original problem (also called the problem of "unintended consequence"). The term "cobra effect" arises from a likely apocryphal anecdote set at the time of British rule of colonial India. The British government, concerned with the high number of wild venomous cobras, implemented a bounty system for collecting dead cobras. While the strategy initially appeared to be successful, an underground cottage industry soon arose in which cobras were specifically bred and raised in order to collect the bounty. Upon learning of the systemic abuse, officials rescinded the program causing breeders to release the now worthless snakes. As a result, the wild cobra population soared. Thus, "the apparent

Hygeia, Goddess of Health
Peter Paul Rubens, c. 1615

---
[19] David and Sharon Covington, "Introduction to Biblical Counseling" notes, 2004

solution for the problem made the situation even worse."[20]

The cobra effect clearly highlights the mechanism for sin as it reveals the heart's instinctive devices for, and sophistication in, circumventing any attempts at exposure. For example, the cobra effect often shows up in church circles where Christians, knowing that idolatry and sin are on the counseling radar for intercept and destroy, simply resort to underground guerilla tactics. In other words, idols are cleverly camouflaged, and sin is recast and concealed. Conversation is scrubbed and appearance sanitized to keep the biblical counselor in the dark. In this way, many Christians devise a means to "game the system," adopting methods to deflect confrontation of heart idols.

Case in point, seasoned Christians are often skilled at what I term "Sunday-morning-parlance chess," avoiding diction which, in church circles, raises red flags, while injecting red herrings. For example, the words "want" and "need" (connoting godless desire) are replaced with "would like to have"; "worried" and "anxious" are replaced with "concerned" (which connotes a certain intermingled resting), and "successful" (carrying worldly connotations) is replaced with "meaningful." And the silver spike through any potential questions concerning one's faith is to inject the word "repent" into discussion. (The issue of repentance can be highly-misleading as often Christians just mean that they are sorry for an emotional outburst, a word or action, rather than desiring a radical turning from sin before the face of God.[21]) The point is that certain words are eschewed, and others are marshaled, to cloak the heart's true motives. Christians easily put on "a form of godliness while denying its power."[22] Thus, the skilled counselor sees past semantics and diction into the intentions surrounding language.

Genesis 3:1 states, "Now the serpent was more crafty than all the other animals the Lord God had made." This craftiness, a hallmark of Satan, employs a deceptive form of pseudo-wisdom in an attempt to out-maneuver God (the cobra effect in play). The very mechanisms God puts in place to ferret out idols and bring them to light can easily be manipulated to allow idols to flourish unmolested and unimpeded. Those who fear having their hearts exposed become masterful at ducking behind a veil of silence, playing "Sunday-morning-parlance chess," and maintaining all the proper outward signs to keep other Christians unsuspecting. De facto, this weaves a feathered nest for idols to thrive.

> "Who is more foolish, the child afraid of the dark or the man afraid of the light?"

---

[20] "The Cobra Effect," Wikipedia.com
[21] Consider, for example, that Pharaoh twice stated that he repented (Exodus 9:27; 10:16, 17). However, he did not repent of a heart inclined toward evil. He merely used the concept of repentance as a manipulative strategy to avoid God's judgment.
[22] 2 Timothy 3:5

> (Maurice Freehill)

Sinners instinctively set up diversions so as to shroud the heart's machinations. In order to resist the exposure of idols, many routinely raise the following issues as diversionary tactics:

1. Current or past abuse or neglect
2. Current or past pain, disappointment, or suffering
3. Current or past loss, or regret
4. Current or past disabilities and impairments
5. Current or past poverty or humiliation
6. Current or past unemployment or financial losses
7. Current or past suicidal ideations
8. Current or past sacrifices or displays of noble character

A counselee often refers to, or emphasizes, these issues as a diversionary tactic. The counselee's objective is to steer attention away from heart issues through some method that will make the counselor appear cold and heartless if he does not sympathize with, comfort, or praise the counselee. While there are certainly times when sympathy, commiseration, consolation, and even celebration, are appropriate, loving, and glorifying to God, needed heart confrontation should never be neglected in the process. (The counselor may even mention the awkwardness of raising heart issues in light of the counselee's self-revelations.) The wise counselor must recognize that often the counselee's self-revelation is a cunning strategy to short-circuit, and siphon energy from, any attempted rendezvous with the heart.

While each person seeks to distill his plight down to a situational problem, God impresses a competing narrative which exposes errant worship. This is why the sinner resists God's form of change so vociferously. He wants to remain comfortable in placating idols of his own making. Yet, God continually assails idolatrous covenants, so as to expose the sinner's worshipping core.

Constituents and Contours of the Counseling Engagement

Once as I traveled abroad, I was introduced to a Bible study group whose participants welcomed me warmly. After the study, I mentioned that I was on my way to a neighboring city to teach a counseling seminar. On the spur of the moment, one of the group members stated that she would accompany me to the seminar. Soon, two other women stated that they too would attend. I had just met these Christian sisters, yet they seemed magnetically drawn to this counseling message. There was an almost instantaneous sense of trust, as if we were kindred spirits.

There are other Christians, I have sometimes known for decades, with whom every meeting seems like a reintroduction. The relationship seems marred by a wispy suspicion, a hinted hesitance, and an ill-defined opposition which we never seem to get past. These may be faithful brothers and sisters in Christ, but our spirits seem somehow at odds, like a subtle tremor of distrust that unsettles the relationship.

The point is that among counselees there are either raised or lowered shields, resistance or compliance, to God's intentions for the heart. Some seem instinctively joyful to receive gospel-centered counsel, as if it is a homecoming celebration. With others, it is as if the counselor perennially shouts with cupped hands across a fortress moat. Despite the promise of Christ's healing, the drawbridge is rarely, if ever, lowered and the counselor receives sniper fire (jabs, barbs, accusations, etc.). How does the counselor bridge this often trenchant spiritual divide?

Guillame de Clermont Defending Ptolemais Acre in 1291
Dominique Louis Papety, 1845

Much of this divide in the way the counselee receives the counselor has to do with the counselee's posture toward counseling. Often the counselee vehemently seeks to leverage each interaction into a confidence-builder, a means for garnering attention, a quest to feel loved, a desire to be understood, and even to be afforded a means for assuaging the qualms of a guilty conscience. The counselor who does not cooperate with this agenda will be tacitly, if not propositionally, criticized.

> As a counselor, I never want to be a distraction in any life, except for the purposes of the gospel. If I must disrupt lives with the gospel, if I must ruffle feathers with the

> gospel, or if others at times lose sleep over the gospel, then I have entered into lives for a godly ambition. Any other source of distraction, anything outside of the gospel, is of the world, and ultimately breaks down God's work in others' lives.

Likewise, the counselor who does not make the counselee feel better about himself will at times be labeled "hurtful." The counselor will find himself at a crossroads - either cave to the interpersonal pressure or lovingly, but firmly, remain on task so that Jesus might have his way. Thus, the counseling session is a highly-sophisticated battle of wills. The counselor may rightly cede non-essentials, but with regard to the essentials he must remain as immovable as granite. Those who hunger and thirst for righteousness will be drawn to this message,[23] as others glare from across a protective moat. Some counselees will feel like kindred spirits, while with others each meeting is like a fumbling first encounter.

In the movie "The Wizard of Oz" (1939) Dorothy says to the cowardly lion, "Don't you know the wizard's going to give you some courage?" The lion's response, "I'd be too scared to ask him for it." As previously stated, idols are operative during counseling process itself,[24] not just those of the counselee, but the counselor's as well. The counselor, often eager for assurance that the counselee views the counseling as a success, wants the counselee to leave with a tangible answer, a concrete pragmatic solution (which may not be God's objective). Thus, there is a propensity to make the seemingly abstract (repenting at the feet of Jesus) into the seemingly concrete (a list of principles or procedures for managing life). The counselor, hoping not to lose the counselee to the world's counsel, often casts his message from the world's foundry, all in the futile hope that he can trump the world's offerings.

Aware of Satan's schemes,[25] the wise counselor pays attention to the right issues, loves the counselee with a God-defined love, and is vigilant for God's work of change. The counselor, when subject to the counselee's pressure, must not resort to a passive or morally-neutral stance. Instead, he remains a stalwart champion of God's sanctifying work. Recognizing the rhythms, times, and seasons of the heart, the counselor offers all that God longs to provide, in God's timing and in God's way, to incarnate the gospel with all of its force and fury, comfort and invitation, so as to effect eternal purposes at the expense of the praises of men.

> "He that gives good advice, builds with one hand; he that gives good counsel and example, builds with both; but he that gives good advice and bad example, builds with one hand and pulls down with the other." (Francis Bacon)

When not based in obvious sorrow, crying is frequently a means of winning sympathy

---

[23] Matthew 5:6
[24] Paul Tripp, Westminster Theological Seminary, Philadelphia, Pennsylvania
[25] 2 Corinthians 2:11

when an idol is exposed. Weeping can be a "weapon of mass distraction" used to gain the upper-hand in conflict,[26] especially when idols are under siege. In an attempt to keep the counselor off-balance, tears seek to deflect attention from the sinful heart, and so the one who cries enjoys a tactical advantage (although not a strategic one). Weeping can also serve as a means to maintain moral superiority through signaling a supposed offense, since it is generally assumed that the one who cries has in some way been violated. The counselor, if himself ruled by man-pleasing idols, may easily succumb to the temptation to abandon the chase, rejigger the conversation toward innocuous goals, chart a non-intrusive course, and adopt an indulgent agenda.[27]

As with Daniel in the lion's den, to merely remove the source of fear leaves the heart unchecked and God's work undone.[28] While the counselor never allows anyone to remain in an overtly dangerous situation, he at times recognizes that God has a deeper purpose than to simply remove the object of fear. God often allows a manageable threat (whether real or perceived) to remain until the idols of the heart have been altogether abandoned, or at least substantially weakened. Recognizing that the fearful counselee seeks the most immediate and efficacious means to remove his trepidation, the counselor holds forth the gospel in the midst of the fear, and not always a situational escape.

> Numbers 19:12 stipulates that a man must purify himself with the water of cleansing on both the third and seventh days. The phrase used for "purify," *bo yithchatta* (בו יתחטא) is literally "he shall sin himself with it." The Hebrew idiom "to sin oneself" means to remove one's sin. It is similar to the concept of "to skin an animal" or "to bark a tree."[29]

Often the well-wishing counselor, seeking to look like a hero, functions as little more than Satan's co-conspirator when he seeks immediate solutions without regard for God's eternal purposes. The wise counselor keeps God's objective front-and-center, regardless of the exigencies of the moment, remembering that God is always personally present in the work he undertakes. God never allows one to remain in fear without his ready assistance. God himself defends the defenseless and protects the oppressed for the singular purpose of exposing heart idols and replacing them with abiding faith. Thus, in summary, God never desires that one face the object of his fears alone, but himself offers clear and present grace to choose the path out of fear and into faith.[30]

Excursus: Counseling and the Coming Apocalypse: Renovating Wardenclyffe

---

[26] This term "weapon of mass distraction" from an unknown source
[27] Incidentally, I have found that when tears do not work, a counselee rapidly shifts to anger or hostility as a means of intimidation to repel besieging counsel.
[28] Daniel 6:16-23
[29] Adam Clarke Commentary, Bible Study Tools, 2012
[30] Psalm 23:4

Tower[31]

> "The future influences the present just as much as the past." (Friedrich Nietzsche)

Exodus 8:26 states, "But Moses said, 'That would not be right. The sacrifices we offer the Lord our God would be detestable to the Egyptians. And if we offer sacrifices that are detestable in their eyes, will they not stone us?'" This verse draws out the contrast between the world (symbolized by the Egyptians) and the Lord's people. The world finds worship of God "detestable" and rushes forward to "stone" those who offer this worship.[32] There is clearly a life-and-death struggle (always spiritual, but often physical) between those in Christ and those in the world, a struggle vastly more acute than most Christians want to admit.

Procession of the Apis Bull, Frederick Arthur Bridgman, 1879

Some years ago, while working overseas, I found myself under the threat of imminent physical attack on account of my faith. The threat was pointed and specific. By God's grace, I escaped the situation without bodily harm. However, that event left me with nightmares for years afterwards, and a habit of glancing over my shoulder. While that was an isolated event long since past, according to the Bible a day is coming when such pointed and specific persecution will be a daily threat to all believers.[33] A time is rapidly approaching when believers will be in continual fear for their lives.[34]

---

[31] Using the earth as a giant conductor, Nikola Tesla (1856-1943) envisioned an electromagnetic transmitting tower for sending radio waves around the globe.
[32] Acts 7:54-58
[33] Consider Acts 8:1-3 in this regard.
[34] Millions of Christians throughout the world, especially in the Middle East, already live under the daily scepter of torture and death, a kind of foreshortened and accelerated eschatology.

> "Then you will be handed over to be persecuted and put to death, and you will be hated by all nations because of me. At that time many will turn away from the faith and will betray and hate each other, and many false prophets will appear and deceive many people. Because of the increase of wickedness, the love of most will grow cold, but the one who stands firm to the end will be saved. And this gospel of the kingdom will be preached in the whole world as a testimony to all nations, and then the end will come." (Matthew 24:9-14)

Eschatological events include:

1. A seismic shift in social and moral standards[35]

2. Rising awareness of not just the world's hatred of Christians, but of its willingness to act on that hatred

3. A certain justified "paranoia" on the part of Christians as a result of rising persecution[36]

4. Greater social isolation for Christians as they are deliberately excluded from ever-broadening aspects of society[37]

> Revelation 17:18 reads, "[The harlot of Babylon] you saw is the great city that rules over the kings of the earth." For the implementation of apocalyptic events, the world's population is rapidly being urbanized. This is attended by the rise of anomic communities (a component of the Bible's apocalyptic vision), a vision which sees the rise of satanic forces and intensified persecution. The anomic community is a crucial cog in the turning apocalyptic wheel.[38]

5. The growing financial slavery cycle may become so intense that Christians are unable to maintain a viable livelihood and family life.[39]

> "The second beast was given power to give breath to the image of the first beast, so that the image could speak and cause all who refused to worship the image to be killed. It also forced all people, great and small, rich and poor, free and slave, to receive a mark on their right hands or on their foreheads, so that they could not buy

---

[35] 2 Timothy 3:1-5
[36] Under one totalitarian government, in particular, Christians are currently being identified for eventual genocide.
[37] Luke 6:22
[38] For further discussion of anomic communities see "The Disintegration of Community" in chapter 10: "Counseling and the Church: Syndicating the Vision"
[39] The slavery cycle is outlined in the second book in this series, *What Agreement Is There Between the Temple of God and Idols?: The Accidence of Sin and Idolatry*, chapter 2: "The World, The Flesh, and the Devil: Assessing the Threat Matrix"

> or sell unless they had the mark, which is the name of the beast or the number of its name." (Revelation 13:15-17)

The Bible is clear that the world hates the faithful Christian;[40] this is often palpable. Thus, a Christian may sense that others oppose him, do not like him, and even actively seek to harm him. This is rapidly becoming a universal reality, not isolated flashes of evil.[41] As end times events march closer, there is a rising intensity to the world's hatred of Christians. There will invariably be a greater proportion of false believers among church attendees, especially as Scripture warns of the rise of antichrists and false prophets.[42] Thus, as the Christian is acutely aware of heightened persecution, this will invariably affect his psyche, his emotional state, and the texture of his social interactions.

> "Be always on the watch, and pray that you may be able to escape all that is about to happen, and that you may be able to stand before the Son of Man." (Luke 21:36)

It would appear that as the end approaches Christians will experience more difficulty succeeding in the world.[43] End times descriptions tell of more people willing to forfeit their souls for money.[44] Thus, access to many of society's institutions constricts as it becomes increasingly difficult to succeed through honest means. This is a kind of soft persecution, the inability to simply survive through a humble métier. The Christian should expect to experience more persecution concerning basic lifestyle choices. For example Matthew 14:3-5 reads,

> Now Herod had arrested John and bound him and put him in prison because of Herodias, his brother Philip's wife, for John had been saying to him: 'It is not lawful for you to have her.' Herod wanted to kill John, but he was afraid of the people, because they considered John a prophet.

John the Baptist was imprisoned and finally beheaded for opposing Herod's unlawful marriage. However, Herod, wanting to kill John, was afraid of the people. A time is rapidly approaching when, on a mass scale, Christians who uphold absolute morality will be similarly persecuted. However, unlike Herod, those in authority will not withhold their wrath because there will be no fear of the people. The world will celebrate such persecution.

Additionally, consider the stoning of Stephen. In Acts 7:60 Stephen asked God not to hold this murder against the Sanhedrin. In Acts 8:1, "Saul was there, giving approval

---

[40] John 15:18
[41] 2 Peter 3:3
[42] 1 John 2:18; Matthew 24:11
[43] Revelation 13:16
[44] 2 Timothy 3:3-5

to [Stephen's] death." Consider that in the months ahead Saul would be confronted by Jesus himself, and renamed "Paul." Thus, it is likely that Stephen's prayer produced some tangible effect, and may have been used by God to effect Saul's conversion. As end times events approach, the prayers of the persecuted may no longer produce such conversions, may not turn enemies into exponents of the faith.

The Fall of Phaeton, Peter Paul Rubens, 1604

> "But mark this: There will be terrible times in the last days. People will be lovers of themselves, lovers of money, boastful, proud, abusive, disobedient to their parents, ungrateful, unholy, without love, unforgiving, slanderous, without self-control, brutal, not lovers of the good, treacherous, rash, conceited, lovers of pleasure rather than lovers of God – having a form of godliness but denying its power." (2 Timothy 3:1-5)

In the recesses of this discussion is an implicit challenge to the assumption that the world, flesh, and the devil constitute a static backdrop to the Christian's experience, or exist with a predetermined form and level of intensity. What if that backdrop is not static but dynamic (in motion), so that the world, the flesh, and the devil advance toward an eschatological crescendo? In other words, what if the face of evil, in its triadic form, presently takes on sharper contours and intensity boosts? How would that affect, not just the individual Christian's life, but the biblical counseling endeavor in, and through, the church?

> Often people are eager to hear the latest news concerning world events. In actuality the Bible tells one more about modern world than the evening news, since the Bible alone explains human nature, and its depravity, with precision and persuasion. So it is in fact history which reveals the future.

The point is that an epoch rapidly approaches when the very fabric of the universe will rend as evil pierces space and time. Consider Matthew 10:21, "Brother will betray brother to death, and a father his child; children will rebel against their parents and have them put to death." Matthew 24:10 reads, "At that time many will turn away from the faith and will betray and hate each other…" Even the most trusted and intimate relationships in a Christian's life will be cast into peril as the social order implodes. Human relationships, marked by wrenching betrayal, will be dismantled (along with society as a whole). This offers a window into the gravity and horror of end times events, a time in which people will commit the most heinous acts for the sake of mere survival, and even as supposed service to God himself.[45]

> "Don't let anyone deceive you in any way, for that day will not come until the rebellion occurs and the man of lawlessness is revealed, the man doomed to destruction. He will oppose and will exalt himself over everything that is called God or is worshiped, so that he sets himself up in God's temple, proclaiming himself to be God." (2 Thessalonians 2:3, 4)

The theory offered here is that as eschatological events approach, a certain temporal asymmetry or skew occurs with regard to the Christian experience, namely in targeted and intensified persecution. Consider an example. Life is designed in such a way that as one displays grace a gracious cycle forms in which one generally receives grace in return. Thus, as one lives a godly life, displaying good fruit, one tends to reap a certain blessing from others.

However, as end times events approach this gracious cycle may come off of its axis, so that Christian grace is repaid with insults and threats, hatred and exclusion. In other words, end times events seem to represent a certain paradigm shift in which gracious and vicious cycles are reversed (or at least severely impaired) on account of a radical shift in morality and worship (a systematic and pervasive implementation of the old adage that "no good deed goes unpunished.") How does this topsy-turvy social climate, which will even infiltrate the church, affect the Christian, his psyche, his relationships, and his walk with God? How does the Christian maintain a handle on his world when everything around him swirls and swoops with confusing uncertainty?

> "Do not trust a neighbor;

---

[45] John 16:2

> put no confidence in a friend.
> Even with the woman who lies in your embrace
> guard the words of your lips." (Micah 7:5)
>
> "For then there will be great distress, unequaled from the beginning of the world until now—and never to be equaled again." (Matthew 24:21)

This rising persecution poses the question, "Does anything change in terms of biblical counseling?" For example, before I was threatened overseas, if I had told other Christians that I feared imminent bodily harm, I might have been labeled "paranoid." However, once that threat materialized I was no longer paranoid but clairvoyant.

> "While people are saying, 'Peace and safety,' destruction will come on them suddenly, as labor pains on a pregnant woman, and they will not escape." (1 Thessalonians 5:3)

How does this coming paradigm shift or eschatological skew affect the way a counselor offers counsel? How does the counselor direct others in a world operating under new terms of engagement, terms which send percussion bombs through the existing social order, even through the church itself? For example, will the relational directives of Ephesians 5:22 to 6:9 offer sanctuary when relationship with Christ is severed and persecution wends its way into even the most imitate of human relationships? When "a man's enemies will be members of his own household,"[46] how does one offer marriage and family counseling? During eschatological events, what are the new expectations and standards with regard to Christian life, work, and social interaction?

> Luke 18:8 states, "When the Son of Man returns, will he find faith on earth?" Does this verse refer to widespread persecution of Christians, or is it an indictment of Christians who have fallen away to follow the world?[47]

Excursus: Alien Abduction[48]

Several years ago one of my students (a college freshman at the time) shared with me a chilling account. He claimed that as a high school student he was abducted by aliens. My knee-jerk reaction was to dismiss his story as a delusional fantasy. However, something in this young man's words sounded eminently rational. He included certain details, and excluded others, which seemed to fit with what his claims. He told me that his parents and others did not believe him, and that he had been searching for

---

[46] Matthew 10:36
[47] Os Guinness raised this question in his interview with the Gospel Coalition, March 4, 2010.
[48] Some ideas from the film "Age of Deceit: Fallen Angels and the New World Order," director Gonzo Shimura, 2012.

answers.

I was at a complete loss. My thought had always been that aliens, unequivocally, do not exist and that, therefore, any claim of alien abduction must be spun from an overactive imagination. But here in front of me was one who was recounting the story. The fire in his eyes and the tremor in his voice told me that something real had happened, but what?

A source of shame to me in this case is that I have always asserted that the Bible speaks comprehensively to every issue of the human experience. There is no experience which the Bible does not decisively address, convincingly illuminate, and ultimately clarify (although the question of evil is shrouded in mystery). Yet, as I stared into this man's fear, not one Scripture verse came to mind. I had no integration point to disentangle this ethereal experience. I could share the gospel, as I always do, but to this man the gospel was meaningless unless it demonstrated some ability to navigate his confusion. (As a side note, I taught this young man for a year during which time I kept an eye on him in class. He showed himself to be intelligent, clear-minded, articulate, and emotionally-balanced. I detected nothing to indicate that he had fabricated his story.)

I hesitate even to raise this issue for fear that it will prove a speculative distraction to the larger objective at hand. However, if I profess that the Bible can, and does, address every human experience, and if I profess to be able to understand and counsel any person from any starting point in his life, then I had better search the Scriptures until I find an answer.

Analysis of alien abduction begins in Genesis 3:15, which reads, "And I will put enmity between you and the woman, and between your offspring and hers; he will crush your head, and you will strike his heel." This verse states that Satan literally has "seed" (offspring). There are two ways to construe this. The first is that Satan will beget, not literal offspring, but figurative offspring as he deludes mankind into serving him. Thus, every sinner is Satan's figurative seed.[49] The second interpretation is that Satan himself (or demons) will beget *literal* offspring, sire actual beings to serve him and do his bidding.

The second interpretation has merit if one considers Genesis 6:2 which reads, "the sons of [the gods] (הָאֱלֹהִים בְּנֵי, *elohim ben*) saw that the daughters of humans were beautiful, and they married any of them they chose." Additionally, Genesis 6:4 reads, "The Nephilim (גִּבּוֹרִים) were on the earth in those days—and also afterward—when the sons of God went to the daughters of humans and had children by them. They

---
[49] Matthew 13: 38, 39

were the heroes of old, men of renown."[50] The implication is that the sons of the gods, referred to in Genesis 6:2, are "fallen angels,"[51] or demons, since their offspring are also referred to as fallen. Thus, fallen angels, doing Satan's bidding, impregnated women in order to spawn depraved and wicked offspring who would take up Satan's rebellion against God.

The Great Flood, Anonymous

There is also a theory that Satan's goal was to disrupt the human genetic code.[52] Based on this, God sent the Great Flood to annihilate Satan's offspring which, through his fallen angels, had propagated upon the earth. God's objective was to expunge the tainted DNA in order to thwart Satan's plan of world domination. Since the human race was thus contaminated, God chose to make a clean sweep and start again by means of the primogenitor Noah and his sons.

Despite the Great Flood, it is clear that Satan's fallen angels or demons continue to harass mankind. Second Corinthians 11:14 states, "And no wonder, for Satan himself masquerades as an angel of light." In modern times, demons likely take on the appearance of aliens in order to beguile unsuspecting onlookers. While post-scientific people have largely rejected the notion of demons as childish superstition, these same

---

[50] *Nephilim* is translated both "giants" and the "fallen ones." The traditional interpretation is that these were enemy beings. The Hebrew word *Nephilim* is found in Genesis 6:4, and later in Numbers 13:33, to refer to the hostile inhabitants of Canaan.
[51] 2 Peter 2:4, 5; Jude 1:6
[52] "Age of Deceit: Fallen Angels and the New World Order," director Gonzo Shimura, 2012. (interview with Douglas Hamp)

people see aliens as highly-evolved highly-intelligent beings who have achieved all for which mankind strives, the mastery of physical laws and immortality. So, essentially aliens are masked demons, Satan accommodating the modern *Zeitgeist*.

Aliens appear to be god-like creatures having power over the laws of physics, and over the material world more generally. They give the impression that through their intelligence they have achieved immortality. (This fits with Satan's scheme to deceive mankind into thinking that he can achieve this same god-like status through his own effort, as well.) Additionally, these aliens appear to be saviors, drawing attention away from the true Savior. This fits with Satan's plan to install the antichrist over the New World Order and place upon him the mantle of human salvation. The mystery shrouding aliens sets the stage for a supernatural world leader.

Satan's objective then is to dangle news of aliens in the media, with periodic sightings which can neither be confirmed nor denied. This raises intrigue in the general public, yet keeps the question veiled from direct scrutiny. Aliens and UFOs open the way for an atheistic world religion in which mankind worships his own potential, the rejection of Jesus as savior, the vindication of evolution, genocide as a way to cull the undesirables, and the rule of the antichrist as a supposed highly-evolved supernatural being.

> "Science has made us gods before we are even worthy of being men." (Jean Rostand)

From Scripture it is clear that Satan is never original.[53] He can only imitate God's work. Thus, Satan seeks to mimic God's heavenly displays with his own deceiving spectacles.[54] Therefore, UFOs could be Satan's work to beguile the world into believing that aliens can defy the laws of physics, warp time and space, and possibly serve as surrogate saviors of mankind. UFOs may merely be celestial mirages, images Satan projects in order to chicane onlookers.

Possibly hundreds of thousands of people throughout the world claim to have been abducted by aliens. Is there truth in these claims? It seems entirely possible that, as before, Satan seeks to alter the human DNA so as to form a new race of *Nephilim*. Maybe alien abductions are Satan's attempt to initiate legions into occult practices. The motive is not clear, but it would appear that abduction accounts are actual, that something beyond the limits of science is taking place.

The most fascinating development in all this is that many who study alien abduction

---

[53] This idea from Vern Poythress, Westminster Theological Seminary, Philadelphia, Pennsylvania, primarily based on Revelation 13

[54] One might consider Elijah's flaming chariot, in 2 Kings 2:11, as a kind of prototypical "heavenly display" which Satan seeks to imitate using some image like that of a UFO.

have uncovered that calling upon the name of Jesus causes the alien abduction to end suddenly. This is has been well-documented, even by atheistic researchers, yet this truth has been systematically concealed because it is such obvious confirmation of the gospel.[55]

When the Dust Settles God is There

The Tulip Folly, Jean-Léon Gérôme, 1882

Andrew Carnegie (1835-1919), the American steel magnate, spent his retirement gifting $350 million to various causes. He petitioned for world peace and, in 1913, met with Germany's Kaiser Wilhelm II (1859-1941) to promote that country's alliance with the United States. However, Carnegie's efforts were in vain as one year later World War I broke out. On the eve of the war, Carnegie completed his autobiography, concluding it by heralding his efforts to ensure world peace. Yet, on the day war erupted Carnegie penned his final journal entry, and never wrote again. He died five years later a broken-hearted man.

Like Carnegie, those who are wise, mighty, and noble in the eyes of the world are often deeply distracted,[56] even mesmerized, by their perceived earthly advantage.[57] Yet, God does not summarily disregard such people. He recognizes a far deeper plane of human existence, beyond the purely existential. God seeks out those who, regardless of their *Sitz im Leben*, have lost all faith in the world, or in their ability to

---

[55] "Age of Deceit: Fallen Angels and the New World Order," director Gonzo Shimura, 2012. (interview with Douglas Hamp)
[56] 1 Corinthians 1:26
[57] James 1:10, 11 offers some insight into this.

successfully negotiate that world. Those who renounce their earthly pursuits are often the ones who finally transcend them to become the blessed as they place their entire reliance upon God himself.

> "One man pretends to be rich, yet has nothing; another pretends to be poor, yet has great wealth." (Proverbs 13:7)

God seeks those who hunger and thirst for righteousness.[58] These are usually the one's whose lives have not just failed in some crucial way, but who have lost faith in themselves. God, therefore, runs to those the world might deem "failures," not necessarily material failures, but self-confidence failures (the fear of God finally being allowed to take root). God longs to care for the inwardly crushed, bruised, broken, and rejected, regardless of outward appearance.[59] Those who have lost assurance in themselves, and have given up on meeting perceived needs, are the ones who are enabled to see their desperate need for God. It is not so much the externally forlorn and forsaken, but the internally forlorn and forsaken, who are prepared for the good news.

> "Learning the gaze of God, we come to weigh life aright." (David Powlison)

Throughout the Bible, the widow, the orphan, and the alien were the most vulnerable in society and, therefore, the most in need of a kinsman-redeemer. This gave them a greater understanding of God, and of their need for salvation. However, God does not restrict the classification of widow, orphan, and alien to a mere literal definition. He uses these terms somewhat fluidly, as metaphorical categories for the lonely and brokenhearted, the vulnerable and destitute, the lost and dejected. Thus, from God's perspective destitution is not merely a socio-economic condition, but operates in a worship dimension. The poor in spirit, regardless of situation, turn to God for help in the recognition of God's faithfulness as kinsman-redeemer.[60]

---

[58] Matthew 5:6
[59] Isaiah 42:3
[60] Leviticus 25:25; Ruth 4:4, 6

- 6 -

THE BASIC PLOTLINES WHICH EMERGE IN COUNSELING

Introduction

First Corinthians 10:13 begins, "No temptation has overtaken you except what is common to mankind." The concept "what is common to mankind" offers a glimpse into the basic plotlines which routinely emerge in counseling. In listening to people's stories, their descriptions of their own lives, a certain set of themes emerge time and again. While each person's particular experiences are unique, life-story plotlines seem to follow prescribed patterns and set channels, almost like experience boilerplates.

This chapter catalogues and analyzes the principle plotlines which emerge in counseling. The objective is to clarify for the counselor the types of stories he will inevitably encounter, so that in the process of counseling he can tune out the background noise. This will permit him to pinpoint the crux of each life-story. As the counselor is more attuned to prototypical narratives, he is better prepared to bring the gospel to bear upon the counselee's story.

> "…We are living characters, set in a story not from the mind of man, but from the mind of God." (David Kupelian)

Why is Classic Literature Still Read Today?

> "There is nothing more wonderful than a book! It is a message to us from the dead, from human souls whom we never saw, and lived maybe thousands of miles away. Books are small sheets of paper but they speak to us, make us laugh, terrify us, teach us and comfort us. They are like looking into the open heart of a friend or brother." (Charles Kingsley)

Great literature adeptly captures the human experience, giving voice to inchoate and universal aspirations, fears, passions, and joys. It unravels human intent and offers a window into man's existential plight. When properly interpreted, literature proffers a vivid, and often highly-impactful, description of the human condition.

Eminent literature causes the reader to enter into the most vexing human conundra and mysteries, feeling that, with just a glimmer of light, they have in some way been reckoned with. Not all questions are adequately answered, but the questions themselves are lent dignity. A society's treasured literature in a sense functions as a form of wise counseling, offering a cathartic glimpse into the human existence.

> Larger-than-life heroes and villains are increasingly the subjects of movies and television. The quiet dutiful common man, the frequent subject of classic novels, poems, and paintings, is often overlooked today.

Sir Isumbras at the Ford, John Everett Millais, 1857

Literature offers the reader friendship, to know people possibly as one has never known them before. In a world of transient and fractured relationships, literature galvanizes the human resolve, records its existence for posterity, and attunes one to a larger grander story outside of himself.

> Mankind has gone from *MacBeth* to McDonald's for its cultural enrichment, from *Excalibur* to X-Box for its sense of courage, from the *A Tale of Two Cities* to "Sex and the City" for its understanding of human relationship.

In a world in which many wear relational masks, and cunningly cloak their true feelings and intentions, literature offers a privileged look below the surface of the human experience, allowing the reader a peek into the deepest recesses of the heart, a gaze rarely allowed in life's jostle and tussle. Thus, literature plunges the reader into the hidden world of the psyche so as to offer an understanding of desire, intention, and the rhythm of life. Great literature is so exhilarating to the student of the human condition because it is a treasure trove of examination, investigation, and inquiry into the nature of reality, the purpose of mankind, the question of good and evil, right and wrong, as well as the often muted quest for absolution and salvation.

> "People who read good literature have lived more than others who have not. We only have one life to live but when we read we live many more lives." (S.I. Hayakama)

Literature as a Conduit into the Heart

In what way is the study and use of classic literature a profitable venue and vehicle for counseling? Classic literature offers remarkable insight into the human condition, as the psyche is explored with a piercing discernment, intuition, and sagacity. Thus, students of literature seem to be more acquainted with humanity's pitfalls, perils, and pursuits, able to peer into the dark recesses of the heart, so as to uncover its tides and intention, loves and languishment.

> "All the world is a stage
> And all the men and women merely players;
> They have their exits and entrances;
> And one man in his time plays many parts." (*As You Like It*, Act II, scene vii)

While classic literature often offers a persuasive analysis of the psyche, the danger is that literary interpretations are usually based upon psychology (namely that of Carl Jung (1875-1961)), to the detriment of the literature and the reader, and often in defiance of the authorial intent. How can the Bible be used to understand these stories so that they are rightly analyzed, and thus used for counselees' edification and sanctification?

In Shakespeare's (1564–1616) tragedy, *Macbeth* (c. 1606), consider Macbeth's desperate attempt to cleanse his murderous hands. This is a classic example of what the psychologist might term obsessive-compulsive (OCD) behavior. However, the Bible alone offers the correct analysis. Macbeth's frenzied hand-washing is a flailing effort to somehow purge himself of his sin, the desperate act of an anguished conscience. The Bible alone understands the agency for this behavior because it alone sees the with-regard-to-God (*coram Deo*) reality of man's existence.[1] Thus, Shakespeare offered the story; the Bible interprets it. The Bible understands that Macbeth's first evil deed soon metastasized, that the guilt of his sin could not be exculpated through human effort. Shakespeare presented the plight and perplexity of mankind; the Bible lends it clarifying resolution.

---

[1] Romans 1:19-22; For additional development of the *coram Deo* concept see the first book in this series, *Ask for the Ancient Paths: From Art to Artifice to Arisen*, chapter 6: "Man Before the Face of God: The Imperium of the Psyche"

> "The Prince of Cumberland! That is a step
> On which I must fall down, or else overleap,
> For in my way it lies. Stars, hide your fires;
> Let not light see my black and deep desires.
> The eye winks at the hand; yet let that be
> Which the eye fears, when it is done, to see." (*Macbeth*, Act I, Scene IV)

Echoing this same frenzied flailing for absolution is Edgar Allen Poe's (1809–1849) "The Tell-Tale Heart" (1843) in which a murderer, as he sits in his study, cannot silence his victim's pounding heart, the corpse hidden under his bedroom's floorboards. In Fyodor Dostoyevsky's (1821–1881) *Crime and Punishment* (1866) a young man, Raskolnikov, conceives and commits the perfect murder. Yet, he is daily haunted by his conscience, so much so, that he confesses to the authorities. Raskolnikov throws himself upon their mercy to duly punish him, so as to purge him of his unendurable guilt. The Bible alone describes the heart's internal mechanism because the Bible alone understands the heart's architecture.

Competing Stories

> "Those who tell the stories rule society." (Plato)

Aristotle spoke of four central conflicts:

1. Man against man
2. Man against himself
3. Man against nature
4. Man against the supernatural

The counselee's stories invariably revolve around one of these archetypical conflicts. The counselee places himself in the center of that conflict as somewhat of a tragic hero. In the course of his struggle, he either achieves victory through his own strength, or else fails to attain what he desires. Then he must assign blame for his failure. Counseling should begin with the counselee's presenting core conflict, but fundamentally seek to recast that conflict in radically biblical terms. There must be movement within that story toward an encounter with Christ.

> Is there a pattern of threes in a counselee's stories? Does he frame his story in the intersection of three main characters?[2]

In each of these four core conflicts one either embraces a man-centered, or a God-centered, story. The man-centered story usually presents mankind struggling

---
[2] Christopher Booker, *The Seven Basic Plots: Why We Tell Stories* (New York: Continuum, 2005)

against a harsh cruel world that makes him suffer. Suffering compels him to do regrettable things, but he cannot stop himself. He must overcome the burden of suffering by changing his situation. His heart is basically good and noble, but he needs help (God's, if he exists) to overcome his situation. Man's only hope for change is to change his situation (rather than his worship commitments). Man is the author and hero in his story, and God, at best, plays a supporting role. At worst, God either enjoys seeing people suffer or is too weak to stop suffering.[3]

Marshall Ney at Retreat in Russia, Adolphe Yvon, d. 1893

For example, Acts 16:25-34 offers diametrically opposed interpretations of the same situation. While in prison, Paul and Silas interpreted their situation as God's working, and they showed their faith through singing hymns. Their jailer, however, interpreted his situation (the supposed breach of the jail) as loss, and he showed his hopelessness through seeking to commit suicide, a form of suppressing the truth in unrighteousness. To Paul and Silas, their location (the prison) was of no ultimate significance. Thus, they experienced joy in all situations because God was their reality.

To the jailer, God was a meaningless concept, and so, he experienced desperation because the prison was his reality. Paul and Silas correctly interpreted their experience; the jailer did not. To the jailer, the loss of his honor was the ultimate indignity since his god was himself, his position, and his performance. The failure of his gods resulted in a plan for self-inflicted capital punishment, because there was no solution beyond that. Quite ironically, Paul and Silas were prisoners, yet free. The jailer was in

---

[3] David and Sharon Covington, "Introduction to Biblical Counseling" notes, 2004; also see Genesis 3:4, 5

charge of the prison, yet a prisoner. Paul and Silas displayed their freedom in their joy. The jailer showed his imprisonment through his attempted suicide.[4]

> "Instead of saying that man is a product of his circumstances, it would be more accurate to say that he is the architect of his circumstances. From the same material one man builds a palace and another hovel." (Thomas Carlyle)

A key to effective counseling is knowing what to listen for. The counselor is careful not to let the counselee's personal story overrun the overall objective (to confront the heart with its need for radical worship reform). This means that sometimes the counselor does not allow a particular storyline to distract. He shifts to other issues and questions which the counselee may deem secondary, superfluous, incidental, or non-instructive. Often, rightly at cross-purposes with the counselee, the counselor hunts for pivotal themes, patterns, quests, drives, and motives. At times a seemingly uninspiring story can present highly-significant revelations. Sometimes it is these incidental stories which most reveal the counselee, since he may unmask himself in the most inconsequential details. The skilled counselor knows what to listen for, as the right data reveals the heart.

> Postmodern man tends to think in stories, so this is often the most effective means for reaching the modern mind. However, the major prophets of the Old Testament generally did not communicate with their audience in story but, rather, in motif or symbol (commonly referred to as word-pictures).[5] For example, Ezekiel used the following symbols to illustrate his message:
>
> 1. The use of the iron pan and clay tablet[6]
> 2. Eating the siege rations[7]
> 3. Shaving his beard and dividing the hairs[8]
> 4. Clapping his hands and stomping his feet[9]
> 5. Packing his belongings and digging through a wall[10]
> 6. The sword dance and map in the sand[11]
>
> Ezekiel's word-picture method, labeled "street theater," is often efficacious for communicating abstract concepts. In counseling practice, the use of motif or symbol to illustrate points may be profitable.

---

[4] For a more detailed discussion of the issue of suicide see the case study, "Suicide: Idols in Death Throws" in chapter 2: "Suffering: The Kintsugi Objective"
[5] Raymond Dillard and Tremper Longman III, *An Introduction to the Old Testament* (Zondervan, 1994) chapter on Ezekiel.
[6] Ezekiel 4:1-8
[7] Ezekiel 4:9-17
[8] Ezekiel 5
[9] Ezekiel 6:11
[10] Ezekiel 12:1-20
[11] Ezekiel 21:8-23

The Question of Literary Interpretation

The question may be posed, where is the meaning or substance found in literature? Is it in the author's intent, in the text itself, or in the reader's interpretation? In other words, is the author's intent the sole arbiter of truth in the story he unfolds? Is the author separated from truth, so that the text itself is the only source of meaning? Is the reader the sole arbiter of truth, regardless of authorial intent? Thus, there are three literary horizons:

1. The author
2. The text
3. The reader

Assigning truth to the reader's interpretation, separated from authorial intent, is called deconstruction. This is a post-modern phenomenon which strips literature of its meaning so that it is merely a ready vehicle for modern voices and stories. However, in renunciation of deconstruction, the proper literary interpretation firstly looks to the author to determine the meaning of his own writing.

> "Books are the quietest and most constant friends; they are the most accessible and wisest counselors, and the most patient of all teachers." (Charles Eliot)
>
> "When you reread a classic you do not see more in the book than you did before; you see more in you than there was before." (Clifton Fadiman)

One could apply this analysis to the counseling endeavor in which the reader (the counselor), interprets a text (the counselee's psyche and experience), based on the intentions of the author (God himself). The proper analysis first looks to authorial intent so as to uncover the text's nascent meaning. The counselor, as Spirit-filled reader, holds true to authorial intent while not projecting onto the text his own personal biases. Like a fleur-de-lis, the author, text, and reader work in concert to uncover the heart's Kelvin-Helmholtz waves (its tidal movements and subterranean currents). Yet, the author (God himself) is the central petal clarifying the other two interpretive elements.

> The theory of evolution is so compelling because it is cast as a "story"; it employs a kind of narrative plot to explain how man came into being. The story enthralls us because it has a protagonist – "life," and an antagonist – "death" or "chaos." For some mysterious reason, chance favors, even champions, life. With equal mystery, chaos comes to defeat. The story is easily understood, and therefore blindly believed. That is why it has been so effective, even with children. As with all stories, evolution

requires a believing audience.¹²

Jungle Tales, James Jebusa Shannon, 1895

Excursus: Bible Characters[13]

The Bible contains some of the most magnificent literature ever written, employing literary devices which are often subtle yet poignant. One device is the use of tiered characters. The Bible contains the following types of characters:

1. One-dimensional

These are shadowy and often ill-defined characters merely mentioned so as to form the backdrop for other characters. These characters do not exhibit any personality traits but simply illumine the features of other characters (for example, the shepherds at Jesus' birth,[14] the wise men from the East,[15] or the crowds[16]).

2. Two-dimensional

---

[12] The one who subscribes to evolution's basic principles does not weigh facts on an objective scale, but rather espouses a religious perspective, one that masquerades as verifiable science.
[13] Jack Dean Kingsbury, *Matthew as Story* (Augsburg: Fortress Press, 1988); for additional discussion of Bible interpretation see the first book in this series, *Ask for the Ancient Paths: From Art to Artifice to Arisen*, chapter 3: "The Centrality of Scripture in Counseling"
[14] Luke 2:8-18
[15] Matthew 2:1, 2
[16] Luke 23:18-23; John 6:15

These are developed characters who display strong personality traits and experience some transformation in the course of events (for example, King Herod,[17] Judas Iscariot,[18] the Samaritan woman at the well,[19] or the man born blind[20])

3. Three-dimensional

These characters are vivid and fully-developed. They show a broad range of emotion and exhibit dramatic change through the unfolding of a story's events. Peter and the Pharisees are highly-dynamic three-dimensional personalities throughout the gospels. Yet, Jesus himself is the quintessential three-dimensional character, and functions as the hub of the Gospels. Each Gospel narrative, in its entirety, revolves around Jesus' personal identity, so that his actions continually unfold that identity to those around him. (What is remarkable is that, when in contact with others, Jesus does not change; others are compelled to change when in contact with him.[21])

This three tiered approach to characters may be instructive for counseling, as one presents stories in which one-dimensional, two-dimensional, and three-dimensional characters emerge. Such varied characters offer treasured insight into the counselee's functional worship commitments. The counselor should pay careful attention to one, two, and three-dimensional characters in the counselee's stories as, to some degree, idols cluster around three-dimensional renderings.

Analyzing the Plot: Narrative, Metanarrative, Subtext

There are a fixed number of basic plots in all of literature, so that any given story is simply a variation on one of these plots. Thus, an understanding of plotlines may be instructive, as a counselee will likely offer one or more basic plots to frame his presenting problem.

Literary scholars debate the number of foundational plots, whether seven, twenty, or thirty-six. A seven plotline schema is so rough-cut that it does not offer much real assistance in understanding the heart, while a thirty-six plotline approach is overly detailed, so that one loses the import of such an analysis. Thus, the use of twenty basic plots appears to be suitable since this offers enough detail to draw out crucial distinctions and nuance, yet is not so detailed that it overwhelms the endeavor.

The following twenty plotlines could be thought of in two ways:

---

[17] Matthew 2:3-ff
[18] John 6:70, 71
[19] John 4:7-ff
[20] John 9
[21] For further discussion of the nature of Jesus' interaction with others see the case study, "Prayer as Life-Blood of Relationship with Jesus" in chapter 4: "The Umbilicus of Personal Relationship with Christ"

1. As the counselee's metanarrative, his grand storytelling

2. As the framework for the counselor's application of the gospel (the gospel being injected through various thematic apertures)

In other words, these basic plotlines serve to organize and structure the storytelling data and, conversely, they serve as the portals into the gospel. For example, stories of rescue are a perfect introduction to Jesus' deliverance on the cross. Stories of revenge indicate the trenchant evil within the heart (highlighting the need for salvation). The counselor can thus use these plotlines to expand his repertoire for highlighting the gospel, to tailor his approach based upon the ascendant themes within the counselee's heart.

Saul and the Witch of Endour, William Sidney Mount, 1828

In dissecting any plotline one may consider the following tripartite structure:

Metanarrative	The counselee's overarching worldview: the global themes and grand story being conveyed
Narrative	The counselee's actual words
Subtext	The often subtly implied or silent messages, hidden intentions, and governing motives behind the counselee's actual words

Upon listening to the counselee's narrative (sometimes a confused scattering of data), the counselor infers a particular metanarrative taking shape, a set of global themes, or a grand story emerging. In this way the counselor slowly draws into focus the counselee's interpretive lenses, his functional worldview.

Additionally, there is a subtext. This is the counselee's hidden messages, his true intentions, and his governing motives (of which he may be somewhat unaware). The counselor seeks to draw out this subtext to reveal the contours of the heart.[22]

> "A wise man hears one word and understands two." (Yiddish proverb)

Consider Norman Rockwell's (1894-1978) work *Triple Self-Portrait* (1960) in which Rockwell, seated at a mirror, paints himself. The painting contains three "Rockwells":[23]

1. Rockwell himself seated on a stool (The viewer only sees his back.)

2. Rockwell in the mirror (Here the viewer glimpses the artist's visage.)

3. Rockwell's representation of himself (a somewhat caricatured and idealized sketch)

Triple Self-Portrait offers some insight into narrative, subtext, and metanarrative. The narrative is the artist himself. The subtext is his image in the mirror. The metanarrative is his self-rending.

Observations on the Painting	Implications for Counseling
1. In the mirror image one cannot see Rockwell's eyes, as if the artist denies the viewer a window into his soul.[24]	Often the counselee deliberately conceals the intentions of his heart. The purpose behind discerning subtext, and drawing a focus upon metanarrative, is to gain a window into the soul.
2. There are five portraits tacked to the artist's easel. On the right are portraits of Albrecht Dürer (1471-1528), Rembrandt van Rijn (1606-1669), Pablo Picasso (1881-1973), and Vincent van Gogh	The counselee's depiction of himself often arises from unstated heroes. The wise counselor discerns the outline of admired personalities emerging from the depths of the counselee's narrative. Like Rockwell, the counselee has a tendency

---

[22] For additional discussion of this topic see "What Christians Often Say and What They Mean" in chapter 8: "Diagnosis: Vanishing Secrets"
[23] Due to copyright restrictions Norman Rockwell's art cannot be reproduced here.
[24] Andrew Hamilton, "Norman Rockwell's *Triple Self-Portrait*" (Counter-Currents Publishing, website)

(1853-1890). On the left, one sees Rockwell's practice sketches of himself.	to aggrandize himself based on prized associations.
3. Rockwell deliberately interjected various humorous incongruities into his painting. The artist holds a paintbrush but the image on the canvas is a pencil sketch. The sketched pipe is propped at a higher angle than the one in his mouth. Smoke rises from the trashcan next to Rockwell. (Rockwell possibly poked fun at himself for once starting a fire in his workshop by dumping hot ash into a trashcan filled with oil-covered materials.)	Often a counselee presents incongruities which caricature or idealize himself. Sometimes such incongruities offer treasured insights into a cloaking mechanism for the heart, or indications of where idols nest themselves.

The counselee's narrative advances a particular global theme (metanarrative) into which the counselee has invested himself, or out of which he lives. This is the overarching story that gives the counselee meaning and structure. Beneath the narrative is the subtext. This is the sometimes stated, often implied, or wholly silent messages behind the actual words, the hidden intentions and supervisory motives which often must be painstakingly deciphered and disentangled.

> Listen carefully to people's stories, whether of sadness or happiness, and what they subsequently seek. In both instances, idols will be revealed. Stories of sadness often reveal dysfunctional idols, idols in peril. Stories of happiness reveal functional idols, idols in splendor. In both cases, the stories reveal something of the contents of the heart.

The general contours of the counselee's narrative follow either justice or injustice plotlines. For example, an injustice plotline could be the assertion that bad things happen to good people, or that good things happen to bad people, making God the antagonist and his work clouded with suspicion. This perceived injustice makes God into a rival to those who feel they deserve better.

Justice plots often take comfort that bad things happen to bad people, fulfilling the counselee's sense of cosmic order. This brings a measure of inner peace and confidence that God is both vigilant and willing to act. A variation on the justice narrative is the idea that bad things happen to good, but highly-flawed, people. This makes for engaging drama, a hope that change is possible so that flawed characters can be transformed. Often the counselee expresses this form of the justice narrative with the greatest passion because the heart is drawn to exhilarating drama.

The Counselee's Story Commonalities with Literature

As an image-bearer, each person is naturally adept at assigning cause and effect.[25] Thus, each person instinctively seeks out patterns and explanations for often befuddling life experience. However, on account of sin, man assigns cause and effect erroneously, so that, the unregenerate heart is highly-maladroit at decisive pattern recognition. In other words, the sinner seeks, but cannot ascertain, a cogent and conclusive motif which gives rise to his story. Employing a kind of Hegelian dialectic (thesis and antithesis giving rise to a new thesis), the sinner continually assesses and reassesses whether or not he has the story correct (concerning that which gives

Deluge
Anne-Louis Girodet de Roussy-Trioson, 1806

rise to the pattern). Incidentally, in response to his flawed pattern recognition, mankind often engages in confabulation, making up a story he can believe in order to explain behavior he does not understand (or refuses to understand).

In an attempt to make sense of his befuddling world the counselee shares a narrative, which includes major players and his interpretation of life events. There is a stated or implied:

1. Setting
2. Protagonist
3. Antagonist
4. Plot

---

[25] David McRaney, *You Are Not So Smart* (Gotham Books, 2011)

5. Moral

Thus, the counselor receives the counselee's narration of events, with the implied protagonist and antagonist operating in a particular setting. There is a plot out of which a moral eventually emerges. While generally the counselee views himself as the protagonist, there may be times when he also views himself as the antagonist, sensing a struggle within himself.[26]

Additionally, as with literature, the counselee's narrative shadows the following general pattern: exposition, rising action, climax, falling action, and denouement. In detecting this pattern, the counselor can trace the heart's interpretative drive, idols in ascent and in descent, taking flight and plummeting, seeking mastery and peaceful resolution (although such a drive is never satisfied).

> "There is a condition worse than blindness, and that is, seeing something that isn't there." (Thomas Hardy)

The issue is that the counselee's various narrative features (setting, protagonist, antagonist, plot, and moral) are generally misconstrued with regard to God's Word. Thus, the wise counselor must dismantle the counselee's story, reconstructing it upon a sound footing, so that future stories adopt a new basis for exposition, climax, and denouement. The rightly construed story offers a satisfying interpretation.

What is the Difference Between Literature and Psychology?[27]

Psychology is a false religion foisted upon the world by Satan and his servants to draw attention away from the gospel of Jesus Christ. However, could the same charge be leveled against literature? Is literature, as a structured and prescriptive form of story-telling, repackaged psychology which engages the imagination rather than the reason? In short, is literature simply well-disguised psychology?

The Bible itself is literature and, as such, interprets other literature. The Bible's literary qualities derive from the fact that it was written by men (and inspired by God), so as to make it accessible to men. Extra-biblical literature therefore, when interpreted through the gaze of the Bible, reveals something of the timeless human condition. The Bible, as literature, unlocks all other literature.

While psychology actively seeks to direct its adherents toward a humanistic

---

[26] For further discussion of the topic of mankind's self-glorifying storytelling see "Counseling as a New Set of Lenses (as a Presuppositional Endeavor)" in the first book in this series, *Ask for the Ancient Paths: From Art to Artifice to Arisen*, chapter 2: "The Counseling Ambition," and "Interpreting the Bible," also in the first book, chapter 3: "The Centrality of Scripture in Counseling"

[27] For a comprehensive response to psychology see the first book in this series, *Ask for the Ancient Paths: From Art to Artifice to Arisen*, chapter 8: "What Has Jerusalem To Do With Vienna?: The Case Against Psychology"

worldview, literature is less intent on this. Thus, well-crafted literature is an artful portrayal of the human drama which, when viewed through the lens of Scripture, offers an edifying and insightful look at the psyche. Psychology, on the other hand, already dons a godless set of lenses to interpret the drama. While literature offers the raw data of the human experience, psychology has already plotted that data using its own co-axial grid.

> "Art is a microscope which the artist fixes on the mysteries of his soul, and shows to people these mysteries which are common to all." (Leo Tolstoy)

Twenty Basic Plotlines[28]

The following plotlines are common metanarratives at work within mankind. One or more of these plotlines may be operative at any given time in the psyche.

Movement Plots

1. **Quest** - daring enterprise; seeking to overcome evil, deficiency, and perceived need

Three kings from the East travel to Bethlehem	Matthew 2:1-12
The Odyssey (8th century BC)	Homer (8th century BC)

2. **Adventure** – voyage to procure a needed entity with a measure of thrill in the travel

Beowulf (c. 8th – 11th centuries) – a tale of conflict, recounts the hero's ordeals, an escape from death, and ends with the community delivered from evil	Author unknown
Robinson Crusoe (1719)	Daniel Defoe (1660-1731)
Alice in Wonderland (1865)	Lewis Carroll (1832-1898)
Around the World in Eighty Days (1873)	Jules Verne (1828-1905)

3. **The Riddle** – the desire to uncover an enigma; being subject to erroneous judgment

The Legend of King Arthur (5th century AD, although it was	

---

[28] The idea for these plotlines, and their labels, borrowed from Ronald B. Tobias, *Twenty Master Plots* (Cincinnati: Writer's Digest Books, 1993). This material complemented and enhanced with Georges Polti, *The Thirty-Six Dramatic Situations* (translation by Lucille Ray) (Polti reconstructed the thirty-six plots that Johann Wolfgang Goethe (1749–1832) claims a literary critic Carlo Gozzi (1720–1806) developed).

not codified until about 1100) is an epic tale of a glorious king who united the Britons, and repelled their enemies, using the magical sword, "Excalibur." Arthur is thought to have established a round table for his knights so that each was equal in his kingdom.	
King Lear (c. 1606)	Shakespeare (1564–1616)

4. **Discovery** – the disloyalty or disgrace of a loved-one

Judas as traitor	Matthew 26:21

Jephthah, John Everett Millais, 1867

5. **Pursuit** – vaunting ambition

Pharaoh's army pursing the Israelites into the Reed Sea[29]	Exodus 14
Moby Dick (1851) contains a peculiar dilemma: Is the whale or Captain Ahab the real villain of the story? Is the enemy nature, in all its rage and fury, or is the true enemy man himself in all his rage and fury?	Herman Melville (1819-1891)

---

[29] According to Exodus 13:18 that which is traditionally called the "Red Sea" is correctly translated "Reed Sea."

6. **Rescue** – recovery; deliverance

| Daniel in the lion's den | Daniel 6 |

7. **Escape** – extrication from the cruelty of misfortune; movement from destitution to prosperity through talent, determination, or moral superiority

| Israel's deliverance from slavery to Egypt | Exodus 14:29-31 |
| *David Copperfield* (1850) tells of modest downtrodden characters whose special talents or beauty are at last revealed to the world with a favorable ending. | Charles Dickens' (1812-1870) |

| Dickens' novels expose the horrors of London life in the middle to late 19th century when children were forced into grueling labor, pollution was suffocating, and disease and death were rampant. The London that Dickens described was a place of unspeakable filth; the stench alone was enough to make one sick. Food was infested with insects. Winters were especially hard since there was insufficient warm clothing and coal. In the 1830s and 1840s half of the deaths in London were children under age ten. |

Conflict Plots

8. **Rivalry** – enmity of foes or even family; conflict; jealousy; adversity

King Saul was praised by Israel's townswomen for slaying thousands, David for tens of thousands; this caused Saul to grow angry and develop burning envy toward David. (From that point on Saul kept a suspicious eye on David.)	1 Samuel 18:7-9
Paul confronted Peter as rivals for the supremacy of Christ in the hearts of Gentile believers.	Galatians 2:11-14
"The Cask of Amontillado" (1846)	Edgar Allen Poe (1809-1849)

9. **Underdog** – an inferior vying for superiority

| David and Goliath | 1 Samuel 17 |

10. **Revenge** – seeking and achieving vengeance; justice

| Samson against the Philistines | Judges 15 |

11. **Ascension** – victory in revolt; overcoming a "monster"

The Legend of Robin Hood (late 11th century) is the story of a British nobleman treated unfairly by the invading Normans in 1066. Robin Hood, skilled with the longbow, dwelled in Sherwood Forest with his band of "merry men." He took on the persona of a criminal who robbed the rich and distributed their money to the poor.	Author unknown

The Duel After the Masquerade, Jean-Léon Gérôme, c. 1859

12. **Descent** – loss; tragedy; disaster sustained; death

Nebuchadnezzar became a beast	Daniel 4:33
In *Don Giovanni* (1787), at the finale, the Don stubbornly stood up to the Commendatore's ghost and was pulled down to hell on account of it.	Lorenzo Da Ponte's (1749–1838) libretto (opera by Mozart (1756-1791))
Frankenstein (1818)	Mary Shelley (1797-1851)

People tend to be drawn to a conflict narrative where it should not exist (such as between spouses or family members). However, when conflict occurs between those who should be in conflict (between the Christian and the world, for example), there is often little human interest.

Love Plots

13. **Love** – whether romantic or familial

Jacob loved Rachel	Genesis 29:18
Jane Eyre (1847)	Charlotte Brontë (1816-1855)

14. **Forbidden Love** – secretly requited love; adultery, crimes of love; obstacles to love; the desire to love a rival

David and Bathsheba	2 Samuel 11
Romeo and Juliet (1599) concerns two "star-crossed lovers" whose families are enemies. Romeo and Juliet meet secretly but are soon discovered. In the final scene, Romeo, finding Juliet in an unconscious stupor, thinks that she is dead. Consumed with grief, he kills himself with a dagger. When Juliet awakes and discovers Romeo dead she commits suicide. The play explores life's bitter calamity, that a love so pure and heartfelt was crushed by hatred, envy, and pitiable circumstance.	Shakespeare (1564–1616)
The Scarlet Letter (1850)	Nathaniel Hawthorne (1804-1864)

15. **Sacrifice** – sacrifice for an ideal; the pain of sacrificing for loved ones; remorse

A Tale of Two Cities (1859)	Charles Dickens (1812-1870)

Identity Plots

16. **Temptation** – to be lured by one's passions

Jesus tempted in the desert	Matthew 4:1-11

17. **Wretched Excess** – rebellion and subsequent insanity from overleaping desire; fatal imprudence

King Solomon was led astray by foreign wives	1 Kings 11:4-11

18. **Metamorphosis** – a complete change of identity

| *The Metamorphosis* (1915) | Franz Kafka (1883-1924) |

19. **Transformation** – rebirth of character

| In "A Christmas Carole" (1843) a curmudgeon, Ebenezer Scrooge, treats his employee, Bob Cratchit, with brutal frugality. Scrooge makes Cratchit work long hours with only one lump of coal for warmth during the bitter winter. Eventually, Scrooge is visited by three ghosts; one shows him his past, another his present, and the third his future. In the future Scrooge sees that because of Cratchit's penury his crippled son, Tiny Tim, dies. Scrooge is warned that he will be condemned unless he changes his ways. On Christmas morning Scrooge awakes a new man. Filled with Christmas joy, he runs to Bob Cratchit's house with a goose to be prepared for dinner. | Charles Dickens (1812-1870) |
| The parable of the Prodigal Son | Luke 15:11-31 |

A Christmas Carol
Charles Henry Granger, d. 1893

Charles Dickens considered Jesus' parable "The Prodigal Son" to be the greatest short-story ever written.

20. **Maturation** – personal growth

| *The Mayor of Casterbridge* (1886) | Thomas Hardy (1840-1928) |

The counselee authors storylines which accord with his sinful response to a God-shaped, God-infused, and God-directed universe. This plotline analysis reveals for the counselor the major theme (or themes) which occupy the counselee's psyche. Once that theme is identified the counselor can hone-in on the attached idols (in the process blocking out background noise which only clouds the counseling endeavor). Thus, this plotline analysis should uncover idols of the heart, understanding how those idols have often surreptitiously embedded themselves in the counselee's larger life story. The hope is that in the context of that story the heart's covenant alliances will emerge, so that the counselor can help lead the counselee to repentance. Without a penetrating look at the heart, there is no purpose to this analysis. However, as the heart is exposed a new plotline can be written with Jesus as hero, and counselee as supporting cast. The theme of the counselee's plotline may remain the same, but it is approached from a distinctly new angle and redefined in a Christ-centered manner.

That said, it must be noted that, from a biblical perspective, there is a single master plotline: God seeks and saves sinners who in turn worship him, as he is opposed by Satan who seeks worship for himself. Every human story could ultimately be resolved down to this central understanding of life events. However, the counselee, as fallen sinner, generally does not see this plotline operating.

Concluding Thoughts

People are instinctively drawn to stories since the psyche so readily traffics in them. This is one of the reasons that people crave drama, whether in literature, sports, or in family life. They long to both witness drama, and to live out that drama. Desire is the driver of human drama. For example, the desire for the praise of men leads to emotional pain in the experience of rejection, vengeful ideations, or, conversely, soaring jubilation when one achieves what he desires. The love of money leads to panic in times of economic turmoil, anguish over lost wealth, desperation concerning the future, or conversely elation over newfound riches.

For the Christian, there is no need to live out frivolous human drama because he has already experienced the great cosmic drama of Jesus Christ conquering evil on the cross. The Christian now lives in the story of redemption and participates in its ongoing unfolding within history. For this reason, the Christian does not need to create drama for himself. He does not crave additional stories for self-gratifying purposes; he merely basks in the story of his saving God. The most earth-shattering drama that could ever be imagined – God himself battling Satan, the world, and sin and defeating each through God's own humiliating death – has already been accomplished. God has written the story of his victory in vivid strokes throughout the Bible.

Artisanal Counseling:
A Foray into Methods

The Wounded Cavalier, William Shakespeare Burton, 1855

Introduction

Leviticus 14:14-18 states that one healed from an infectious skin disease was to bring a lamb to the priest for cleansing. Blood from the lamb was placed on the healed person's right earlobe, right thumb, and right big toe.[1] Incidentally, this was the same procedure prescribed for consecrating priests. Likely God intended to send a message that the highest and lowest in society were equals on account of their common need for salvation through the shedding of blood.

Beyond this, the one healed of an infectious skin disease had now experienced God's grace through healing, having been set free from social ostracism. For the one healed of an infectious disease, the priest placed oil over the blood smeared on the earlobe,

---
[1] Leviticus 14:14

thumb, and big toe.[2] The blood represented justification, the oil, sanctification. Oil signified healing, renewal, and anointing. One was declared cleansed and purified through the blood, to which God added the sanctifying oil of the Spirit to make that declared cleansing complete. God renews those he saves.

> The purpose of sanctification is never that one should become proud but rather that one should become pure.

It is fascinating that at the priests' consecration this anointing with oil was not stipulated.[3] It may be that the one healed of an infectious disease now enjoyed a greater experience of God than the priest himself. The healed person had previously lived outside the camp. Yet, he was now reinstated into the community, in effect raised from death to life. The healed person had seen God's wonder in a way that others had not, and therefore, through his trials, had experienced something of the wonder of sanctification. Those in Christ are like the one healed of an infectious skin disease, brought from death to life and subsequently sanctified.

Artisanal Counseling

Chinese cuisine is carefully balanced according to the concepts of *yin* (阴) and *yang* (阳). *Yin* is the feminine represented by cooler softer foods. *Yang* is the masculine, spicier solid foods. A true Chinese chef plans dishes with exactly the right balance. For example, meat (*yang*) must be balanced by vegetables (*yin*), and ginger (*yang*) is combined with scallions (*yin*). Sweet and sour is countered by spicy, and cold and hot dishes combine for proper digestion. There is also attention to the aroma, color, and texture of dishes, following carefully prescribed ancient rules.[4]

Artisanal pertains to "a high-quality or distinctive product made in small quantities, usually by hand or using traditional methods," such as artisanal bread or cheese.[5] Like the preparation of fine Chinese cuisine, with its keen attention to detail, so too, counseling is, in many ways, an artisanal endeavor, not merely stating biblical doctrines, but knowing how to rightly apply those doctrines so that they are winsome and rightly balanced. There is nothing in counseling which is "mass-produced," but rather all counseling is highly-personalized and specifically tailored for the counselee.

On account of the Bible, the biblical counselor can speak to any issue facing any person at any stage in life in any culture. The reason is that the Bible offers wisdom which transcends the limitations of human experience (whether of age, gender, culture, or sin pattern). Therefore, even if, for example, one were never a parent he is able to

---

[2] Leviticus 14:17
[3] Leviticus 8:23, 24
[4] Hugh Thompson and Kathryn Lane, *China: An Eyewitness Guide* (Dorling Kindersley, 2005) 421.
[5] Dictionary.com

wisely counsel parents (and their children) using God's Word. (Prioritizing experience is an outgrowth of psychology which sees human reason and experience as conduits for truth.)

> Artisanal counseling could be summarized by the question, "How does God influence the problem, diagnosis, strategy, solution, insight, and the type of counselor needed?"[6]

The wise counselor holds a vision of sanctification for the counselee under his care. That vision of sanctification is:[7]

1. **Specific.** The vision of sanctification should be clearly articulated otherwise the counselee will never know if he is advancing toward it.

2. **Relevant.** The sanctification goal must be in accordance with God's declared will (as stated in his Word) for the counselee's life.

3. **Attainable.** One's expected growth in sanctification should accord with the measure of one's faith in Christ. If one's faith does not measure up to one's expectation for sanctification, he will likely doubt Christ's ability to effect sanctification in his people. (The point is that some Christians expect to be free from besetting sin, while not being willing to take the steps required by faith to do battle with that sin. The counselor should hold expectations for sanctification in accord with the counselee's level of faith.)

4. **Measurable.** Sanctification may be difficult to quantify, but there should be an ongoing qualitative assessment of its progress. One should be able to in some sense gauge how closely his life accords with God's will. Are there observable benchmarks, models, or evaluators for the degree of sanctification one experiences?

5. **Ongoing.** While most set goals based on a set beginning and end, the Christian's growth in sanctification is an ongoing quest requiring daily repentance and continued vigilance, in order to maintain and advance his already attained victory in Christ.[8]

A prevalent problem that I find in a church setting is that much is spoken in generalities. It is common to hear, "love God," "trust God," "obey God," and "glorify God." While these statements are all supremely true, another facet of artisanal counseling is making the counseling message specific and detailed so as to avoid

---

[6] David Powlison, Westminster Theological Seminary, Philadelphia, Pennsylvania
[7] Some ideas borrowed from Kathleen Allen and Peter Economy, *The Complete MBA for Dummies*, 1st edition. (For Dummies Press, 2000)
[8] 1 Timothy 6:20

nebulous generalities. When statements are obscure the sinner is afforded too much leeway to interpret them based on his vagary. There is simply too much "play" in the concepts, and like a moth to a flame, the sinner feels a magnetic pull to abstractions which offer no substantive bulwark against the heart's maraud.

Undertow, Winslow Homer, 1886

For example, to simply advise that one should trust God usually translates into trusting God to meet one's idolatrous desire.[9] Telling one to glorify God in his personal life can easily be hijacked into, "Do what makes one happy." The logic may go, "After all, wouldn't God be glorified if I were happy?" Thus, the artisanal counselor does not allow concepts to remain "radioactive" abstractions, but develops them in sufficient depth, and with adequate detail, to cause them to be wielded with sanctifying purpose.

Biblical Counseling Introduces a Person, Not a Set of Principles[10]

Jamestown, Virginia, was settled by the Cavaliers, both aristocrats and servants, who traveled from England in search of gold in the New World. They cared little for hard work, conservative values, or goodwill toward the Native Americans. The Cavaliers squandered their time sending "fools gold" (pyrite) back to England. In fact, many starved on account of their lazy, frivolous, and debauched lifestyle. They preferred chasing riches to building a stable and productive community. It was the Cavaliers' spirit which permeated the South, eventually embracing the heinous practice of

---

[9] This observation from Paul Tripp, Westminster Theological Seminary, Philadelphia, Pennsylvania
[10] For a more comprehensive look at this topic see chapter 4: "The Umbilicus of Personal Relationship with Christ"

slavery.[11] In some ways, this is a fitting introduction to this section on person-over-principles. Principles are pyrite; the person of Jesus is the equivalent of building a "stable and productive community" which will stand the test of time.

Biblical counseling is not therapeutic in the world's sense, not cognitive therapy, not behavioral therapy, not self-actualization (meeting perceived needs). The Bible does not present the human dilemma as arising from mere wrong thoughts, mere wrong behavior, or the scars of unrequited emotional needs. The Bible does not offer a set of principles, how-to steps, or coping techniques. The Bible, with laser-like intensity and focus, pinpoints heart worship, the nouthetic core.[12]

> Counseling is not the gathering of helpful personal facts, nor the cold intellectual rehearsal of doctrine. Counseling is God himself seeking out, ravishing, and rebuilding hearts.

The Bible offers an encounter with a person – Jesus Christ. Its message is that each human being was created by a person, sin exists vis-à-vis that person, and its absolution, indeed the very reason the universe exists, is revealed in that person as savior. Thus, human design, the human problem, and its solution are all profoundly personal. The Bible centers upon introducing and inducing faith in the person of God himself. Anything less than this is ultimately a devious plan masterminded by Satan, which leaves the personhood of man untouched and un-impacted.

To reduce the Christian message to principles is a travesty of epic proportion in that this subverts the gospel, deifies man, and glorifies man's attempts to change himself through his own effort. To reduce the Christian message to a set of principle is to rend the very fabric of the gospel. The sinner's quest for a prism which refracts (and thus isolates) the Bible's teaching into discrete principles is the devil's errand. This desire for principles is an attempt to wrest from Scripture all that mankind needs to conclusively live without God, like erecting a Xanadu for the psyche. In contriving a system, the sinner's futile hope is that Scripture would cede the means to no longer need relationship with its author. For this reason, the wise counselor does not try to merely plug principles into the gaps in a counselee's life; he tries to rescue the fool from his foolishness.[13]

> If one gives an idolater better tools he will just use those tools to strengthen the effectiveness of his idolatry.[14]

---

[11] Peter Marshall and David Manuel, *From Sea to Shining Sea: God's Plan for America Unfolds* (Grand Rapids, Michigan: Fleming H. Revell, 1986)
[12] David Powlison, Westminster Theological Seminary, Philadelphia, Pennsylvania
[13] Paul Tripp, *Instruments in the Redeemer's Hands: People in Need of Change Helping People in Need of Change* (Presbyterian and Reformed Publishing Company, 2002)
[14] Paul Tripp, *Instruments in the Redeemer's Hands: People in Need of Change Helping People in Need of Change* (Presbyterian and Reformed Publishing Company, 2002)

Scripture exists to confront the human person with the person of God. While the counselor daily prays for those he counsels and seeks to bring Scripture to bear upon the issues of the heart, the wise counselor seeks far more. He engages in information gathering, and probing analysis, to bring God himself into the inner sanctum, into the concealed workings of the counselee's heart. The counselor places the dots close enough together that they can be connected, the final image revealing that the counselee's only hope is in surrendering his will to Jesus, and inviting Jesus to do the work that the counselee has tried in vain to accomplish.

Socrates Tears Alcibiades from the Embrace of Sensual Pleasure
Jean-Baptiste Regnault, 1791

If one encountered a physically disabled person, one would certainly not offer him a lesson on anatomy and physiology as a supposed cure. Such a person needs more than right understanding; he needs profound healing. So too, the sinner needs an actual and ongoing encounter with Jesus Christ.[15] The Bible does not offer an intellectual understanding of God and man; it brings God and man into communication, and ultimately into relationship, so that man can be healed.

Consider that Israel's battles against Jericho and Ai are recorded with highly-detailed

---

[15] Paul Tripp, *Instruments in the Redeemer's Hands: People in Need of Change Helping People in Need of Change* (Presbyterian and Reformed Publishing Company, 2002)

descriptions.[16] These two cities serve as opposite poles in Israel's approach to holy warfare. Jericho was a high-walled city, difficult to lay siege, yet Israel was able to take it with ease, as it relied upon the Lord. On the other hand, Ai was a vulnerable city against which Israel was quickly decimated, because it did not inquire of the Lord and did not do battle in the Lord's strength.

In like manner, Christians are called to do battle with sin, a battle under the Lord's direction and in his strength. In this way, the Christian is surely victorious, even when the sin involved is seemingly formidable and indominable. Conversely, when the Christian does battle in his own strength he is easily defeated, even when the sin at hand looks relatively manageable.

> Every year 100 people throughout the world choke to death on a pen cap. Consider the tragic lead up to such an event, the seemingly nugatory act of placing a cap in one's mouth only to find it fatally lodged in one's windpipe. Such is the plight of mankind when he seeks to deal with the heart's evil as an adjustable moral aberration.

The Christian is to receive that which God imparts through Christ, and is not to view Jesus as merely a moral teacher or exemplary model of faith. Christians are not called to be mere imitators of Christ. Christ actually imparts life-changing power as he sanctifies the Christian. Jesus, working in the believer's heart, seeks to change:

1. One's loves[17]
2. Where one places his confidence[18]
3. One's fears[19]
4. One's anxieties[20]
5. One's longings[21]
6. One's demands[22]
7. What one places before his eyes and surrounds himself with[23]
8. One's willingness to act upon his own good pleasure[24]
9. One's compulsive self-interest[25]
10. One's preoccupation with personal concerns, comforts, or riches[26]
11. What one desires to install as God[27]

---

[16] Joshua 6:1-27; Joshua 7, 8
[17] Hosea 2:12-17
[18] Philippians 3:3-7
[19] Luke 12:4, 5; Philippians 1:28; Acts 16:27
[20] Psalms 127:2; Philippians 4:6, 7
[21] Ephesians 2:3-7
[22] Matthew 18:28-35; Luke 7:47
[23] Philippians 3:19
[24] Philippians 2:13-15
[25] Philippians 1:17; 2:3, 21
[26] Philippians 4:6, 12; Acts 16:19
[27] Philippians 3:19

> "Let the message of Christ dwell among you richly as you teach and admonish one another with all wisdom through psalms, hymns, and songs from the Spirit, singing to God with gratitude in your hearts." (Colossians 3:16)

There is a root error in thinking that the counselor can just present "data" and the counselee will arrive at the truth and accept it. This assumes that human reason functions properly, so that it rightly sees fact and dutifully assesses it as God would. In reality, the counselee often reinterprets the evidence to fit his self-serving views of God. He falls back on his presuppositions to reinterpret reality as he believes it should be interpreted. Idols giggle with impish delight in the face of evidence, unless that evidence is attended by an actual confrontation with God's Spirit.

> "Each had his past shut in him like the leaves of a book known to him by heart; and his friends could only read the title." (Virginia Woolf)

The counselor must guide the counselee to rightly interpret the evidence in submission to God. He assists the counselee in seeing the evidence as God sees it, so as to align the counselee's interpretation with God's. In this way, the counselor draws the counselee into God's story, entices him to enter into a new plot in which Jesus is the beginning and the end of his personal story.[28] As one's personal story then becomes the story of Jesus death and resurrection this is the dawn of change.

While the Bible's teaching, when stripped of the personhood of God and reduced to mere abstraction, is often co-opted for nefarious purpose, that teaching, when presented under the protective gaze of the gospel, takes on the meaning God intended. Hebrews 4:12 states, "For the word of God is alive and active. Sharper than any double-edged sword, it penetrates even to dividing soul and spirit, joints and marrow; it judges the thoughts and attitudes of the heart." When the Word of God is viewed through the prism of the gospel, Jesus crucified and raised, alive and relational, it cannot be manipulated for self-serving purpose.

The Fractal Method of Counseling

The term "fractal" refers to the entire design being found in each individual part. For example, a tree is composed of branches and leaves which themselves bear the design of the entire tree. The tree's shape is replicated in each limb, branch, leaf, and even in the capillaries within each leaf. Each part, no matter how small, manifests the design of the whole. In like manner, the fractal method of counseling means that the entirety of the message (creation, fall, redemption) permeates every topic of discussion. It is an approach which brings the central truths of God's Word to bear

---

[28] David and Sharon Covington, "Introduction to Biblical Counseling" notes, 2004

upon every issue, so that the gospel is always present, even in the most minute detail.

In the fractal method the Biblical counselor weaves into every conversation a recognition of design (image of God), sin, and redemption. So, for example, a counselor would not confront idolatry as an isolated entity since he recognizes that a worship vacuum can never exist within the heart. Renunciation must be followed by redemptive faith, "put off" must be followed by "put on."[29] Thus, the counselor seeks the destruction of idols only within the larger context of repentance and renewal in Christ. The counselor, thus, while confronting the idolatry problem, simultaneously offers the gospel solution. This ultimately gives the gospel prominence in the discussion.

> "Wisdom begins at the end." (Daniel Webster)

Counseling as Incarnational Ministry

I asked one of my students which career she hoped to pursue. Her reply, "I want to be a translation" (she, of course, meant a "translator"). We all enjoyed a good chuckle. But as I thought about her response, it occurred to me that this seemed to be more than just a simple error. Her response revealed something about the nature of people. My student does not just want to perform the function of translator; she wants to be the translation itself. She wants to identify so closely with her work that her words flow through her, that her very being is present in those words.

This in some way fits the Bible's concept of a counselor. When asked what one wants to be, the Christian might respond, "I want to be counsel." In other words, one does not merely seek to be a *counselor*, but the *counsel* itself, to be an incarnation of the true Counselor, God himself. In seeking to incarnate God's counsel, one hopes to be a living manifestation of that counsel so as to cause the counselee to desire to "do business with" God himself.[30]

> "Most of history is a record of the triumphs, disasters, and follies of famous people. What we forget is the lives of quiet, common men and women who accomplished great things in secret." (Philip Howard)

Some time ago there was a fad among American churches to raise the thought-provoking question, "What would Jesus do?" This points to a grave misunderstanding in the church today, using Jesus as simply a good example or a good moral teacher. Such a question is fundamentally misguided because it assumes that one can do what Jesus did. In fact, one does not need a model of good behavior, he needs one to save

---

[29] Ephesians 4:22-24
[30] This term "doing business with God" from Sharon Covington, Biblical Counselor

him from himself; he needs daily repentance and growth in faith, so that he is changed by Christ directly.

Portrait of Andrea Odoni, Lorenzo Lotto, 1527

In the same way, the counselor is not merely an example of Christ, nor does he only try to model Christ. The counselor confronts people with the living Christ himself. He does not just hold forth an exemplary model, but introduces them to the model-maker, Jesus as *personal* savior. As incarnational ministry, counseling is daily meaningful confrontation with Jesus himself so as to effect progressive incremental change, changing what people live for, how they see their lives, and what they desire.

> "I expect to pass through life but once. If, therefore, there is any kindness I can show, or any good I can do, let me do it now, for I shall not pass this way again." (William Penn)

The Counselor as Prophet, Priest, and King

> "…I have become all things to all people so that by all possible means I might save some. I do all this for the sake of the gospel, that I may share in its blessings." (1 Corinthians 9:22b-23)

The Counselor as Prophet

The prophet speaks truth, interprets, and offers a sense of meaning. The prophet's objective is that the sinner's deliberate ignorance should turn to wisdom.[31] For this Israel's prophets were hated, insulted, stoned, and callously murdered.[32] When the counselor speaks truth into a sinful heart he will often be vociferously, if not violently, opposed. He will be subject to *ad hominem* attacks and excoriated. This is to be expected, especially when the counselee is particularly wed to his idolatry.

An aspect of being a prophet is that the counselor does not wait for counseling opportunities. He steps forward (when appropriate) to speak truth to power (the heart's stronghold), never to tear out healthy tissue, but to surgically remove cancerous lesions. The counselor's intrusion is always to remove that which brings death, and to instill that which gives life.

That being said, there is a pesky cultural expectation that one will not poke his nose into another's business. This expectation, at times, must be defied in order for God's work to move forward. God does not always wait for people to ask for help (because they generally do not know that they need help until it is too late). For example, John the Baptist did not wait for Herod to ask about the legality of marriage to Herodias.[33] John courageously spoke, and was eventually beheaded for it.[34] Just as God struck out in search of the lost coin and the lost sheep, or ran toward the prodigal son,[35] so too, the prophet steps forward to persuade the sinner of his glaring need, recognizing that, more often than not, the counselee has no idea of the severity of his imperiled state.[36]

> John Woodford said, "Silence is a powerful tool in negotiation; the one who speaks first loses." Often the counselor can wrongly become the de facto "voice of God" in the counselee's life. Therefore, there may be moments when the counselor is rightly silent, when he patiently allows the counselee to arrive at the truth (albeit with some gentle nudging). Silence may be best when the counselor has already given the counselee a great deal of guidance, and to continue to cover the same ground will prove unfruitful. Therefore, at key junctures, the counselor's silence may be the needed hiatus for the counselee to find his own answers in God's Word.

Like John the Baptist, a counselor after God's own heart does not "play it safe," only entering into those relationships and situations that are most promising, or likely to produce the desired effect. Sometimes the counselor pours water on his own firewood,[37] puts himself in a measure of peril in order to reach others. The wise and

---

[31] Michael Bobick, *From Slavery to Sonship: A Biblical Psychology for Pastoral Counseling* (1995) 43. (class notes)
[32] Luke 13:34
[33] Mark 6:18
[34] Mark 6:27
[35] Luke 15
[36] Acts 18:4; 2 Corinthians 5:11
[37] 1 Kings 18:33-35

faithful counselor pours out his life for others,[38] in the process forgetting to save or protect his own life from possible harm (physical, emotional, financial, legal, etc.). There have been many I counsel who represent a liability to me, a situation that threatens to capsize other endeavors. Yet, I am willing to take measured risks for the sake of helping some know Christ, and be known by Christ.

The Counselor as Priest

> "Every high priest is selected from among the people and is appointed to represent the people in matters related to God, to offer gifts and sacrifices for sins. He is able to deal gently with those who are ignorant and are going astray, since he himself is subject to weakness." (Hebrews 5:1, 2)

The priest offers comfort through empathetic understanding and mercy. His objective is that the sinner's fear should turn to peace.[39] The counselor, as priest, rightly rejoices with those who rejoice, and mourns with those who mourn,[40] coming alongside the broken-hearted with the soothing balm of a compassionate God. While the counselor is called to extend comfort to a suffering soul, show understanding in the midst of paralyzing loss, and express sympathy to the downtrodden, this must not come at the expense of the counselor's other stations, the prophetic and the kingly. However, the modern "feminization" of the church tends to prioritize and over-emphasize the station of priest, so that counsel is prone to permissive abstraction with regard to the description of God's love.

> "Therefore I will give their wives to other men and their fields to new owners. From the least to the greatest, all are greedy for gain; prophets and priests alike, all practice deceit. They dress the wound of my people as though it were not serious. 'Peace, peace,' they say, when there is no peace." (Jeremiah 8:10, 11)

The Counselor as King

First Corinthians 4:8 reads, "Already you have all you want! Already you have become rich! You have become kings--and that without us! How I wish that you really had become kings so that we might be kings with you!" The counselor is called to exhibit a type of kingship in Christ's place. Such a king asserts authority and speaks with power. The counselor-as-king's objective is that the sinner's rebellion should be surrendered.[41] The kingly function may at times offer a taste of God's wrath and hints of the impending punishment upon sin. As a representative king, there are times when

---

[38] Philippians 2:17
[39] Michael Bobick, *From Slavery to Sonship: A Biblical Psychology for Pastoral Counseling* (1995) 43. (class notes)
[40] Romans 12:15
[41] Michael Bobick, *From Slavery to Sonship: A Biblical Psychology for Pastoral Counseling* (1995) 43. (class notes)

faced with a fool, that the counselor must firmly assert the consequence of sin to those who refuse to turn in repentance. (This may require an appropriate display of godly anger in order to emphasize the severity of the matter.)

The Capture of Kazan by Ivan the Terrible on October 2, 1552
Grigoriy Ugryumov, c. 1800

"The one who has real vision sees things that are invisible." (Jonathan Swift)

In modern times the church has experienced "the death of outrage" as it becomes increasingly comfortable with transgression within its own members.[42] The church has grown weak in its display of the kingly function, likely out of the fear of being labeled a "hellfire and brimstone" church. On account of the fear of man, and a desire for the praises of man, the kingly function is essentially non-existent in most churches. There is no outrage for sin and no burning consumption for purity among God's people.

Perennially donning a priestly demeanor is far safer, more socially acceptable, potentially avoids litigation, conveniently avoids conflict, and generally guards the church from negative perceptions in the surrounding community. The church has grown "chronically nice" so that it essentially displays one-dimensional interpersonal relationship, never courageously calling others to repentance, to exhibit discipline, or

---

[42] This term "the death of outrage" from William Bennett

to show passion for purity in Christ. A chronic priestly demeanor severely hobbles God's work, renders the church impotent and impoverished in its growth in sanctification, and spawns feckless and flaccid leadership. (This is the curse of what might be termed the "feminization" of the church.)

The counselor reflects Jesus himself as prophet (instructs), priest (atones for), and king (sovereign over). The counselor, while functioning as prophet, priest, and king, both abides in Jesus (the perfection of all previous prophets, priests, and kings),[43] and presents Jesus to those he counsels. That is his sole objective.

The counselor's mission is to show the counselee areas of the heart in need of repentance and areas surrendered in life-giving faith. The right counsel should make one uncomfortable with sin, so as to effect change. It should also make one comfortable with faith that God longs to praise and magnify. The counselor as prophet, priest, and king is called to participate in this winnowing effect.[44]

In the final analysis, the counselor should be both present and "invisible." The counselor, as God's delegate, incarnates Scripture as he displays God's mind, emotions, invitation, and at times, wrath. Yet, there is a sense in which the counselor should be invisible so as to let God, through his Word, speak to, direct, and change hearts. The counselor never draws attention to himself and never stands on his own understanding, but rather in every interaction showcases God's Word. Thus, the counselor as functioning prophet, priest, and king draws attention to the savior.

The Counselor's Love:[45] "I Love Mankind – It's People I Can't Stand"[46]

In each interaction Jesus perfectly loved those with whom he interacted. To the Pharisees Jesus spoke in harsh and confrontational tones. Matthew 23:15 states "Woe to you, teachers of the law and Pharisees, you hypocrites! You travel over land and sea to win a single convert, and when you have succeeded, you make them twice as much a child of hell as you are." At other times Jesus stated the truth directly and boldly. Matthew 10:21, 22 states,

> Looking at him, Jesus felt a love for him and said to him, 'One thing you lack: go and sell all you possess and give to the poor, and you will have treasure in heaven; and come, follow me.' But at these words he was saddened, and he went away grieving, for he was one who owned much property.

---

[43] Charles Hodge, *Systematic Theology* (Nabu Press, 2010)
[44] Matthew 3:12
[45] For a more complete discussion of the Bible's description of love see the case study, "God's *Sui Generis* Love," in chapter 2: "Suffering: The Kintsugi Objective"; also see "The Counselor's Compassion" in the same chapter.
[46] Quote from Charles Schulz (1922-2000)

To the broken in spirit, Jesus spoke in gentle ways. Luke 23:43 recounts, "Jesus answered him [the crucified thief], 'Truly I tell you, today you will be with me in paradise.'"

Jesus perfectly loved the Pharisees in his rebuke; he perfectly loved the young rich ruler in his command; he perfectly loved the repentant thief in his promise of salvation. In every interaction Jesus displayed the entirety of God's love, not merely isolated aspects of it. Thus, in each interaction Jesus manifest God's love as judging and compassionate, fighting for and fighting against the sinner, hating sin, defending, personal, pursuing, suffering, desiring repentance, and ultimately nurturing relationship.

The Good Samaritan
Vincent Willem van Gogh, 1890

Like Jesus, and in submission to Jesus, the counselor's love (albeit imperfect) follows the contours of God's love for sinners. The counselor's love seeks to facilitate heart change, pursues, gently intrudes, cares for, displays grace, suffers with, perseveres, confronts, hates the evil within, judges that which ought to be judged, moves forward with energy, watches, defends, teaches, fights for, fights with, is personal, is specific, seeks repentance, and desires restoration with God and others. Therefore, the counselor's love is never non-directive, detached, passive, impersonal, judgment-less, or neutral.[47]

Love is, without question, the limiting reagent in the counseling endeavor.[48] Counseling will only bear fruit to the extent that the counselor truly loves the counselee. The counselor's love arises from the continual recognition that he has been extended a high honor in Christ, the charge of the cure of souls. The counselor cares

---

[47] David Powlison, "Is God's Love Unconditional?" *The Journal of Biblical Counseling* (Glenside, Pennsylvania: The Christian Counseling and Education Foundation)
[48] 1 Corinthians 13:13

for those who belong to Christ, those for whom Jesus shed his blood. This should cause the counselor to enter into the counseling relationship, and execute his craft, with a profound sense of godly fear and trembling.[49] (This same fear and trembling should apply to any Christian offering counsel in any context.)

> When faced with one in the grip of suffering never say that you know how he feels.[50] While this may seem like a sensitive and kind approach, it is not. Such a statement does not build trust or rapport; it fosters simmering resentment. One does not, and cannot, know how another feels in midst of his particular experience of suffering.

Love dictates that the faithful counselor does not just sympathize with those who seek his counsel; he empathizes with them. The counselor does more than just listen to another's story. He figuratively enters into that story, imagining his own life within the others' context. He mentally explores the facets of a life lived under certain threats, faced with challenges, burdened with disappointments, tyrannized by suffering, in the grip of addiction, and living with the burning regret of stinging loss. Only when the counselor has adequately understood something about the life in front of him, should he be so bold as to offer counsel. (Remember that Job's friends sat with him in silence for seven days and nights before daring to speak.[51])

> "A wise old owl lived in an oak;
> The more he saw the less he spoke;
> The less he spoke the more he heard.
> Why can't we all be like that wise old bird?" (Old Mother Goose Nursery Rhyme)

The Willingness to Disrupt Harmony

In Genesis 33:10, a fearful Jacob encountered his brother Esau and told him, "For to see your face is like seeing the face of God, now that you have received me favorably." It is remarkable that just prior, in Genesis 32:30, Jacob had, in fact, seen the face of God, and said that his life had been spared. Jacob seemed to quickly forget the experience of wrestling with God and so resorted to craving a ready sedative, peace with his brother.

In certain cultures interpersonal harmony is prized above all else. To break harmony, for any reason, is to break relational bonds and rend the fabric of the social order. This focus on harmony is merely neatly wrapped fear of man, and craving for the praise of man. While harmony can often be a manifestation of God's common grace, it is usually maintained at the expense of truth. Additionally, God prioritizes sanctification above harmony, so that often harmony must be sacrificed for the sake of

---

[49] Philippians 2:12
[50] The Larry Crabb biblical counseling seminar, Wayne, Pennsylvania
[51] Job 2:13

inducing heart change. Discord and confrontation are frequently necessary if one is to battle evil within himself and others. Those who worship harmony miss the blessing God seeks to bestow.

> "Do not suppose that I have come to bring peace to the earth. I did not come to bring peace, but a sword." (Matthew 10:34)

Harmony built on falsehood is not harmony at all. Lies ultimately result in greater disharmony, distrust, distance, misunderstanding, and eventually open conflict. The desire for harmony has become one's god when it controls each interaction and is the highest goal, above God's truth.

In the modern world often those who disrupt harmony are condemned, denounced, pressured, manipulated, and reasoned with to simply comply, accept, acquiesce, and abandon their integrity. The objective is to deify human feelings and desires over God's. Sadly, as placation is reinforced people lose their desire to persist in social interaction. Life devolves into a web of lies, a charade of upholding false pretenses, the mere posture of relationship, and simply guarding one's reputation.

> "They dress the wound of my people as though it were not serious. 'Peace, peace,' they say, when there is no peace." (Jeremiah 6:14)

While the sinful heart reflexively eschews conflict, especially when that conflict appears threatening, conflict may be clear evidence of growth in holiness. The Christian must recognize that as he draws closer to God he will at times find greater opposition, discord, and isolation. Conversely, the Christian who blindly lives at peace with the world has invariably fallen into a measure of complacency and compromise. As a backslidden Christian lives in the flesh and disregards God, his peace with the world will likely increase, so that he is more comfortable with sin but continually unsettled with regard to God.

Romans 12:18 is clear, "If it is possible, as far as it depends on you, live at peace with all men." Thus, the Christian makes every effort to live at peace through sacrificing personal desires and overlooking offenses. However, to fully obey Jesus is to at times experience conflict, not just with the world, but with Christians who love the world and their own sin. The wise counselor is willing to experience disharmony with others, and even cause others to live in disharmony, where that produces peace with God.

> "No doubt there have to be differences among you to show which of you have God's approval." (1 Corinthians 11:19)

Establishing the Terms of Engagement

In John 6:15 the crowds sought to seize Jesus and make him king. They did not want a Messiah; they craved a king. They wanted one who would give them power, command over their fears, respect among the nations, success in the eyes of the world, safety from marauding tribes, and a sense of pride. However, God himself was to be their king, so that each of their longings was to be met in him directly. Yet, the crowds wanted someone to offer them the things of the world – an abundant life in the here-and-now. It was because of this love for the world, and its systems, that the people refused to countenance their sin, or Jesus as savior.

As previously mentioned, Jesus would not allow the people to pull him off of his Father's plan. Jesus was like a hub with spokes attached (the spokes being relationships with others).[52] Those spokes continually pressured Jesus in an attempt to pull him off-center. However, Jesus would not allow those around him to displace him from his center point, his Father's will.[53] This was always the source of glaring conflict between Jesus and others. While others held a sinful agenda for Jesus, he would not permit himself to be distracted or diverted.

In this same way, the wise counselor remains fixed on a certain center-point of uncompromised truth, and he is not seduced into deviating from God's plans. As winsome and irenic as he may be, as sensitive and improvisational, the counselor does not allow himself to be sidetracked by the counselee's agenda, an agenda that would invariably short-circuit a steady gaze at the heart. The counselor does not allow the counselee to install the counselor as an accomplice in sin. This causes him to set rigorous terms of engagement, to hold to an agenda which accords directly with God's.

> As part of both my ministry and leisure time, I travel to several new cities each year. I love jogging, and have established a tradition of running through a city as a way to see it at a relatively slow place on the street level. That being said, I have learned the hard way that when running on unfamiliar streets often my sense of direction fails me; so it is easy to get lost. Thus, my usual plan is to travel in straight lines, to remain on a main thoroughfare and follow it to an obvious landmark. In other words, I make few diversions.
>
> When counseling those with whom I have little familiarity, I operate in "straight lines," focused on the gospel (and its related development). I only make turns at obvious "landmarks," and refuse to rely on my own sense of direction (as that may produce an unfruitful point of departure). In other words, it is easy to get sidetracked by a counselee's agenda, if one is not careful.

---

[52] For additional discussion of this topic see the case study "Prayer as Life-Blood of Relationship with Jesus" in chapter 4: "The Umbilicus of Personal Relationship with Christ"
[53] Jack Dean Kingsbury, *Matthew as Story* (Augsburg: Fortress Press, 1988)

Both Upholding and Vacating the Social Contract

In Stephen Vincent Benet's (1898-1943) short story "The Devil and Daniel Webster"[54] (1937) a New Hampshire farmer, Jabez Stone, no longer willing to tolerate his spate of bad luck, swears to sell his soul to the devil. The next day the devil, using the pseudonym "Mr. Scratch," shows up at Stone's home with an offer to buy Stone's soul in exchange for seven years of prosperity. Stone accepts the offer. However, when the payment date arrives, Stone seeks to break the contract and hires the renowned attorney Daniel Webster (1782-1852) to represent him in the case. Webster calls for a jury trial at which he presents compelling arguments for the dissolution of the contract. Through his shear force of eloquence (even though the trial is stacked against Webster), he wins the jury's agreement, releasing Stone from his contractual obligation. (Incidentally, as part of the court's judgment the devil was barred from ever again bothering anyone in New Hampshire.)

Patrick Henry in the House of Burgesses
Peter F. Rothermel, 1851

The point is that while Stone entered into a legally-binding contract with the devil, he was the beneficiary of a social contract with his advocate Daniel Webster (which ultimately saved his soul). Webster fought for something far greater than legal right because he believed in the cause. That was the basis for the social contract.

Likewise, there is a certain tacit social contract between the counselor and the counselee, to which, under the dictates of biblical wisdom, both should adhere and

---

[54] Stephen Vincent Benet, "The Devil and Daniel Webster" (Farrar and Rinehart, 1937)

also disregard. What is the social contract? It is an often unspoken collection of boundaries and invitations which society has established in order to guard and prosper proper relationships. The social contract shifts and adjusts based on the nature of relationships, from a stranger on the street to a lifelong friend. How does the counselor rightly take advantage of social openings, while not abusing assumed restrictions?

Recently, a former student contacted me with news that she had become a Christian. (I had taught her four years prior at which time she regularly attended a Bible study at my home.) We had lost contact after I left the school, but she recently emailed me for advice on some personal matters. In the course of our discussion it surfaced that she had found a boyfriend. After some prayer and careful consideration, I shared with her my grave concerns for dating, and my admonition to seek a Bible-directed form of courtship. I sensed that she was taken-aback by my warning, as if this was out-of-bounds from her initial questions. Maybe I had indeed overstepped the perceived social boundary. Yet, I felt I had to offer some help before mistakes were made that might bring a lifetime of regret, mistakes I have seen hundreds of times in even the most well-intentioned Christians.

Did I vacate something of the tacit social contract? I think so. But I did so under the dictates of love for another, and under the guidance of the Holy Spirit. I did it to counsel a whole person concerning her potentially imperiled relationship with Jesus. This vignette offers a window into upholding and vacating the social contract. I upheld the contract where it was proper and respectful to do so, but vacated it when necessary for seeking the highest good of another.

> While having a faithful Christian to whom one is accountable holds untold benefits, unless that accountability relationship is built upon the proper perspective it can serve as a deflector for dealing with heart issues. The fear of man may cause one to merely uphold external appearances, while allowing the heart to remain unchallenged (more akin to a "fraternity" or "team player" approach than to promoting actual relationship with Christ). Accountability relationships are therefore only as good as the state of the hearts on either side of the relationship.

Does the Counselor Hold a Measure of Rightful Authority Over the Counseling Interaction?

As is the way of the world, when two people meet, in the course of introductions and formalities, there is a jockeying for position, a civilized struggle to establish one as the superior and the other as the inferior in the context of the interaction. Sometimes such relationships are already clearly demarked as with a teacher and student, boss and employee, or police officer and citizen. But in the course of everyday interactions, in which a clear authority structure has not been established, there is often an imperceptible tussle for position.

This is much of the point of introductions and formalities, to mark out the terms of engagement, to determine dominance. Usually within one minute of meeting, one party has established his dominance, and the other his relative submissiveness. This "domination-submission axis" can base itself on one of many possible criteria such as perceived wealth, intelligence, appearance, experience, age, or relational energy. The point is that, in the world's system, two people do not remain as equals, one must ascend and the other must submit, one leads, the other follows.

The biblical counselor, however, does not conduct himself in this way. For the counselor, there is no sense of worldly dominance or submission. Counselor and Christian counselee are rightfully equals in submission to Christ. This means that the counselor never asserts dominance over the counselee, and likewise does not allow the counselee to assert dominance over him. Additionally, the counselor does not resort to worldly tactics to maintain this relational balance. He does not resort to manipulative strategies to tweak the equilibrium of social authority (whether through self-effacement, man-pleasing, esoteric language, or the like). Rather, since Jesus is the dominant party to whom subservience is due, the counselor continually draws the conversation back to Jesus for the natural restoration of the balance of power.

That being said, the counselor should be afforded a certain measure of authority in the counseling interaction (regardless of gender on either side of the counseling equation). That authority is never used to maintain control, or to manipulate, but to serve as a reminder of the need to come under the authority of Christ. This is a way to teach the counselee Ephesians 5:21, "Submit to one another out of reverence for Christ." The counselor, while exercising a measure of authority (exhibiting a measure of godly gravitas, if you will), simultaneously maintains a certain measure of "invisibility" so that the conversation always comes back to relationship with Jesus himself. Thus, the authority structure is never mediated through the counselor, but through direct submission to Christ.

The Judah and Tamar Syndrome[55]

Genesis 38:15-26 recounts the story of Judah and his daughter-in-law Tamar. Not recognizing Tamar, Judah thought that she was a prostitute. He slept with her and she became pregnant. Three months later Judah was informed that Tamar was guilty of prostitution and with child. He ordered that she be burned to death. In a kind of Shakespearian irony, Tamar produced Judah's seal, cord, and staff as proof that he was

---

[55] For additional discussion of the topic of confronting sin see "The Question of Judgment" in the first book in this series, *Ask for the Ancient Paths: From Art to Artifice to Arisen*, chapter 2: "The Counseling Ambition"

the father. Judah admitted his guilt stating, "'She is more righteous than I, since I wouldn't give her to my son Shelah.'"

This story, while an extreme example of hypocrisy, tends to characterize the counselor's approach to those who have sinned. The counselor recognizes, and rightly so, that he is often guilty of exactly the same sin that he sees in others.[56] However, the danger is that he resorts to permissive silence for fear of being labeled a hypocrite. This could be thought of as the "Judah and Tamar syndrome," the unwillingness to confront another's sin (when such confrontation is warranted and lovingly restorative) under the misguided assumption that because one has committed the same sin (or comparable sin) he is disqualified to speak on the matter.

Farewell of Hector and Andromache, Anton Losenko, 1773

The source of the counselor's integrity and social right is that he himself experiences daily repentance before the cross of Christ. The counselor is changing, growing in knowledge, deepening his faith, continually reinterpreting his life, and striving to experience joy in the midst of his own suffering. Only the counselor who is actively involved in his own change is equipped to help others find similar change. This, of course, does not imply that the counselor is by any means perfect, but rather that he is being sanctified.

---

[56] Although this is certainly not necessarily the case. For a comprehensive discussion of this topic see "The Question of Judgment" in the first book in this series, *Ask for the Ancient Paths: From Art to Artifice to Arisen*, chapter 2: "The Counseling Ambition"

> "But if we were more discerning with regard to ourselves, we would not come under such judgment. Nevertheless, when we are judged in this way by the Lord, we are being disciplined so that we will not be finally condemned with the world." (1 Corinthians 11:31, 32)

The world and worldly Christians obsessively eschew all confrontation with sin, hating nothing more than to be exposed and called to repentance. The main reason people despise confrontation with their sin, the reason they frequently quote Matthew 7:1 ("Do not judge, or you too will be judged"), is because they love their sin, and rue the thought of renouncing it. That is the reason why many Christians are quick to assert that love overlooks, but does not point out, transgression. This reasoning fundamentally rejects the notion that sanctification is the highest priority in a Christian's life, and that freedom from indwelling sin demands one's whole and immediate attention. Those Christians who are merely saved eschew confrontation with sin, while those who are disciples recognize its implacable wisdom.

Augustine of Hippo (354–430) stated, "Hate the sin and love the sinner." While many wrongly assume that the confrontation of sin is an aggressive and hurtful act, in the hands of the biblical counselor it is quite the opposite. Confronting sin is often the most loving act one can do for another, intended to initiate or restore broken relationship with God. To hate the sin *is* to love the sinner. However, most sinners, loving their sin, cunningly redefine the counselor's hatred of sin as hatred of the sinner himself in an attempt to shame the counselor.

> "The art of being wise is the art of knowing what to overlook." (William James)

The counselor's own, sometimes grievous, past should not preclude him from helping to free others from their sin. On the contrary, having committed similar transgressions should spur one on to greater vigilance in helping others not to fall into the same pain and regret. The counselor's only true means for loving others is to forget about himself, his past transgressions, and to focus on helping those around him find living faith.

Illegitimate Totality Transfer[57]

Illegitimate totality transfer refers to turning legitimate confrontation into a supposed targeted impugnment, so that the counselee wrongly assumes that the counselor, when addressing sin issues, is launching a personal invective. Rattled by what he casts as a direct affront, the counselee easily imports concepts into the confrontation that are not

---

[57] The term "illegitimate totality transfer" borrowed from Moises Silva, Westminster Theological Seminary, Philadelphia, Pennsylvania

part of the discussion, and thus, does not allow the confrontation to remain localized to the specific sin issue. In many ways, the illegitimate totality transfer is a red herring or smokescreen used to divert attention from the besetting sin. Another problem may be that the sinner has so wrapped his identity around his sin that he no longer segregates sin from personhood. His sin has become his identity. Thus, the confrontation, while surgically-focused on the sin alone, is irrevocably viewed as an assault upon the person.

Marius at Minturnae, Jean Germain Drouais, 1786

Two observations:

1. In the counselor's confrontation with sin, the counselee routinely finds a single statement that troubles him, one that draws his ire, and remains fixated on that statement to the exclusion of all others. How does the wise counselor rightly direct his focus, and properly couch statements that might derail the entire counseling endeavor?

2. During confrontation, rarely is that person listening to what is said about the specific sin issue. He is intent on quelling his own guilty conscience and, therefore, raises an irrelevant argument in response to an internal voice of accusation. How does the counselor detect and amplify that internal voice of accusation if it is of God's Spirit, or silence that voice if it is Satan's?

This question of illegitimate totality transfer can be seen from the opposite side as well - with regard to the counselor. Counselors tend to be people-pleasers. That is often why they are drawn to counseling. Does the counselor merely long to see people "fixed" so that he can feel he has earned a certain reward, or is the counselor motivated by a genuine passion in seeing people renewed in Christ? When the counselor loses his passion for Christ, and longs for the accolade of tangible results, he runs the risk of becoming overly-invested (enmeshed) in the counselee. The desire for ostensible change can easily become an idol to the counselor. The counselor often wrongly believes that the counselee's sanctification is based upon the counselor's own words and effort. Likewise, he may erroneously assume that the counselee's inability to change is the result of the counselor's own personal failure. In other words, the counselor may live vicariously through the counselee, so as to make perceived short-term results into a referendum on his worth or wisdom.

> Luke 6:26 states, "Woe to you when all men speak well of you, for that is how their fathers treated the false prophets." The counselor's objective is not that the counselee would speak well of him; his objective is that the counselee would be a fully-sanctified disciple of Christ alone.

Recording Evidence

First Peter 4:8 counsels that "love covers over a multitude of sins," and 1 Corinthians 13:5 states that love "keeps no record of wrongs." While the Christian forgives the wrongs committed against him, never again mentioning nor remembering them, this posses a certain challenge and tension with regard to counseling. A central aspect of counseling is helping others see their sin, which means offering clearly-defined evidence (and may include documented examples). Retaining that evidence often requires recalling past transgressions. However, this recall is never for the sake of criticism, accusation, or for withholding forgiveness. It is for the sake of loving another, longing for him to be free from his sin.

That being said, there should be a certain "statute of limitations" on recounting past transgressions for the purpose of pointing out sin patterns. The examples should be recent and relevant to the current state of the heart. The recall should also be done in a loving manner so as to help another see the transgression without dredging up murky personal history, or an unwelcomed recounting of distant experiences.

When I have identified an "alleged" sin issue that I feel must be addressed, I build a body evidence to marshal in the presentation. I find that the most effective means for gathering the proper evidence is to write it down and then to erase it from my memory. Otherwise, I tend to rehearse that evidence, so as to be able to recall it at the proper moment of confrontation. By writing it down, I remove myself from it so that I can simply review the record at the proper time. This also guards my own heart so that as

I continue to interact with that person, our dealings are not clouded by this recorded evidence. Maintaining the written record, and then forgetting the issues, allows me to deal with others in a more unfettered way until the time is right to initiate the proper confrontation.

> "The palest ink is better than the best memory." (Confucius)

The Art of Confrontation: Confronting Sin, Not Sinful Confrontation

Three types of diplomacy have been historically used with regard to China:

1. **Ping-pong diplomacy** (1971). This involved light-hearted competition to build friendship.

2. **Panda diplomacy** (from the Tang Dynasty (AD 618–907) to the present). This involves a "soft" display of goodwill and gratitude.

3. **Gunboat diplomacy** (1842). This involved the threat of military action in the event of a diplomatic breakdown.

This may be a little creative, but consider each of these diplomatic approaches, ping-pong (prophet), panda (priest), and gunboat (king), operating simultaneously in the confrontation process. Thus, confrontation is at the same time a prophetic, priestly, and kingly diplomatic effort. While diplomacy serves to build or maintain relationship between nations, in this case, it is between the confronted and God. The three aspects of confrontation symbolized by ping-pong, panda, and gunboat encapsulate God's three-pronged method for reaching the sinner, an intertwining of liberating truth, curative mercy, and measured wrath.

While biblical counseling is built upon loving confrontation of the heart, most think of confrontation in secular terms, bellicose, angry, and resulting in interpersonal tension and distrust. The Bible's concept of confrontation is vastly different; it is grounded in love, so as to build relationship with God and others. With restored relationship as the ultimate goal, the Bible's examples for confrontation take on a wide-array of textures depending on the recipient's heart-set. The Bible's sense of confrontation may at times carry with it the pungent taste of God's burning anger and impending wrath (gunboat).[58] It may favor a reasoned approach (ping-pong),[59] or it may traffic in soft tones and conciliatory language (panda).[60] As previously stated, all three components simultaneously attend each occurrence of confrontation, although particular instances may rightly skew toward one of the three.

---

[58] Exodus 4:14
[59] Isaiah 1:18
[60] Luke 7:47

The Anger of Achilles, Jacques-Louis David, 1825

In confronting the naïve and simple-minded, the approach will weigh toward the prophetic (speaking truth), and go light on the kingly (expressing wrath). For the one who is weak-willed or "small-souled," confrontation will weigh toward the priestly, (extending mercy), and again will go light on wrath. For the fool set in his ways, confrontation will weigh toward the kingly, the scepter of impending wrath, and will tread lightly on the prophetic and priestly.

Thus, confrontation can center on a rational look at the trajectory of one's life, a gentle prodding, or a strong-armed battle of worldviews. Regardless of the particular form confrontation takes, the objective is the same, that the holy living God would himself directly impact, communicate with, and deal face-to-face with sinners; that the confrontation would be daily, ongoing, and ultimately seek to effect restoration of relationship.

Paul Confronts Peter

In Acts 10:9-16 Peter had a vision of the large sheet lowered from the sky presenting various species of animals. God commanded Peter to eat freely, and to not call anything impure that God had made clean. In Acts 10:28 Peter said to Cornelius' household, "'You are well aware that it is against our law for a Jew to associate with a Gentile or visit him. But God has shown me that I should not call any man impure or unclean.'"

Galatians 2:11-14 states,

> When Peter came to Antioch, I opposed him to his face, because he was clearly in the wrong. Before certain men came from James, he used to eat with the Gentiles. But when they arrived, he began to draw back and separate himself from the Gentile because he was afraid of those who belong to the circumcision group. The other Jews joined him in his hypocrisy, so that by their hypocrisy even Barnabas was led astray. When I saw that they were not acting in line with the truth of the gospel, I said to Peter in front of them all, 'You are a Jew, yet you live like a Gentile and not like a Jew. How is it, then, that you force Gentiles to follow Jewish customs?'

Peter clearly evidenced the fear of man in his dealings with the Jerusalem contingent. He feared their judgment and criticism. Paul, zealous for the truth and not willing that any should be deceived by Peter's error, forcefully confronted Peter's disobedience. Paul did not mince words, especially with a captive audience of impressionable new believers and seekers.

> I notice that relationships rarely progress past the initial interaction. The first interaction between two people tends to be the way those people will always interact. If the first interaction is based on hostility, that tends to color every future interaction. If based on fear, covering, or transparency, then these will dictate future interaction. If the first interaction is based upon mutual respect and genuine love, that will permeate and pervade the relationship going forward. It would appear that in the interaction between Peter and Paul there is some truth to this.

As with Peter, the Christian receives an incomparable gift when he is shown his sin. While Peter seems to have humbled himself, most eschew being shown their sin, rail against it, and often launch strenuous counterattacks. Paul showed eagle-eyed foresight and singular courage in confronting Peter in love, and he is commended for it. This manner of godly confrontation is one of the rarest events in the modern church and, yet, was a mainstay of the early church, a pillar upon which the church was built.

Jesus offered the perfect model for godly confrontation: direct, concise, easily apprehended, and as part of a larger plan for freedom from one's sin, and most importantly, conducted in love. Jesus never left his audience with bad news but always dovetailed that bad news with his message of salvation. Thus, Jesus' confrontation, while it carried with it a piercing sting, was always attended by a triumphant message of forgiveness and reconciliation for those who chose to receive it. Additionally, Jesus spoke with a tone, and in a manner, appropriate to the type of person with whom he was speaking. He did not allow the conversation to be hijacked with distraction. He focused his words like a laser into the heart with timely and persuasive brevity.

> "Wounds from a friend can be trusted, but an enemy multiplies kisses." (Proverbs 27:6)

Anyone who lovingly confronts another with sin should be commended as an incomparable friend. False friends (often ensnared by the trap of unconditional love) are silent when they see others headed for trouble or robbed of joy. A true friend has vision, and steps forward in faith, to put the friendship at risk for a higher purpose in God's economy.

> Thank your critics because they have done you a favor. (adapted from quote by Mel Gibson)

The Baths of Caracalla
Lawrence Alma-Tadema, 1899

This entire discussion of godly confrontation is predicated on an absolutely essential element: that the confronter is himself daily confronted by Christ. If not experiencing ongoing submission to Christ, the confronter will invariably err. Any confrontation is only permissible, any right to speak into another's life is only granted, as one is himself being challenged, searched, and sanctified by Christ. Without this intimate connection to Christ, otherwise godly confrontation invariably devolves into what I term the "complaint-criticism-condemnation spiral." The spiral is this:

1. Complaint soon arises as otherwise faithful Christians feel their perceived needs going unmet.

2. This quickly devolves into stinging criticism of others for not meeting those needs.

3. Condemnation soon follows in often bitter disputes as the aforementioned criticism goes unanswered. Otherwise faithful Christians are even branded as false believers simply for failing to meet other's perceived needs.

Much church interaction sadly falls into this trap as Christians cannibalize their own church body with derelict counsel.

Wise confrontation must never be confused with complaint, criticism, or condemnation. However, those who do not know Christ, or who are currently not living in relationship with him, often twist wise confrontation into something it is not. They easily leverage godly confrontation (which is specifically directed toward sin alone) into an opportunity to launch complaint, criticism, and condemnation (*ad hominem* attack of one type or another). The church must never become a breeding ground for warlike gossip and slander. Yet, sadly that is what materializes in a counseling-oriented church which is severed from relationship with Christ. That which was meant to bring life (godly confrontation), ends up bringing death when not done in Christ, for Christ, and by Christ.

> **The Guideline of Three**[61]
>
> Once is an anomaly; twice is a pattern; three times is a precedent.
>
> 1. The first time a counselor observes some seemingly minor, but questionable, behavior or words he should not pursue it.
>
> 2. The second time a counselor observes the same he should make a careful mental note of it.
>
> 3. The third time, he begins to formulate a theory on the idol which gives rise to this. The counselor raises the issue and asks questions to gather further information. He looks for a heart pattern (whether idolatrous or faith-based) to emerge, and seeks to either confirm his theory or else abandon it in light of the evidence.
>
> Why a guideline of three? This guards the counselor from chasing down blind alleys. Often people spout errant words, or unwittingly display seemingly questionable behavior, when in fact there may be nothing substantive behind those words or acts.
>
> For example, a friend who arrives late to a social event may have encountered unforeseen traffic. A counselee who, in passing, mentions needing more

---

[61] This idea from David Powlison, Westminster Theological Seminary, Philadelphia, Pennsylvania

> self-confidence may have simply misspoken. A colleague who seems gluttonous may be involved in intense physical training or may be recovering from an illness. The point is that it is best not to question every adumbration, but rather to gather evidence and formulate a theory of heart worship. Once the evidence illumines a particular pattern then the counselor has solid ground to build a case for a call to repentance.

Advice for Godly Confrontation

1. Pray daily for the person to be confronted.[62] As one prays for another his entire demeanor toward that person changes. There is a conspicuous absence of malice and palpable love for the subjects of one's prayer.

2. Live with integrity as a follower of Christ.[63] Be careful that the same ongoing sin could not rightly be leveled against oneself.[64] Thus, one should confess his own sin first, if needed (privately or, if appropriate, publicly).[65] This may also offer a hedge against *ad hominem* arguments to be leveled against the confronter. (Such arguments are always a red herring to derail the confrontation, and thus should never be allowed.)

3. Show a Christian his sin privately following Matthew 18:15-17.[66] However, if he has already made the matter public (an open display or statement which could have a damaging effect on others) then it should be handled publicly.[67]

4. A church leader should be confronted in front of the church, if his sin clearly imperils the church's vitality.[68]

5. Before confronting ask questions.[69] Seek clarity in order to resolve seeming contradictions. Take every opportunity to thoroughly investigate the matter before rushing to judgment.

6. Offer the benefit of the every doubt. The counselor does not serve as a prosecuting attorney in an adversarial system. He serves an impartial adjudicator seeking to help the confronted rightly arrive at, articulate, and understand the truth about himself. Where there may be gray areas, the counselor helps the counselee articulate that in a fair way. The issue must be clearly established, or it should be shelved for the time-being.

---

[62] Ephesians 6:18
[63] 1 Timothy 3:2
[64] Matthew 7:5
[65] James 5:16
[66] 1 Corinthians 6:1
[67] 1 Corinthians 5:4, 5
[68] Galatians 2:14
[69] James 1:19

7. Be clear about that which is sin and that which is not. Sin should be supported with evidence and have grounding in Scripture. Be sure that the issue is definitively sin, and sharply delineate its parameters, so as to segregate the sin from that which may be mere annoyance, intellectual limitation, memory lapse, or simple miscommunication. Filter out the later so that the specific sin issue stands out in vivid detail.

Reading Room Discussion on Anti-Slavery, Charles Henry Granger, d. 1893

8. Godly confrontation is never criticism, and should not come across that way. While the world either blindly accepts sin or criticizes the sinner, the Christian does neither. The Christian tests all things through a godly set of lenses,[70] and when appropriate confronts in genuine love for the sole good of the confronted (and the church). The one being confronted should be able to recognize that he is being shown love in the matter.

9. Timing is everything.[71] Confrontation should not come in the middle of distractions, or at inopportune moments, which will siphon attention from the issue. It is vital to be sensitive to life events, whether joyful or sorrowful, so as to not inappropriately draw the confronted away from those special moments.[72]

10. Be sure the sin issue is well-substantiated with obvious evidence. What I have termed "The Guideline of Three" means that an issue should not be raised unless

---

[70] 1 John 4:1
[71] Ecclesiastes 3:1
[72] Romans 12:15

it has been observed at least three times (except when faced with the imminent threat of danger). This guards against reacting to something that may be an outlier (an anomaly) on the general backdrop of faith. After the sin has been observed a third time, it is appropriate to raise it.

11. Do not consider confrontation based on the seeming severity of the sin. There should be frequent light confrontation as an ongoing corrective to what otherwise might be seen as trivial sin.[73] The Bible observes that seemingly trivial transgressions quickly escalate into far greater ones, so one is to deal with perceived inconsequential sin before it snowballs into that which is life-altering.[74]

12. Confront in love.[75] This does not mean merely putting on a loving demeanor, but possessing a heart that truly loves another. One's demeanor may rightly vary based on the severity of the issue and on the immediacy of the consequences.

> If you see any brother or sister commit a sin that does not lead to death, you should pray and God will give them life. I refer to those whose sin does not lead to death. There is a sin that leads to death. I am not saying that you should pray about that. All wrongdoing is sin, and there is sin that does not lead to death. (1 John 5:16, 17)

One's demeanor should reflect God's in the matter. This means showing the appropriate emotion to fit the type of person (simple, fool, mocker, etc.) and the nature of the sin. For example, measured godly anger, as Jesus often displayed, is appropriate when confronting the hardhearted.[76]

13. Always offer a "from-to" dynamic for change. The sin is not just confronted, but the way out is always offered. For example, Jesus encouraged the rich young ruler, "...go, sell your possessions and give to the poor, and you will have treasure in heaven. Then come, follow me."[77] An additional example, "But when [John the Baptist] saw many of the Pharisees and Sadducees coming to where he was baptizing, he said to them: 'You brood of vipers! Who warned you to flee from the coming wrath? Produce fruit in keeping with repentance.'"[78] Jesus said,

> 'Woe to you, teachers of the law and Pharisees, you hypocrites! You give a tenth of your spices--mint, dill and cumin. But you have neglected the more important matters of the law--justice, mercy and faithfulness. You

---

[73] Paul Tripp, *Instruments in the Redeemer's Hands: People in Need of Change Helping People in Need of Change* (Presbyterian and Reformed Publishing Company, 2002)
[74] Matthew 18:8, 9
[75] Galatians 6:1
[76] John 2:17
[77] Matthew 19:21
[78] Matthew 3:7, 8

should have practiced the latter, without neglecting the former.'[79]

In each example, the sinner, while confronted with his sin, was also offered a path of repentance and reconciliation. God always holds forth such a path.[80]

14. Never get into a quarrel.[81] State your case persuasively and cogently and leave it at that. If the one being confronted refuses to listen terminate the conversation and follow the instructions offered in Matthew 18:15-17.[82] If, after involving another believer, and later the church, the Christian still refuses to repent he becomes God's direct charge as one under discipline.[83]

15. The goal of all confrontation is restoration of both relationship with God and fellowship with the church. In confrontation, there should be a plan for restoration, and when the sin has been renounced, that plan should be implemented as quickly as possible.

16. Once sin is brought to repentance, and all needed forgiveness is offered and received, the matter is closed and is never to be raised again.

What Is the Difference Between Criticism and Biblical Confrontation?

Criticism…	Biblical Confrontation…
1. Seeks to harm another's spirit	Seeks to restore one's spirit
2. Is done with no regard for the good of the one criticized	Is done only for the good of the one confronted[84]
3. Creates alienation and isolation	Seeks to restore fellowship
4. Brings lingering emotional damage	Brings healing and life[85]
5. Comes from Satan for the purpose of destroying relationship with God	Comes from God for the purpose of reigniting relationship with himself

Criticism arises from a performance-oriented view of life. Godly confrontation grows out of the Bible's teaching on sanctification. The objective in all confrontation is to restore the Christian to relationship with God, child to father, servant to master, friend to friend. In this sense, a counselor, as he helps the counselee see his sin, is not critical but constructive of building a bridge with, and through, Christ. Thus, repentance, and the blossoming faith that follows, takes center stage in an atmosphere of celebratory thankfulness. Godly confrontation is never an end in itself, but always for the purpose

---

[79] Matthew 23:23
[80] 2 Peter 3:9
[81] Romans 12:18
[82] Matthew 10:14
[83] 1 Corinthians 5:5, 13
[84] James 1:4
[85] John 6:68

of conciliation.

> Modern society seeks to eliminate all struggle and strife from life. The church is often no different. Sometimes there needs to be struggle and strife; that is a necessary part of the sanctification process. Thus, there are times when interpersonal relationships will be marked by a controlled measure of struggle.

The counselor does not just expose idolatry and sin, but with equal frequency commends and praises faith. The counselor looks for areas of both sin and faith, so that the former may be eradicated, and the latter may be magnified. Where the Christian lives with a sinful regard for himself and God, the counselor seeks to help him see his need for repentance. Where the Christian lives in obedience, the counselor helps him recognize and celebrate this, so that he may praise God for this work and continue to walk in supplication to his God. While the Christian is often blinded to his own idols, quite surprisingly, he is often equally blinded to the faith operating within him. The Christian may not recognize that many aspects of his life are driven by genuine faith. Thus, in highlighting that faith, celebrating it as such, and seeking to expand it, the Christian can continue to cede territory within his own heart.

Counseling as Confession

James 5:16 states, "Therefore confess your sins to each other and pray for each other so that you may be healed. The prayer of the righteous man is powerful and effective." First John 1:9 states, "If we confess our sins, he is faithful and just and will forgive us our sins and purify us from all unrighteousness." Counseling offers an opportunity to confess sins for restored relationship with God.

Confession is a tearing-down and a rebuilding; it is painful sorrow and soothing healing. Confession stares into the soul's darkness and brings it to light. John 3:21 states, "But whoever lives by the truth comes into the light, so that it may be seen plainly that what they have done has been done in the sight of God." First Corinthians 11:28-32 states,

> Everyone ought to examine themselves before he eats of the bread and drink from the cup. For those who eat and drink without discerning the body of Christ eat and drink judgment on themselves. That is why many among you are weak and sick, and a number of you have fallen asleep. But if we were more discerning with regard to ourselves, we would not come under such judgment. Nevertheless, when we are judged in this way by the Lord, we are being disciplined so that we will not be finally condemned with the world.

Confession is never an opportunity for stealth criticism. Its purpose is to help the

Christian uncover wrong worship and seek repentance. Confession should be accompanied by joy, never by humiliation or embarrassment. God desires that his people confess their sin as the means for their relational (both vertical and horizontal) healing.

Lear and Cordelia, Ford Madox Brown, c. 1854

> "Therefore, if you are offering your gift at the altar and there remember that your brother or sister has something against you, leave your gift there in front of the altar. First go and be reconciled to them; then come and offer your gift." (Matthew 5:23, 24)

The Christian should both offer his confession and provide a safe harbor for others to confess when needed. Matthew 18:15-18 states,

> 'If your brother sins, go and point out their fault, just between the two of you. If they listen to you, you have won them over. But if they will not listen, take one or two others along, so that 'every matter may be established by the testimony of two or three witnesses.' If they still refuse to listen, tell it to the church; and if they refuse to listen even to the church, treat them as you would a pagan or a tax collector. Truly I tell you, whatever you bind on earth will be bound in heaven, and whatever you loose on earth will be loosed in heaven.'

It is imperative to hold to Matthew 18:15-17 in handling issues concerning perpetrating sin and being sinned against. Yet, rarely in my church dealings have I seen this command followed. I usually observe those sinned against immediately turning to a sympathetic advisor for support, airing complaints which end up as divisive gossip or slander. The Christian is not at liberty to deal with sinning, and being sinned against, as he so chooses. He is to follow God's directive, and the counselor must be vigilant for this directive. (When any situation comes with clear stipulations and directives in Scripture, I admonish a counselee to follow the biblical command to the letter, and I refuse to entertain that issue until he does.)

Not every transgression needs to be confessed. If, for example, one lies to another, but that lie does not directly affect that person (such that the lie is not specifically directed toward that person), there is no need to confess it to that person. However, if a lie does directly affect that person, then it must be confessed immediately. For example, in a conversation with a friend, if I were to lie about an outside matter to which the friend is unrelated, I would not be under compunction to confess that lie to him, although I am, of course, compelled to confess it to God.[86]

Counseling as Evangelism

Biblical counseling is traditionally thought of as the provenance of Christians, one to another. However, the biblical counseling model could equally well be applied to unbelievers as a means for evangelism. The book of Acts presents three models for evangelism, that which is directed to:

1. "A synagogue audience with a rudimentary understanding and respect for Scripture"

    Acts 13:13-52 recounts major prophecies found throughout Scripture indicating Jesus' death and resurrection. This approach appeals directly to Scripture.

2. "Pagan peasants focused on weather and crops"

    Acts 14:15-17 offers a general introduction to "heaven and earth," coupled with a persuasive logic on life experiences.

3. "Athenian poets and philosophers"

    Acts 17:22-31 appeals to the philosophical system of the age.

Each of these models finds a place in the counseling endeavor: the direct appeal to

---

[86] This insight from David Powlison, Westminster Theological Seminary, Philadelphia, Pennsylvania

Scripture, the logic of life experiences, and a more in-depth philosophical discussion (such as polemics against psychology).

One might be surprised to know that I counsel the non-Christian using often the exact same images, Scripture verses, and means of confrontation as I would a Christian. The unbeliever, while he is not in Christ, can be extended a vision of what faith in Christ could produce in him, what life could look like for one being transformed by God's Spirit. Thus, universally, with the unbeliever and believer, I present the gospel, often in exactly the same way. (Tangentially, while the Christian lives in a new identity in Christ, his functional identity is often identical to that of the non-Christian.) The hope is that regardless of the audience, the gospel, viewed through the lens of "from-to" counseling, will radically transform the unbeliever, and gradually restore the believer.

> Just as Jesus admonished the Laodiceans for their lukewarm attitude toward him,[87] so too, I would much rather counsel an angry opponent than an apathetic false believer. The former, while outwardly diffident, can be reckoned with, and his arguments exposed. The latter offers little or nothing to work with, and thus renders the counseling endeavor vacuous.

Matters of Sound Practice

The Hippocratic Oath states, "First, do no harm." This may be an apt starting point for addressing the counselor's approach.

1. Every counseling conversation is strictly *sub rosa*, private, guarded, and held in confidence. The counselor must never betray anything revealed in a private session; this is absolutely vital. Only that which the counselee has specifically made public should be shared with others (and that only on a need-to-know basis).

2. The counselee should be encouraged to bring his counseling needs before the church, but this is his responsibility, not the counselor's. The counseling session may operate under the auspices of the church, or it may function as a parachurch mission.

3. "The counselor speaks and thinks newly-minted recreations and applications of Scripture into the exigencies or the moment, updated at every point by Jesus Christ."[88] Thus, it is more effective to speak biblical concepts to the particular person than to quote verses.[89] For example, it is better to say that the particular person is in the Spirit than to talk about being in the Spirit as a general concept.

---

[87] Revelation 3:15, 16
[88] David Powlison, Westminster Theological Seminary, Philadelphia, Pennsylvania
[89] David Powlison, Westminster Theological Seminary, Philadelphia, Pennsylvania

4. It must be emphasized that the counselor does not judge the heart; he points out evidence of what lies in the heart.⁹⁰ That being said, while the evidence may at times be incontrovertible, the heart is under God's sole authority. Therefore, the counselor can only present the evidence and encourage the correct analysis, but must leave the work of actually changing the heart to the Holy Spirit. Just as Job's counselors were horribly deceived concerning Job's nouthetic state, so too, those in Christ may make grave mistakes regarding the heart's motives and intent.⁹¹

5. Often the use of visual models, charts, or diagrams (such as a "third-way" diagram⁹²) can be crucial to understanding.

Saint Augustine
Philippe de Champaigne, c. 1650

6. Homework should be assigned and completed. A self-counseling project is an excellent way to cause the counselee to see his own heart worship and continually draw himself to repentance before Christ.⁹³

A crucial issue in counseling is the question of whether the counselor is trying to help the counselee be completely free of enslaving thought and behavior, or simply to live by faith in the midst of such thought and behavior? For example, should the vision for one traditionally labeled obsessive-compulsive (OCD) be to completely free him of his obsession, or should he learn to live by faith in the midst of this condition? Is the counselor's goal to merely manage the problem or to progressively eradicate the

---

⁹⁰ David Powlison, Westminster Theological Seminary, Philadelphia, Pennsylvania
⁹¹ For a comprehensive discussion of this topic see "The Question of Judgment" in the first book in this series, *Ask for the Ancient Paths: From Art to Artifice to Arisen*, chapter 2: "The Counseling Ambition"
⁹² For a discussion of the "third-way" see the first book in this series, *Ask for the Ancient Paths: From Art to Artifice to Arisen*, chapter 10: "The Third-Way of Sanctification: From Abominable to Indominable"; the third-way concept from David Powlison, Westminster Theological Seminary, Philadelphia, Pennsylvania
⁹³ For discussion of the self-counseling project see chapter 8: "Diagnosis: Vanishing Secrets"

problem so that one day there is not even a trace of it?

As another example, should the counselor's goal be to completely free a counselee of homosexual ideations, or should the counselee simply be directed to live by faith in the midst of such thoughts? One school of thought sees that the counselee may never be completely free from these thoughts, but can live by faith in daily denying their power over him. Another approach sees that the goal should be total freedom from the thoughts, utter reform, so that that person no longer entertains any thought outside of Christ.[94]

A Summary of Crucial Truths about Counseling

1. The counselor seeks to illuminate the heart so as to make the need for greater faith in Jesus stand out. The counselor must not exacerbate preexisting problems by merely breathing new life into dysfunctional idols.

2. The counselor himself continually draws closer to Jesus and desires his own change. The counselor never forgets that he is a sinner saved by grace. This gives him the humility, wisdom, and integrity to draw others to faith.

3. The counselor does not seek to merely manage problems, but seeks the renewal of whole people. He recognizes that he deals with comprehensive, often complex, and conflicted lives, not simply isolated aspects of those lives.

4. The counselor builds trust through repeated communication of compassionate understanding.

> "People won't care what you know until they know that you care." (Richard Craven)

5. The counselor holds a clear vision for change and communicates that to his counselee. In this way, the counselor inspires the counselee to desire change.

6. The counselor continually intensifies the counselee's quest to seek deeper relationship with Jesus and, thus, to desire change.

7. The counselor fights for something far greater in the counselee than the counselee seeks for himself. Just because the counselee is satisfied with a particular outcome does not mean that God is. Thus, the counselor acts for God's interests in the situation, not the counselee's.[95]

---

[94] 1 Corinthians 2:16; 2 Corinthians 10:5
[95] Mark 8:33

8. The counselor recognizes that counseling can at times appear fraught with awkward and uncomfortable conflict, but he is not afraid of this. He pursues a deeper purpose than mere happiness or harmony.

9. A counselor cuts across standard expectations, not merely reciting Scripture verses, but introducing Scripture in a way that brings the person of Jesus Christ to bear upon the counselee's heart.

10. Just as the prophet Ezekiel used "street theater" with props to make his message come alive, so too, the counselor innovates so as to be creative in his presentation. He knows when to silently listen, when to rouse attention, when to display anger, and when to inject humor. He is rich with analogy and metaphor so as to create visual images in the counselee. The counselor is willing to take calculated risks and experiment.

11. The counselor seeks to "work himself out of a job." The counselor is not just performing counseling, but training the Christian to counsel himself. This means that the counselor becomes less vital as the counselee is more capable of diagnosing his own heart, and more disciplined in bringing himself to repentance before Jesus.

12. The counselor eagerly anticipates celebrating the counselee's victories in Christ, recognizing advances, no matter how seemingly insignificant. Often small victories are the precursor to far greater ones.

Note to Counselors: Seize the Day!

The ancient Greek physician Hippocrates (c. 460 – c. 370 BC) began his medical tome, *Aphorismi*, with the following Greek saying:

> Art is long;
> Vitality is brief,
> Occasion precipitous,
> Experiment perilous,
> Judgment difficult.[96]

By this Hippocrates meant that in comparison to the time needed to perfect one's craft, the life of the practitioner is relatively short. The requisite investment in training is followed by a relatively brief time in which to apply one's training to those in need of it. The idea is that time is a scarce commodity and, therefore, one must cherish the brief opportunity to apply his expertise.

---

[96] Translation from Wikipedia article "Hippocrates"

> A variant on Hippocrates' saying comes from the first century rabbi Tarfon who wrote, "The day is short, the labor vast, the workers lazy, the reward great, the Master urgent." (Avot 2:20)

What do Hippocrates words mean for the biblical counselor? Second Timothy 4:2 states, "Preach the word; be prepared in season and out of season; correct, rebuke and encourage--with great patience and careful instruction." The wise counselor, through careful study and patient obedience, prepares himself to lead others out of sin and into relationship with God. The preparation time is great; the application time is short. The counselor acts on every opportunity which God provides, to facilitate the change he knows that God desires for those with whom he interacts.

> What's the point of singing if one sings the wrong song in the wrong tune?
> What's the point of running if one runs the wrong race to the wrong place?
> What's the use of working if one pursues the wrong métier and the wrong gain?
> What's the use of loving if one loves the wrong lover in the wrong way?
> What's the point of life? Not merely to sing the right song, run the right race, do the right work, and love rightly. Life, and all its pursuits, was designed to be directed by, and to, the person of God. Indeed, the very universe is personal.

- 8 -

Diagnosis:

Vanishing Secrets

God Seeks to Thoroughly Cleanse His People

onsider Leviticus 14:33-57 which gives instruction on cleansing a house from mildew. Mildew here could be thought of as a metaphor for sin, sin that enters those who "live in the land of Canaan."

Instruction in Leviticus	Application to the Issue of Sin
1. In Canaan certain houses may be afflicted with mildew.[1] (In some instances the Lord gave a house over to its mildew.)	"Therefore God gave them over in the sinful desires of their hearts to sexual impurity for the degrading of their bodies with one another." (Romans 1:24)
2. A priest examined the house to determine if the mildew penetrated below the wall's surface.[2]	"I myself am convinced, my brothers and sisters, that you yourselves are full of goodness, filled with knowledge and competent to instruct one another." (Romans 15:14) "…not giving up meeting together, as some are in the habit of doing, but encouraging one another--and all the more as you see the Day approaching." (Hebrews 10:25)
3. If the mildew had spread then the priest ordered the contaminated stones to be torn out and "thrown into an unclean place outside town."[3]	"If your hand or your foot causes you to stumble, cut it off and throw it from you; it is better for you to enter life crippled or lame, than to have two hands or two feet and be cast into the eternal fire. If your eye causes you to stumble, pluck it out and throw it from you. It is better for you to enter life with one eye, than to have two eyes and be cast into the fiery hell." (Matthew 18:8, 9) "Dear children, keep yourselves from idols." (1 John 5:21)

---
[1] Leviticus 14:34
[2] Leviticus 14:37
[3] Leviticus 14:40

4. Additionally, the wall must then be scraped and the debris dumped outside the town.[4]	"Come near to God and he will come near to you. Wash your hands, you sinners, and purify your hearts, you double-minded." (James 4:8)
5. New stones were then to replace the old, and new clay was to plaster the house.[5]	"You were taught, with regard to your former way of life, to put off your old self, which is being corrupted by its deceitful desires; to be made new in the attitude of your minds; and to put on the new self, created to be like God in true righteousness and holiness." (Ephesians 4:22-24)
6. If the mildew returned, it was a "destructive mildew" and the house must be torn down, its stones, timbers, and all its plaster taken outside the town to an unclean place.[6]	"There will be weeping there, and gnashing of teeth, when you see Abraham, Isaac and Jacob and all the prophets in the kingdom of God, but you yourselves thrown out." (Luke 13:28)

Leviticus 14:33-57 shows the extent to which God calls his people to go in eradicating sin. Each is to aggressively pursue even seemingly minor manifestations of sin (a "mildew"), tear them out, and cast them away. God desires that each, in God's own strength, and at his direction, then "scrape" the surrounding facets of his life to make sure that not the slightest semblance of the sin remains. For even a trace residue spreads, soon contaminating the entire house.[7]

> "But among you there must not be even a hint of sexual immorality, or of any kind of impurity, or of greed, because these are improper for God's holy people." (Ephesians 5:3)

If the mildew reappears the entire house must be torn down, stones (structure), timbers (roof), and plaster (interior), and discarded. This means that God desires the complete demolition of entrenched and besetting sin. He desires to vanquish sin so as to initiate total renewal. God may forcefully remove that which is contaminated, and even dismantle one's "home." God may remove that which his people idolatrously call home, rendering them psychically "homeless" until they find their home in him.[8]

Christians are to be alert to the "mildew," vigilant to eradicate it, and willing to allow godly inspectors (counselors) to help identify it. Each must be willing to do violence to his sin, tear out stones, and cast them away. He must be willing to scrape the walls of his life, obliterating anything that hints of rebellion against God.

---

[4] Leviticus 14:41
[5] Leviticus 14:42
[6] Leviticus 14:45
[7] Esther 1:18 offers another example of this concept
[8] Luke 15:5, 6

Why did God command that the house be razed in the event the mildew returns? Mildew spreads quickly; it can contaminate clothing, bring dire health effects, and proliferate to adjacent houses. Likewise, sin is a contagion that easily metastasizes to infect families, communities, and nations. It is fascinating that God eventually allowed the Babylonians to raze the Jerusalem temple.[9] The temple was demolished because of the people's protracted and trenchant sin;[10] such devastation serves as a symbol of the ravages of sin upon a nation. The violence with which the Babylonians tore down the temple was the violence with which the people should have torn down the idols in their hearts.

Bringing Idols to Justice

The Scapegoat, William Holman Hunt, 1854

Leviticus 16:21 recounts the implementation of the scapegoat,

> He [Aaron] is to lay both hands on the head of the live goat and confess over it all the wickedness and rebellion of the Israelites – all their sins – and put them on the goat's head. He shall send the goat away into the desert in the care of a man appointed for the task.

That which died alone in the desert was obliterated from thought and record. The concept of death in the desert is an image of God forgetting his people's sin, that sin simply withering and dying with the forlorn goat. When sins were transferred to the head of the scapegoat, the people were released from the punishment that would

---

[9] 2 Kings 25:9; Lamentations 2:6
[10] Matthew Henry Commentary, Bible Study Tools, 2012

normally accompany their sin. (Of course, the death of the scapegoat was of no actual consequence to God. It was merely a symbolic deferral of the penalty which Christ would one day take upon himself.[11])

Notice that Aaron was appointed to confess *all* the sins of the Israelite people. God did not provide Aaron with a set prayer to recite; he was simply to admit the people's sin. The implication is that Aaron would actually know those sins, and that he would speak from the heart as one intimately familiar with their transgressions. How could Aaron know the people's sins except that he probe into their worship commitments? Likewise, counselors are to uncover the worship commitments of those they shepherd, to recognize the sin of those whom they serve, so as to help them confess their sin and subsequently grow in holiness.

In order to confess the people's sins, the Levitical priests were given three methods for discerning a matter:

1. Aaron possessed the *Urim* and *Thummim* placed over his heart.[12] Discerning God's will involved a binary question with a "yes" or "no" answer.

2. A priest used prescribed rituals for discerning God's will, such as the test for an unfaithful wife.[13]

3. A priest made direct inquiry into matters, investigating them for God's purposes and rendering judgment.[14]

In what way do these models offer a proleptic indicator of the way in which those in Christ are to discern his will? Unlike the Levitical priests, the counselor is not to use either an *Urim* and *Thummim* approach or ritualistic tests. The counselor has that which is far superior, the indwelling Holy Spirit, which relationally leads believers into truth. Like Levitical priests, the counselor is called to direct inquiry, so as to render certain God-honoring judgments. In this way, the counselor is called to discern matters and situations, such as John's call to "test the spirits."[15] The counselor searches for that which is invisible (intentions of the heart) by exploring that which is visible. The counselor uses direct inquiry until the invisible finally comes to light. (This is the purpose of the "X-ray questions" which follow.)

> The old adage, "If you want to know the real reason for anything ask 'Why?' seven times," seems to apply here. Each time one asks "Why?" the analysis deepens.

---

[11] Hebrews 9
[12] Exodus 28:30
[13] Numbers 5:11-31
[14] Leviticus 27:8, 11, 12
[15] 1 John 4:1

For most, their idols are preserved in amber, their most sacred treasures, the high-places at which they daily worship. Though often concealed, those idols eventually surface when ferreted out with the right questions. However, do not ask a person what his idols are;[16] he will not reveal them, or else he will offer socially acceptable idols which serve as a red herring. Idols must be uncovered through select questions. If one asks the right questions, and listens in the right way, people will eventually reveal their idols (albeit indirectly). While the idolater desperately seeks to deceive others about his worship commitments, those commitments invariably surface.[17] They cannot help but surface with focused and persistent analysis, and that is to the counselee's eternal benefit.

> When speaking to a counselee stay attuned to worship-charged words such as: avoid, believe, desire, fear, hope, love, seek, trust, and want. These words may indicate that idols are not far off.

The Search for Themes and Patterns: Initial Observations

A Chinese physician of holistic medicine would consider a broad spectrum of information before deciding on a treatment plan. He would take into account a patient's behaviors, body odors, gestures, language, least favorite foods, lifestyle, living environment, personal relationships, personality type, and usual diet. Physicians may also use touch and listening to determine a patient's health. The technique, *kan mian xiang* (看面相), involves reading a patient's face in order to determine the health of vital organs. For example, if a one's face is red his body contains too much "fire." While neither recommending nor gainsaying holistic medicine, it is helpful for the counselor to consider a similar range of data. Rather than merely relying on verbal evidence, the counselor should consider a panoply of visual clues to spy the heart's posture (while being cautious about such clues).

The counselor initially observes details, some more overt than others, to gain indications of the inclinations of the counselee's heart. This information may offer clues as to the idols operating below the surface. Examples include:

1. One's manner of dress

Dress reveals one's functional beliefs. Appearance can offer clues to self-discipline, self-image, perfectionism, lust, desires, and hopes. It is as if clothes are an "X-ray of the soul," broadcasting what one lives for, and what one holds to be true. There is an old saying, "Clothes make the man." They also divulge who a man is.

---

[16] Paul Tripp, Westminster Theological Seminary, Philadelphia, Pennsylvania
[17] Luke 12:3

> It is fascinating that during economic booms fashion trends toward shorter women's skirts. Is there a similar causality that could be observed concerning idols of the heart and clothing choices?

A young Christian woman wears floor-length dresses or long slacks, even in oppressive heat. She is careful to remain almost compulsively covered in all circumstances. While at first blush there is something refreshing and commendable in a woman who seeks to be demure, I soon surmised that this woman's clothing choices grew out of a fear of people. There was a desire to be concealed. The long skirts and heavy clothing kept her shielded from others, like armor to repel possible intruders. Noticing this crucial piece of data became an entrance point into counseling. It turns out that this woman, while a highly-regarded worship leader in her church, is a false believer. Her clothing may have been chosen to cloak her deception and chicanery, to shroud a heart filled with contempt for God and his people.

Portrait of Marie-Antoinette of Austria
Jean-Baptiste Gautier Dagoty, 1775

2. The form and content of one's speech

One's diction reveals a great deal about what one worships. Is the counselee a careful speaker or undisciplined in speech? Which topics tend to surface and how are those topics handled?

An older Christian woman, who for a time attended the church I pastor, displayed an undisciplined tongue. It was not so much what she said, but the manner in which she said it, which caught my attention. Her words seemed brash and unruly, even when sharing scriptural truths. Finally, the woman spread malicious gossip in the church. I sensed this coming for months, as there was something in her words that hinted of a heart dominated by gossip and slander.

> Listen carefully to others' prayers and jokes. Prayers and jokes both expose the heart, since people pray for, and joke about, what they desire. Jesus told his followers to pray that God's will would be done,[18] but people usually pray that their own will would be done. Even the non-Christian's prayer (although he only speaks to himself) is a window into heart worship. Likewise, a person is truly revealed in his jokes; the mask comes off and the heart is exposed. If handled cautiously, a transcript of a counselee's prayers and jokes offer an accurate road map of the heart.

3. Gestures (related to the form and content of speech)

The way one gesticulates communicates volumes about how his words should be interpreted. The astute counselor notices shifting eyes, the ability or inability to make eye contact; changes in body posture, slouching or upright shoulders; when the counselee seems to pay careful attention, and when he seems to lose interest in the conversation. A handshake or absence of one, an icy stare or a warm smile, and even how one handles everyday items, indicate heart inclinations.

> Notoriously, gamblers meticulously study one another's faces. As one's face, in its most minute detail, often reveals his hand. (Of course, this study is only for the love of money.) The biblical counselor also studies faces, but for God's purpose to uncover evidence of the heart.

4. One's family situation

Family life reveals something about the pressures and joys facing the counselee. However, drawing too much out of family life can lead to erroneous assumptions about the heart, so the counselor holds such observations tenuously.

5. One's profession

One's profession, like his family life, may offer clues to particular pressures to conformity, as well as the idols one crafts which serve that profession well.[19]

While some initial observations about the counselee are valuable, there is a danger of being blinded by social stereotypes. It is easy to categorize a counselee based on what the counselor thinks he will find. The counselor must recognize that heart worship is

---

[18] Matthew 6:10
[19] Acts 19:24-27

never dictated by circumstance, or *Sitz im Leben*. Worship is tempted by circumstance, so *Sitz im Leben* may offer clues on where to probe more deeply. But until there is strong evidence, the counselor must hold judgments in abeyance.

Additionally, the counselor must not draw assumptions from an isolated data point. He should chart his observations into an overall theory. This means that the counselor does not draw too much from any one observation, but amalgamates observations so as to trace trajectories of the heart.

> "Everything we hear is an opinion, not a fact. Everything we see is a perspective, not the truth." (Marcus Aurelius)

For example, in women and children the theme of "injustice" tends to surface. Those typically outside of traditional authority structures often are highly-sensitive to perceived injustices or neglect from those in authority.[20] Women and children may easily harbor contempt for authority and seek to undermine it, albeit subtly.[21] Conversely, men tend to be alert to perceived disrespect for authority. Men are often attuned to acts of rebellion as well as subversive words and actions. They may grab for control so as to ensure respect from others.

The counselor is rightly attuned to particular themes which tend to surface in those both outside of, and in, authority. But such a generality will prove dangerous if not tempered by a more detailed understanding of those he counsels. While women in general may be traditionally sensitive to perceived or real injustice, a particular woman may be a company vice-president who is leery of perceived insubordination from those lower on the corporate ladder. While at work she expects to be in command and her directions followed.

However, when she returns home she is rightly under her husband's authority, and simultaneously an authority over her children. She may face particular temptation to rebel against her husband's God-given authority, especially if she earns a higher salary and commands more social respect than he. While in theory there should be no difference between the way she treats her children and the way she treats her employees (caring, concerned for their welfare, guiding, disciplining), there may be temptation to renege on her responsibility to serve as an authority to her children. She may even be tempted to use her children as pawns in a smoldering offensive to undermine her husband's authority.

Likewise, while men in general are traditionally more attuned to acts of disrespect, a particular man may serve as a clerk, harboring resentment that those in authority keep

---

[20] The following discussion based heavily on David Powlison, "Ephesians," *The Journal of Biblical Counseling*, (Glenside, Pennsylvania: The Christian Counseling and Education Foundation)
[21] 1 Corinthians 11:1-34

him in a low position, denying him prosperity. This man is married but does not have children. When he returns home he may either become overly assertive with his wife as a way to garner the respect he feels he lacks at work, or he may be overly compliant as a result of adopting a daily pattern of submission. His wife may become belligerent toward his lackluster domesticity, as he fails to be the proper type of authority.

The Seven Ages of Man, William Mulready, 1838

The counselor must parse the counselee's particular life situation to understand in which ways that counselee rightly or wrongly functions as an authority, and in which ways he rightly or wrongly sees himself as a victim of injustice. The wise counselor recognizes that the idolatrous heart operates regardless of situation, but at the same time that heart is tempted in particular directions based on the exigencies and pressures of one's positions and responsibilities.

> "As a species we're really bad at understanding costs that come later on. Instead, we assign a disproportionate amount of importance to what's immediate and tangible." (Hai Yan Shui)

The Search for Themes and Patterns: Data Gathering

First Samuel 2:12 states that Eli's sons were wicked, having no regard for the Lord. They grabbed the choicest sacrificial meat for themselves at the expense of those around them. Further, they fornicated with the women serving at the Tent of Meeting.[22] In this context, consider Eli's statements to his sons in 1 Samuel 2:23, "So he said to them, 'Why do you do such things? I hear from all the people about these wicked deeds of yours.'" Quite revealing is Eli's question, "Why?" This shows a fundamental blindness toward his son's rebellion. Eli should have known something about the motive for his sons' behavior, the wickedness of their hearts, and their disregard for God himself.[23]

Similar to the priest Eli, when one commits heinous sin invariably his kith and kin offer the same response, "I had no idea he could do this. I didn't see this coming." (This response may be self-protective to avoid potential litigation.) However, such statements reveal a root blindness in sinners with regard to evidence of the heart. Estranged from God, people often lack the most rudimentary skills to accurately assess the condition of those in their immediate relational circle.

As themes and patterns emerge in counseling, the counselor seeks to understand their meaning and import. Which of these themes indicate ruling idols? In dealing with the counselee, which issues emerge time-and-again in conversation, actions, prayers, and discussions of God and self? Additionally, discrete actions reveal certain heart themes, pointing to worship patterns. Some examples of discrete actions ("red flags") which offer clear evidence of idolatry include:

1. Biting one's finger nails (anxiety)
2. Waiting until last minute to pay bills (mammon worship)
3. Needing "a little confidence boost" (performance as idol)
4. "Having the munchies" (escape)
5. Rolling one's eyes (rebellious grumbling)
6. Sleeping when faced with difficult task (escape)
7. Procrastination (fear of failure)
8. Eating two desserts[24] (lack of self-restraint)
9. Voyeurism (lust of flesh)
10. Excessive apologizing (fear of man)
11. Moments of conspicuous silence
12. Moments of loquaciousness

Focusing on these (and other) seemingly innocuous or inconsequential acts may look

---

[22] 1 Samuel 2:22
[23] This insight from Jay Adams, *Competent to Counsel: Introduction to Nouthetic Counseling* (Zondervan Publishing, 2009)
[24] Edward Welch, Westminster Theological Seminary, Philadelphia, Pennsylvania

like over-scrupulosity. However, little things mean a lot in the discernment of the heart's patterns. At issue is not the seriousness and severity of the act, but the idols which stand behind it. As the counselor analyzes even the slightest thoughts and actions, he sees patterns emerge, patterns which could quickly snowball into more pronounced sin. Thus, properly understood, counseling recognizes and confronts even minute sin, since one does not know which of those will end up metastasizing and overtaking one's life.[25]

> "The power of accurate observation is commonly called cynicism by those who don't have it." (George Bernard Shaw)

The counselor must assess how deeply the idol's roots wend their way into the heart, and the extent of the worship. The counselor also seeks to ferret out the presence of genuine faith in the context of this idolatry. How might the counselee be growing in faith so that the idolatry is in remission? How is God already exposing and assailing idols so that the counselee is being brought to distinct junctures of repentance? How does the counselor come alongside to augment, magnify, and further the work God is already doing in the counselee's heart?

Thus, a central counseling question involves worship trajectory and motion. Is the counselee furthering idolatrous worship, or is he daily seeking to renounce idols and grow in faith? Is the idolatry metastasizing, or is it in remission? The answers to these questions reveal trajectory, the global scope and direction of the counselee's life, so as to discern if he is on an arc of faith or rebellion. These answers also reveal the "velocity" of the heart's movements, so that the counselor can discern if change is rapid or tepid, if the counselee is surging forward or stagnating.[26]

Chipping Away at the Façade

Just as Foucault's pendulum precisely traces the rotation of the earth, so too, people's words are a "pendulum" in tune with the rotation of their hearts.[27] Listen to people carefully. They will tell you exactly what they worship. The following are a few worship-laden statements which mimic neutral observation or noble character:

1. "I thought she was taller than me. I'm glad she is not."
2. "I must help her. She needs my love."
3. "I want to earn a lot of money so I can build a church."
4. "Thank you for helping me improve my self-confidence."

---

[25] Sinclair Ferguson, Westminster Theological Seminary, Philadelphia, Pennsylvania
[26] For additional discussion of this topic see "The 'Heisenberg Uncertainty Principle' of Biblical Counseling" in the second book in this series, *What Agreement Is There Between the Temple of God and Idols?: The Accidence of Sin and Idolatry*, chapter 8: "The Search for Eldorado Ends: Repenting of Idols of the Heart"
[27] Matthew 12:34b, 35

5. "This morning I was so self-absorbed. Then I went to the worship training and I felt better about myself."

Oscar Wilde (1854-1900) wrote, "Give [a man] a mask, and he will tell you the truth." How does the counselor unmask those he counsels while incentivizing truth-telling? Just because someone uses a particular word does not necessarily mean he intends the concept. This unmasking is a process of uncovering the intended concepts behind words.

Every person is both a twisted and tangled knot of deception as well as forthright evidence about his inner state. In other words, each person both cloaks and reveals at the same time. Each routinely maintains a smokescreen while simultaneously revealing the idols within his heart. The counselor endeavors to peer behind the Emerald City curtain, acts to remove the psyche's Venetian mask, and vies to glance into those "portals of discovery" into the heart.[28] If the counselor listens carefully, patterns will emerge, subtle and recessed, behind otherwise false fronts. He will slowly disentangle that which is genuine data from that which is a diversionary tactic.

Asking Analytical Questions: The Stealth "Truth Serum"

Return of the Bucentoro to the Molo on Ascension Day, Canaletto, c. 1732

I have spent significant time traveling on Italian public buses. To describe Italian bus drivers as loquacious is an understatement. They speak with passengers in quite an animated manner (even removing both hands from the steering wheel to emphasize a

---

[28] This term "portals of discovery" borrowed from author James Joyce (1882-1941)

point). Italian buses (and Italy, in general) function as a mass counseling session where riders offer and receive counsel freely and without reservation. Counseling, of one form or another, is endemic to the Italian lifestyle.[29]

Conversely, I have traveled to nations formerly, or currently, under totalitarian rule in which to reveal a personal problem, or to even ask a question about the meaning of life, is to subject oneself to scrutiny, spying, and possible unpleasant social consequence. In other words, in some nations is it simply not safe to share anything of a personal nature, especially information which seems to communicate perceived or real doubts or failings.

North American society stands somewhere between the Italian and the totalitarian. In the United States one is expected to respect others' privacy. Likewise, it is considered inappropriate to say too much about one's personal life.[30] People usually seek to guard intimate details, sharing generalities which cannot be used as future ammunition. How does a counselor function in a society which encourages people to keep themselves somewhat concealed from view? How does a counselor become privy to the right level of detail about another's life while not gaining inappropriate amounts of detail? This raises the further question, how detailed should counseling analysis be anyway? On what level should the counselor analyze problems so as to shed light on them?

> Listen as much to what is unsaid as to what is said. What is unsaid speaks volumes, and may be a truer indicator of the heart, than what is said. Listen to the way concepts are phrased and matters are postured, often so as to sidestep the crucial heart issues.

The answer to any personal question depends upon the context into which the answer is voiced. For example, if one were to ask me, "How are you today?" the answer will depend upon who is asking, and why. To a student, as class is about to begin, the answer is "Fine, thank you, and you?" My answer will justifiably vary to an unbelieving friend, a believing friend, or a close confidant. The issue is that I am simultaneously in many states, so that my chosen self-revelation depends on the purpose that the query serves. I am concurrently joyful in Christ, and burdened by grief for dying souls. I am at the same time content in my life, and beleaguered by persecution on various levels. In this sense, the counselor must expect that questions will solicit varied responses based on context, setting, and the degree of familiarity between those interacting. Communication can at times exhibit a certain crumbling coarseness or a sharpened steel blade; it all depends upon the context.

---

[29] In this regard, I find it fascinating that Italians live the longest of all Europeans.
[30] Peggy Post and Peter Post, *The Etiquette Advantage in Business*, 2nd edition (William Morrow Publishers, 2005)

The point is that one's cultural environment will render more or less attractive the Bible's call to bear and share burdens and to engage in sound counsel. Thus, the biblical counselor must be aware of his cultural setting, the proclivities of, and threats to, those with whom he interacts. Which leads to another crucial point, the church should be a place of safety from the world (regardless of the particulars inherent in that part of the world). The church ought to function as an incubator for trustworthy relationships in which one engages in transparent counsel free from the threat of criticism or rejection.

Leo Tolstoy (1828–1910) wrote, "All, everything that I understand, I understand only because I love." There is a profound truth in this statement. The counselor's wisdom is built on genuine love for those he counsels. Heart-felt compassionate unflagging love sparks the insights, lights the dark chambers, and assembles the soul's "Ryline's fragments" into whole and living texts. In fact, as counseling is actually taking place the counselor ought to silently pray for love for his counselee, that the God of love would invade the counseling process, wresting it from the fascism of dead platitudes and callous theological abstraction.

"X-Ray Questions" Which Uncover Idols or Faith[31]

> "It is better to ask some of the questions than to know all of the answers." (James Thurber)

In 1753 Benjamin Franklin (1706-1790) invented the lightning rod. Aristocratic European women soon had them installed on their hats with a ground-wire trailing below their gowns. There is something in this amusing historical note which lends insight into the issue of analytical questions. Often people figuratively install lightning rods on their hats with an accompanying ground-wire. When lightning strikes (any life event or situation) it travels alone the path of least resistance so that it discharges with no sanctifying effect. How does the wise counselor install himself in the lightning's path? How does the counselor make sure that lightning is not summarily discharged, but channeled through the heart so as to illuminate and regenerate it? One could think of the following analytical questions as "heart electricity meters," indicators of the relative condition of the heart in the midst of life's lightning strikes.

Exposing idols is an onerous task because the sinner tends to serve plausible idols.[32] Besides, idols often are not evil in and of themselves. Thus, the following questions are carefully designed to delve into the heart in order to reveal its functional gods. These questions pry under surface irritability, selfishness, hopelessness, escapism,

---
[31] This section largely borrowed from David Powlison, "X-ray Questions," *The Journal of Biblical Counseling* (Glenside, Pennsylvania: The Christian Counseling and Education Foundation)
[32] Paul Tripp, Westminster Theological Seminary, Philadelphia, Pennsylvania

self-righteousness, self-pity, fears, pusillanimity, and complaining, so as to enter into the worshipping core. It is crucial to understand that while the following analytical questions are usually used to uncover idols, they may also uncover areas of vibrant Christ-centered faith.

In the Conservatory, James Jacques Joseph Tissot, c. 1878

1. What makes one angry?

   One fiercely guards whatever he believes his life depends upon. Anger generally surfaces when idols are threatened. However, anger can also be used in faith to display the righteous wrath of God.

   Saul was handsome, tall, and "remarkable," but the more he was enamored with himself, the greater his insecurity, envy, anger, and fear of David. In fact, Saul's burning anger was closely tied to his envy of David. Saul worshipped control over his kingdom and was inflamed with murderous rage at the thought that it could be taken from him.[33] Also consider that King Xerxes honored Haman, "…elevating him and giving him a seat of honor higher than that of all the other nobles. All the royal officials at the king's gate knelt down and paid honor to Haman…"[34]

---

[33] 1 Samuel 18:8-11
[34] Esther 3:1, 2

However, one man, Mordecai, refused to rise or show fear in Haman's presence. The absence of that one man's honor enraged Haman.[35] Haman worshipped his honor, and so furor attended any assault upon that honor.

2. What does one feel he *must* have?

   Questions of "must" reveal inordinate desire. It is often not so much what one wants, it is that he wants it too much, which is the problem.

3. What does one treasure?

> "For where your treasure is there your heart also will be." (Matthew 6:21)

4. For what is one most thankful?

5. What does one think about most of the time?

   Does one create a fantasy world in which he is loved, admired, powerful, concealed, or suffering? Do one's thoughts gravitate toward Christ, thinking about how to glorify him in a given situation, how to change in order to become more like him, and how to better bear witness to him?

> Pay careful attention when others quote Scripture, especially those sections upon which they focus a great deal of attention. This offers a window into the heart. The Bible can often be misused to justify sin, placate a guilty conscience, or advance a personal agenda. The counselor should be vigilant to how Scripture is being subtly misinterpreted, or deliberately twisted to serve a purpose. For example, a Christian woman often quotes 1 John 4:8, "God is love." What she means by this is that God loves her unconditionally and does not want her to change. She also means that she should accept everyone exactly as they are, and not focus attention on sin issues. "God is love" has merely become a convenient justification for her passivity toward, and neglect of, those around her, like a mantra that she recites to squelch the guilt of sin.

6. What would make one happy?

   The pursuit of happiness can be the pursuit of idolatrous desire. The Christian does not speak about happiness, but about joy. Joy comes from within, is not subject to circumstance, and is renewed day-by-day. Happiness evaporates quickly in the burning sun of trials, because it is circumstance-based.

---

[35] Esther 5:9

> A counselee's stories, and the details upon which he focuses in any given situation, reveal a great deal about his heart. For example, a Christian friend pays careful attention to others' height, mentioning physical attributes before other factors. This seems to indicate a certain abiding lust of the flesh. This friend seems to invest value and meaning in the physical, possibly because he lives in fear of physical confrontation. His focus upon, and praise of, height and strength may indicate that he craves such attributes as a means to alleviate a trenchant fear of people.

Related to the issue of happiness is the question of humor. Humor offers two valuable insights. First, it is an unguarded, yet coded, peek into the heart, as humor reveals worship commitments. Secondly, humor often functions as a cover for anxiety. Note when a counselee interjects humor; this could flag an issue for further investigation.

> "Many a truth is said in jest."[36]

7. What would make one's life complete?

    What does one feel would demark his life as a success in the eyes of others? What does one feel he must have, attain, or achieve in order to be fulfilled?

8. What is one unwilling to sacrifice for Jesus?

    This question often reveals an idol. Another way to come at the issue is to ask, "What one would be willing to sacrifice for Jesus?" Listen for the lacuna between the two questions.

9. What would break one in life? What could one not possibly live without (or live with)?

10. Whom or what does one fear?

    Fears are the opposite side of wants, and usually point directly to idolatrous worship. When one fears God he recognizes God's sovereignty in each situation, and is not swayed by anything that seems to indicate the contrary.

11. When is one most anxious?

12. When is one most confident?

---

[36] This concept is attributed to Geoffrey Chaucer (1343-1400), William Shakespeare (1564-1616), or "Roxburghe Ballad" (circa 1665) depending on the degree to which the original accords with this modern expression.

13. What would success look like in one's life?

> Listen carefully to the subject of a counselee's praises. What does he routinely find praiseworthy, and what does he routinely overlook?

The Gallery of the HMS Calcutta, James Jacques Joseph Tissot, c. 1877

14. Upon what does one hang his hope?

People sacrifice everything for their hopes, and fall into deep despair when those hopes fail. The Christ-centered Christian puts the entirety of his hope in the assurance of salvation, and in the promise of a future inheritance.[37]

> It is noteworthy that when people feel disenfranchised, isolated, rejected, or in emotional pain they tend to pay more attention to the eschatological and apocalyptic sections of Scripture. A focus on the apocalyptic gives those who feel hopeless the expectation of God's imminent vengeance and wrath upon injustice. However, the Bible's apocalyptic message was written to encourage those who suffer to endure a little longer.[38]

15. Whose approval does one seek, that of men or God?

---
[37] Ephesians 1:14
[38] 1 Peter 4:12

16. What does one believe God is doing in his life right now?

17. What does one see as his rights?

> Pay careful attention to where a counselee assigns blame in a given situation. This can be an indicator of that from which he himself seeks exoneration.

18. What makes one tired?

Asking what makes one tired offers a revealing glance at the heart. There is a difference between being physically tired and existentially tired. Everyone grows physically tired,[39] but only those enslaved to idols grow existentially tired. Existential tiredness arises when fallen mankind works in his own strength, for his own purposes, persisting in the service of enslaving idols.

Those who work in God's way, with God's Spirit, and for God's glory do not grow existentially tired.[40] Their body may need rest but they enjoy a certain enduring mental and emotional vitality. The heart that is free from enslaving passions, unshackled to man-centered effort, does not grow existentially tired since it is sustained and energized by God.[41]

19. What battles is one fighting right now?

20. Does one feel a craving to eat between meal times? Does one have a tendency to control food?

Idolatry tends to drive cravings. Food is a convenient means for soothing a soul vying for comfort and escape. Thus, the way one handles food offers a window into idolatrous cravings.

21. When one enters a room filled with strangers, what is generally the first thing that enters one's mind?

22. Which Bible character most resonates with one's personality? What does one identify with in this person?

Blaise Pascal (1623-1662) wrote, "We are more convinced by reasons we have found ourselves than by those which have occurred to others." With this in mind, it is often better for a counselor to ask questions than to make statements. For example, rather than stating, "You seem defensive" it may be more effective to ask, "Do you feel that

---

[39] Matthew 8:20
[40] Matthew 11:29, 30
[41] Isaiah 40:31

you are defensive?" With those who are somewhat at odds with the counseling process (or even with the counselor himself), a well-worded question may do far more to lasso the heart than a blunt statement. In fact, a timely question is itself wise counsel, even if it does not receive a response.

Case Study: Questions Which Might Uncover the Lust of the Eye[42]

1. Is one filled with anxiety concerning his appearance, or concerning his ability to attract a person with the right appearance?

2. Is one consumed with envy, self-loathing, competitiveness, or feelings of inferiority or superiority? When does this occur?

3. Has one developed brooding comparisons, out of control consumer spending, despair, eating disorders, hatred toward or obsession with one's body image, preoccupation with physical appearance, or extreme self-consciousness?

4. When one enters a room, does he immediately notice others' appearance and compare himself?

5. Does one often indulge in a vivid fantasy world?

6. Does one carry a mirror, or frequently seek one out before meeting others? Is one intent on frequently snapping his own picture or, conversely, on avoiding having his picture taken?

7. Does one, at times, deliberately seek to make himself unattractive?

> Intentional ugliness could result from having given up on the image game altogether. One willfully makes himself ugly as a way to communicate a smoldering hatred of the world. However, the same lust of the eye is no less operative. Often those who fail to meet the standard set on account of their lust deliberately seek out rejection as a form of self-righteousness and supposed moral superiority. In this way, the one who rebels against a certain image standard (by trying to appear ugly or strange) plays the same image game, just from the opposite side. The goal is to make oneself into an anti-image martyr, to let rejection feed simmering self-pride. Thus, regardless of the outward manifestation, the same sybaritic ambition lives in the heart.

Assessing Responses

---

[42] Many of the following questions inspired by David Powlison, Westminster Theological Seminary, Philadelphia, Pennsylvania

When confronted with sin, nearly all sinners zealously seek to escape a direct light upon the heart. People are highly-skilled at cloaking their sin, evading questions, or using the Socratic method to turn the questions on the questioner. The following are some common tactics used to divert attention from the heart when the stronghold of idolatry is under siege.

1. The red herring (the *non sequitur*)

The red herring refers to a smoked fish used to distract hunting dogs in order to get them off the quarry's trail. The term means injecting something irrelevant into a discussion in order to distract one from the real issue. The red herring may even be completely true, but is nevertheless unrelated to the central point. (Incidentally, this technique is common in film in order to divert attention from the main plot.)

2. The *ad hominem* attack

Who Shall Be Captain?
Howard Pyle, 1911

Ad hominem in Latin is literally "against the man." This manner of social aggression refuses to address the topic at hand, but instead seeks to personally discredit the opponent. The idea being that if the questioner is personally discredited his arguments are as well.

3. The false appeal fallacy

This is using an expert in one field as an authority in a completely unrelated field. For instance, an unbelieving physician may enjoy legitimate credibility when speaking on certain health issues, but has no such warrant to speak authoritatively on matters of the heart.

4. *Hoc ergo poster-hoc*

This is falsely assuming a causal relationship between events A and B simply because B follows A. There may be a *correlation* between events, but not necessarily causation. For example, if a supposed blessing follows an idolatrous decision the perpetrator may feel exonerated in his sin.

> "His argument is as thin as the homeopathic soup that was made by boiling the shadow of a pigeon that had been starved to death." (Abraham Lincoln)

What Christians Often Say and What They Mean[43]

An oronym is a literary device in which a word, or word sequence, can easily be mistaken for another word sequence.[44] Oronyms are based on the length and position of pauses in the phrases, and sometimes upon the emphasis placed on particular syllables. A discrete set of pauses results in a different meaning. Likewise, varied syllable emphasis also generates different meaning. (For example, "ice cream" and "I scream," or "night train" and "night rain" are oronyms. Disambiguation is only achieved through context.) Oronyms reveal that the mind must insert meaning into what it hears; that it must interpret sounds so as to make sense of them. Thus, even in language there is no objective fact. All fact must be mated with an interpretation which makes sense of it. This offers a loose introduction to the issue of interpreting statements.

Isaiah 29:13 states, "These people honor me with their lips, but their hearts are far from me." First John 1:8 also warns, "If we claim to be without sin, we deceive ourselves and the truth is not in us." Christians routinely seek to honor God in word only, a convenient masking agent for hearts far from God. Most of the statements listed below I have personally heard from Christians. Each statement appears to function as a fig leaf, camouflage for idols of the heart. Thus, although some statements may be true, nestled within them is an implicit denial of sinfulness. The wise counselor, therefore, reads the subtext underlying such statements to discern the machinations and deflective efforts of a deceptive heart.

---

[43] For additional discussion of this topic see "The Herod Effect" in the second book in this series, *What Agreement Is There Between the Temple of God and Idols?: The Accidence of Sin and Idolatry*, chapter 8: "The Search for Eldorado Ends: Repenting of Idols of the Heart"; also see "Analyzing the Plot: Narrative, Metanarrative, Subtext" in chapter 6: "The Basic Plotlines which Emerge in Counseling"
[44] The term "oronym" was coined by Gyles Brandreth, *The Joy of Lex: An Amazing and Amusing Z to A and A to Z of Words* (1980)

Statement	What Is Meant by This Statement
1. "No one is perfect."; "We're all human."; "I'm a flawed person"; "I'm no choir boy."	It is true that human beings are morally frail, but the import of this statement is a petition to not make one change. The message is, "If you love me accept me exactly as I am." "…for he knows how we are formed, he remembers that we are dust." (Psalm 103:14)
2. "We're all sinners, aren't we?"	The answer to this query is a resounding, "Yes." However, the intent behind this statement is to short-circuit any attempt at counseling sin issues. The objective is to divest the counselor of authority and stymie any attempts to bring sin to light. This statement seeks to diffuse any forthcoming confrontation.
3. "God is not finished with me yet."	It is, of course, true that God's sanctifying work is not complete in any Christian, and will not be until heaven.[45] However, the intention of this statement is often to induce tolerance for sin, to overlook transgression, and to deflect potential confrontation. This statement tends to breed a certain comfortability and complacency with sin.
4. "Everything is by grace"	The Bible is clear that everything is in fact by grace.[46] However, what most mean by this statement is that one is not to make any judgments, that since one was shown grace one is to overlook every flaw. This is really a statement that God holds no expectations for obedience in his people. The Bible's concept of grace is not blind acceptance of all things. Grace comes in a context of repentance, and results in demonstrable change. Grace is a free gift at Christ's expense, but it is not a *tabula rasa*; it is a directed gift imparted to bear fruit.
5. "It's not my fault that…"	The actual statement may be correct, but look below it to uncover blame-shifting or for the intension of justifying sin. This is of the same ilk as the excuse that since God hardened Pharaoh's heart he was not to blame. Pharaoh was not neutral; he allowed his heart to be hardened by his rebellion.[47]
6. "I have a weakness	This statement is implicit blame-shifting, or at least

---

[45] 1 Corinthians 13:12
[46] Romans 6:1; Ephesians 2:8
[47] Exodus 9:12

for…"	seeks to minimize the severity of sin. It makes the transgression look minor and relatively insignificant.
7. "I sometimes snap at people when I'm cold, tired, or hungry."	Being cold, tired, or hungry may offer the occasion to sin but is never the cause for sin. Sin arises from the recesses of the heart. Cold, fatigue, and hunger only expose that sin, but must never serve as the excuse for it. The one who points to his bodily condition in the discussion of sin usually grasps for a credible scapegoat. The implication behind such a statement is that if the cold, fatigue, or hunger were removed so would the sin. That is not the case as sin is "a man for all seasons." *Portrait of Pere Tanguy* Vincent Willem van Gogh, 1888
8. "I didn't choose my sin."	If one did not choose his sin the implication is that God made that choice. Therefore, one presumes not to be responsible for acting upon something that was never his choice. In reality, one does choose his sin.

9. "I am crossing my fingers that I don't lose my temper today."	The assumption is that losing one's temper is a matter of chance, dictated by the forces of chaos.[48] This statement implicitly shirks responsibility for one's actions, as if one's actions are utterly the work of fate.
10. "Sometimes my temper just gets the best of me."; "I just snapped."	The assertion is that one's temper is outside of his control, that against his will, it robs one of his good and reasonable qualities. The objective is to shift-blame to something outside of one's own psyche. Additionally, the idea that one just snapped places the blame on situation. Like a floor joist that simply gives under the strain of excessive weight, so too the excuse is that one simply cannot stand under the load placed upon him. This makes God into the villain for allowing an unsustainable load, for making the "force of gravity" (life's trials) so excessive that the floor joist has no choice but to snap. The assertion that one just snapped implicitly denies 1 Corinthians 10:13. "No temptation has overtaken you except what is common to mankind. And God is faithful; he will not let you be tempted beyond what you can bear. But when you are tempted, he will also provide a way out so that you can endure it."
11. "Sometimes I feel insecure. That's why I…"	In assigning insecurity as a driver for human behavior, this statement takes a page from the Adler-Maslow pyramid of needs - the idea that a security need was not met, resulting in sin.[49] In reality, the heart is vastly more complex than this. Its problem is never a lack of security, but faulty worship.
12. "I just have mood swings."	This implies that one's emotions are outside of his control.[50]
13. "I have no idea what came over me."	This statement shows a callow disregard for one's own worship commitments so that one is seemingly blindsided by emotion.
14. "I just did something stupid."	This statement makes sin the result of a sudden decline in intelligence. Sin is never a function of, nor driven by, intelligence. The sinner would rather blame a momentary lapse in reasoning than admit to a worship problem.[51] Admitting to stupidity may sound humble

---

[48] 1 Corinthians 10:13
[49] Psalm 23:1
[50] For an in-depth discussion of the topic of emotions see "The Hydraulic View of Emotions" in the first book in this series, *Ask for the Ancient Paths: From Art to Artifice to Arisen*, chapter 8: "What Has Jerusalem To Do With Vienna?: The Case Against Psychology"
[51] Luke 6:45 refutes the notion that sin arises through a lapse in intelligence.

	but it actually places blame upon God for designing the faulty mental machinery.
15. "I just let my guard down for a minute."	This statement makes sin the result of a momentary lapse in self-protective measures. Sin never arises *ex nihilo* and is never the result of simply forgetting to shield oneself. Sin arises from well-cultivated roots deep within the heart.
16. "I'm learning not to beat myself up over every little mistake."	The Bible's message is never that one should "beat himself up." Jesus took that beating in the Christian's place.[52] The spirit behind this statement, however, is to excuse sin, to turn a blind eye to the workings of a depraved heart in desperate need of ongoing repentance.
17. "I'm just having a bad day."	This statement makes sin the result of one's situation (the day). In fact, there is no such thing as a bad day. Every day is to God's glory, to reveal his goodness, and the sinner's towering need for him.[53]
18. "I just cannot forgive myself."	While this statement sounds quite noble and innocent, in reality it is just one among many masks for human pride. It is establishing a standard outside of Christ so that one evaluates Christ's sacrifice as insufficient to handle one's sin.[54] The implication is that one must pay for this sin on his own without Christ, and more importantly, against Christ.
19. "Today is my day."	Romans 11:36 states, "For from him and through him and for him are all things. To him be the glory forever! Amen." Therefore, no day belongs to any person. Each day was made by God, for God, to glorify himself. A bride who, for example, expects her guests to focus their attention on her has hijacked a day meant to glorify God and to serve others.
20. "I just need to vent."	This statement assumes a hydraulic view of emotions, the idea that emotions, such as anger, simply occur outside of one's control. The biblical view is that emotions are chosen based on what one worships, desires, and craves.[55]
21. "I am passionate about	This is usually just a covering for idolatry. If one can

---

[52] Luke 22:63
[53] Psalm 118:24
[54] Romans 8:1 and 1 John 1:9 offer an implicit rebuttal to this way of thinking.
[55] For an in-depth discussion of the topic of emotions see "The Hydraulic View of Emotions" in the first book in this series, *Ask for the Ancient Paths: From Art to Artifice to Arisen*, chapter 8: "What Has Jerusalem To Do With Vienna?: The Case Against Psychology"

_____." ("I guess I just care too much.")	camouflage his idolatry as passion this often makes the idolatry appear noble and praiseworthy to the world.
22. "I'm just strong-willed."	The implication is that one's design is flawed, so that one's actions operate outside of his will. This statement is also a clever covering for idolatry. According to Galatians 5:23, the Christian is never to be strong-willed with regard to Christ, but rather, submissive and gentle-spirited. *The Secret* Adolphe William Bouguereau, 1876
23. "I fell into sin."	When one falls he cannot control the process, and so he is not to blame. The assumption is that sin occurred without one's conscious will being engaged.[56]
24. "The situation got the best of me."; "The devil made me do it."	This states that the situation is to blame, as if the situation thieved one's moral character against his will.[57]
25. "I'm battling my demons."	This statement makes sin into the work of non-descript demons. This is usually a cunning way of deflecting sin

---

[56] Galatians 6:1; 1 Corinthians 10:12
[57] James 1:14

	onto an abstract ethereal plane where blame cannot be assigned. It also makes the sinner look like a tragic hero doing battle on his own, as one besieged by war. The objective is to diffuse all possible criticism for wrongdoing. (After all, only a heartless person would discourage one in the midst of heated battle.)
26. "I'm just not a good Christian."	This is a red herring intended to deflect others from one's pride; as it indicates that one has failed to uphold his own moral standard. The Christian faith is not about trying to become a good Christian, as if one seeks to maintain a set of moral principles in his own strength. Instead, it is about abiding in Christ, letting Christ himself become one's righteousness.[58]
27. "I am just trying to be a good example of Christ."	This statement is quite deceptive because on the surface it sounds so eminently Christ-centered. Who, after all, would disagree with being a good example of Christ, especially in light of 1 Corinthians 11:1, Ephesians 5:1, and 1 Peter 2:21, which all speak of Christ as example? The problem is not in what is said, but in what is not said. Seeking to be a good example of Christ often diverts attention from the need to first be indwelled and changed by Christ. Thus, the Christian first invites Jesus to daily confront and change him so that he can be given the power to live in obedience. Thus, seeking to first be a good example of Christ is often based in the arrogant assumption that one can imitate Christ in his own strength, and in this way is an attempt to avoid the indwelling Christ who seeks to bring heart change.
28. "It was just a sin of omission."	While this may sound fair enough,[59] there is a subtle implication that the sin occurred through forgetfulness. Inserting the word "omission" seems to strip sin of its active and deliberate quality. In God's eyes, supposed sin of omission is just as heinous as sin of commission, but the former sounds far less threatening.
29. "I have not been given the level of grace required to live by faith in this regard."	Deciphering this statement is tricky because it involves a masterful slight of hand. It is true that some have not been given grace in certain regards, but this never pertains to renouncing sin. This statement is a cunning manipulation calculated to induce guilt in anyone who

---

[58] 1 Timothy 1:15, 16
[59] James 4:17 speaks about the sin of omission.

	confronts one's sin. The implication is that it is hardly one's fault that he cannot obey God.

"…And God is faithful; he will not let you be tempted beyond what you can bear. But when you are tempted, he will also provide a way out so that you can endure it." (1 Corinthians 10:13) |
| 30. "I was born this way." | This statement is used to justify sin by placing the blame firmly upon God as designer. The implication is that it is God's fault for designing one in a certain way so that he is destined to moral failure.

The Inundation of the Biesbosch in 1421
Lawrence Alma-Tadema, 1856 |
31. "It's a genetic problem. I am 'hardwired' this way."	This excuse places the blame for sin upon God since the sinner is a victim of his design. If God created one with a genetic flaw that makes him sin, only a cruel God would then condemn one for that sin. More often than not, the excuse that one is hardwired in a particular way is a cunning concealment for idolatry.
32. "I'm left-brained (right-brained)."	The theory is that left-brained people tend to be concrete thinkers, visual and literal, while right-brained thinkers tend to be abstract thinkers, auditory and artistic. This can easily become an excuse for sin, the idea that God "wired" one's brain in a certain way, making it prone to certain moral failings.
33. "I'm a visual/auditory/kinesthetic learner."	One's learning style easily becomes a ready excuse for moral failure. Learning style also becomes a means to shield oneself from criticism, since one simply cannot act in accord with certain moral standards which run

	counter to his design characteristics. God is once again saddled with the blame for faulty design.
34. "I'm a type-A (type-B) personality."	This is an excuse for impulsive (or passive) behavior. It puts the blame for sin squarely upon one's design.
35. "I had a difficult childhood. That is why I…"	This excuse puts the blame for one's sin on his upbringing, that one was in some way deprived. That deprivation then becomes the scapegoat for one's subsequent sin. It is assumed that it is not one's fault that he did not receive the requisite upbringing to live a life of obedience to God.[60] *Mitate no Kinko* Suzuki Harunobu, d. 1770
36. "I'm the oldest (middle, youngest, only) child."	Birth order can become a convenient excuse for any errant type of behavior. The blame for sin is implicitly placed upon God for his faulty timing and flawed ordering of events.
37. "I'm just living the way I was taught to." ("I was not taught well.")	The implication is that if one's lifestyle and choices comply with the authorities above oneself (parents, teachers, government, etc.), then they should be acceptable to God. This statement makes one appear to

---

[60] Matthew 7:11 acknowledges that parents will at times fail their children but this is never an excuse for sin.

	be an innocent victim of imperfect authorities so that one is not culpable for sin, since there is no way for one to know any better.
38. "That's just my culture."	The idea is to hide behind one's culture as the reason for sin. This lays a cunning counseling trap in that to question another's actions, attitude, or words is viewed as implicitly attacking the perpetrator's culture. Thus, the excuse that culture is the driver diverts attention away from the heart and short-circuits any attempt to confront sin (since to do so would be labeled "culturally insensitive").[61]
39. "I have Mediterranean/Teutonic blood"; "I caught California fever."	The implication is that one is not culpable for his emotional state (such as angry outbursts or intractable sang-froid) since one has no control over the "blood" coursing through his veins. This excuse places blame upon design ("blood") and environment.
40. "I am not as bad as _____."; "It's not like I _____."	This statement is an example of the "continual comparison to the extreme." As long as one finds others with whom he compares favorably, he feels more comfortable in his sin.[62]
41. "If only I had …."	This statement implies that God is not good because he does not provide what one needs to pursue a life of holiness. God is capricious for withholding that which would prosper one's life, and because God has withheld his gift one feels he is not to blame for his sin.[63]
42. "I will never allow that to happen again."	This statement is a form of "playing God" in that it seeks to strong-arm the future from God.[64] The implication is that if God fails to deliver in a certain way, then one is justified in his sin.
43. "I'm learning to maintain relational boundaries."	This statement, while it contains a measure of wisdom,[65] is often used to deny the imperative to love others as God desires. While this statement sounds like blind tolerance and the avoidance of inappropriate judgment, usually, the spirit behind such a statement is the fear of man.
44. "I just want freedom	This is another version of the theme that one's situation

---

[61] Galatians 2:20 and Colossians 2:8 are, in some sense, implicit rebukes to culture.
[62] In Matthew 12:35-37, Jesus short-circuited the continual comparison to the extreme as each sinner is held accountable to his own words.
[63] Proverbs 30:8, 9 offers the view that wealth and poverty may present a temptation to sin, but are never the excuse for sin.
[64] 1 Samuel 18:6-9 is a good example.
[65] Ephesians 5:22-6:9

from…"	is the problem. If one could only achieve freedom (which God is withholding) then one could live a life of faith. God's callousness enslaves the sinner so that he is conscried to sin.
45. "I'm an adult. I should be allowed to do what I want."	This statement really reads, "I'm autonomous. I should be allowed to live without accountability to God." In this specific context, "adult" is not a biblical category. The Bible describes believers as "children," "sheep," and "saints," but not as adults with the right to live autonomously. The statement that one is an adult is really a clever disguise for craving the authority to sin with impunity.
46. "It's 2015."	This statement makes immorality (usually sexual immorality) look like a natural response to human progress. The implication is that Byzantine forms of morality (namely arising through a literal reading of the Bible) should be abandoned as outdated and repressive.[66]
47. "I suffer from low self-esteem."	This statement is used when one's idols are not working for him. One wants to be significant in the eyes of others but he can't meet the standard he set, a standard raised in rebellion against God. What usually follows this statement is its next of kin, "I lack self-confidence." This becomes the excuse for why one cannot do something, has failed morally, or is suffering emotionally.[67]
48. "God helps those who help themselves."	This statement, routinely attributed to the Bible, is the opposite of biblical truth. God helps those who with humble hearts admit their inability to help themselves, and fall upon his mercy in Christ.[68] This statement is usually summoned to explain why one must act without God, in one's own power, and for one's own purposes. Such a statement is the height of human arrogance.
49. [excessive apology]	Excessive apology grows from the fear of man and the craving of others' approval and acceptance. This can be a way to meet one's perceived needs without appearing "needy," since one seems so noble and humble. There may also be a prideful self-righteous in appearing

---

[66] Romans 1:21-25 offers an implicit polemic against the notion of human progress. Hebrews 13:8 makes clear the view that absolute morality is a historical constant maintained by Jesus, who never changes.

[67] For further discussion of self-esteem see the second book in this series, *What Agreement Is There Between the Temple of God and Idols?: The Accidence of Sin and Idolatry*, chapter 9: "Marauding Visigoths: The Autocratic Self"

[68] Luke 18:13; John 15:5

	morally superior through profuse gratitude. People often praise this kind of behavior, so it serves as a red herring keeping others diverted from one's sin.
50. "Do not judge and you will not be judged…" (Luke 6:37);[69] "Let any one of you who is without sin be the first to throw a stone at her." (John 8:7b)	The command not to judge, in Luke 6:37, is a warning against withholding forgiveness from others, which can arise when one places himself in the position of God. It never indicates that one is not to make judgments about right and wrong, good and evil. Christians are called to test the spirits,[70] to judge matters within the church,[71] and to critically evaluate that which pertains to the body of Christ.  *The Love of Helen and Paris* Jacques-Louis David, 1788 Listen carefully when one injects, "Do not judge and you will not be judged," or "Let him who is without sin cast the first stone." Often such statements are invoked when the counselor closes-in on a poignant sin issue.

---

[69] For a more complete discussion of this topic see "The Question of Judgment" in the first book in this series, *Ask for the Ancient Paths: From Art to Artifice to Arisen*, chapter 2: "The Counseling Ambition"
[70] 1 John 4:1
[71] 1 Corinthians 5:12

	This is a flailing attempt to force the counselor off course, to cause him to abandon his pursuit.

Most counselees themselves readily judge when it is convenient and expedient to do so, but then are quick to denounce judgment which seems to challenge their own sin. There is a root hypocrisy in this practice, and the counselor is wise to point this out for the sake of repentance. |
51. "I do not hold to any doctrine or theology. I just follow Jesus and the Bible."	First Timothy 4:16a reads, "Watch your life and *doctrine* closely..." The Bible presents myriad truths which are to be categorized and summarized as doctrine (the Trinity, the hypostatic union, the perseverance of the saints, etc.). The Bible presents a theology (the study of God) which must be interpreted and applied under the direction of his Spirit. While certainly the Christian is called to only follow Jesus and the Bible, the subtext in this statement is an anti-intellectualism which tends to compartmentalize and reduce faith to pietism. This compartmentalization and reduction makes one vulnerable to secular thought.[72] A rejection of the need for sound doctrine and theology is usually a statement that one does not want to "work out" his faith,[73] does not want his faith challenged, and does not invite change. At the heart of this statement is a denial of the need for gospel-directed reason and analytical assessment with regard to issues of the heart.
52. "God is love."[74]	Quoting this verse is usually for the purpose of deflecting potential confrontation with sin. The objective is to show blind tolerance rather than seeking to understand the distinctive nature of God's love.[75] This verse must be interpreted through the lens of the entire Bible, viewed in the context of the Father sending his Son to die for sinners. It should never serve to blindly make people feel good about themselves, or to find comfort in their sin.
53. "I want to be loved	This statement really says that one does not want to

---

[72] Consider 1 Corinthians 3:2, 3 which links remaining as a child in the faith with worldliness. Additionally, Hebrews 5:12 bemoans the fact that some believers have not progressed past "elementary truths."
[73] Philippians 2:12
[74] 1 John 4:8
[75] For a more detailed discussion of God's love see the case study, "God's *Sui Generis* Love," in chapter 2: "Suffering: The Kintsugi Objective"

unconditionally."	change but rather remain comfortable in his sin. The clandestine objective is that others should accept and assist one in his Kabuki theater-like drama.
54. "I just can't feel God's love"	Such a statement usually arises in the context of excuse for one's sin and is just rebadged human pride, another means of self-focus. The implication is that if one could just feel God's love, then he would stop sinning against God. However, I usually find that those who most assertively claim to not feel God's love themselves have no love for God. Thus, their feeling reflects the state of their own hearts, rather than that of God's. Besides, feeling God's love was never the prerequisite for obedience by any of the Bible's faithful. Those who showed faith did so regardless of feeling.
55. "God would not want me to be unhappy."	A recently divorced Christian woman stated that she had the right to search for a man who would meet her "needs," because, in her words, "God would not want me to be unhappy." Therefore, it behooves God to give her what she wants. Her logic pivots upon the notion that one should seek his own happiness first (while implicitly neglecting holiness),[76] because that must be the will of a good God. The objective is to keep oneself pampered with acceptance and the feeling of being loved. This is the recipe for justifying every form of evil.
56. "As long as my wife is happy, that's all that matters."	This statement, while it sounds other-centered,[77] is based on seeking to meet perceived needs in another (in this case, one's wife). The speaker also seems to exhibit a pressing fear of man. When the day comes that his wife is not happy his world will feel like a train wreck, and he will fall into a lugubrious state. From the Bible's perspective there is only one thing that matters - growth in holiness.
57. "I am trusting God for _____."[78]	The completion of this statement is usually the idol of one's heart. People usually trust God for whatever they worship.
58. "Pray, pray, pray."	While the call to prayer is certainly God-honoring and 1 Thessalonians 5:17 admonishes Christians "to pray

---

[76] 1 Thessalonians 4:3; 1 Peter 1:16
[77] Ephesians 5:25
[78] This concept from Paul Tripp, Westminster Theological Seminary, Philadelphia, Pennsylvania

	without ceasing," the intention behind pressured carnal prayer is to strong-arm God into granting one's request.

Theologian John Murray (1898–1975) said that the heart divides on a "razor's edge." By this he meant that there is often a hair's breadth between godliness and idolatry. The heart so subtly transforms godly intent into idolatrous craving. The first observation about the statements listed above is that some of them contain a measure of truth. It is true that no one is perfect; it is true that God is love. However, these verities are used to mislead others in order to exculpate the sinner. These statements generally make the speaker appear to be a victim so as to offer some form of plausible deniability for sin. The

Officer and Laughing Girl
Johannes Vermeer, c. 1657

speaker sees himself as not responsible for his sin, since he is either conscried to play out a predetermined script, or is shackled to the whim of circumstance. The wise counselor spies the nascent deception in each statement. He ferrets out the self-delusion, blame-shifting, and desire to escape God's plan for change.

"Believe not all that you see, nor half of what you hear."

Counseling Threats: Stigmas and Stereotypes, Straw Men and Shibboleths[79]

At the time of this writing I have either been a student at, or taught at, a dozen institutions of higher education. With the exception of a few, each of those institutions bills itself as internationally-minded, committed to a certain pluralism (although that takes on various hues in various contexts). At some location in most of those institutions, there is a hall draped with flags from around the world. There may even

---

[79] For additional development of this topic see "The Question of Judgment; The Tendency toward Transference (Projection)" in the first book in this series, *Ask for the Ancient Paths: From Art to Artifice to Arisen*, chapter 2: "The Counseling Ambition"

be a world map with red dots showing the location of alumni. The point is, with some of these institutions, this is a propaganda technique to counter an assumed parochialism; the international flag hall looks like a convincing antidote to bigotry and intolerance. In reality, much more than this is required.

At this point in our discussion there is a needed counterbalance, the call for diagnostic caution. Often the biblical counselor may unwittingly hold to a certain soft-bigotry. He may assume that those of a particular ethnicity, Christian tradition, or educational background, approach and respond to God in a particular way. While wisdom alerts the counselor to certain heart patterns, wisdom also dictates that he hold to expectations tenuously. Rarely do people function in lockstep with their faith traditions, nor are they homogeneous with regard to socio-economic or cultural upbringing.

> I once attended the lecture of an older Christian educator whom, I believe, presented some heretical ideas. At an opportune moment after his talk, I introduced myself and asked if we could discuss a few of his points. In the course of exchanging pleasantries, I mentioned my Westminster Theological Seminary background. The man's affect hardened as he blurted out, "You Calvinists..." I can't remember what he said next, but I knew that further conversation was futile (and it turned out to be).

This brings us to the point at hand, the tendency in counseling toward four related threats: stigmas and stereotypes, straw men and shibboleths.

1. A stigma is a "mark of disgrace, stain, or reproach, as on one's reputation."

2. A stereotype is an unfair characterization of another, offering a fixed form where one does not exist.

3. A straw man is "a fabricated or conveniently weak or innocuous person, object, or matter, used as a seeming adversary or argument."

4. A shibboleth is "a custom, phrase, or use of language that acts as a test of belonging to, or as a stumbling block to becoming a member of, a particular social class, [or] profession."[80]

One danger in counseling is to attach a certain stigma to a counselee who may have a sorted past, or who may have sinned in a particularly vivid way. Past sin is not necessarily indicative of the current condition of the heart. A counselee may so distain his past sin that he eschews it like a plague. Thus, the counselor must evaluate evidence in the present, along the heart's current trajectory. He wades through the

---

[80] These four definitions from Dictionary.com

excuses, the mitigating factors, and the situational ethics, to uncover the truth of the psyche. The wise counselor blocks out distractions and background static, to give ear to the salient issues surrounding the heart. Then he goes after those issues with a persuasive intent.

> Generally, I don't want to know much about a counselee's past sins or experiences. Some cursory data offers context, but nothing more is needed. I find that too much discussion of the past skews my assessment. I would rather focus on the current state of the heart. (Besides, past experiences often serve as a diversionary tactic to showcase some excuse for present transgression.)

The counselor may stereotype a particular counselee based on appearance or superficial issues without adequate evidence to either confirm or refute that stereotype. For example, since 1955 blue jeans have been loosely associated with teenage rebellion. Recognizing this as nothing more than a stereotype, I strike such an observation from evidence, until such evidence is irrefutable.

Setting up a straw man is zeroing-in on another's weakest and most vulnerable argument, without giving adequate attention to more substantive ones. In the counseling context this might mean focusing on secondary concerns without considering the primary thrust of God's work in that person's life. God has a particular intent and focus in the counseling session; the counselor seeks to plumb God's own concerns.

> "Every time I paint a portrait I lose a friend." (John Singer Sargent)

Lastly, a shibboleth is seeking indicators of inclusion in one's own faith tradition or worldview. This may include catch-phrases, certain behaviors, or customs which either accord with (or else contradict), one's own assessment of truth. For example, most Christians pray before a meal. Those who do not may be considered less committed Christians (when they are not necessarily).

There is the danger of making sweeping generalities about a counselee without adequate knowledge, possibly using a single data point or a particular observation to extrapolate the counselee's entire heart condition. (Incidentally, this danger grows as the counselor gains more experience, since he has invariably identified certain sin patterns time and again. This sets the stage for distortions which warble the counseling purview.) The counselor must suspend all judgment until evidence is clear and pervasive. Thus, there should be a preponderance of evidence to back up claims concerning the heart. How does the counselor distill sin from issues of deficient intelligence, giftedness, personality traits, or mere situational conditions?

> "The greatest obstacle to discovery is not ignorance – it is the illusion of knowledge." (Daniel Boorstin)

For example, a young Christian woman often arrives to appointments late and forgets to handle responsibilities. I could easily assume that a sin issue lies behind this, a certain self-centered quality that must be confronted. However, in studying the patterns carefully, I concluded that this woman may have slightly below average intelligence, and may simply have trouble remembering her responsibilities, or may lack to mental foresight to think through issues before they arise. This is certainly not a sin problem, but simply an issue of not having the mental equipment to handle details adequately.

The Jewish Money Lender
Auguste Charpentier, d. 1880

The point of this section is that any person could be implicated with just about any sin on any given day. While each person is vastly more sinful than he can ever imagine, the counseling endeavor should focus on the most pressing besetting sin. The counselee should be loved in a way that allows him to see his heart as God himself sees it. That requires a focused and directed look, an incremental and systematic dealing with the heart.

How do stigmas and stereotypes, straw men and shibboleths infiltrate the counseling process? I propose a set of four deficiencies in "visual acuity" with regard to counseling. These I term the tetrad distortions of the:

1. Myopic
2. Hyperopic
3. Astigmatic
4. Presbyopic

These terms refer to faulty "focal lengths" in the counseling horizon.

Condition	Definition	Implication for Counseling
1. Myopia	Nearsightedness - the ability to focus on close objects but not those at a distance	The counselor may atomize data, becoming so attentive to minute details in the counselee that he "hyper-reads" or over-analyzes data. For example, there are times when people are simply making light conversation without deep intent. Additionally, the counselor's attention may be drawn to peccadilloes, idiosyncrasies, and annoyances so that he misses the actual issue at hand. The counselor rightfully looks for legitimate patterns, so as not to become distracted by minutiae. For example, while studying at Westminster Theological Seminary, I routinely met with a Nigerian friend. As I soon discovered, in African culture setting a place and time to meet is merely a guideline. So my friend might arrive a half-hour late. For him, stopping to greet each person along the way is far more important than holding to a set appointment time. In had to shed my myopic vision to enter into my friend's world.
2. Hyperopia	Farsightedness - the ability to focus on distant objects, but not those close-up	The counselor so aggregates data, keeps such a broad and far-reaching vision, that he cannot adequately apply the gospel to specific life events. The counselor may tend to "auto-counsel" so that he offers counsel which is not specific to the counselee, not attuned to his particular questions and motives. This counselor may fear propinquity so as to somewhat distance, or even dehumanize, the counselee.
3. Astigmatism	A toric distortion - the eye's vertical and horizontal planes do not align so that vision is	The counselor may hold a distorted view of the counselee's life so that, while the counselor is attuned to details and rightly hunting for patterns, he skews those details and patterns. The counselee must be careful

	non-uniformly blurred at various distances.	to focus on the crux of the heart's malady, firstly its "vertical" (with regard to God) dimension and secondarily the "horizontal" (the implications for relationships). The astigmatic counselor may warp these dimensions, essentially compromising the gospel.
4. Presbyopia	The cornea loses elasticity so that it cannot adjust to near small objects. (As those objects are extended a distance they come into focus.)	The counselor loses a certain "elasticity" to draw into focus the heart's often confusing mosaic of both sin and faith. The counselor must not be fixated on sin to the exclusion of commending and encouraging growth in genuine faith. Presbyopia tends to set up straw men since one is not able to focus on details and, thus, forms a convenient caricature of the counselee.

The Scout, Friends or Foes, Frederic Remington, c. 1905

"Beware lest you lose the substance by grasping at the shadow." (Aesop)

The Christian receives corrective lenses supplied by God's Spirit. Those lenses are progressively sharpened by Scripture so as to rectify all manner of spiritual distortion. Renewed by God's Spirit, and refined by Scripture, one's spiritual eyes function as they were designed. Thus, the Christian does not seek either a jeweler's loop or a set of field binoculars. He seeks a properly fitted set of spectacles adjusted by Christ and worn for Christ's purposes. In other words, he seeks to see exactly what Jesus himself seeks.

The same analogy could be applied to the counselor as he engages in counseling. He needs corrected vision to see the counselee as God sees him, neither myopically, hyperopically, astigmatically, or presbyopically. In other words, the counselor seeks an Archimedean point at which God himself stands to rightly assess the near and far, micro and macro matters of the heart. One could think of this Archimedean point as gaining the ability to rightly interpolate and extrapolate counseling data. Counseling interpolation is the ability to precisely maneuver between data points (heart evidence), while extrapolation is the ability to accurately extend data points, to discern the logical trajectory of heart allegiances.

> "…to a clear eye the smallest fact is a window through which the Infinite may be seen." (Thomas Henry Huxley)

Diagnosis: "Tree Diagrams"[81]

Uncovering, Analyzing, and Shaping the Motives of the Heart

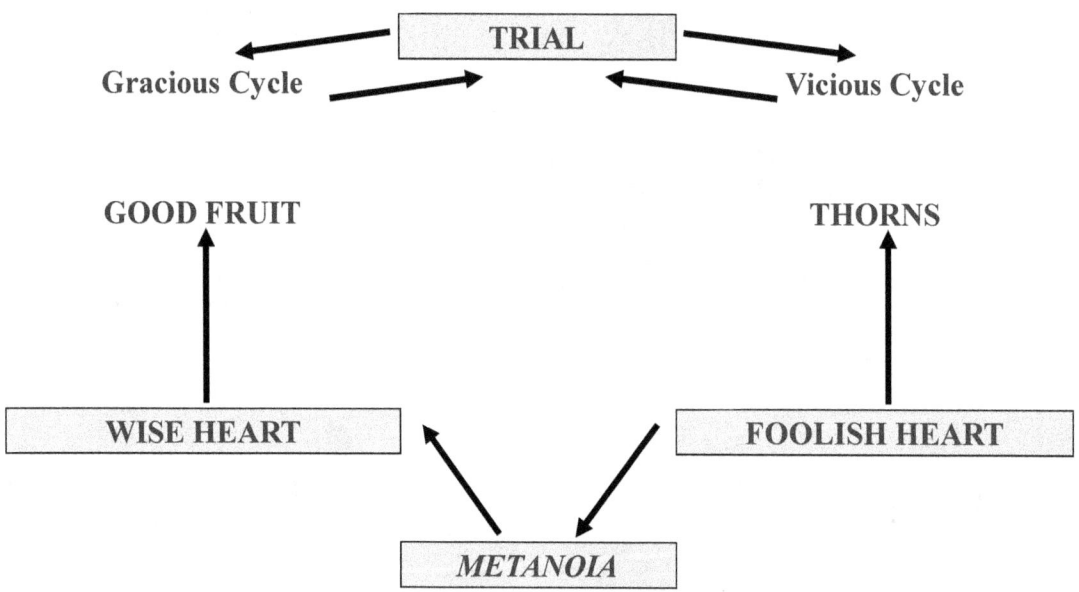

1. The Trial

Symbolized by a burning sun (which harkens back to the Israelites complaint and demand to return to Egypt), the trial is any trying situation – minor or major.[82] Picture the heart to be an opaque cup. One cannot see the cup's contents until it is disrupted; then the contents are exposed. This is the purpose of trials, to disrupt the heart so that its contents are exposed.

---

[81] This model derived from David Powlison's "Dynamics of Biblical Change" class, Westminster Theological Seminary, Philadelphia, Pennsylvania; most of the content from this section borrowed from David Powlison
[82] Jeremiah 17:5, 6

> "[Jesus] learned obedience from what he suffered." (Hebrews 5:8)

God deliberately orchestrates trials. Thus, God plans every situation as a crucible out of which emerges the truth about who he is and who we are. In that contrast, the glaring need for heart change becomes obvious. God is behind each situation to reveal the worship (whether faithful or faithless) of those involved. That is why trials exist. However, in encountering trials the vast majority of Christians stop there, merely focusing on removing them and recasting the situation. This misses the deeper, and infinitely more important, heart change that God desires to draw out of the trial.

Three Trees, Rembrandt van Rijn, 1643

> "The LORD works out everything to its proper end -- even the wicked for a day of disaster." (Proverbs 16:4)

The issue at hand is not about escaping the situation, but about being confronted with, and conformed to, Jesus. To simply remove what one deems to be an undesirable situation (that God has allowed to remain in place for a time) leaves the heart unconfronted, and God's crucial work undone. God does not rest until hearts are conformed to his glory. In this way, the blind attempt to simply remove trials, before they have accomplished their purpose, is an act of defiance against God, one that is destined to failure.

> "I form the light and create darkness, I bring prosperity and create disaster; I, the LORD, do all these things." (Isaiah 45:7)

The trial could be thought of as a trigger or spark that sets in motion the desires of the heart. Unless unmasked by the trial, the heart would likely remain highly-guarded.

Thus, the trial is not valuable in and of itself, but only so far as it exposes heart. There is also a distinct trajectory to each trial which closely traces the contours of the heart, so that the trial precisely matches the targeted elements of the heart's worship.

> "Moses said to the people, 'Do not be afraid. God has come to test you, so that the fear of God will be with you to keep you from sinning.'" (Exodus 20:20)

In drawing attention to the heart, God seeks to clarify and cleanse it. As the heart is continually exposed and repentance occurs, it is then tested anew so that God's sanctifying work is progressively deepened, broadened, and made permanent in the believer. With regard to the unbeliever, trials are calibrated to drive him to the foot of the cross in supplication, to serve as a catalyst to saving faith.

> "Those who sow in tears will reap with songs of joy." (Psalm 126:5)

What constitutes a "burning sun" is itself a reflection of the heart. A burning sun for one person may have no effect on another since one's desires, loves, and cravings determine what becomes a trial. That which becomes a burning sun can therefore reflect either idolatrous commitments or genuine faith. Sinful desires forge their own particular set of purging trials. Likewise, living by faith triggers another distinct set of confirming trials.

For example, in tabloid fodder there are frequent stories about two Hollywood starlets seen wearing the same dress to an awards show. Reporters establish an impromptu "beauty competition" to determine which star wore the dress best, or which star attracted more attention. A starlet who craves the praises of men, who longs to be the center of attention and an object of beauty, may feel a burning sun surrounding this situation. However, for one living by faith in a holy God, one who does not crave the praises of men and places no value on external beauty, this situation induces no angst.

Conversely, one who witnesses God's honor demeaned and Jesus' name maligned and trampled will likely experience a trial where others do not. A burning sun to the faithful may be drastically different than one to the reprobate.

Additionally, a burning sun can often first appear as a blessing, but later bring a curse. For example, a student tells her teacher that he is handsome. There is initially exhilaration in the compliment, but subsequent anxiety in the thought that such compliments may soon evaporate as the body ages. Thus, what, at first blush, looks like gain actually carries with it a profound fear of loss, leading to the exposure of heart idols.

> "I consider that our present sufferings are not worth comparing with the glory that

> will be revealed in us." (Romans 8:18)

2. The Heart

The heart, as the "worship-generation plant,"[83] could best be summarized as "what one does to God." The heart either faithfully obeys God or else rebelliously defies him. There are only two types of hearts, the wise and the foolish, each exposing what one desires, believes, identifies with, and trusts. The unbeliever's heart is unadulterated foolishness; the believer's heart is a patchwork of faith and faithlessness. God vies to shatter the unbelieving monolith and lay claim to greater territory within the tessellated believing heart.

Allegory of Hearing, Jan van Kessel, Sr., d. 1679

> "I the LORD search the heart and examine the mind, to reward each person according to their conduct, according to what their deeds deserve." (Jeremiah 17:10)

The foolish heart is overrun with defective and addictive false worship which spawns a distorted view of reality, oneself, and God. The unbeliever can only live in a foolish heart, a heart that subscribes to self-deluding lies, and operates under the theme of "I must."

> "What causes fights and quarrels among you? Don't they come from your desires

---
[83] Proverbs 12:20; Matthew 15:17-20; Mark 7:21-23

> that battle within you?" (James 4:1)

Examples of defective worship within the foolish heart:

1. I must get as much as I can.
2. I must be respected at work.
3. A loved one must accept me.
4. I must remain in control, have influence, and maintain an image of success.
5. God must make me happy.
6. The world must treat me fairly.

Sometimes the heart wants that which is good, but wants it too much. At other times it wants what is wrong, and likewise wants it too much. This captures the sinner's "must" posture with regard to God and the creation. Additionally, defining the foolish heart as a must-driven entity explains its worship dysfunction. However, a distinction must be made between desires which are good but inordinate, and those which are inherently rebellious.

For example, the heart may live under the idolatry of, "I crave my spouse's love." Is it wrong to want the love of one's spouse? No, the problem is that one wants this too much. The sinner corrupts a good desire so that it transmogrifies into an object of worship (this is the basic definition of idolatry). The sinner willfully brainwashes himself into making all cravings into needs, when in reality they are not.[84] In this way, the sinner absolutizes needs, redefining them as part of his design, so that if he is deprived of those needs he can blame God for his design, or for withholding that which would complete his design.[85] The more plausible the perceived need the greater its toxicity within the heart.

> "Give me five minutes and I can justify any sin." (Edward Welch)

In the following example a wife is controlled by a craving for her husband's love. This leads to various responses driven by the foolish heart.

Idolatry: Craving the Husband's Love	Possible Responses		
	Set #1	Set #2	Set #3
The idolatry initially:	Frustration	Frustration	Frustration

---

[84] David Powlison, Westminster Theological Seminary, Philadelphia, Pennsylvania
[85] For a more detailed discussion of the topic of needs see the first book in this series, *Ask for the Ancient Paths: From Art to Artifice to Arisen*, chapter 7: "The Needs Imperative"

	Anger	Suicidal fantasy	Being loving, but for a manipulative purpose
	Guilt	Anxiety	Seductive, yet receiving no response
	Escape		
	Adulterous fantasy		
	Guilt		
The idolatry finally:	Despair	Confusion	Anger

One, or all, of the emotional progressions listed above may take place when faced with frustrated idols. The idolater may go through these scenarios several times a day, retracing the same path time-and-again, with the futile expectation of a different outcome. This is the nature of idolatry; it is always a just-one-more experience. God frustrates idols out of his soaring mercy to mankind; he will not allow idolatry to satisfy the sinner.

Unlike the foolish heart, the wise heart is faith-directed reliance on God, a resting in the belief that God's promises are trustworthy. The Christian has been given the opportunity to live in a wise heart, but does not fully avail himself of it.

Wise Worship	A Progression of Possible Responses
The worship initially:	Abiding godly desire
	Joyful, loving
	Peaceful
	Firmly in the grip of reality; a sense of assurance
The worship finally:	Experiencing the blessing of seeing good fruit

Examples of worship within the wise heart:

1. How much more can I rely on God? What would most glorify God?

2. I will gladly give my life away for the service of others.[86]

3. I will not respond in the way I have been mistreated. I will love those who hate me.[87]

4. I will seek eternal purpose, and not the dictates of the here-and-now.

---
[86] Philippians 2:17
[87] Matthew 5:44; Romans 12:14

3. Thorns and good fruit.

The good fruit and the thorns arise from the heart, and are "what one does to others."

> By their fruit you will recognize them. Do people pick grapes from thornbushes, or figs from thistles? Likewise, every good tree bears good fruit, but a bad tree bears bad fruit. A good tree cannot bear bad fruit, and a bad tree cannot bear good fruit. Every tree that does not bear good fruit is cut down and thrown into the fire. Thus, by their fruit you will recognize them. (Matthew 7:16-20)

Garden, Pieter Gijsels, d. 1690

> No good tree bears bad fruit, nor does a bad tree bear good fruit. Each tree is recognized by its own fruit. People do not pick figs from thornbushes, or grapes from briers. A good man brings good things out of the good stored up in his heart, and an evil man brings evil things out of the evil stored up in his heart. For the mouth speaks what the heart is full of. (Luke 6:43-45)

Thorns are the outgrowth of a foolish heart. The thorns are either obviously sinful thoughts, words, and actions, or else false fruit masquerading as good fruit. While life-depriving, thorns may cloak themselves to appear life-giving.

Good fruit is the outgrowth of a wise heart. The good fruit may include:

1. Knowledge of God[88]
2. Praise for God[89]
3. Patience and endurance[90]
4. Holy conduct[91]
5. A pure conscience (accurate, active, at peace)[92]
6. The ability to offer wise counsel[93]

> The Biblical counselor searches out the root of sin, not its branches and leaves (which are mere outgrowths of the roots). To focus on the branches and leaves is to miss the opportunity to eradicate the source of sin.[94]

4. Vicious and gracious cycles

A vicious cycle develops as one produces hurtful words and actions so that others do the same. One's trials increase as harsh words stir up anger, and evil actions beget greater evil. Additionally, others glimpse one's foolish self-centered heart and often keep a distance. They may view the thorns, one's manipulative and seductive behavior, and sense the "hook in the bait." The greater the thicket of thorns the greater the strife one experiences with others.

On the contrary, a gracious cycle arises as one speaks loving and life-giving words, so that one finds that others often do the same. Godliness (of certain types) begets favor with others resulting in a measured blessing.[95] The greater one's lush verdant fruit the more others will seek and find refreshment in one's company, and will in turn offer refreshment.

5. *Metanoia* (μετάνοια) (sanctification as literally the "turning" of the heart)[96]

Metanoia is movement from foolishness to wisdom through relationship with Jesus Christ. Such movement is propelled by repentance, which is always the Holy Spirit's work. Notice that the crossover from foolishness to wisdom takes place through the heart, and not by means of thorns turning to good fruit. In other words, sanctification

---

[88] 2 Corinthians 1:8
[89] 2 Corinthians 1:3
[90] 2 Corinthians 1:6
[91] 2 Corinthians 1:12
[92] 2 Corinthians 1:12
[93] 2 Corinthians 1:4
[94] Michael Bobick, *From Slavery to Sonship: A Biblical Psychology for Pastoral Counseling* (1995) 37. (class notes)
[95] Proverbs 15:1
[96] For a more detailed discussion of sanctification see the first book in this series, *Ask for the Ancient Paths: From Art to Artifice to Arisen*, chapter 10: "The Third-Way of Sanctification: From Abominable to Indominable"

is accomplished through change of heart worship, not through mere change of behavior.[97]

There are three basic metaphors for change:

1. Inviting and allowing God to do violence to one's sin through forcibly removing that which impedes growth in Christ.

> "If your right eye causes you to stumble, gouge it out and throw it away. It is better for you to lose one part of your body than for your whole body to be thrown into hell. And if your right hand causes you to stumble, cut it off and throw it away. It is better for you to lose one part of your body than for your whole body to go into hell." (Matthew 5:29-30)

2. Renouncing the flesh and living according to the Spirit

> "For if you live according to the flesh, you will die; but if by the Spirit you put to death the misdeeds of the body, you will live." (Romans 8:13)

3. The command to put off the old self and put on the new self.

> "You were taught, with regard to your former way of life, to put off your old self, which is being corrupted by its deceitful desires; to be made new in the attitude of your minds; and to put on the new self, created to be like God in true righteousness and holiness." (Ephesians 4:22-24)

The "put off, put on" dynamic of Ephesians 4:22-24 contains a mystery at its center, an imperative passive verb. The grammar implies that something must to be done to the believer that he cannot do to himself. Thus, the Christian is called to personally cry out for help, so that God himself puts on the new man, with new desires, out of which flow new actions. This new action influences the situation so that gracious circles, instead of vicious ones, result.[98]

Case Study: The Ping-Pong Match

One afternoon a friend knocked on my door and asked to play ping-pong. I gladly agreed, seeking a relaxing time to chat and enjoy the bucolic weather. While I was not interested in competition, my friend was. As we practiced, he pestered me for a competitive game. I finally acquiesced. From the start my friend dominated our play,

---

[97] For additional development of this topic see the section "The Third-Way of Sanctification" in the first book in this series, *Ask for the Ancient Paths: From Art to Artifice to Arisen*, chapter 10: "The Third-Way of Sanctification: From Abominable to Indomitable"
[98] David Covington, Biblical Counselor

so that I was soon under ping-pong duress. Making matters worse, after every point he yelled, "I win." He seemed to relish winning and making sure I knew who was ahead. Since I consider myself a good player, the situation unsettled me.

My reaction:

THORNS	GOOD FRUIT
Inward:	
1. Brooding, scheming how to get a measure of civilized revenge	1. Play fairly and without a desire to either dominate or kowtow
2. Angry that I could not play better and that he insisted on keeping score	2. At peace with the outcome
3. Entertaining a fantasy world in which I am a superlative player	3. Content with the ability God gave me, and honestly praising my friend's superior ability
4. Depressed to be losing when I felt like I needed to win at something	4. Can, in humility, ask my friend to help me improve my game
5. Planning to use diction that I knew my friend would not understand, so as to appear more intelligent as a way to regain a sense of dignity in the situation	5. Recognize my future to be in Christ, not in my performance for people, or in their perception of my performance
Outward:	
1. Becoming taciturn and distant, as if I was not really focused on the game but my thoughts were elsewhere	1. Give my full attention to the game as a way to love my friend; no need to find a convenient escape
2. Become aggressive so as to gain control of the match through a display of force	2. Play well, but not with idolatrous intent
3. Make excuses for my poor play, such as "I was up all night working," "I am not feeling well today," or "I have not eaten today"	3. No need to explain my play; let it stand as it may
4. Stop playing competitively; turn off my emotions and effort; conveniently forget the score	4. Play and compete with a joyful heart
5. Secretly practice every day so that I will never be humiliated again	5. To practice or not practice is not the issue, but rather the motive for practice

As I played, my heart was a war-zone of various idolatrous desires and schemes. However, I prayed for Jesus to have victory in my heart. I surrendered my will and emotions to him. I rehearsed the gospel and God's intention in bringing this friend into my life. My eyes were opened to no longer see the game as the purpose of the afternoon, but to see my friend as a soul in need of Christ. My heart shifted from a self-serving and self-protective pursuit, to genuine love of God and my friend. As my friend continued his ping-pong onslaught, I could remain at peace, harboring an abiding sense of joy in a God who had far greater plans for that game (in me and in my friend) than just the final score.

Max Decugis
François Flameng, d. 1923

The outcome is that over our remaining two years working together, my friend and I played ping-pong frequently. This became a fruitful point of contact for our growing friendship. I had the opportunity to share the gospel with this friend, and he soon read parts of the Bible. (Incidentally, at our final match we were split, two games each.)

The Counseling Practicum[99]

Each summer our family travels to Tanglewood nestled in the Berkshires of western Massachusetts. As is our tradition, we attend a concert of the Boston Symphony Orchestra, but not the black-tie event of Saturday night. We prefer the rehearsal concert held on Saturday morning. The rehearsal is preceded by a lecture on the particular piece where one gains an appreciation of its history and its unique place in the classical music corpus, as well as a more intimate look at the featured musicians. During the rehearsal the conductor occasionally stops the symphony to discuss crucial elements, maybe asking the violin section to play a particular note with more vigor, or directing the clarinets to slow down a touch. In the unfolding process, musicians may discuss the score, share a laugh, or even exchange tense words. We find the rehearsal

---

[99] This section almost entirely from David Powlison, "Dynamics of Biblical Change" class, Westminster Theological Seminary, Philadelphia, Pennsylvania (originally labeled "The Self-Counseling Project")

far more edifying, entertaining, and engaging than the finished product. Being privy to the types and frequency of refinements is much more gratifying than simply witnessing a perfectly polished final product.

There is something in this anecdote which offers a glimpse into the wonder, beauty, and thrill of helping others know, and be known by, Christ. There is something in the process which builds stunning appreciation for the final "polished product" (the heart fully-surrendered to Christ). There is something in the dialogue, questioning, and searching which offers the feeling of having mined hidden treasure, to recognize the towering achievement of the piece at hand.

> "In great affairs men show themselves as they wish to be seen, in small things they show themselves as they are." (S. Chamfort)

Choose an issue to work on. This may involve minor or major behavior or thought patterns. Minor issues are always linked to deeper problems, like "a handkerchief pulled out of the magic hat with twenty more attached to it."[100] Break down major besetting sins into particular actions, thoughts, and feelings.

Examples:

1. **Anxiety.** What are the pressures, stresses, worries, cares, and demands that routinely surface in one's life? How does one respond - snacking, brooding, or fidgeting?

2. **Athletics.** Sports offer a window into pride, fear, competitiveness, and living on basis of one's successes or failures.

3. **Authority.** Is one's stance toward parents, teachers, or bosses, rebellious and strong-willed, or timid and overly-compliant? Does one enter into a private world of his own rule? As an authority is one harsh or neglectful?

4. **Broken relationships.** Is one prone to drawing up battle lines, playing the peacemaker, resorting to anger, avoiding conflict all together, using bullying tactics, manipulating, or seeking to keep others in a state of insecurity and confusion?

5. **Comforts and escapes.** In what way does one turn to drugs, food, hobbies, the newspaper, sexuality, sports, or television as an escape? Does one entertain a fantasy world of success or failure? When and why does this happen?

6. **Driving habits.** Driving is a microcosm of one's lifestyle and approach to people.

---

[100] David Powlison, Westminster Theological Seminary, Philadelphia, Pennsylvania

Is one law-abiding and scrupulous, aggressive and hurried, fearful and guarded, courteous and protective of others?

7. **Fear of people.** Is one consumed with the desire for approval, or with the fear of rejection? Does one lie, flatter, cower, tower, avoid, play the chameleon, or wear a relational mask? Does one find himself defined by other's opinions? Does one find himself suddenly silent, insecure, or self-confident?

8. **Grumbling.** Is one negative, complaining, or ungrateful? Is one sour and disappointed in life?

9. **Leisure and work.** Is one a workaholic with a counterbalancing self-indulgence in comforts? Is one driven and restless? Does one frequently procrastinate and resort to avoidance? Is one's rest a time to truly bask in Christ, or is it a camouflaged form of self-promoting work?

The Green Lizard, Charles Perugini, d. 1918

10. **Money and possessions.** The vast majority of people run off the rails in their handling of money. When money is involved some become obsessed with hording, fearful of poverty, worried about each expenditure, overly-generous, using money to "buy friends," impulsive spenders, or consumed by feelings of inferiority or superiority.

11. **Romance and sex.** How does one handle sexuality? Does one use seduction as a weapon of interpersonal war? Does one succumb to lingering eyes or flagrant actions? What does one do when encountering the media's images?

12. **Self-absorption.** Is one highly-opinionated and excessively talkative? Does one use listening as a bargaining chip to leverage one's own agenda?

13. **Being sinned against or victimized.** How does one react to being wronged? Does one resort to anger, denial, escape, launch a plan for future self-protection, or cultivate a sense of moral superiority?

Describe the problem in detail.

1. How does the problem show up in behaviors, words, thoughts, and emotions?

2. When, where, and with whom does the problem surface?

3. How often, how intense, and how recidivistic is the problem?

4. What is the trigger or starting point?

5. What intensifies the problem?

6. Who are good and bad examples that one follows in dealing with the problem?

7. What has helped in bringing the problem to repentance in the past?

8. Why has this issue arisen at this time?

Bring the Word of God to bear on this issue.

1. What is God's character and the nature of his promises?

2. What does change in Christ look like?

3. How does one daily search the Scripture with this issue in view, so that one continually asks God to author repentance and faith?

4. In what way is one following the Bible's imperative to "put off" and "put on"?[101]

---

[101] Colossians 3:9, 10

Specific goals which indicate change

  1. What does headway look like, and what is one aiming for?

  2. What does good fruit look like?

  3. Pray in advance for situations that one knows will offer temptation. Rehearse godliness in the face of temptation.

  4. When one sees the false fruit he rightly resolves to repent and remove the idolatrous focus.

Enlisting encouragers

  1. Who is a trusted counselor on this issue? Who knows God and his Word well so as to offer valuable counsel?

  2. Keep oneself accountable to a godly counselor, and allow that person to question one about his walk with Christ. In the context of accountability, one commits to being transparent and confessing his idolatrous focus.

Journal progress

  1. What happened? What did one do, say, feel, and think?

  2. What came to mind? Did sinful desires or Scripture surface in the heart's battlefield? Did one conjure godly or sinful models of others?

  3. Through experiencing victory in this matter, how is one now equipped to counsel others more effectively?

  4. Sanctification often looks like "a yoyo walking-upstairs."[102] There are moments of both victory and defeat. Chart that which brought victory and that which brought defeat.

  5. Draw a "tree diagram" about a specific situation, and how one moved from a foolish heart to a wise heart.

An Example of the Counseling Practicum

The Presenting Problem

---

[102] Clair Davis, Westminster Theological Seminary, Philadelphia, Pennsylvania

One has a tendency to become defensive when he feels under attack. This defensiveness arises when faced with either a real or perceived threat. How does one analyze this, and bring it into submission to Christ?

A Summary of the Evidence

　1. If belittled, one lashes out.

　2. If ignored or overlooked, one becomes aggressive and overly assertive.

　3. If contradicted, one must prove his point.

A Group of Danish Artists in Rome, Constantin Hansen, 1837

　4. If accused (either rightly or wrongly), one searches for excuses and mounts an overly energetic defense (as if the accuser is the ultimate judge).

　5. If one feels overwhelmed by perceived adversaries one becomes depressed.

More Detailed Evidence

1. When speaking with others, one's thought often is, "Does he know to whom he's speaking? How dare he speak to me in that way!"

2. If one has been overlooked, one may speak in a curt manner, brood, or assume an authoritative tone of voice.

3. One owns an expensive car and wears ostentatious clothing.

4. When driving, the surrounding traffic becomes an adversary with which one is engaged in combat.

5. If the boss criticizes one's work, one launches into a spirited rebuttal replete with well-articulated excuses and documented rationalizations.

6. If a friend is curt on the phone, one may think, "He will pay." One may refuse to call the friend until he has been made to suffer a little.

7. One seeks any means to feel superior to others (such as advanced academic degrees).

8. A friend or relative receives an award or honor and one burns with envy. One feels he must be the most highly-decorated. To gain ascendancy one may engage in covert character assassination or issue backhanded compliments. ("This is a big accomplishment for you.")

9. One easily lies to maintain the illusion that he is worthy of respect.

10. One may surround himself with sycophants who will never question him. One searches for a doting spouse who will be enamored with him.

11. On the opposite side, maybe one surrounds himself with highly-prestigious people. Thus, only those who are respected by the world are allowed in one's circle. One feels he must be associated with "winners," so that he can bolster his own image.

12. One may search for the perfect spouse, a "trophy wife." This is part of indulging a fantasy world in which one is the star of his own show.

13. One may violently strike objects or people in order to feel dominant, in control, and respected.

14. One uses his cell phone as a social shield so as to avoid personal interaction in the face of daunting threats.

15. One may seek to live in the shadows, and long to go unnoticed, so as to escape criticism or attack.

16. One may become a loner so as to avoid being subject to any threat. (It is far easier to be alone than to negotiate potential relational threats.)

The evidence shows a pattern of self-protection, escape, and amassed artillery for interpersonal assault. The one who is fearful of attack installs relational bulwarks (defensive) and siege works (offensive).

The Death of King Saul
Elie Marcuse, 1848

What is the underlying idol? The idol is respect, more specifically that one *must* be respected (the operative word being "must"), at all times, in all places, and by all people whom one deems to owe him respect.

When the idol appears to be working, one feels an adrenaline rush, such as the boss just complimented one in front of his peers. Therefore, one feels that rebellion against God is working, that one is finally winning praise in his carnival of self-glory. Receiving the respect that one craves feels exhilarating. There is a sense of power and victory, blessing and peace. But this is false fruit destined to become a wanion.

The idol's sense of peace is fleeting as it finally brings chaos and disorder. When the idol is frustrated one may descend into depression. In the midst of the searing pain of failed idolatry, one may seek escapes, a shopping spree, a divorce, a scheme to gain money quickly. As he assesses himself through others' eyes, one may claim that he suffers from low self-esteem. He may decide he needs new friends, people who will really love him as he desires to be loved.

There is, in all this, the self-delusion in seeking out that which will serve a dysfunctional idol and make it work. Finally, if an idol cannot be adequately rehabilitated, one installs a new one that appears primed for success. Thus, the process starts over again.

As the idolater studies himself, recognizing his trenchant rebellion and stubborn resistance to God's advances, he is brought to the realization of his abject spiritual poverty. He soon longs for freedom from the tangled web, the dark labyrinth, the serpentine contortions of his heart. God has brought him to the brink of deliverance, poised him to surrender his heart to Christ. God seeks to ravish the desires of his heart, so that they might be replaced by life-giving faith. The question is, "Will the idolater conclusively renounce the remnants of recalcitrant sin, finally shedding its menace?" Will he lay down his arms at the foot of the cross, allowing Jesus to be his bulwark and siege works?

Excursus: The Anxiety Game Plan[103]

> "Light grief speaks, but deep ones are silent." (Latin proverb)

Consider moments of anxiety, preoccupation, and fretful concern:

1. **The past**. Something happened and one can't get it off his mind.

2. **The present**. Something is happening and one is consumed by it.

3. **The future**. Something will happen and one's mind turns it over and over, chewing on every possible contingency.[104]

As worry tightens its grip on the soul perhaps one reaches for some convenient escape or quick fix: raid the icebox, watch television, read a novel, go shopping, drink a beer, or play a game. Perhaps one mobilizes to seize control: make a string of phone calls, work all night, build a faction of supporters, or clean one's house.

In dealing with anxiety:

---

[103] This excursus mostly borrowed from David Powlison, Westminster Theological Seminary, Philadelphia, Pennsylvania
[104] David and Sharon Covington, "Introduction to Biblical Counseling" notes, 2004

1. Name the pressures. What tends to hook one's emotions?

2. Identify how one expresses anxiety.

   a. Is the experience best described as "suffocating"?

   b. Is there an obsession with the object of the anxiety such as in replaying thoughts?

   c. Does one resort to anger as a perceived means of warding-off fears?

   d. Does one exhibit an uncontrollable desire for relief such as gluttony, smoking, sexuality, or shopping?

3. Ask oneself why one is anxious. What is the inner logic?

   a. What "form of greed" is one expressing?

   b. What does one want, need, crave, expect, demand or lust after?

   c. What does one fear either losing or never gaining?

4. What are Jesus' promises to those who belong to him?

5. Go to the Father. Leave one's requests with God and let him handle them.

6. Give oneself away to abandoned love for God and others.

Bible Study: Insights into the Heart from the Book of Philippians[105]

Study Acts 16:6-40 and Philippians 1-4

1. What were the varied pressures that Paul faced? What were Paul's hardships? What burdens, temptations, stresses, problems, failures, threats, and pains – actual and threatening – did Paul face? How did people sin against Paul?

2. What in Paul's situation was positive? What successes, triumphs, vindications, and blessings did Paul experience? What positive impact did he have on events and people? What was God doing around and through him?

3. What are people's typical reactions to circumstances? How do people react to the

---

[105] This Bible study adapted from David Powlison's "Dynamics of Biblical Change" class, Westminster Theological Seminary, Philadelphia, Pennsylvania

pressures that Paul was under? How do you react when things weigh on you? What are your thoughts, words, attitudes, emotions, and actions? What did Paul command the Philippians not to do?

4. How do people react when good things happen? What are the temptations that you face when life abounds with good things? What are your thoughts, words, attitudes, emotions, and actions? What problems can arise when a person experiences blessings?

5. How do sinful reactions affect a situation? What vicious or gracious cycles are created when Christians react to a situation out of the flesh or out of the Spirit? What could have happened in Paul's life, or in the lives of those around him, if he had reacted to events in the flesh?

Ruins with Scene of the Apostle Paul Preaching, Giovanni Paolo Panini, 1744

6. Take a look at motives. Sometimes motives can be shown to directly link to actions, at other times the link is more tenuous. What causes underlie various bad fruit (such as in Philippians 2:14)?

7. How do particular sins flow directly from motives? How might grumbling, anger, worry, compulsive eating, or manipulation flow directly from the "god" or "mindset"

described in Philippians 3:19?

8. What happens when people try to change thoughts, behaviors, or emotions, or their circumstances without addressing the heart? What happens when people try to put on a behavior without dealing with motivation? What happens when people never really address what rules them?

9. Who is God in Paul's world? What was Paul presupposing about God? How was God Paul's actual environment? In what way does this show itself?

10. What ruled Paul? How was Paul's life driven by faith? What controlled Paul's interpretation of circumstances and his response to them? What was Paul's secret of contentment, source of peace, thankfulness, and joy? What did Paul believe, trust, fear, hope in, love, and seek to obey?

11. How does faith make the world look very different? How does faith as a ruling motive reinterpret our circumstances in the midst of suffering or success?

12. How does genuine faith change people in discernable ways? How was Paul's thankfulness, peacemaking, and contentment a direct outgrowth of believing and fearing God?

13. How does this account portray repentance and change? How does faith enable one to experience lasting change? How does one find deliverance from:

   a. Compulsive self-interest (Philippians 1:17, 2:3, 2:21)
   b. Confidence in oneself (Philippians 3:3-7)
   c. Making one's desires into gods (Philippians 3:19)
   d. Living for what is before one's eyes and surrounding oneself (Philippians 3:19)
   e. Willing and acting upon one's own good pleasure (Philippians 2:13-15)
   f. Preoccupation with anxieties, comforts, or riches (Philippians 4:6, 4:12; Acts 16:19)
   g. Fear of people and what they can do to oneself (Philippians 1:28; Acts 16:27)

What does moving toward Christ in these areas look like? (Use specific examples from Philippians to show this "from-to" structure of repentance.)

14. How does Philippians describe the ongoing process of change? Everyday Christians experience repentance as an ongoing process. (Explain this from the perspective of Philippians 1:6, 1:9, 1:14, 1:25, 2:12, 2:15, 3:12-16; 4:2; 4:12)

15. What were Paul's commands to his readers? How did Paul's interpretation of his

world result in good fruit? What did he say, do, and feel in the midst of both trials and victories? Was Paul a Stoic (one who feels no emotion)?

16. What gracious cycles can one imagine Paul had created through his display of faith?

17. What does this study of Philippians mean to you personally? What is the deepest area of change that God is asking you to work on?

- 9 -

EMERGING FROM THE CHRYSALIS:
Issues the Counselor Observes and Seeks to Change

Joseph Reveals Himself to His Brothers, Jean-Charles Tardieu, 1788

Deuteronomy 6:4-25

Hear, O Israel: The Lord our God, the Lord is one. Love the Lord your God with all your heart and with all your soul and with all your strength. These commandments that I give you today are to be on your hearts. Impress them on your children. Talk about them when you sit at home and when you walk along the road, when you lie down and when you get up. Tie them as symbols on your hands and bind them on your foreheads. Write them on the doorframes of your houses and on your gates.

When the Lord your God brings you into the land he swore to your fathers, to Abraham, Isaac and Jacob, to give you—a land with large, flourishing cities you did not build, houses filled with all kinds of good things you did not provide, wells you did not dig, and vineyards and olive groves you did not plant—then when you eat and are satisfied, be careful that you do not forget the Lord, who brought you out of Egypt, out of the land of slavery.

Fear the Lord your God, serve him only and take your oaths in his name. Do not follow other gods, the gods of the peoples around you; for the Lord your God, who is among you, is a jealous God and his anger will burn against you, and he will destroy you from the face of the land. Do not put the Lord your God to the test as you did at Massah. Be sure to keep the commands of the Lord your God and the stipulations and decrees he has given you. Do what is right and good in the Lord's sight, so that it may go well with you and you may go in and take over the good land the Lord promised on oath to your ancestors, thrusting out all your enemies before you, as the Lord said.

In the future, when your son asks you, 'What is the meaning of the stipulations, decrees and laws the Lord our God has commanded you?' Tell him: 'We were slaves of Pharaoh in Egypt, but the Lord brought us out of Egypt with a mighty hand. Before our eyes the Lord sent signs and wonders—great and terrible—on Egypt and Pharaoh and his whole household. But he brought us out from there to bring us in and give us the land he promised on oath to our ancestors. The Lord commanded us to obey all these decrees and to fear the Lord our God, so that we might always prosper and be kept alive, as is the case today. And if we are careful to obey all this law before the Lord our God, as he has commanded us, that will be our righteousness.'

Deuteronomy 6:2-25 offers a picture of all-encompassing relationship with God:

Command (Deuteronomy 6:6-9)	**Make God the focus...**
1. These commandments that I give you today are to be on your hearts. (6:6)	...as the wellspring of one's life[1]
2. Impress them on your children. (6:7)	...of one's future, one's inheritance
3. Talk about them when you sit at home. (6:7)	...in everyday matters
4. Talk about them when you walk along the road. (6:7)	...in travel, commerce, in communication
5. Consider them when you lie down. (6:7)	...when considering one's life, the meaning and purpose of one's existence
6. Consider them when you get up. (6:7)	...when one begins his day, making sure God directs one's steps
7. Tie them as symbols on your hands.	...when one works

---

[1] Proverbs 4:23

(6:8)	
8. Bind them on your foreheads. (6:8)	…of one's mind, what one remembers, what one considers
9. Write them on the doorframes of your houses. (6:9)	…of a "welcome mat" to the outsider, to know who reigns in one's house
10. Write them on your gates. (6:9)	…of a kind of public notice to neighbors and the authorities, like a sign broadcasting one's social commitment

Deuteronomy offers a comprehensive picture of change in relationship with God. Likewise, how is the Christian's life marked out for change on account of Christ? The Christian attends church where he studies the Bible, prays, and sings hymns. But what happens the rest of the week? Is there a radical transformation which takes place? Does the Christian, in all his ways, show the fruits of a life transformed by Christ? Is it evident in even the smallest detail that one has been brought from life to death, that one is sanctified?

> Have Christians fallen into the "soft-bigotry of low expectations"?[2]

Issues the Counselor Observes and Seeks to Change

Once, at a fine restaurant, I overheard a patron at the next table order a Bordeaux. When the wine arrived, the man indignantly asserted that the type of glasses on the table were inappropriate for that particular wine. The waiter promptly gathered up the offending glasses and returned with taller more bowl-like ones. What the waiter learned is that oenology is an exacting discipline. The type of glass dictates the amount of air which comes in contact with the wine, the opportunity to sample the bouquet, and the ability to channel the wine to various parts of the mouth (directly to the back of the mouth or to the tip of the tongue). The glass is precisely chosen to best uncover the subtle treasure in that particular wine. God is even more exact with regard to changing his people's lives. He longs to transform every corner of the Christian, to resurrect and recreate hearts which blossom into Christ-like thoughts, words, and actions.

> Life is not about finding yourself; it is about allowing yourself to be recreated. (adapted from George Bernard Shaw)

1. How one views God

Does God exist to glorify mankind, or does mankind exist to glorify God? Of course,

---

[2] The phrase the "soft-bigotry of low expectations" from Daniel Patrick Moynihan (1927–2003), former New York State senator

mankind exists to glorify God. God is reality and primary; the creation is derivative and secondary. Sin reverses the primary and the secondary; it makes the concrete (God) into an abstraction (such as a "higher power"), and the abstraction (concepts such as love) into the concrete (that which is falsely deified).

> "The heavens declare the glory of God; the skies proclaim the work of his hands. Day after day they pour forth speech; night after night they reveal knowledge." (Psalm 19:1, 2)
>
> "Jesus answered: 'Don't you know me, Philip, even after I have been among you such a long time? Anyone who has seen me has seen the Father. How can you say, "Show us the Father"?'" (John 14:9)
>
> "'For in him we live and move and have our being.' As some of your own poets have said, 'We are his offspring.'" (Acts 17:28)

2. How one views himself

The Lictors Bring to Brutus the Bodies of His Sons, Jacques-Louis David, 1789

> "By the sweat of your brow you will eat your food until you return to the ground, since from it you were taken; for dust you are and to dust you will return." (Genesis 3:19)
>
> "Have mercy on me, O God,

> according to your unfailing love;
> according to your great compassion;
> blot out my transgressions.
> Wash away all my iniquity
> and cleanse me from my sin.
> For I know my transgressions,
> and my sin is always before me.
> Against you, you only, have I sinned
> and done what is evil in your sight;
> so you are right in your verdict
> and justified when you judge.
> Surely I was sinful at birth,
> sinful from the time my mother conceived me.
> Yet you desired faithfulness even in the womb;
> you taught me wisdom in that secret place.
> Cleanse me with hyssop, and I will be clean;
> wash me, and I will be whiter than snow.
> Let me hear joy and gladness;
> let the bones you have crushed rejoice.
> Hide your face from my sins
> and blot out all my iniquity.
> Create in me a pure heart, O God,
> and renew a steadfast spirit within me." (Psalm 51:1-10)
>
> "You have neither heard nor understood; from of old your ears have not been open. Well do I know how treacherous you are; you were called a rebel from birth." (Isaiah 48:8)
>
> "But there is a place where someone has testified: 'What is man that you are mindful of him, the son of man that you care for him?'" (Hebrews 2:6)

3. How one views his situation

Situation is never the reason for the heart's worship. Situation is engineered by God to reveal the contents of the heart, to expose sin. Mankind's problem is a heart that gravitates to godless answers, methods, and outcomes. God carefully directs each situation to reveal the heart, and to draw each to repentance. Therefore, when one seeks to merely alter his situation, he often short-circuits and circumvents God's purposes.

> "The man said, 'The woman you put here with me--she gave me some fruit from the tree, and I ate it.'" (Genesis 3:12)

> "When tempted, no one should say, 'God is tempting me.' For God cannot be tempted by evil, nor does he tempt anyone." (James 1:13)

On the Swing
Nikolai Yaroshenko, 1888

The Bible's saints were often self-serving and consumed with personal ambition.[3] They frequently looked out for their own interests, seeking protection through their own godless means. However, it was a willingness to take a leap of faith, at a potentially disastrous moment, for which God called them "righteous." Thus, the Bible commends those who at an eternal juncture chose faith.[4] At the nexus of life and death, the faithful jeopardized their futures to obey God.[5]

4. What one worships

Each is a worshipping being so that each either strikes treasonous covenants with idols, or a faithful covenant with the true God. This is the most fundamental reality of human existence, that each was made to worship, that each worships in every thought, word, and action. Mankind's deepest problem is firstly one of worship, not one of cognition, behavior, or situation.

> "Jesus answered, 'It is written: 'Worship the Lord your God and serve him only.''"

---
[3] Luke 9:46; Philippians 1:17
[4] Hebrews 11
[5] Esther 4:16; 5:2 is a good example of this.

> (Luke 4:8)
>
> "God is spirit, and his worshipers must worship in the Spirit and in truth." (John 4:24)

5. What one considers good or evil, right or wrong

What one considers good or evil is usually based on subjective feelings, or on the way in which one's desires are advanced or not. God defines good and evil based on his panoptic understanding of reality with clear commands about pursuing good and shunning evil.[6]

Those who are consumed with themselves, with only protecting their own interests, see good and evil, right and wrong, as it pertains to their own personal ambitions and desires. They become selectively blind to what is happening around them, viewing their surroundings through a polarizing lens that only filters self-serving concerns. As one is brought into greater submission to Christ, as one increasingly fears God, one's vision is radically renewed so that one suddenly sees God's concerns. In this way, good and evil, right and wrong, are redefined so as to accord with God's understanding and desires. This renewed understanding becomes the fountain from which flows the courage to stand up for God. David's statement in 1 Samuel 17:26b is a good example, "Who is this uncircumcised Philistine that he should defy the armies of the living God?" Forgetting about himself for a moment, David was consumed with God's glory. He neglected the lethal threat towering in front of him and simply focused on honoring God's name.

> "Against you, you only, have I sinned and done what is evil in your sight, so that you are proved right when you speak and justified when you judge." (Psalm 51:4)
>
> "The wicked accept bribes in secret to pervert the course of justice." (Proverbs 17:23)
>
> "Woe to those who call evil good and good evil, who put darkness for light and light for darkness, who put bitter for sweet and sweet for bitter." (Isaiah 5:20)

6. What one considers a blessing or a curse

That which one considers a blessing or curse is usually based on transient feelings and sinful desires. Those with the eyes of Christ see every situation as a blessing when God orchestrates a change in heart worship.[7]

---

[6] 1 Corinthians 14:20; Romans 16:19
[7] Romans 8:28

> "Those who cling to worthless idols forfeit the grace that could be theirs." (Jonah 2:8)
>
> "Three times I was beaten with rods, once I was stoned, three times I was shipwrecked, I spent a night and a day in the open sea, I have been constantly on the move. I have been in danger from rivers, in danger from bandits, in danger from my own countrymen, in danger from Gentiles; in danger in the city, in danger in the country, in danger at sea; and in danger from false brothers. I have labored and toiled and have often gone without sleep; I have known hunger and thirst and have often gone without food; I have been cold and naked." (2 Corinthians 11:25-27)
>
> "Consider it pure joy, my brothers, whenever you face trials of many kinds," (James 1:2)
>
> "But even if you should suffer for what is right, you are blessed. Do not fear what they fear; do not be frightened." (1 Peter 3:14)

7. What it means to be wise or foolish

The Bible says that wisdom begins with the fear of God; yet the fool says in his heart there is no God.[8] The wise knows what to keep separate and what to join together; the fool joins and separates to his destruction.[9]

> "And he said to the human race, 'The fear of the Lord—that is wisdom, and to shun evil is understanding.'" (Job 28:28)
>
> "The fear of the LORD is the beginning of knowledge, but fools despise wisdom and instruction." (Proverbs 1:7)
>
> "…then you will understand the fear of the LORD
>   and find the knowledge of God.
> For the LORD gives wisdom;
>   and from his mouth come knowledge and understanding.
> He holds success in store for the upright,
>   he is a shield to those whose walk is blameless," (Proverbs 2:5-7)
>
> "Do not be wise in your own eyes; fear the LORD and shun evil." (Proverbs 3:7)
>
> "Therefore everyone who hears these words of mine and puts them into practice is

---

[8] Psalm 14:1
[9] Cornelius Plantinga, *Not the Way It's Supposed to Be: A Breviary of Sin* (Wm B. Eerdmans Publishing Co., 1996)

> like a wise man who built his house on the rock. The rain came down, the streams rose, and the winds blew and beat against that house; yet it did not fall, because it had its foundation on the rock. But everyone who hears these words of mine and does not put them into practice is like a foolish man who built his house on sand. The rain came down, the streams rose, and the winds blew and beat against that house, and it fell with a great crash." (Matthew 7:24-27)
>
> "At that time the kingdom of heaven will be like ten virgins who took their lamps and went out to meet the bridegroom. Five of them were foolish and five were wise. The foolish ones took their lamps but did not take any oil with them. The wise ones, however, took oil in jars along with their lamps. The bridegroom was a long time in coming, and they all became drowsy and fell asleep.
>   At midnight the cry rang out: 'Here's the bridegroom! Come out to meet him!'
>   Then all the virgins woke up and trimmed their lamps. The foolish ones said to the wise, 'Give us some of your oil; our lamps are going out.'
>   'No,' they replied, 'there may not be enough for both us and you. Instead, go to those who sell oil and buy some for yourselves.'
>   But while they were on their way to buy the oil, the bridegroom arrived. The virgins who were ready went in with him to the wedding banquet. And the door was shut.
>   Later the others also came. 'Lord, Lord,' they said, 'Open the door for us!'
>   But he replied, 'Truly I tell you, I don't know you.'
>   Therefore keep watch, because you do not know the day or the hour." (Matthew 25:1-13)

8. What one calls slavery and freedom

Every civilization throughout history has engaged in slavery. The Bible does not make light of this when it speaks of a far greater slavery which holds mankind captive, the slavery to sin. Sin holds each in fierce bondage vastly too powerful for any to break. That is why each needs Jesus Christ to set him free from the bondage to sin.

Each is a slave to what he worships, to his fears, to his desires, and to his perceived needs. Freedom is being forgiven for one's sins, so that one is no longer burdened by condemnation nor plagued by guilt. The one whom Jesus sets free is free indeed.[10]

> "Take my yoke upon you and learn from me, for I am gentle and humble in heart, and you will find rest for your souls. For my yoke is easy and my burden is light." (Matthew 11:29, 30)
>
> "Jesus replied, 'I tell you the truth, everyone who sins is a slave to sin.'" (John 8:34)

---

[10] John 8:36

> "You have been set free from sin and have become slaves to righteousness." (Romans 6:18)
>
> "It is for freedom that Christ has set us free. Stand firm, then, and do not let yourselves be burdened again by a yoke of slavery." (Galatians 5:1)

Brothers Sell Joseph into Slavery, Konstantin Flavitsky, 1855

9. What one considers success and failure

According to evolutionary thinking the strong and proud survive. In reality, based on the way God has ordained the creation, the opposite is true. The strong and proud ultimately fail, being sent away empty.[11] It is the poor in spirit who are blessed, the one's who recognize their desperate need for God who ultimately survive as they find Christ and, in him, eternal life. Thus, that which the world calls success God might call failure; that which the world might call failure, God might call success.

> "Do not be overawed when a man grows rich, when the splendor of his house increases;" (Psalm 49:13)
>
> "Woe to those who are heroes at drinking wine and champions at mixing drinks,"

---

[11] Luke 1:53

> (Isaiah 5:22)
>
> "He has filled the hungry with good things, but has sent the rich away empty." (Luke 1:53)
>
> "Jesus replied: 'A certain man was preparing a great banquet and invited many guests. At the time of the banquet he sent his servant to tell those who had been invited, 'Come, for everything is now ready.'
> But they all alike began to make excuses. The first said, 'I have just bought a field, and I must go and see it. Please excuse me.'
> Another said, 'I have just bought five yoke of oxen, and I'm on my way to try them out. Please excuse me.'
> Still another said, 'I just got married, so I can't come.'
> The servant came back and reported this to his master. Then the owner of the house became angry and ordered his servant, 'Go out quickly into the streets and alleys of the town and bring in the poor, the crippled, the blind and the lame.'
> 'Sir,' the servant said, 'what you ordered has been done, but there is still room.'
> Then the master told his servant, 'Go out to the roads and country lanes and compel them to come in, so that my house will be full. I tell you, not one of those who were invited will get a taste of my banquet.'" (Luke 14:16-24)
>
> "So from now on we regard no one from a worldly point of view. Though we once regarded Christ in this way, we do so no longer." (2 Corinthians 5:16)
>
> "What is more, I consider everything a loss compared to the surpassing greatness of knowing Christ Jesus my Lord, for whose sake I have lost all things. I consider them rubbish, that I may gain Christ." (Philippians 3:8)

10. What one puts his hope in, confidence in

> "I do not know what tomorrow holds, but I know who holds my tomorrow." (Tim Tebow)

What does one put his hope or confidence in? Is one's hope in himself? Is one's hope in science or society? Whatever one places his hope in will fail if it is not truly in God himself. The only thing worthy of one's hope is God's promises, made in and through himself.

> "Blessed is he whose help is the God of Jacob, whose hope is in the LORD his God." (Psalm 146:5)
>
> "This is what the Lord says:

> 'Cursed is the one who trusts in man,
> who draws strength from mere flesh
> and whose heart turns away from the LORD…
> But blessed is the man who trusts in the LORD,
> whose confidence is in him.'" (Jeremiah 17:5, 7)
>
> "Now faith is confidence in what we hope for and assurance about what we do not see." (Hebrews 11:1)

11. What one sees as the source of his problems and trials

Are one's problems based solely on what happens to him, or are they also based upon how one responds to what happens to him? Do one's trials exist because God is communicating a need for change?

> "If you do what is right, will you not be accepted? But if you do not do what is right, sin is crouching at your door; it desires to have you, but you must rule over it." (Genesis 4:7)

12. How one views suffering[12]

The Christian neither exalts suffering nor sees it as worthless.[13] The Christian recognizes that people were not designed to suffer, yet are subject to suffering as a result of the fall. The blame for general suffering is not rightly placed upon oneself (as Job's counselors asserted) nor upon God.[14] Suffering, as a general phenomenon, is the mark of a world under the control of Satan. Jesus' suffering and death was for the purpose of redeeming believers' suffering, not a promise to remove it from one's life. In Jesus, suffering bears fruit for eternity.

> "Not only so, but we also glory in our sufferings, because we know that suffering produces perseverance…" (Romans 5:3)
>
> "For our light and momentary troubles are achieving for us an eternal glory that far outweighs them all." (2 Corinthians 4:17)

> Numbers 19:6-9 prescribes that a priest was to throw cedar wood, hyssop, and scarlet wool onto a sacrificed red heifer. The burned heifer's ashes were to be kept in a clean place outside the camp for use in the water of cleansing; this was purification for sin.

---

[12] For a more detailed discussion of the topic of suffering see chapter 2: "Suffering, The Kintsugi Objective"
[13] Paul Tripp, Westminster Theological Seminary, Philadelphia, Pennsylvania
[14] Andrew Field, "Introduction to Redeemer," p. 6, Westminster Theological Seminary, Philadelphia, Pennsylvania

> There is an obvious reference to Jesus Christ in the cedar wood (cross), hyssop (used to put wine vinegar in his mouth during the crucifixion),[15] and scarlet wool (blood). These articles became intermingled with the heifer's charred remains (possibly a veiled reference to Christ's death). The ashes were then placed into water of cleansing used for purification from sin. The Christian's trials and suffering, represented by the ashes, are part of the cleansing that God affects in the heart. This cleansing process is purification from sin.

Aeneas Flees Burning Troy, Frederico Barocci, 1598

13. What one fears

What one fears reveals where he places his trust. Those who fear people have made others into their gods, as those who determine their ultimate fate. Those who fear God believe that he alone dictates their future. Believers fear nothing else.

> "Even though I walk through the valley of the shadow of death I will fear no evil for you are with me." (Psalm 23:4)
>
> "The righteous cry out, and the Lord hears them; he delivers them from all their troubles." (Psalm 34:17)
>
> "Surely God is my salvation; I will trust and not be afraid.

---
[15] John 19:29

> The Lord, the Lord himself, is my strength and my defense;
>   he has become my salvation." (Isaiah 12:2)
>
> "So do not fear, for I am with you; do not be dismayed, for I am your God. I will strengthen you and help you; I will uphold you with my righteous right hand." (Isaiah 41:10)
>
> "'Do not be afraid of them, for I am with you and will rescue you,' declares the Lord." (Jeremiah 1:8)
>
> "Do not be afraid of those who kill the body but cannot kill the soul. Rather, be afraid of the One who can destroy both soul and body in hell." (Matthew 10:28)
>
> "There is no fear in love. But perfect love drives out fear, because fear has to do with punishment. The one who fears is not made perfect in love." (1 John 4:18)

14. Whom one calls a friend or enemy

Friends are not those who simply tell one what he wants to hear. Friends seek to make one better through the proper means. A real friend is just as likely to tell one when he is wrong as when he is right. On the other hand, one's enemies are those who seek to position one far from God, from his plans, and from his love.

> "Wounds from a friend can be trusted, but an enemy multiplies kisses." (Proverbs 27:6)
>
> "You adulterous people, don't you know that friendship with the world means enmity against God? Therefore, anyone who chooses to be a friend of the world becomes an enemy of God." (James 4:4)

15. What one does with his time

Time is the most precious commodity in the creation. Once a moment is gone it is impossible to replace. Does one see his time as his own, or does he see it as a gift given to him for God's glory? In light of God's glory, what is the best use of one's time?

The world's slavery is designed to convince one to use every moment to demonstrably advance his life. In other words, the world focuses on doing, so as to have something to show for one's time. Time is to be spent either acquiring, experiencing, or improving one's social standing. In defiance of the world, the Christian life is not so much about *doing* but more about *being*. The Christian's life is less about amassing experiences, and more about simply being in relationship with one's God. That often means letting the world race by as one lives simply, humbly, and quietly at the foot of the cross.

Someone may ask me, "What have you been doing with yourself?" My response is sometimes a hackneyed assortment of seemingly inconsequential undertakings. There are times when I have done nothing of worldly significance, and have nothing demonstrable to show for my efforts. Often I have merely engaged in vibrant relationship with my God, something of incalculable significance. Often the times of greatest change in the Christian's life come when he does nothing of worldly importance, but instead focuses on simply sitting at Jesus' feet and listening to him.

> "Better is one day in your courts than a thousand elsewhere; I would rather be a doorkeeper in the house of my God than dwell in the tents of the wicked." (Psalm 84:10)

16. How one views the future; what one see as his eternal fate

What happens upon death? Does one just cease to exist? Will one live forever in heaven or hell? The Bible is clear about the fate of sinners and saints, the former on a wide path leading to death, and the latter on a narrow one leading to life.[16]

> "So we fix our eyes not on what is seen, but on what is unseen, since what is seen is temporary, but what is unseen is eternal." (2 Corinthians 4:18)
>
> "But our citizenship is in heaven. And we eagerly await a Savior from there, the Lord Jesus Christ," (Philippians 3:20)
>
> "Dear friends, I urge you, as foreigners and exiles, to abstain from sinful desires, which wage war against your soul." (1 Peter 2:11)

17. What one loves, and what one looks for in love[17]

Upon what has one fixed his love? Does one love that which God loves? What is true love? Is it simply a feeling, or is it a display of God's goodness and character?

> "Therefore, I tell you, her many sins have been forgiven—as her great love has shown. But whoever has been forgiven little loves little." (Luke 7:47)

18. What makes one happy, sad, or angry

---

[16] Matthew 7:13, 14
[17] For a more comprehensive discussion of the nature of God's love see the case study, "God's *Sui Generis* Love," found in chapter 2: "Suffering: The Kintsugi Objective"

Emotions are never neutral; they are deeply connected to what one worships, and in what one has invested his hope. Does one feel joy, sadness, and anger for that which God feels joy, sadness, and anger?

Moralism dictates that one control his emotions out of fear of moral failing or punishment (called the "volition-based approach"). Conversely, liberalism tells one to express himself, to explore and cultivate his emotions for his own self-serving purpose (called the "emotion-based approach").[18] The Christian's emotions are neither suppressed nor cultivated as such. Rather, they reflect the emotion that God himself feels. Thus, the Christian expresses emotion freely from a regenerate heart as an outworking of honoring God.

God Speed
Edmund Blair Leighton, d. 1922

> "Have I not commanded you? Be strong and courageous. Do not be afraid; do not be discouraged, for the Lord your God will be with you wherever you go." (Joshua 1:9)
>
> "A happy heart makes the face cheerful, but heartache crushes the spirit." (Proverbs 15:13)
>
> "He took Peter, James and John along with him, and he began to be deeply distressed and troubled. 'My soul is overwhelmed with sorrow to the point of death,' he said to them. 'Stay here and keep watch.'" (Mark 14:33, 34)
>
> "Jesus wept." (John 11:35)

---

[18] Andrew Field, "Introduction to Redeemer," p. 7, Westminster Theological Seminary, Philadelphia, Pennsylvania

> "Rejoice always, pray continually, give thanks in all circumstances; for this is God's will for you in Christ Jesus." (2 Thessalonians 5:16-18)
>
> "For the Spirit God gave us does not make us timid, but gives us power, love and self-discipline." (2 Timothy 1:7)
>
> "Is anyone among you in trouble? Let them pray. Is anyone happy? Let them sing songs of praise." (James 5:13)

19. What it means to show grace

The Bible's concept of grace is vastly more than just being socially gracious (well-mannered and polite). The Christian's display of grace shows forth God's character, offering forgiveness and mercy, as well as engaging in needed confrontation for the purpose of change. God's display of grace is for the purpose of affecting salvation in the unbeliever, and sanctification in the believer. It is far more than merely being magnanimous, but wields the full range of God's work and intent. Thus, sometimes it is just as gracious to display godly anger as it is to extend hospitality.

> "Because Joseph, her husband, was faithful to the law, and yet did not want to expose her to public disgrace, he had in mind to divorce her quietly." (Matthew 1:19)
>
> "Let your conversation be always full of grace, seasoned with salt, so that you may know how to answer everyone." (Colossians 4:6)

20. What one is thankful for[19]

> "Give thanks to the LORD, for he is good; his love endures forever." (Psalm 107:1)
>
> "Give thanks in all circumstances; for this is God's will for you in Christ Jesus." (1 Thessalonians 5:18)

21. What one remembers

Life is fundamentally about what one remembers. Is one's memory controlled by a man-centered interpretation of experiences? Does one remember the work of a holy God leading one in paths of righteousness for his name's sake?[20]

---

[19] For additional discussion of thankfulness see "Incentivized Repentance: Gratitude Reversal" in the second book in this series, *What Agreement Is There Between the Temple of God and Idols?: The Accidence of Sin and Idolatry*, chapter 8: "The Search for Eldorado Ends: Repenting of Idols of the Heart"

[20] Psalm 23:3

> "[Love] does not dishonor others, it is not self-seeking, it is not easily angered, it keeps no record of wrongs." (1 Corinthians 13:5)

22. How one describes events; how one views history[21]

The Thanks Offering
Adolphe William Bouguereau, 1867

All of history is organized around Jesus Christ, and for good reason. Jesus Christ is the reason for the creation, the center point of time and space. All of history is God leading people to the knowledge of himself, so that they would find Jesus as their savior. Thus, all of history exists to reveal Jesus. When one becomes a Christian he is instantly connected to history as God's willing participant. He is no longer an enemy to God's work in and through history, but rather an instrument for bringing Christ into the world. The Christian, thus, works in accord with the purpose and movement of history.

The Christian views history (both in aggregate and in individual lives) through a Christ-centered set of lenses. Thus, what the Christian points out about events, what he sees and does not see, reflects his faith in a God who orchestrates all things for the good of those who know and love him.[22]

> "Then Moses and the Israelites sang this song to the LORD: 'I will sing to the LORD, for he is highly exalted. The horse and its rider he has hurled into the sea.'" (Exodus 15:1)
>
> "For from him and through him and to him are all things." (Romans 11:36)

---

[21] For a more comprehensive discussion of the correct view of personal history see chapter 1: "Memories Preserved in Amber: Adopting God's Retrospective"
[22] Romans 8:28

23. How one describes himself and others

How one describes people reflects his deepest beliefs about who people are, and how they should be assessed. Likewise, what one says about himself reflects how he reckons his own value. The Christian does not countenance nationality, race, ethnicity, appearance, height, age, talents, or socio-economic status. The Christian sees only one presiding truth for humanity, the all-consuming need for relationship with Jesus Christ. In this way, the wise Christian is blind to that to which God himself is blind. Conversely, he sees that which God sees: lost and desperate sinners in need of salvation, and fellow believers in need of greater sanctification.

> "To some who were confident of their own righteousness and looked down on everyone else, Jesus told this parable: 'Two men went up to the temple to pray, one a Pharisee and the other a tax collector. The Pharisee stood by himself and prayed: 'God, I thank you that I am not like other people—robbers, evildoers, adulterers—or even like this tax collector. I fast twice a week and give a tenth of all I get.'
>
> 'But the tax collector stood at a distance. He would not even look up to heaven, but beat his breast and said, 'God, have mercy on me, a sinner.'
>
> 'I tell you that this man, rather than the other, went home justified before God. For all those who exalt themselves will be humbled, and those who humble themselves will be exalted.'" (Luke 18:9-14)

24. How one treats his own body

Does one's body exist for his own pleasure and purposes? Can one do anything he wants with it? The Christian recognizes that his body was designed as a temple where God himself lives. Therefore, his body does not belong to him, and is never to be used for self-serving pleasure.

> "'Do not cut your bodies for the dead or put tattoo marks on yourselves. I am the LORD.'" (Leviticus 19:28)

> "Do you not know that your bodies are temples of the Holy Spirit, who is in you, whom you have received from God? You are not your own; you were bought at a price. Therefore honor God with your bodies." (1 Corinthians 6:19, 20)

> The Christian's view of sexuality is neither to lust for it (hedonism) nor to deny the pleasure inherent in it (asceticism). The Christian, within the covenant of marriage, is invited to enjoy sex, while recognizing it to be under the authority of God's second Great Commandment, to love another as oneself. In other words, a husband and wife rightly see sexuality as an other-centered act intended to magnify God's character

within themselves.

25. What one considers beautiful and ugly[23]

What God calls "beautiful" is a matter of the heart, so that beauty radiates from within. Likewise, ugliness also radiates from within, the manifestation of one completely consumed with himself. The Christian trains himself to see people as God sees them, not according to appearance but according to matters of faith.[24]

The Overthrowing of the Rusty Knight
Arthur Hughes, c. 1898

> "For God, who said, 'Let light shine out of darkness,' made his light shine in our hearts to give us the light of the knowledge of the glory of God in the face of Christ." (2 Corinthians 4:6)

> "Your beauty should not come from outward adornment, such as elaborate hairstyles and the wearing of gold jewelry or fine clothes. Rather, it should be that of your inner self, the unfading beauty of a gentle and quiet spirit, which is of great worth in God's sight. For this is the way the holy women of the past who put their hope in God used to adorn themselves. They submitted themselves to their own husbands, like Sarah, who obeyed Abraham and called him her lord. You are her daughters if you do what is right and do not give way to fear." (1 Peter 3:3-6)

---

[23] For additional discussion of this topic see "'I'm a Nightmare Dressed Luke a Daydream': The Quest for Flawless Beauty" in the first book in this series, *Ask for the Ancient Paths: From Art to Artifice to Arisen*, chapter 5: "Redefining the Pygmalion Effect: Exploring the Image of God in Man"

[24] 1 Samuel 16:7

26. Whom one considers to be a true man or woman

Feminism has, to a large degree, emasculated men. Hollywood plays upon this notion of the emasculated man to caricature and twist manhood through the portrayal of gross-motor actions and large splashy events. (This deception seems to have gained a vast following.) Men often seek to re-emasculate themselves through demonstrable acts such as smoking, drinking, womanizing, and even violence. In this way, they seek to recapture that which makes them feel like real men again. Men were uniquely designed by God to combat evil, to vanquish Satan with acts of God-derived power. In order to accomplish God's work, men (like women) are to first allow God to conquer their hearts through his indwelling Spirit.

How does one view manhood and womanhood? Is this through the lens of beauty, strength, competence, or possessions? Is manhood and womanhood actually attained through invisible qualities related to knowing and serving God in distinctive ways?

> "A wife of noble character who can find?
> She is worth far more than rubies.
> Her husband has full confidence in her
> and lacks nothing of value.
> She brings him good, not harm,
> all the days of her life.
> She is clothed with strength and dignity;
> she can laugh at the days to come.
> She speaks with wisdom,
> and faithful instruction is on her tongue.
> She watches over the affairs of her household
> and does not eat the bread of idleness.
> Her children arise and call her blessed;
> her husband also, and he praises her:
> 'Many women do noble things,
> but you surpass them all.'
> Charm is deceptive, and beauty is fleeting;
> but a woman who fears the LORD is to be praised." (Proverbs 31:10-12; 25-30)
>
> "Like an apple tree among the trees of the forest is my lover among the young men. I delight to sit in his shade, and his fruit is sweet to my taste." (Song of Songs 2:3)
>
> "Wives, in the same way submit yourselves to your own husbands so that, if any of them do not believe the word, they may be won over without words by the behavior of their wives, when they see the purity and reverence of your lives." (1 Peter 3:1, 2)

27. How one views marriage

> "Jesus replied, 'The people of this age marry and are given in marriage. But those who are considered worthy of taking part in the age to come and in the resurrection from the dead will neither marry nor be given in marriage, and they can no longer die; for they are like the angels. They are God's children, since they are children of the resurrection.'" (Luke 20:34-36)
>
> "Husbands, love your wives, just as Christ loved the church and gave himself up for her to make her holy, cleansing her by the washing with water through the word, and to present her to himself as a radiant church, without stain or wrinkle or any other blemish, but holy and blameless. In this same way, husbands ought to love their wives as their own bodies. He who loves his wife loves himself." (Ephesians 5:25-28)

28. How one relates to authority

Christians recognize that authority (husbands, employers, parents, teachers, government, police) is instituted by God to restrain mankind's waywardness. Thus, submitting to authority is part of fearing God. A Christian submits to and obeys authority, except when that authority contradicts God himself.

> "Let everyone be subject to the governing authorities, for there is no authority except that which God has established. The authorities that exist have been established by God. Consequently, whoever rebels against the authority is rebelling against what God has instituted, and those who do so will bring judgment on themselves." (Romans 13:1, 2)

29. How one treats those who are vulnerable

> "This is the final test of a gentleman: his respect for those who can be of no possible value to him." (William Lyon Phelps)

Does one care for the widow, alien, and orphan (the weak and imperiled) as God cares for them? Does one treat the vulnerable as valuable members of God's creation? God designs the weak to manifest his hidden qualities. Does one treat the vulnerable as displaying something of God's power and goodness? While the Bible mentions the needs of the widow, orphan, and alien, one could rightly include the disabled, victims of injustice, and even, injured animals. The Christian is gracious toward, and respectful of, the poor because he is ever cognizant of his inner poverty with regard to

God,[25] a poverty that was eradicated by Jesus' death on the cross. This leads him to compassion with regard to the poor without any sense of moral superiority.[26]

> "Then he asked them, 'If one of you has a son or an ox that falls into a well on the Sabbath day, will you not immediately pull him out?'" (Luke 14:5)

> "But God chose the foolish things of the world to shame the wise; God chose the weak things of the world to shame the strong." (1 Corinthians 1:27)

30. How one relates to those under his care

The Christian is first a servant of God, so he is able to exercise authority in the right way, with consideration for those under his care.

> "Fathers, do not exasperate your children; instead, bring them up in the training and instruction of the Lord." (Ephesians 6:4)

Our Village Clockmaker Solving a Problem
James Campbell, d. 1893

31. How and why one studies and works

The purpose of work is not firstly about making money; Christians work to the glory of God. This means that they see work as an opportunity to serve and better others, offering one's skills to improve others. Pay ought to be a secondary concern. A Christian works without regard for the respect he will receive from others, and without seeking to improve his plight in life. One's actual job is finally of no consequence; whom one works for is of eternal consequence.

If one is assured success he works harder because he knows that his labor will actually produce the result he seeks. That is the blessing upon a Christian's work. His work will actually produce results in keeping with God's will, so he works

---

[25] Andrew Field, "Introduction to Redeemer," p. 5, 6, Westminster Theological Seminary, Philadelphia, Pennsylvania
[26] Andrew Field, "Introduction to Redeemer," p. 6, Westminster Theological Seminary, Philadelphia, Pennsylvania

with passion and with focused intent, because he knows that the Lord works through him for cosmic purposes.

> "Then some soldiers asked him, 'And what should we do?' He replied, 'Don't extort money and don't accuse people falsely--be content with your pay.'" (Luke 3:14)
>
> "Therefore, my dear brothers, stand firm. Let nothing move you. Always give yourselves fully to the work of the Lord, because you know that your labor in the Lord is not in vain." (1 Corinthians 15:58)
>
> "Whatever you do, work at it with all your heart, as working for the Lord, not for human masters, since you know that you will receive an inheritance from the Lord as a reward. It is the Lord Christ you are serving." (Colossians 3:23, 24)

32. How one spends money

> "Riches are gotten with pain, kept with care, and lost with grief."

Money, for most, is the first concern when faced with any life question. However, it is often God's last concern. The way one views money reveals what he puts his hope in. Does one buy things that he hopes will fill his deepest longings? Does he place his trust and worth in what he owns? Is one hoping to win friends, and maintain their attention, through his possessions?

> "Why spend money on what is not bread, and your labor on what does not satisfy? Listen, listen to me, and eat what is good, and your soul will delight in the richest of fare." (Isaiah 55:2)
>
> "He who has been stealing must steal no longer, but must work, doing something useful with his own hands, that he may have something to share with those in need." (Ephesians 4:28)

33. How one treats possessions

Does one treat his possessions as though they belong to him alone? The Christian recognizes that his possessions do not exist for his own purposes. He, therefore, holds onto them loosely. Christians live a simple life recognizing that this world is not their home. They do not invest themselves in things that are perishing.

> "Whoever has will be given more, and he will have an abundance. Whoever does not have, even what he has will be taken from him." (Matthew 13:12)

> "For you know that it was not with perishable things such as silver or gold that you were redeemed from the empty way of life handed down to you from your ancestors," (1 Peter 1:18)

34. What one considers valuable

What is truly valuable? The Christian recognizes that value is invested into the creation by God alone. Thus, he never views the creation through the lens of economics, but based on how God defines it in terms of an eternal schema - that which manifests his glory.

As eternal beings, people are infinitely more valuable than possessions, achievements, or experiences (that which is perishable). Yet, the modern tendency is to devalue human life as just another expendable commodity. The Bible recognizes that there is nothing more worthwhile than helping a soul find relationship with God.

> "The law of the Lord is perfect,
>   refreshing the soul.
> The statutes of the Lord are trustworthy,
>   making wise the simple.
> The precepts of the Lord are right,
>   giving joy to the heart.
> The commands of the Lord are radiant,
>   giving light to the eyes.
> The fear of the Lord is pure,
>   enduring forever.
> The decrees of the Lord are firm,
>   and all of them are righteous.
> They are more precious than gold,
>   than much pure gold;
> they are sweeter than honey,
>   than honey from the honeycomb." (Psalm 19:7-10)
>
> "Enter through the narrow gate. For wide is the gate and broad is the road that leads to destruction, and many enter through it." (Matthew 7:13)
>
> "The kingdom of heaven is like treasure hidden in a field. When a man found it, he hid it again, and then in his joy went and sold all he had and bought that field. Again, the kingdom of heaven is like a merchant looking for fine pearls. When he found one of great value, he went away and sold everything he had and bought it." (Matthew 13:44–46)

> "What good will it be for someone to gain the whole world, yet forfeit their soul? Or what can anyone give in exchange for their soul?" (Matthew 16:26)

35. What one eats and drinks, and how one eats

Isabella, John Everett Millais, 1849

A Christian does not eat to survive but eats as part of God's purpose and glory. Since Jesus is the bread upon which the Christian feeds, he can eat actual bread modestly, not in a gluttonous manner. The Christian looks for ways to show hospitality and friendship over shared meals. He also eats in a respectful and quiet manner, not drawing attention to himself.

> "For life is more than food, and the body more than clothes." (Luke 12:23)
>
> "Then Jesus declared, 'I am the bread of life. Whoever comes to me will never go hungry, and whoever believes in me will never be thirsty.'" (John 6:35)
>
> "Do not get drunk on wine, which leads to debauchery. Instead, be filled with the Spirit," (Ephesians 5:18)

36. How one dresses

A Christian dresses modestly, not drawing attention to himself either through flashy or slovenly dress. He also seeks to guard other's hearts, so as not enslave them, recognizing that anything which distracts from God's purposes is the work of Satan. Additionally, since a Christian is clothed in the righteous robe of Christ,[27] he can dress modestly knowing that his earthly clothing is not the source of his glory.

> "If not, what did you go out to see? A man dressed in fine clothes? No, those who wear expensive clothes and indulge in luxury are in palaces." (Luke 7:25)
>
> "I also want women to dress modestly, with decency and propriety, not with braided hair or gold or pearls or expensive clothes," (1 Timothy 2:9)
>
> "I counsel you to buy from me gold refined in the fire, so you can become rich; and white clothes to wear, so you can cover your shameful nakedness; and salve to put on your eyes, so you can see." (Revelation 3:18)

37. What one finds humorous

"Many a truth is said in jest."[28] What one finds humorous reveals a great deal about his character, so that those in rebellion toward God laugh at that which God finds disgraceful. The counselor listens carefully to jokes so as to discern something of the heart's desires.

> "Laughter,' I said, 'is foolish. And what does pleasure accomplish?'" (Ecclesiastes 2:2)
>
> "Godly sorrow brings repentance that leads to salvation and leaves no regret, but worldly sorrow brings death." (2 Corinthians 7:10)
>
> "Nor should there be obscenity, foolish talk or coarse joking, which are out of place, but rather thanksgiving." (Ephesians 5:4)

38. How one entertains himself

Has one's source of entertainment become nothing more than a frivolous waste of time? Has the desire for a moment's thrill left one addicted to wanting just one more flight of fantasy?

> "My people come to you, as they usually do, and sit before you to hear your words, but they do not put them into practice. Their mouths speak of love, but their hearts

---

[27] Revelation 6:11
[28] This concept is attributed to Geoffrey Chaucer (1343-1400), William Shakespeare (1564-1616), or "Roxburghe Ballad" (circa 1665) depending on the degree to which the original accords with this modern expression.

> are greedy for unjust gain. Indeed, to them you are nothing more than one who sings love songs with a beautiful voice and plays an instrument well, for they hear your words but do not put them into practice." (Ezekiel 33:31, 32)

39. How one competes

The way one competes in sports, for example, reveals something about his level of selfishness or service to others. Competition should be an opportunity to help and encourage others, to better them, not to better or promote oneself. A Christian can certainly win in competition, but that is never his chief objective.

> "Do you not know that in a race all the runners run, but only one gets the prize? Run in such a way as to get the prize." (1 Corinthians 9:24)

40. How one drives

Few activities display a person's character like his driving habits. How one drives reveals a great deal about what he worships, in that behind the wheel one is lured into a false sense of control, a surge of power, and the delusion that one is impervious to threats. Consider that one's propensity to speed is the extent to which he will steal. His treatment of other drivers reveals his level of cowardice, and his care around pedestrians reflects the degree to which he fears God. Thus, the automobile reveals one's character whether aggressive, controlling, punishing, or gracious.

> "'Love the Lord your God with all your heart and with all your soul and with all your mind and with all your strength.' The second is this: 'Love your neighbor as yourself.' There is no commandment greater than these." (Mark 12:30, 31)

Excursus: The Psychology of the Speedometer

Speedometers seem straightforward enough, but in reality they are a deceptive component of the automobile. On the one hand, they should offer a welcomed measure of caution; on the other, they are a cleverly-designed marketing gimmick. Even the size and color of speedometers are chosen to elicit certain emotions during the driving experience.

Since the vast majority of drivers desire a fast car, the speedometer is designed to make the driver feel that the car is faster than it is. A speedometer dial that goes to a high number stokes the promise of driving excitement. However, a speedometer must also alert the driver to potential danger and induce a measure of caution. Thus, it assumes this "schizophrenic" presence in the driver's psyche.

In the 1970s, with the implementation of a national speed limit, speedometers' high speed displays were relatively low. This meant that at normal highway speed the needle registered far to the right. The idea was to cause a driver to overestimate his speed and slow down. Today, however, manufacturers generally design speedometers to register in the middle of the dial at highway speed. This seems to make drivers the most comfortable.

In speedometer design one sees the clever machinations of the human heart and the ease with which it is manipulated. The speedometer's intended purpose is to offer a measure of caution, but it is leveraged as a marketing tool to prompt sales.

41. How one views science, technology and medicine

Does one view science and technology as his savior? Does one think that science is neutral, and therefore above religion (which appears to be subjective)? The Christian rightly recognizes that science is heavily based on religious assumptions. He also recognizes that, although it appears to do so, the vast majority of technology does not truly better the Christian's life. In fact, technology often makes life more oppressive and enslaving. The Christian recognizes that there may be a certain utility to technology and scientific knowledge, but he never places blind trust in their ability to deliver mankind from its most pressing plight of sin.

> "My son, pay attention to what I say;
>   turn your ear to my words.
> Do not let them out of your sight,
>   keep them within your heart;
> for they are life to those who find them
> and health to a man's whole body." (Proverbs 4:20-22)
>
> "Gracious words are a honeycomb,
>   sweet to the soul and healing to the bones." (Proverbs 16:24)
>
> "He replied, 'When evening comes, you say, 'It will be fair weather, for the sky is red,' and in the morning, 'Today it will be stormy, for the sky is red and overcast.' You know how to interpret the appearance of the sky, but you cannot interpret the signs of the times.'" (Matthew 16:2, 3)
>
> "She had suffered a great deal under the care of many doctors and had spent all she had, yet instead of getting better she grew worse." (Mark 5:26)

42. How one views culture

Culture is "things loved in common,"[29] and as such is an inherently man-centered system of interaction between people (often structured by means of a God-fearing lattice work). One's approach to culture should neither be that all cultures are inherently equal (multiculturalism), nor that one's culture ought to be worshipped as superior. Even in the most godless cultures there are redeemed or redeemable elements, and even in the most God-fearing there are misguided elements. The Christian upholds those aspects of culture which accord with God's truth (the sanctity of marriage, for example), while renouncing those aspects which are in rebellion against the truth (as with alternative lifestyles). How does one evaluate culture using God's Word, so as to transform that culture and bring it into submission to God?

The Sporting Ladies
James Jacques Joseph Tissot, 1885

> "Your New Moon feasts and your appointed festivals I hate with all my being. They have become a burden to me; I am weary of bearing them." (Isaiah 1:14)
>
> "The Lord said to me, 'Go, show your love to your wife again, though she is loved by another and is an adulteress. Love her as the Lord loves the Israelites, though they turn to other gods and love the sacred raisin cakes.'" (Hosea 3:1)

There is a helical relationship between culture and the individual. Culture shapes the individual, and in turn, the individual shapes the culture of which he is a part. Thus, the salvation and sanctification which the counselor seeks to visit upon individuals could also be applied more broadly to culture.[30] In fact, the Christian should both witness to individuals, and engage the larger cultural milieu with the gospel, so that

---

[29] Augustine of Hippo (354–430)
[30] This concept is inspired by David Covington, Biblical Counselor

that message impacts and permeates both.

Conclusion

There is something about the Christian life which looks highly-unattractive to a defiant and depraved world. God, in shaping living temples for himself, fashions people who look as though, from the world's perspective, they suffer from elephantitis - grotesque, misshapen, and horrific to behold. There is something in the Christian that looks disfigured, undeveloped, and repulsive when viewed through the world's prism. Yet, there is something eminently glorious and attractive about the faithful Christian to those who honestly seek God. (The Christian even emanates the aroma of Christ to those who are being saved, and the smell of death to those who are perishing.[31]) Regardless of the world's impression, God is no mere impresario. The Christian is being rebuilt in the forge of God's own being so that, in God's sight, the Christian is glorious and radiant, a reflection of Christ himself. Thus, there is something about the Christian life which is excruciating, exquisite, extreme.

> "When you were born, you cried and the world rejoiced. Live your life in such a manner that when you die, the world cries and you rejoice."

I'd like to offer a parting thought on this topic. When, after a span of years, one becomes reacquainted with an unbelieving friend, one resigns himself that sin patterns have become more deeply entrenched, that the spirit has darkened. There is an ill-defined expectancy that, for the non-Christian, life tends center around what he has done and acquired, who he knows, or what he feels, with little, or no sense, of *becoming*.

Conversely, when one is reacquainted with a Christian friend, there is a thrill to see how God has worked in that life during the intervening years. There is an ill-defined excitement in glimpsing the metamorphosis of a heart that progressively takes on more of the form and texture of its Savior, a comfort in listening to speech which drips with the honey of God's Word, a passion for seeing God's shepherding hand in another's life. So, for the Christian, the exhilaration of meeting a long lost brother or sister in Christ is less about cataloguing of what he has *done*, and more in a discovery what he has *become*, a sharpened and more luminescent portrait of Jesus himself.

---

[31] 2 Corinthians 2:15, 16

- 10 -

Counseling and the Church:
Syndicating the Vision

Fronleichnoms Procession in Hofgastein, Adolph von Menzel, 1880

Introduction

At the end of the 19th century over one thousand Italian immigrants founded the town of Roseto in the foothills of western Pennsylvania.[1] Nearly all of them emigrated from a single town in central Italy by the same name. Upon founding Roseto, the immigrants cleared farmland, set up factories, built churches, and cut stone from the surrounding mountain quarries.

In the late 1950s a doctor named Stewart Wolf, while visiting western Pennsylvania, met to a fellow physician from Roseto. This physician told Wolf that he had rarely seen heart disease in his patients (at that time the leading cause of death for men sixty-five and under).

---

[1] Malcolm Gladwell, *Outliers: The Story of Success* (New York: Little, Brown and Company, 2008) 3-11.

Intrigued, Wolf set out to investigate the cause. In 1961 he undertook an extensive study which revealed that the inhabitants of Roseto were markedly healthier than the general population. Although not wealthy, Roseto experienced a decidedly high quality of life in which suicide, alcoholism, crime, and poverty were nearly non-existent. Premature death was almost unheard of as everyone lived well into old age and died from natural causes.

Wolf first studied their diet and found that they ate an abundance of fattening and sweet foods all year-round. This caused many to be obese. They also smoked heavily and got little exercise outside of their daily chores. Next he studied their genetics and found that their Italian relatives were not nearly as hearty. Was there something special about this region of Pennsylvania? No, surrounding towns experienced heart disease at three times the rate of Roseto.

Wolf eventually discovered the secret of Roseto's health: its community life. They visited each other often, cooked and ate with family and friends. Grandparents enjoyed high social status and were afforded weighty responsibility in the care of their grandchildren. People regularly participated in social events, attended church, and put little emphasis on material wealth. The town's people were socio-economically identical, and when a family experienced financial hardship the community mobilized to get it back on its feet.

The people of Roseto were largely shielded from the pressures and vicissitudes of modern life. There was an almost enchanting quality to the town as families ate, laughed, and talked with ease. People routinely sat outside their homes chatting with neighbors well past dusk. Even work was pleasurable as each experienced a sense of camaraderie. Doctor Wolf concluded that Roseto's citizens experienced such remarkable health because the community as a *whole* was healthy.

How can the lessons learned through Roseto be applied to the church? How can the church experience this kind of community health, this oneness of spirit? What does it take for a church to gain a certain measure of vitality so that its members are built up, encouraged, and growing in sanctification? How can the church regain the Acts 4:32 vision, "All the believers were one in heart and mind. No one claimed that any of their possessions was their own, but they shared everything they had."?

The Disintegration of Community

I was shocked the first time I heard someone say that he only occasionally attended our church, but that he usually attends his home church in a nearby town. My thought was, "Why are you not at your home church?" One of the reasons Christian's church-hop is to maximize their degree of social connection while minimizing their exposure to meaningful biblical counsel. This is a crafty way to keep others at a distance and to create a sense of superiority (the idea that one's Christian experience is broader and deeper than those in one's immediate company). This arrangement offers an escape hatch so that as some get too close, or fail to meet one's perceived needs, one has a ready refuge. I find that this church-hopping phenomenon is largely driven by pride. The objective is to prioritize one's own desires for a church experience, to gain some sought-after outcome such as finding a spouse or cultivating a career network (although certainly these are not wrong in, and of, themselves).

A Moor Presenting a Parrot to a Lady, Nicholaes Berchem, c. 1660

The church-hopping phenomenon is a symptom of a far deeper problem. In modern times there has been a marked shift in the nature and make up of communities, a shift which has profoundly affected the church. This shift is along the following lines:[2]

1. **Integral community**. This community is highly-cohesive, with individual members identifying with the community's concerns and successes. It has a near unanimous participation rate among its constituent members. This type of community characterized distinct precincts of American cities until the 1960s.

---

[2] Rachel B. Warren and Donald I. Warren, *The Neighborhood Organizer's Handbook* (Notre Dame, Indiana: University of Notre Dame Press, 1977).

(The Roseto, Pennsylvania community was the quintessential integrated community.)

2. **Parochial community.** This is a community which demarks itself along strong ethnic lines. It is self-contained and views itself as independent from the broader society. It has a highly-homogeneous makeup and set of values.

3. **Diffuse community.** This tends to be an extrinsically homogeneous community, but with little internal sense of connection. Constituent members share only a loose common identity.

4. **Launch community.** This community constitutes itself, not for the sake of community, but as a "way-station" for the tacit purpose of allowing members to move into a higher social echelon. Thus, community members see themselves as unified only in their mutual desire to leave the community, and are merely biding time until they can "launch" to another more prestigious community.

5. **Transitory community.** This is a community with a high degree of flux. There is little continuity or collective identity. This community is extrinsically highly-heterogeneous and, therefore, members see themselves as having little connection.

6. **Anomic community.** This is the post-modern "non-community." These are people who merely live in proximity to one another, but share no common identity and no cohesion. There is no shared vision for the community, and therefore each acts almost exclusively for self-serving purpose.

Whether rural, urban, or suburban, there has been a steady progression toward anomic communities. As communities lose their cohesion and, likewise, as families are fractured, there is a loss of natural counseling mechanisms in society. Thus, people become more isolated, fearful, introspective, self-absorbed, and prone to violence. As society gradually disintegrates the occurrence of deviant behavior proliferates, and built-in checks-and-balances, as well as natural forms of catharsis centered on informal social interaction, slowly evaporate. How does the church avoid this disintegration so as to maintain a healthy integrated community, even when the surrounding culture fails to? How can the church become an earthly home for believers, a taste of eternal unity with Christ?

> It is fascinating to note that as modern society increasingly moves in the direction of anomic communities, there is often a counterbalancing rise of makeshift parochial communities (such as street gangs). Parochial communities tend to serve as safe-havens in a fractured world. Thus, as society disintegrates there are

> countervailing forces (tribalism) which tend to reconstitute it (albeit in often derelict forms).

A Friendly Visit, William Merrit Chase, 1895

A Christian woman engaged in slander and gossip after our church meeting. I confronted her with her transgression, and asked for a meeting of reconciliation with the one whom she had slandered. She refused, instead blaming the church for the unpleasant situation. This woman then stated that she would no longer attend our church but, from then on, would attend another church which is her frequent Sunday fellowship. She stated that she was more comfortable with the other fellowship anyway.

The question must then be raised, "If she is a worldly Christian, with a lose tongue, what is it about the other church which makes her feel comfortable?" Likely, the comfort comes from its permissive attitude toward sin, one which allows her to maintain her worldliness unchallenged. While the church is charged with disciplining its members, the modern church-hopping phenomenon short-circuits this discipline process, rendering it impotent. False believers simply move along to the next welcoming church up the street. This is yet another curse of anomic church life.

Defining the Church

The New Testament church traces back to the Old Testament concept of the *qahal* (קהל), meaning "to meet or come together at an appointed place." The New Testament uses two terms to name the church. The first is *ekklesia* (ἐκκλησία) (*ek* = out; *kaleo* = call), the "called out ones." (Jesus was the first to use this term.) The second term is *kuriake* (κυριακῇ) meaning "belonging to the Lord."

> "But you are a chosen people, a royal priesthood, a holy nation, God's special possession, that you may declare the praises of him who called you out of darkness into his wonderful light. Once you were not a people, but now you are the people of God; once you had not received mercy, but now you have received mercy." (1 Peter 2:9, 10)

What is the nature of this "calling out"? It could refer to the people simply being called out of their homes to gather for worship, or it could have the deeper meaning of being called out of the world to holiness. Jesus used *ekklesia* to refer to those gathered around him who publicly recognized him as Lord, and sought to establish his kingdom.[3]

> The New Testament uses four principle metaphors to describe the church:[4]
>
> 1. The body of Christ[5]
> 2. The temple of the Holy Spirit[6]
> 3. The New Jerusalem[7]
> 4. The pillar and ground of truth[8]

The church operates on three horizons:

1. **Worship of God** (vertical). Everything about the church is ultimately to worship God

2. **The church's sanctification** (internal). The church is established to effect holiness within itself.

3. **The salvation of the world** (outward). The church is to hold forth Jesus to the world.

The vertical (worship of God) drives the internal (sanctification) which compels the outward (the gospel to the world). Thus, the proper worship of God drives both sanctification and an efficacious message of salvation. While the worship of God is primary and the other two aspects are derivative, all three horizons: God, church, and world, are simultaneously in focus within the church's life and practice.

---

[3] Louis Berkhof, *Systematic Theology* (Grand Rapids, Michigan: William B. Eerdmans Publishing Co., 1949) 555, 556.
[4] Louis Berkhof, *Systematic Theology* (Grand Rapids, Michigan: William B. Eerdmans Publishing Co., 1949) 557, 558.
[5] Colossians 1:18; Ephesians 5:23
[6] 1 Corinthians 6:19, 20
[7] Galatians 4:26
[8] 1 Timothy 3:15

The Nature of the Church

There is a tension in Scripture between the individual and corporate aspects of calling and salvation. The Christian is individually called and saved, and yet this is not for solely individual purposes. God's purpose is always to draw the individual into a corporate identity and function so that the fullness of God's work in the Christian can be observed, and experienced, in the context of community relationship. This is the backbone of the biblical counseling paradigm. The church is called to be a self-counseling entity as part of its fulfillment of God's boarder vision to sanctify itself, to set itself apart.

Wandering Thoughts
Francis David Millet, d. 1912

> Someone once said that the church exists so that Christians can express, and experience, forgiveness (a spirit of repentance) and thankfulness (a posture of gratitude in all things). In some ways this encapsulates the Christian life, one of continual repentance and gratefulness not just *for* Jesus, but *to* Jesus.

The church, composed of living temples of the Holy Spirit, is both a redeemed institution and a living organism. It is an institution in that it stands in the Word as against the system of world and as an arm of salvation extended to the world. It is an organism in that it is a communion of believers, each exercising gifts and talents. Each Christian is called to exercise his gifts for building the church. Without this, the church, corporately, and its members individually, are impoverished. The church should never allow its counsel to be *solely* an individually-initiated endeavor. All counsel is rightly a church-initiated endeavor.

Certainly counsel can, and does, occur in private, but it should always occur with a vision toward renewed involvement in, and positive impact on, the larger church body.

A counseling paradigm should not allow the counselee to merely consider how sin and sanctification affect him personally, but how the church as a whole is influenced.[9] (This is a crucial lesson which I seek to instill in our congregation.) Sin, however it is expressed - whether in a corporate or private context - necessarily affects the church as a whole. The effect may not be demonstrable or traceable, but it is, nevertheless, presiding and shaping.

> "If one part suffers, every part suffers with it; if one part is honored, every part rejoices with it." (1 Corinthians 12:26)

The State of the Modern Church

In the 17th through 19th centuries in Puritan America the church occupied the central hub around which towns blossomed. The church was steadfast, stalwart, and guiding. Most town activity was in some way under the auspices of, or influenced by, the local congregation. The pastor was the most highly-educated in the town, a guiding influence for each life-event, and a mentor to each profession. The pastor, in line with God's Word, offered a navigable vision and ethical integrity to those under his care. He shaped education, politics, entertainment, family life, and professional practice.[10]

Today, the church has largely been relegated to a tertiary role in American society. It is now considered at best a quaint addendum to society's agenda, and at worst an unwelcomed subversive to progress. The church is frequently tolerated as foolishly irrelevant or arcane, and at times attacked as a vestige of subjugating forces and Byzantine ideologies. The pastor today has been reduced to a community organizer and occasional sympathizer, with little meaningful relevance.

In actuality, those who hold forth God's Word should be the vanguards, the watchmen, the defenders, and transformers of culture. They should minister with profundity and persuasion, not swayed by public opinion, but solidly grounded upon a Christ-centered understanding of people. Today, such a vision seems like a vague and distant dream.

I've visited or studied myriad churches over the past two decades. Long ago I stopped reading statements of faith because they are generally boilerplate documents. How do I determine what a church really teaches and promotes? I observe the children. How disciplined are the children? Is there a permissive atmosphere or one of self-denial and servanthood? Are the children served a diet of secular intoxicants or are they

---

[9] Harvie Conn (1933–1999), "Doctrine of the Church" class, Westminster Theological Seminary, Philadelphia, Pennsylvania

[10] David Wells, *No Place for Truth: Whatever Happened to Evangelical Theology* (Grand Rapids, Michigan: William B. Eerdmans Publishing Co., 1994)

called to feast on the fear of God?[11] The way that a church teaches and disciplines its children provides a litmus test to its functional theology. It speaks volumes to a church's *actual* faith and practice.

For example, I recently visited a Christian school in which children are directed to shout the phrase, "I am the greatest; I am the best!", like a mantra drilled into their impressionable minds. When I asked some teachers about the practice, I was told that this helps promote a healthy sense of self-esteem and noble character. I directed them to Daniel 4:30 in which King Nebuchadnezzar stated, "'Is not this the great Babylon I have built as the royal residence, by my mighty power and for the glory of my majesty?' As a result of his vainglory, Nebuchadnezzar was cursed with isolation, the characteristics of an animal, and insanity.[12] I pointed out that Nebuchadnezzar's megalomania likely started as a phrase similar to that which the children are encouraged to repeat, that, like Nebuchadnezzar, the children are being led down a cursed path. Such a connection fell on deaf ears.

> Matthew 28:19, 20 records: "Therefore go and make *disciples* of all nations, baptizing them in the name of the Father and Son and of the Holy Spirit, and teaching them to obey everything I have commanded you." Jesus' command is not merely to win new believers; his command is to make disciples. This means that he desires more than saved people. He desires complete followers, those totally undivided and fully obedient to him.

One of the greatest tragedies in the church today is that Christians do not see the need for daily change. This is, in fact, God's highest priority in the life of a Christian – change which effects greater holiness. Every situation is carefully orchestrated by God to bring about lasting holiness. If the Christian does not understand this he will never understand what is happening to him. However, Christians often wrongly assume that once they are saved their highest goal is happiness, because their sin has been paid for. While it certainly is true that their sin has been paid for, each believer is still poisoned with indwelling sin, which God longs to purge. Therefore, God's goal is not one's personal happiness, but one's personal and corporate holiness through the ongoing eradication of sin.

The church focuses some attention on justification (eternal salvation), but far less on sanctification (progressive change). The reason may be that the church does not understand sanctification, nor believe it to be necessary. Possibly it does not see the need for change because it does not recognize the depth and damage of indwelling sin. I also believe that the church is afraid of the world, afraid of being branded "hellfire and brimstone." So the church functionally eliminates the concepts of sin and

---

[11] Proverbs 9:10; 1 Timothy 3:4
[12] Daniel 4:32-34

sanctification so as to make the gospel more palatable, like a once-for-all fix that can be tweaked with pragmatic adjustments. The church is so desperate to give the gospel broad appeal that is severely weakens it in the process, and even worse, often twists it into a false gospel.

The Longshoremen's Noon, John George Brown, 1879

Tragically, this undermines its message of salvation to a fallen world, as the non-Christian judges the validity of the Christian message based on its members' lives. If those lives are being transformed and experiencing vibrant growth in holiness, the seeking unbeliever (God-fearer) will be drawn to the gospel. Thus, a message of justification, without a concomitant display of sanctification, leaves the former flaccid and unattractive.

> For each Christian, walking in faith involves a certain commonality, as well as a certain uniqueness. All Christians are called to obey God's commands in Scripture such as maintaining sexual purity,[13] resisting evil,[14] and using speech which edifies others and glorifies God.[15] However, there is a second component to faith. This involves following God's specific will for one's individual life. If God has called one to service then to deny that service is sin, regardless of whether one's life appears faithful.[16] For one suffering from Alzheimer's, faith may involve daily trusting God to help him find his glasses. For a recent college graduate, faith may involve denying

---

[13] Ephesians 5:3
[14] James 4:7
[15] Ephesians 4:29
[16] Jeremiah 16:2; Hosea 1:2; Matthew 7:21

> his lifelong dream to serve God in direct ministry. Faith, thus, involves a variable component based upon one's personal calling and life situation.

The "Disney-fication" of the Church[17]

Upon taking uncompromised command of Warsaw, Poland on July 22, 1952, the former Soviet Union implemented plans to subvert religious expression throughout the city. At the heart of Warsaw is located The Church of Jesus Christ, a historical treasure of the local community. Soviet officials, knowing that they could not shutter the church without riotous backlash, implemented a plan to erect massive government buildings around the church. The idea was to, in effect, "cover over" the church casting it into perpetual shadow. (In an intriguing turn of events, the Soviets ran short of funds for their building project so that the church, to this day, towers over surrounding structures.)

Throughout its history, the church has been routinely attacked by imperialist forces seeking to crush its faith. Quite remarkably, in the face of nearly all extrinsic threats the church not only prevails, but strengthens. Today, however, the church faces a far more insidious enemy, an internal blight which rots it from the inside out. Nothing fortifies the church like the world's assault; nothing subverts the church like worldly Christians.[18]

George Lucas, the producer of "Star Wars," said, "Movies are the church of modern America." Sadly, he is right. The average American adult spends vastly more time watching movies (forty-five movies per year), than he does in church or reading the Bible. Modern people gather in great halls as a kind of worldly community entranced by the images raised up before them. The movie theater has become a kind of surrogate church were the congregation receives a sermon of images and participates in worship of the material world. In this and in other ways, the media shapes American culture with greater fervour and persuasiveness than does the church, so that twenty-nine percent of adults say that movies profoundly influence their views of life. Each year, as the church wars against the world, it loses ground to secular forces inhabiting and controlling hearts and minds.

The "Disney-fication" of the church is the church following the pattern of worldly entertainment as it stokes, and subsequently seeks to meet, perceived needs. In this way, the church has become Balkanized into individual fiefdoms with their attendant concerns and agendas. Additionally, the church's message has been "caramelized" as simply another source of man-glorifying counsel. The church has committed itself to merely making people feel comfortable in their sin, without a strong call to

---

[17] This concept from David Lyon, *Jesus in Disneyland: Religion in Postmodern Times* (Polity Publishing, 2000)
[18] 1 John 4:6

renunciation, self-sacrifice, and suffering for the faith.[19] As the church's message leaves heart commitments untouched, that message forms a self-absorbed patina around the heart making it impenetrable to the gospel.

Court Ladies Bathing in the 18th Century, François Flameng, 1888

Christians do not need sophisticated church programs. They need to faithfully and quietly sit at the Jesus' feet and listen to him. This Christ-centered quietude is the impetus for the church's counseling. Without this sense of meeting with, and being confronted by, the living Christ, counseling becomes nothing more than another program on the carnival carousel. A church which engages in wise counsel will resist a "program-ized" busied church, recognizing that programs are nothing but smokescreens for hearts shielded from God.

> "Never mistake motion for action." (Ernest Hemingway)

In this same vein, the church should never form artificial splits in the body of believers, division that Scripture itself does not sanction. For example, there should not be a children's group, single's group, a young married couple's group, and a senior citizen's group (although at times it may be appropriate to serve a particular subculture within the church). All believers should learn and grow together. Older and

---
[19] Matthew 16:24; Galatians 2:20

younger, single and married, educated and uneducated should all participate in the body together. When there are false splits in the body, the church becomes more worldly and self-centered. All should grow and serve together, learning to forget about themselves in the service of a far higher calling. Wisdom is not age-based or situation-based (single vs. married), so Christians along a wide swath should be counseling, and receiving counsel from, one another in defiance of all circumstantial barriers.

> Former New York senator Daniel Patrick Moynihan (1927–2003) coined the term "the soft-bigotry of low expectations." This encapsulates a danger in counseling (and indeed in the church as a whole), the threat of low expectations for heart change which, not unsurprisingly, result in little or no change. A glaring example of this is that a pastor once described believers who labor in the church as volunteers already burdened with other life commitments. By this he meant that they should not be expected to serve with excellence.

Biblically-sound Christ-centered Christianity is rapidly weakening and slowly dying in the West (although rising in Asia). This state of affairs is not the result of outside persecution (which is clear and present), but the result of Christians having sold their birthright for worldly counsel. Christians have by-and-large followed the world, having allowed the surrounding culture to dictate valid terms of heart engagement, without fundamentally questioning nor seeking to adequately challenge, alter, or reject cultural forms (eg: advertising, childrearing practices, corporate culture, fast food, sports, medical practice, psychology, entertainment, etc.).

Additionally, the church is largely distracted by Disney-like theology which focuses on titillating splashy externalized events. For example, the modern church's focus on eschatology (millennialism), false deliverance from the demonic, miraculous healing, and vacuous ritual serve as debilitating distractions keeping the church blind to its desperate need for sanctification. The more the church remains fixated on "bright shiny objects," the more it loses its ability to experience growth in holiness. Attention to signs and wonders, prophecy and demons, rapture and glossolalia, gilding and pageantry, merely renders the church a willing handmaiden to Hollywood, more akin to the occult than guardian of the gospel. This focus on the miraculous, the super-spiritual, and the ritualistic finally renders the church vulnerable to psychology as it is ill-equipped to offer a biblically-based model of the psyche.[20]

Like Neville Chamberlain (1869-1940) mistakenly declaring "peace in our time," Christianity has tragically permitted psychology a privileged place in its praxis, under the guise of cultural relevance and inclusiveness. Paradoxically, as the church largely

---

[20] For additional discussion of this topic see "The Church's Psychology Affliction" in the first book in this series, *Ask for the Ancient Paths: From Art to Artifice to Arisen*, chapter 9: "Integrationism: The Modern Day Babylonian Captivity"

shapes its functional theology around a secular understanding of people, its cultural relevance evaporates. Even the world seems to know that the church forfeits its counseling treasure in exchange for shards of pottery.[21]

> Ephesians 4:30 warns the Christian not to "grieve the Holy Spirit of God."

By-and-large the modern church, like many of its New Testament counterparts, is lost, adrift in moral relativism, awash with secular thought, shaped by the surrounding culture (but no longer shaping that culture), and held captive to idols (not so much physical idols but heart-generated ones). The modern church has, to some degree, become a tangled web of lies and deception, doctrinal error, and moral confusion. Yet, God loves those who belong to him (the invisible church) and longs to sanctify them by his Spirit. God longs to rebuild his people into his image, and to this end he uses the church to effect heart change.

At the time of this writing, *The New York Times* reported a chilling and disturbing new fad in evangelical churches, the growth of Mixed Martial Arts ministries. These ministries train young men in MMA-style combat offering them the opportunity to fight in church-sponsored events and, according to *The Times*, the fad is catching on like wildfire. These groups selectively troll the Bible for self-justifying verses and engage in a revisionist reading of Scripture to legitimize their absurdity. One of the objectives is to regain true manhood (which seems to be flagging in Christian circles). The plan is to reconstitute emasculated men by teaching them to physically fight one another. This definition of manhood has been so irretrievably poisoned by the world that it essentially bears no resemblance to the Bible's teaching.

True manhood is not about aggression and violence, but about being dominated by a holy God who longs for submission within those he claims as his own. Thus, a true man is one who submits to Christ in humble reverence, choosing to forsake his physical prowess or potential in order to serve a far greater internal reality.[22]

> First Timothy 6:10 mentions those who "have wandered from the faith and pierced themselves with many griefs."

The church experience should be marked by times of quiet thought, prayerful consideration, sitting at Jesus' feet and listening to him. Churches today are so overrun with programs, activities, and seminars that people do not experience the blessing of simply relating deeply with their God, and with one another. I, personally,

---

[21] Eminent psychologist Orval Mowrer (1907–1982) raised this point with Jay Adams (as found in the introduction to Adam's work *Competent to Counsel: Introduction to Nouthetic Counseling* (Zondervan Publishing, 1986))

[22] For further discussion see "Whom one considers to be a true man or woman" in chapter 9 "Emerging from the Chrysalis: Issues the Counselor Observes and Seeks to Change"

would much rather experience a silent time of prayer, carefully taking the pulse of the heart's tides and movements, over a raucous activity that exhilarates for the moment, but delivers an aftershock of waywardness.[23]

"The wise man knows that it is better to sit on the banks of a remote mountain stream than to be emperor of the whole world." (Zhuang Zi)

The Prevalence of False Believers

The Property Room
Arthur Hughes, 1879

"The worst wheel on the cart makes the most noise."

False believers have always infiltrated God's people. Exodus 12:38 speaks of the rabble who wormed their way in among the Israelites, leading Israel into rebellion. Numbers 11:1 states, "Now the people complained about their hardships in the hearing of the LORD, and when he heard them his anger was aroused. Then fire from the LORD burned among them and consumed some of the outskirts of the camp." The "fire consuming some of the outskirts of the camp" was for the purpose of immolating foreign intruders among Israel's ranks.

There is a pronounced dichotomy in the church. The visible church consists of those

---
[23] Psalm 84:10

who gather for community worship. By contrast, the invisible church is constituted by those who are in union with Jesus Christ. Likely, only a small percentage of the visible church is the invisible church. This raises the issue of insincere seekers and false believers who might be counted among the visible church, but not among the invisible church. It is important to note that counseling takes place both within the visible and invisible church; that counseling frequently adopts diametrically opposed approaches (either emphasizing justification or sanctification), but with the same objective, repentance and faith in Jesus.

One of the most difficult situations I face as a pastor is false Christians who infiltrate the body of Christ. While seeking unbelievers are always welcome, false believers offer a particular threat in that they clearly do not show the fruit of repentance and faith, while sometimes professing to do so.[24] False and true believers engage in this masquerade in which the false are called "Christian" while some of the true know that they are not. Additionally, many true believers are led astray so that they blindly accept error from false believers. How can one know who the false believers are?

> Anne Morrow Lindbergh (1906–2001) wrote, "The most exhausting thing in life is being insincere. That is why so much social life is exhausting." There is something in this which offers a clue to discerning false believers. False believers find church involvement, prayer life, Scripture study, and their good works to be exhausting. They find discussion of the gospel to be tedious. The wise counselor notices something awry in those who profess Christ but often show fatigue with the mere mention of his name.

In every church meeting over which I preside, the gospel is clearly preached, not as a stand-alone message, but as the foundation for all discussion. So the gospel is made vivid, life-changing, powerful, and lovingly confrontational. I watch my audience carefully during the direct presentation of the gospel. Some wear a look of peace and joy; others display cold indifference. Some exhibit a muted flash of anger, while still others are anxious and desperate to get up from their chairs. These reactions speak volumes about how audience members view Jesus and the gospel of salvation. Over the course of weeks or months, when the same pattern displays itself time and again, the evidence is incontrovertible.

> Second Corinthians 2:15, 16 states, "For we are to God the pleasing aroma of Christ among those who are being saved and those who are perishing. To the one we are an aroma that brings death; to the other, an aroma that brings life…" The Christian is the aroma of death to those who are perishing. Does this aroma emanate from the believer's existential being, or only as the believer speaks and lives out the Word of God? The answer may be both. The believer's very presence is a stench to the

---

[24] 2 Corinthians 11:26

> hard-hearted unbeliever, and as the believer actively displays and communicates Christ that aroma intensifies.

Many of those who regularly attend gospel-centered churches have built up a formidable resistance to the gospel, shielding themselves from the message while wearing the mere appearance of godliness.[25] Many false believers even know Scripture well, so as to easily deceive others. This is one of the most difficult situations to deal with and, honestly, one of the most frightening. False believers leave a wake of destruction in their path that threatens to capsize even a relatively healthy church.[26]

> Voltaire (1694-1778) said, "A long dispute means that both parties are wrong." In this same vein, society reflexively assumes that, to some degree, both parties in any conflict are to blame. This is a dangerous assumption. Just because conflict exists between two parties does not mean both parties are at fault. Sometimes one party is attacked and must take evasive action.[27] A relentless pursuit can ensue in which the attacker looks for any way to draw his quarry into the fray. Often as one simply points out a particular sin issue he is assailed and maligned. The false believer expends great energy to remove any challenge to the heart, and *ad hominem* aspersions are a convenient means to repel the threat.

I use a quick test to see if one is a Christian.[28] I ask that person to simply state the gospel. I am not looking for an articulate answer. I am not even looking for a logically arranged answer. I am simply asking for the rudiments of the Christian faith: faith in Jesus Christ's death on the cross as payment for one's sin. If that kernel of truth is not present, then I have no choice but to strongly doubt salvation. A vague discussion of knowing God's love, or belief in God, is often a decoy carefully placed to divert naïve Christians from the false believer's path.[29]

The issue is that the wise counselor must be vigilant to uncover false believers. I believe that a litmus test of saving faith must be employed early on in the counseling process to know what the counselor faces. If, in fact, the counselee is not a Christian (while pretending to be one) then the entire counseling endeavor shifts to an evangelistic outreach.

This is a controversial topic because clearly one is not to judge the heart, but Jesus gave his followers an evaluative criterion, "You will know them by their fruit."[30] The

---

[25] 2 Timothy 3:5
[26] Acts 20:29-31
[27] Matthew 13:38, 39 is clear that some are "sons of the evil one," weeds sown by the devil.
[28] Paul spoke about each examining and testing himself to see if he is, in fact, in Christ (2 Corinthians 13:5)
[29] For a comprehensive discussion of the gospel see the first book in this series, *Ask for the Ancient Paths: From Art to Artifice to Arisen*, chapter 4: "The Gospel as Inception Point"
[30] Matthew 7:16

evidence of saving faith is obvious when one knows what to look for. A Christian has been brought from death to life,[31] delivered from darkness to light.[32] It is impossible for this to happen and not to know that it has happened. It is also impossible to mistake that this has happened when it has not. There is no possibility of "maybe" in being a Christian, just as there is no possibility of believing that a stone-cold corpse is alive. One may not know the exact date that he became a Christian, but he knows that he was brought from death to life, from darkness to light. There is absolutely no way to mistake that.

The Lady of Shalott, John William Waterhouse, 1888

In my experience, not just some, but the majority of the visible church is comprised of false believers, many of whom have been deliberately sent by Satan to sow discord, to divide, and to undermine the church's vitality.[33] Usually this occurs through idle chatter and gossip sown surreptitiously into the ears of those who are willing to listen.[34] Quidnuncs quickly spark rebellion, seeking to topple the church through any perceived or real vulnerability. The greatest defense is that the counseling church would ferret out falsehood and bring it to light, calling "sons of the evil one" to repentance. This is not solely the pastor's responsibility, but that of the entire church. (Yet, sadly, I have found that there are precious few willing to take up this charge.)

---

[31] Ephesians 2:1: Colossians 2:13
[32] Isaiah 9:2; John 3:21; Colossians 1:13
[33] Matthew 13:25; 1 Peter 5:8
[34] 2 Timothy 4:3

> In keeping with the Lord's directives, our congregation holds to a high standard of personal responsibility. There is a strong focus on identifying individual and corporate sin, so as to bringing it to repentance. This has two effects. The first is a commitment that sin will not be permitted to divide or poison the church's life and witness. The second is that it regrettably tends to produce guarded people who are reticent to speak or act. However, only the one who loves his sin has reason to be guarded.

As incredible as it sounds, it is entirely possible that most modern churches have no believers present at all. I find it hard to believe that a true believer could continue to worship in a church which ordains practicing homosexuals or admits them as members in good standing.[35] Likewise, how could a true believer would continue to worship in a church in which the gospel has clearly been replaced by a social justice agenda or where there is teaching that salvation is obtained through one's own good works?[36]

> I called most of the 133 registered churches in my county. Generally, I spoke with a secretary, but on occasion I made it through to a pastor. After introducing myself and my ministry, I asked very simply, "Would the church support a gospel-centered radio outreach to the county?" Only a handful stated that they would in theory support such an effort.

Each true believer must be vigilant for the purity of the church Jesus died to make his bride.[37] It is not the pastor's sole responsibility to defend and maintain the integrity of the church's teaching and life. This is the charge of every Christian who loves Jesus and loves his church. Like a pastor, every Christian, as counselor, is called to participate in a vision, to lead the faithful into battle against intrinsic and extrinsic evil.[38]

The Danger of Church Hierarchy[39]

In Numbers 16:2, 3 Korah lead a group of 250 Israelite men, well-known community leaders who had been appointed members of the council. They came as a group to oppose Moses and Aaron. This episode portends of Jesus' struggles with the Pharisees, religious leaders he labeled "blind guides."[40] Sadly, this story highlights a glaring

---

[35] 1 Corinthians 6:9
[36] Ephesians 2:8, 9
[37] Ephesians 5:32
[38] Proverbs 29:18
[39] For additional discussion of the issue of church hierarchy see "The Dangers When Relationship with Christ is Marginalized," and the excursus "Pastor as Servant" in chapter 4: "The Umbilicus of Personal Relationship with Christ"
[40] Matthew 23:24

problem with any leadership structure. Often those entrusted with the guidance and direction of others focus on little more than selfish ambition.[41]

Later in Numbers 16:9, 10, Moses reminded the Levites that the Lord had set them apart for work on the tabernacle, as well as to stand before the community and minister to them. Moses confronted the Levites with trying to usurp the priesthood. This is reminiscent of the first cosmic rebellion mentioned in Ezekiel 28:14-17 in which Satan, the chief cherubim assigned with guarding God's throne, sought to usurp God's position as Lord of the universe. Satan, like the Levites, was, before his fall, set apart for a God-honoring task, yet sought to claim for himself the station of God himself. In this same spirit, the Levites attempted to seize control of the priesthood.

Like the Korahite rebels, modern church life, has in many ways, degenerated into a "groupthink" experience. Interactive and vibrant relationship with God seems to have been replaced by a quest to wield power, a desire for the praises of men, and the drive to advance one's personal agenda. Likewise, church community is often a euphemism, and clever disguise, for seeking to assuage emotional neediness. Often the community experience can easily devolve into self-help with a gloss of Scripture or the mere appearance of Christ-centeredness ("caramelized Christianity"). Churches lose their vibrancy and mission when they become a feelings-based experience, a self-serving escape, or a de facto sin-institutionalizing support group.

When institutions grow, the temptation rises to centralize authority and power. As centralization occurs, bureaucracy grows. This often strips institutions of their strength as members passively wait for those in authority to act. Consider Revelation 2:14-16,

> 'Nevertheless, I have a few things against you: You have people there who hold to the teaching of Balaam, who taught Balak to entice the Israelites to sin by eating food sacrificed to idols and by committing sexual immorality. Likewise you also have those who hold to the teaching of the Nicolaitans. Repent therefore! Otherwise, I will soon come to you and will fight against them with the sword of my mouth.'

What was the "teaching of the Nicolaitans"? The name "Nicolaitan" is the compound of two Greek words: *nikos* (νίκος) meaning "victory" or "conquest," and *laos* (λαός) meaning "people." Thus, Nicolaitan is literally "victory over the people." This group established a hierarchy which dominated the church. In other words, a cabal maintained power, compelling the laity to submit to its authority. First Peter 5:1-3 warns those in church authority not to function as lords over those entrusted to them. Peter exhorts church elders not to seek tight-fisted control for their own personal

---
[41] Philippians 1:17

aggrandizement. When church elders assume a position of superiority this foments envy and finally division. Additionally, forced hierarchy poisons the church's vitality as individual members are kept in a state of subservience, disempowered from exercising their God-given gifts. In this way, the entire church suffers loss.

> "In a hierarchy every employee tends to rise to his level of incompetence." (Lawrence Peter)

Demonstration on October 17, 1905, Ilya Repin, 1907

The Biblical pattern is not toward the centralization of authority but toward the opposite pole, the delegation of responsibility "downward." In short, the biblical model of church polity and ministry is decentralized and representative. Consider Exodus 18:13-27, in which Jethro, Moses' father-in-law, advised Moses to delegate authority as he found himself overwhelmed with governing Israel.[42] Also Acts 6:2-4 states,

> So the Twelve gathered all the disciples together and said, 'It would not be right for us to neglect the ministry of the word of God in order to wait on tables. Brothers, choose seven men from among you who are known to be full of the Spirit and wisdom. We will turn this responsibility over to them and will give our attention to prayer and the ministry of the word.'

This is properly delegated authority. The point is that, unlike the world which grabs for power, the church gives power away so as to let Jesus reign. Counseling is the ultimate display of relinquishing power as the church seeks to bring about greater

---

[42] Douglas Wilson, *Recovering the Lost Tools of Learning: An Approach to Distinctively Christian Education* (Wheaton, Illinois: Crossway Books, 1991) 102.

sanctification through a community effort. This is the church's hidden, yet towering, strength.

How does this issue of delegated authority apply to counseling? Counseling, as with all church ministry, is under the authority and vision of the pastor and elders. However, the actual counseling responsibility is a charge to the entire church. Every Christian is called to counsel (and, in fact, it is impossible not to, to some degree, in every interaction). Although not many should presume to be teachers,[43] every Christian is, to some extent, Holy Spirit-equipped to counsel so as to help others seek greater repentance and faith. As the pastor trains the congregation in God's Word, the congregation is invested with the rudimentary tools for proper counsel. It is then up to the congregation to either exercise those tools or else to allow them to rust through disuse. Thus, the laity's counseling practice is an implicit antidote to the practice of the Nicolaitans since church-wide counseling persistently dissolves and disbands the falsely hierarchical.

An unintended backlash against the unbiblical growth of church hierarchy is the Pentecostal movement which seeks to embolden the laity with the exercise of miraculous powers. Pentecostalism tends to attract the uneducated and those among the lower socio-economic strata.[44] One reason could be its message of empowerment. A glaring danger with Pentecostalism is that it draws attention away from issues of the heart, placing the locus of attention upon the exhibitionistic, upon super-spiritual deliverance, and in engaging evil spirits in battle. The idea is that "average" Christians can feel like "superheroes" through a demonstrable display of power. This runs against the Bible's teaching that the Christian is not to seek external displays but rather internal victories of the heart (which result in the kind of external changes that God desires). (A consequence of Pentecostalism's super-spiritualism is that it tends to blur form and content, thinking that form authenticates, elucidates, or adds to content.[45] In reality, God is not fooled by external displays; he desires change in the "innermost parts."[46])

While Pentecostalism might be commended for its initiative and fervor, fervor from God's perspective is not necessarily a display of emotion but, rather, a passion for sanctification (of which counseling is a servant). While God seeks to empower each Christian to offer and receive wise counsel, this must come within the context of a God-honoring order and structure (under the auspices of God's Word, with a proper interpretive authority, and accompanied by the faithful exercise of church discipline). The proper structure should not be misconstrued as rigidity with regard to one's

---

[43] James 3:1
[44] Harvie Conn (1933–1999), "Doctrine of the Church" class, Westminster Theological Seminary, Philadelphia, Pennsylvania
[45] This concept from David Covington, Biblical Counselor
[46] Psalm 51:6

dealings with God. It is rather a bulwark against the sinful tendencies of the heart to vapid emotionalism and man-centered counsel.

When ecclesiastical order is separated from Christ it becomes a set of oppressive human regulations which stifle church life and tamp down fervor. However, when order is rightly connected to Christ it contributes to an atmosphere in which life-changing counsel is not only expected, but fruitful. Thus, the appropriate church atmosphere is one conducive to analyzing and shepherding the heart, a concern which is to be adopted by every Christian.

The Abdication of the Church's Counseling Birthright

Historically in the United States technological advances and inventions arose out of "craft" industries. This means that individuals or small groups maintained a craft with expertise and tools that they developed. For instance, some of the greatest inventions in history were constructed in a basement or garage using little more than household materials and tools.

Henry Ford (1863-1947) built his first automobile in a backyard garage using hand tools and scavenged parts. The Wright Brothers constructed the first airplane in their store using sundry bicycle parts. Even Alexander Graham Bell (1847-1922), a teacher of the deaf, invented the telephone in a home workshop. These are examples of inventions which grew out of a craft environment. As late as the early 20th century, this was the chief method of innovation and it fueled the growth of industry.

Historically, individuals, even with limited expertise or education, could develop groundbreaking inventions or start highly-successful businesses. This is because until about a century ago the level of skill required, and the sophistication of needed machinery, was often within reach of common men with strong ambition.

Today, there has been a dramatic decline in the likelihood that common people can conceive marketable inventions upon which a successful business can be birthed. The sophistication of modern technology, the esoteric nature of science, the burdens of government regulation, and a hypercompetitive business world, have fostered an environment in which individuals have trouble devising viable technology. New technologies are usually conceived through well-funded corporate or government research and development programs. The dizzying complexity of the modern world has doomed craft industries, replacing them with corporate hegemony and hierarchy. Today, visionaries usually have no choice but to work for behemoth enterprises.

All of this leads to the issue at hand. The church, composed of "common" believers operating under the auspices of Scripture, is fully equipped to handle issues of the psyche. As Paul states in Romans 15:14, "I myself am convinced, my brothers, that you yourselves are full of goodness, complete in knowledge and competent to instruct one another." A lamentable development is that the church has abdicated its rightful role in the cure of souls, handing over authority to an evidence-based licensed mental health juggernaut. While the church should function as a "craft industry" of times past, instead it is taken captive (often complicitly) by a hegemonic ubiquitous corporation-driven medical model. As with the death of the American craft industry (and the rise of the global corporation and dominant government), the church has largely facilitated the diminishment of its growth in Christ. The church has abandoned a craft mentality with regard to counseling its members instead opting for a highly-sophisticated medical model under the auspices of the world's (pseudo-) scientific system.

George III in Coronation Robes
Allan Ramsay, 1762

Compounding the problem, American church life is becoming hollowed out. This means that biblically-sound churches are losing both their sanctification vigor and member participation. Christianity has become more privatized as people approach church with a consumer mentality. They want church to meet their "needs," rather than seeing it as an opportunity to serve others. This consumer mentality has resulted in fading long-term commitment. Likewise, while churches have adopted fads and gimmicks (such as sermons delivered while riding a bull or gun giveaways), the government has stepped-in, through entitlement programs and humanistic education, to fill the worship void within hearts.[47]

A partial reason for the church's decline in the cure of souls has to do with the increased role of government in individual lives. Through a tight system of regulation,

---

[47] For additional development of the role of government see "The World System: Intrusive Government" in the second book in this series, *What Agreement Is There Between the Temple of God and Idols?: The Accidence of Sin and Idolatry*, chapter 2: "The World, the Flesh, and the Devil: Assessing the Threat Matrix"

and an intimidating atmosphere of litigation, government sustains the mental health profession as a stronghold of cultural dominance. The government has in effect propped up a "cure of souls monopoly" through licensure, allowing a secular worldview to ascend and dissenting views to founder.[48]

> An intriguing phenomenon can be observed throughout world history. Political dominance and the Christian faith are inversely related. As Christian fervor declines political influence rises. Conversely, as Christianity gains strength, politics wanes. Thus, the answer for overreaching government is not a political solution but is intimately tied to the vibrancy of the church. Additionally, if the church ever reclaims its authority and cultural cachet, the government-backed medical community's monopoly will be challenged, if not legally, then functionally.

Powerful forces may sometimes fill church pews (but often not that of the Holy Spirit). For example, Christianity is progressively being reduced to an existential or sensory experience. This approach has gained popularity in recent years with the proliferation of social media (and its vexing social isolation), as people search in desperation for some feeling of actually existing. Those churches which most make people feel alive (variations on the concept of "bells and smells") tend to thrive. However, the result is that modern Christianity has largely grafted itself to a cleverly-disguised relativism that wrongly countenances God presence, power, and work in secular terms, methods, and motives. For this reason, Christianity is systematically being stripped of its functional distinctives, namely the outworking of the gospel, and the ability to counsel from God's Word.

> Counseling honors personhood in the way that Christ does, acting as a palladium against the growing church trend of "vanity victories," the tendency to view salvation by numbers and sanctification by the size and scope of church projects.

As a side note, if my memory serves me, Martin Luther King, Jr. wrote, "Discriminate against a man and you will make friends for him." The sometimes vicious cultural attacks on religion drive many to participate in a "spiritual" experience as merely part of a countercultural movement. The objective of church involvement is not so much to positively find life in Christ, but to express distain for a culture in which they feel disenfranchised. Thus, some find in an increasingly persecuted church a handy battleaxe against culture.

One way or another, the modern church allows the majority of its adherents to remain functional atheists, to fashion for themselves some delusive experience of God and to feel exonerated for their sin through a man-derived means of false justification.

---

[48] For additional discussion of the relationship between government and psychology see "Maintaining the Hegemony" in the first book in this series, *Ask for the Ancient Paths: From Art to Artifice to Arisen*, chapter 8: "What Has Jerusalem To Do With Vienna?: The Case Against Psychology"

> The term "Christian" only shows up in the New Testament three times and it is always a noun.[49] The modern church often turns "Christian" into an adjective with disastrous effect.[50]

In 1863, *The Times of London* called Abraham Lincoln's (1809–1865) Gettysburg Address (1863) "dull and commonplace." Often that which is a scintillating treasure is obscured from view, cast aside as common fare and unremarkable. When done for Christ's glory, counseling is an incomparable gift, but it is often overlooked as a trivial trinket of social interaction. As the world becomes more artificial with each passing year, and as social interaction of all kinds is now increasingly arbitrated through mammon and sybaritic concerns, the church's counseling experience offers a refreshing antidote. Spirit-led counseling is meaningful and substantive, bringing with it a certain earthiness and depth of character that is a rare treasure in a technology-weary world.[51]

Impediments to Counsel

Some typical reasons that believers and unbelievers attend church:

1. To find a spouse
2. To find a tolerant support group
3. To search for business connections or job opportunities
4. For childcare and playmates for children

These objectives frequently run at cross-purposes to the counseling imperative, so that when counseling occurs it is often viewed as an interloper to the stated or unstated purpose for one's church attendance. (This can contribute to the proximity problem mentioned below.)

> Once, after visiting our congregation, a young woman told me that she would no longer attend because our church did not meet her "spiritual needs." I found this hard to believe as our church's teaching is solidly biblical, offering a continual feast upon Christ himself in the context of loving community. Soon after, I discovered that she was engaged to a man in another church. I assumed that all along marriage was her motive for church involvement, and that she did not feel our church met that need. (Of course, this is purely conjectural.)

---

[49] Acts 11:26; 26:28; 1 Peter 4:16
[50] The inspiration for this thought from an unknown source.
[51] For further discussion of this issue see the case study "Technology as a Form of Covering" in the second book in this series, *What Agreement Is There Between the Temple of God and Idols?: The Accidence of Sin and Idolatry*, chapter 5: "Metaphors for Sin"

Buying the Wedding Trousseau, Henry Mosler, 1880

There are two chief hindrances to counseling:

1. The proximity problem

    Some possess the wisdom to see the mechanisms and evidences of the heart, but they remain so distant from others (either deliberately or situationally) that they are not afforded the social opportunity to perform the needed intervention.

2. The "visual acuity" problem

    Some are deeply involved in others' lives but do not possess the wisdom to see the heart's machinations. They have opportunity, but lack the understanding needed to offer meaningful counsel.

Rare is the combination of opportunity and wisdom, proximity and insight. A faithful church family endeavors to overcome both the proximity problem and the visual acuity problem. The hope is that the church becomes fertile ground for life-shaping counsel, a body of believers equipped to help others change, and close enough to make change a clear and present priority.

God wants his people to see persons, people who feel pain, are anxious and lost, longing and desperate for hope. He wants his people to uncover slavery to sin in hearts crying out for confrontation and healing. He wants his people to offer the hope of salvation, not with a one-size-fits-all approach, but with a directed vision, exactly as Jesus approached sinners. How did Jesus approach sinners? He first made sure that they knew that he knew them. He focused his message of salvation directly upon their most pressing and glaring worship issues. He confronted the most poignant sin within his listeners, so that the gospel worked with unrelenting force to overthrow the idols of the heart.

> "Wise men learn more from fools than fools from wise men." (Cato the Elder)

The Peter Principle Redefined

In *The Peter Principle: Why Things Always Go Wrong* (1969), Laurence Peter and Raymond Hull advance a management theory concerning what they have termed, "hierarchology," the study of corporate hierarchy. The principle is this: "Anything that works will be used in progressively more challenging applications until it fails."[52]

In specific, the Peter Principle states that managers rise to their level of incompetence. An employee tends to be promoted based on his achievement in his *current* role rather than on the likelihood of success in his *intended* future role. For example, an excellent salesman may not make an excellent sales manager, since the skill set for the former position may not match that of the latter. (Thus, employees are promoted for their achievement when they often should be rewarded in other ways.) The idea is that every management position will in time be occupied by one who is incompetent to carry out its duties. The Peter Principle offers a bleak prognosis for corporate governance and, as such, points to something of the endemic shortsightedness of man-centered assessment.

The concept of promotion through demonstrated success is not foreign to the Bible. In fact, the Bible seems to favor such a concept. For example, the parable of the talents supports the idea of advancement through competence in even seemingly trivial matters.[53] However, the one administering the promotion (the master) draws a keen insight into the nature of each servant - those who are "kingdom-minded" as opposed to those who are not. Additionally, the patriarch Joseph and later the prophet Daniel were each promoted based on a moment's wisdom in serving their respective sovereigns.[54] Their God-invested sense of integrity commended them where others failed.

> "Do your best to present yourself to God as one approved, a worker who does not

---

[52] Lawrence J. Peter, *The Peter Principle: Why Things Always Go Wrong* (HarperBusiness, 1969)
[53] Matthew 25:14-30
[54] Genesis 41:40, 41; Daniel 5:29

> need to be ashamed and who correctly handles the word of truth." (2 Timothy 2:15)

However, while the Peter Principle makes an intriguing observation, the Bible fundamentally overhauls it. The Bible advances the idea that God orchestrates life in such a manner that it will invariably fail without his direct personal intervention. There is a core admonition that those who forsake relationship with God finally find themselves dashed upon the rocks as they venture forward. Additionally, God deliberately chooses and works through those who are of little or no earthly consequence in order to spite those who are the most highly-regarded.[55] He exalts and promotes those among the forgotten and forsaken who place uncompromised faith in Jesus. This is done to showcase God's power and glory.

Therefore, the Bible redefines the concepts of success and promotion so that they accord with a gospel-centered understanding of life. This redefinition includes:

1. Those who know God's Word, administered through his Spirit, possess a wisdom which sets them apart from the world.

2. Those who act upon intimate knowledge of God's declared will finally succeed for God.[56]

3. Those who are in daily submission to God, obedient and faithful, are the one's whom God entrusts with his most poignant work.[57]

4. God rewards faithfulness with increased knowledge of himself, and with an expanded sphere of influence for Christ's sake.[58]

> "Jabez cried out to the God of Israel, 'Oh, that you would bless me and enlarge my territory! Let your hand be with me, and keep me from harm so that I will be free from pain.' And God granted his request." (1 Chronicles 4:10)

What are the implications of this redefined Peter Principle for biblical counseling? God does not assign his counseling responsibilities to those who are most competent in the world's eyes. Rather, such responsibility is assigned to those who are most faithful to his Word, most desirous to know him and to help others know him. Offering wise counsel is a matter of being willing to step forward in faith, to risk public scorn, to put oneself at a measure of risk for an eternal purpose.[59] Thus, those who are most profoundly used to counsel God's people, those who receive the most

---

[55] 1 Corinthians 1:18-31
[56] Proverbs 3:6
[57] Numbers 12:7
[58] Luke 19:17
[59] Revelation 12:11

opportunity to enter into other's lives, have not "risen to their level of incompetence," but rather have wisely recognized their limitations, their inherent foolishness, and their desperate reliance upon God. These, therefore, are no longer defined as incompetent practitioners, but as those who are rightly-oriented and rightly-connected.

The Church Family: Moving from "Church" as Noun to Verb[60]

> The one who is trusted holds tremendous interpersonal power.

The Earthly Paradise
Wenzel Peter, d. 1829

In the theory of evolution there exists the concept "ontogeny recapitulates phylogeny." This means that each organism, from its beginning as a zygote to the moment of birth, retraces its supposed evolutionary path. In other words, as an embryo undergoes gestation it is like a living "movie" replaying evolution. (In fact, embryos do not retrace evolution but merely follow a common pattern of development from the simple to the complex.) While ontogeny does not recapitulate phylogeny in terms of evolution, it could be applied to the church. Each church member, as he grows in sanctification, is like a living "movie" of the mystery of Christ, and in turn replicates his growth in those around him. So, the church experiences a type of ontogeny recapitulates phylogeny as each Christian is a living recollection of Christ's sanctifying work.[61]

God intended that the church would function as an organic unity, as a family.[62] This means that as one member suffers with regard to his relationship with God, the entire body of believers suffers.[63] While one could view this concept through the lens of

---

[60] This concept from Pastor Robert Bell
[61] 2 Corinthians 1:5; 1 Peter 4:13
[62] 1 Corinthians 12:12-27
[63] 1 Corinthians 12:26

one member being neglected or untaught, there is an often forgotten aspect, that of sin. Sin, when unconfronted and unchallenged, operates like a cancer in the church so that it metastasizes in hearts particularly vulnerable to error.[64] The greatest suffering that the church experiences is that of unrepentant sin, and the loss of subsequent growth in holiness. Even if I do not like every person in our church, I love every person. These are people whom God has called me to invest in, to care for, and to counsel (even if some would not necessarily be my choice as friends). I see the church as an inviolable eternal family, and I take seriously the sanctification of fellow members in Christ.

> The wise counselor is on the lookout for unholy alliances between a counselee and anyone who might offer sanctuary for idols. Those who fear having idols exposed tend to befriend idol "shields," anyone to distract, deflect, or otherwise defer a sanctifying gaze at the heart. When the threat of idol exposure is the highest, often these alliances grow the strongest.

In American jurisprudence, under certain circumstances, a plaintiff must press charges against the accused for the accused to be incarcerated. If the plaintiff refuses to press charges, the accused cannot be charged. Many in the church assume a similar posture with regard to sin. The prevailing view is that if the one sinned against is not particularly offended, then nothing should be done. This is not the Bible's perspective. The church, vigilant for Christ's glory, "presses charges" (confronts, rebukes, admonishes, teaches) against rebellion and transgression, even if the one sinned against is willing to overlook the offense and forgiveness has been extended. While, of course, Proverbs 19:11b points out, "…it is to a man's glory to overlook an offense," and 1 Peter 4:8b states, "…love covers over a multitude of sins," the church does not allow transgression to stand unopposed, when such transgression is clearly destructive to the church's witness and vitality (both in the one committing the offense and in those observing it).[65]

If, for example, one church member slanders the good name of another, regardless of the slandered party's response, it behooves the church to address the issue. In this way, the church does not, for the sake of expedience, adopt worldly standards of conduct, but the will of Christ. Functioning as Christ's instrument on earth, the church is a vanguard for maintaining its own integrity and internal purity.[66]

Leviticus 24:16 states that anyone who blasphemes the name of the Lord must be put to death. The entire assembly must stone him, as the nation must be zealous for God's glory. This concept could be applied to the church today. The entire church must be zealous for seeing God glorified and magnified in one another. We are each called to participate in the work of sanctification, each called to figuratively raise up a stone to

---

[64] Esther 1:16-18
[65] 1 Corinthians 5:1-5 and Galatians 2:11-14 offer good examples.
[66] Romans 16:19

crush the sin within the other. While this could be misconstrued as an unloving and hostile act, what is meant is simply that, as with the Israelites, each Christian is beckoned to exhibit zeal for the purity of fellow believers.

There is a saying, "You will never get credit for the disasters you avert,"[67] and another, "No good deed goes unpunished." The Christian who helps another see his sin will rarely receive a commendation. His work to expose the heart will hardly be applauded, nor will he be the honored guest at an awards dinner. He will not be asked to deliver a commencement address on his work to help free others from the bondage of sin, and seldom will he be thanked by those he has impacted. The one who helps others see their sin is the most forlorn and forgotten hero on earth. His reward is in heaven, held in God's hand. For this reason, it is often far easier to do external good works than internal ones. External good works make one a hometown favorite; internal good works, more often than not, make one *persona non grata*.

> "Now I rejoice in what was suffered for you, and I fill up in my flesh what is still lacking in regard to Christ's afflictions, for the sake of his body, which is the church." (Colossians 1:24)

When one is self-focused, and intent on meeting perceived needs, church will always seem uninspiring because its design is in the exact opposite direction. The church community, if focused on God's Word and if committed to the gospel, always works toward an experience of forgetting oneself and implementing the love of God and others.[68] The church is about learning to love Jesus and his Word, and that requires a humble quiet spirit resting at the foot of the cross.

> "The church is not a museum of saints but a hospital for sinners." (Augustine of Hippo)

If one participates in the church with a worldly spirit then that church experience will always be boring. The church cannot compete with the world with its focus on entertainment, sensory experience, the lust of the eye, and the need for continual emotional stimulation. However, a counseling focus is one of God's many stealth antidotes to a lackluster church experience. Engaging in wise counsel (as both contributor and recipient) transforms church involvement into a compelling encounter with the living Christ. That may be terrifying for the unrepentant, and exhilarating for the repentant, but never boring.

Counseling is often misconstrued as a subcategory of mercy ministry - urgent intervention for the emotionally distraught. In actuality, counseling falls under the

---
[67] This quote from an unknown source
[68] Luke 10:27

purview, and within the context of, incarnational ministry. It is rightly seen as a ubiquitous and daily component of the church's life, woven into even the most seemingly mundane interactions between believers. It is not necessarily a formal event but, more often than not, is an eminently casual one, albeit never a light one. Thus, counseling, as an under-girding element of all interaction, serves to draw believers into dynamic and growing relationship with God. Its intent is not merely assent to sound doctrine, but to prompt a living faith which, firstly connected to Christ, acts, moves, purposes, communicates, and participates in the abundant life Jesus died to bestow upon the church.

Crusaders Thirsting near Jerusalem, Francesco Hayez, c. 1850

> The counseling church is not afraid of Christ-centered slowness or silence or sedulity.

Counseling is part of both the church's objective and subjective holiness. Objective refers to its corporate attachment to Christ; subjective refers to the revitalization of the heart. It is crucial to understand that the church's purity is not found in external structures, or in mere intellectual adherence to particular doctrines, but in individual lives being confronted with, and called to daily repentance before, the living God. This is the import and force of the biblical counseling paradigm. Thus, it bears reiterating, that every Christian has a counseling role within the church (and indeed, every person must of necessity offer and receive counsel in every interaction, no matter how trivial). There are to be no spectator Christians, and certainly there are no forgotten Christians.

> Faithfully following Jesus requires humility, a quiet spirit, a sober assessment of one's sin, an honest dealing with others, the willingness to share and bear burdens, and the courage to make oneself appropriately transparent so as to offer and receive wise counsel.

Here is the Morton's Fork of biblical counseling: if you want to know who someone really is, speak to him privately; if you want to know who someone really is, place him in a group. The church offers a unique setting into which to enjoy moments of private conversation and frequent group interaction, often within a compact timeframe. This is vital for uncovering idols of the heart as one can observe personality changes which may surface in either setting. This interplay of private and group setting represents an implicit polemic against a professional model of counseling (although biblical counselors can conduct formal counseling sessions).

A young Christian woman is quite loquacious in private discussion, often speaking with ease for hours on a host of topics. However, in a church setting among others she is suddenly silent and appears anxious. I surmise that she craves attention. Private discussions put her face-to-face with a captive audience of one. In her mind there is a certain assured acceptance as this one person is entirely focused on her. In a group setting, however, the audience is ill-defined and the attention is diffused. Without a clear channel for discussion, and an obviously attentive recipient, this woman seems somewhat lost and confused. How can her relationship with Jesus free her from needing a captive audience? How can Jesus become her only audience, therein allowing her to speak in a group, even when the attention is not necessarily focused on her?

Those in Christ Possess a Core Competency to Counsel

In Numbers 25:6-15, an Israelite man did something revolting; he brought a Midianite woman to his tent right before the eyes of Moses and the whole assembly. When Phinehas, son of Eleazar, saw this he grabbed his spear and followed them into the tent. There Phinehas impaled both the man and his mistress. On account of his zeal, Phinehas turned God's anger away from the Israelites. When God's people decisively turn from their sin they turn back God's punishment (discipline). God's people are called, not to turn away when others are in the grip of life-altering sin, but to rightly adjudge and to take definitive action to encourage repentance and faith. God desires those who are zealous for the purity of his people,[69] and is well-pleased when they

---
[69] Ephesians 5:3

take steps to purge the church of transgression by bringing it to the feet of Jesus.[70] To our knowledge, Phinehas did not have special training with a spear, and he had not specifically attuned himself to see transgression in his midst. However, when he beheld that which was clearly abominable, he acted out of passion for God and his people. Thus, God uses common people, with no particular talent, often to affect his greatest work in the church.

> "The battle is ours; the outcome is God's." (Robert E. Lee)

A married couple asked me for counsel concerning their growing interpersonal conflict. I have never been married, yet I offered sound wisdom. How is this possible? The Bible tells me everything I need to know about people regardless of their circumstance. Thus, the situation of marriage is largely incidental to the conflict issues. I recently counseled a mother on raising her children. I have never raised children, yet she felt that my advice offered piercing insight. How is this possible? The Bible teaches me everything I need to know about people regardless of their circumstance. So whether counseling a feuding couple, a besieged mother, or a failing senior I apply the exact same gospel-centered understanding as I would otherwise. This is not to be misconstrued as using a boilerplate approach since my application of the gospel is highly-pliable. The point is simply that circumstance is incidental, and largely a distraction, in the quest to uncover the heart.

The idea that one must have himself overcome drug addiction to counsel a recovering drug addict, that one must have experienced the loss of a child to counsel one who grieves this loss, that one must have experienced an actual event to understand it, is largely driven by Freudian psychology which prioritizes human experience. Raising experience to the principle position of understanding profoundly misconstrues the human condition, failing to see it as firstly a with-regard-to-God reality. Even though one has not experienced certain situations first-hand, he is still eminently capable of offering biblical counsel on that, or any issue. Wise counsel is never a question of having amassed the right experience, but one of listening to the right voice and donning the proper set of lenses.[71]

Let's be clear on this. Any Christian can counsel any person, anywhere in the world, in any situation, regarding any sin, based solely on the Word of God. The Word is that universal, that relevant, that capable of imparting wisdom. God's Word alone, under the aegis of his Spirit, pierces the heart and imparts wisdom,[72] not the counselor's situation or personal experience. A single person, armed with Scripture, can counsel married couples far better than a married person with a man-centered understanding. One who has never raised his own children can offer far greater wisdom on

---

[70] Esther 4:16; 5:1, 2 offers a proleptic hint of this.
[71] 1 Timothy 4:12
[72] Hebrews 4:12

child-rearing, using the Word of God, than one who has raised children without a thoroughly Christ-centered approach. The Christian is fully-equipped to face every situation using Scripture regardless of his life experience.[73]

Arnaut Blowing Smoke in His Dog's Nose, Jean-Léon Gérôme, d. 1904

> While some may claim that they are not gifted in counseling, the Bible's concept of counseling transcends giftedness. Counseling is an unavoidable element of each social interaction, as each Christian can and does offer counsel in each interaction. The question is not one of giftedness but one of Christ-centeredness. As love for Christ builds, so grows the ability and passion to see others also grow in him.

The point is that Scripture's wisdom trumps all human experience and situations. In fact, to take it one step further, one's experience and situation are only a source of blindness and a hindrance to truth when not thoroughly interpreted through the lens of Scripture.

One of the most exciting developments in seeing the church counsel itself is the steady growth in joy and the family atmosphere that develops. I would submit that the vibrant counseling church is not so much purpose-driven as it is person-driven. Thus, as each grows in relationship with God, each grows in relationship with one another. Thus, the church becomes a living reflection of the vibrant relationship of believers with their God, a flash of heaven itself. Through this counseling vision for the church

---

[73] 2 Timothy 3:16, 17

the goal is both vertical and horizontal renewal. As counseling is Spirit-filled, focused on repentance and renewal, it becomes vivacious, efficacious, and revelatory of the character of God himself. Wise counsel brings restored fellowship with God, resulting in a bounty of restored fellowship within the church. Relationships are alive and flourishing with the poise, import, and promise of God's own presence. When the church is healthy and growing, experiencing forgiveness and manifesting gratitude (a merism for the fullness of God's grace),[74] there is an exhilaration, an inexplicable levity, and a timelessness about the church's fellowship. There is an incarnation of the abundant life that God promised those in Christ.[75] Thus, the church is simultaneously a means and an end, a conduit and a terminus for this jubilant celebration of the Father.

> "Direct my thoughts, words, and work. Wash away my sins in the immaculate Blood of the Lamb, and purge my heart by Thy Holy Spirit…Daily frame me more and more into the likeness of Thy Son Jesus Christ." (George Washington)

The Victory and Vision of the Counseling Church

God's vision for the counseling church (as presented in this three-part series) is something of a utopian dream marching toward fruition, an already accomplished victory, but a not yet fully-realized vision. For years I have labored to implement and sustain this victory and vision, but I find it a weighty and tedious task. The church is cankered with chthonian lesions, swirling in vortices of relational turmoil, and roiled by polycentric interests. The church is a carousel of convalescent souls rising and falling, approaching and departing, as they are pulled along by a power against which they often feel helpless.

The counseling church requires a fervent Christocentric focus, abiding hearts, steady minds, ears sharply attuned, and eyes rightly directed. It requires a consuming passion for Jesus' work in others, a love which is willing to hurdle relational boundaries and shred social convention. Yet, this fervor and passion is steadily channeled along fine filaments into hearts in need of timely counsel in the right dosage. These fine filaments, in aggregate, form the rarest silk chiffon, painstakingly woven and protected with the greatest care. Rogue elements, caliginous constituents, and worldly distractions easily rend this delicate work of sanctification. Jesus Christ himself must direct the counseling church; he must bestow its wisdom, breathe life into it, and chart its course. Even slightly misaligned teaching (that containing subtle secular concepts) in time creates profound deviation from the truth.[76] That is why those who share

---

[74] While the world's conversation tends to orbit around revenge and complaint, of one form or another (like a worldly merism), the Spirit-filled church's conversation tends to orbit around forgiveness and thankfulness (a kind of Spirit-led merism).
[75] John 10:10
[76] Esther 1:16-18 offers an example of this.

Jesus' passion for people are guardians of his vision, men and women of the watchtower observing a supernova of Christ's glory explode before their eyes.

> "Tyranny, like hell, is not easily conquered. Yet we have this consolation within us, that the harder the conflict, the more glorious the triumph." (Thomas Paine)

EPILOGUE

Saint Ignatius in Glory (America detail), Fra Andrea Pozzo, c. 1691

Revelations Are Nothing Without Revolutions[1]

In September, 2011 a church invited me to present a weekend seminar on biblical counseling. While I had taught on this topic for many years, I lacked a unified and comprehensive set of notes. Exhilarated by the prospects, I stayed up most of the night sketching out a thirty-page outline. Over the intervening years that outline slowly grew into this three volume series.

Henry David Thoreau (1817-1862) wrote, "The best an author can write is the best that he is as a person. Every sentence is the result of his experience and his character is evident from the first page to the last." This could not be truer in myself. This series is a testimony to the faith that I daily live out; it is a record of the investment that God has deposited within me, something of the gospel's mystery and treasure stored in a clay jar.[2]

---

[1] The phrase, "Revelations are nothing without revolutions" from Greg Gutfeld's commentary "Small Government is Back" on Fox News, June 6, 2013.
[2] 2 Corinthians 4:7

At numerous stages throughout this project I felt I had reached a dead-end, either my writing was cramped, my technical skill appeared wanting, my heart was pained, or the sands of time seemed to be rapidly slipping through the hourglass. However, guided by an invisible hand, this project surged forward, sometimes by fits, and at other times by leaps. I always sensed that God wanted this project completed, and his vision for this work, both in scope and in presentation, has far surpassed my own. This series has become a kind of God-sent *coup de foudre*, the impossible-with-man becoming possible with God.[3]

Writing this series has been an unforgettable experience. At times it has been a lavish adventure, uncovering what for me was often *terra incognita* in God's Word. At other times it has been a doleful and lonely trek on the barren hinterlands of my soul. There have been times when I have come face-to-face with my own poverty in Christ, my own severe and striking limitations as a disciple.

At moments, I have seen my idolatrous heart wrap around this project like an anaconda twining itself around prey. I have also seen God offer newly-minted liberation from my own sin as a much needed truth was discovered or a vexing question was answered. In the tumble and triumph, vexation and victory, I have encountered Jesus more fully, and he has emerged supreme within my life. For that I am eminently grateful.

Philippians 2:13 reads, "…for it is God who works in you to will and to act according to his good purpose." God has worked vigorously within me over the course of these nearly four years of writing. He has moved with relentless passion to shape my heart, to guard my mind, and to place a protective hedge around my life, so that this work would contribute in small part to his kingdom building efforts. I consider this to be his work in, and through, me because I have personally witnessed the undeniable marks of his presence throughout the entire process.

With each of the thirty chapters in this series it seemed that God worked with surgical precision to make that particular topic come alive within me. For example, while writing the chapter "Suffering: The Kintsugi Objective" I both experienced searing personal suffering and was called upon to counsel others facing similar trials. The chapter entitled, "The Hobgoblin in the Inglenook: Assessing Loneliness" was birthed from a Stygian spell of vexing loneliness. The subsequent chapter, "The Umbilicus of Personal Relationship with Christ," traces the emergence from that episode as I more vividly experienced Jesus as intimate friend.

Francis Bacon (1561-1626) wrote, "Reading makes a full man, discussion a ready

---
[3] Luke 18:27

man, and writing an exact man." Like Odysseus navigating the Scylla and Charybdis, I have sought to thread the Bible's careful balance on each of the topics explored. If I have achieved that balance, and have faithfully plumbed the depths of God's Word, then I pray that this endeavor bears eternal fruit in each who encounters it.

As a final note, this material was birthed in a teaching context and, to some degree, that is where it is most at home. These texts were meant to be taught, and more importantly, to be put into practice by those with the will, giftedness, and opportunity to do so. I pray that some of you will undertake such an endeavor as part of a larger revival and renewal of Christ's body, the church.

Thus concludes the third, and final, book in *The Christian Exceptionalism in Counseling Series.*™ If you have read all three books, I trust you have not just been blessed with a comprehensive look at biblical counseling, but have experienced a personal encounter with Jesus himself. If you have yet to pick up the first two books, I would encourage you to do so as they provide the needed background to this third installment. I want to thank each of you who have invested your time into reading this work. Time is precious, and there is hardly enough of it to read all that is profitable on this topic.

"Read the best books first. There may not be time to read them all." (Anonymous)

The Author

James Venezia studied physics at Haverford College and later divinity and apologetics at Westminster Theological Seminary. He currently serves as a college instructor and pastor.

Please direct comments or questions concerning this series to jamesvenezia@yahoo.com.

The Christian Exceptionalism in Counseling Series™

The first book in the series, *Ask for the Ancient Paths,* is an introduction to biblical counseling.

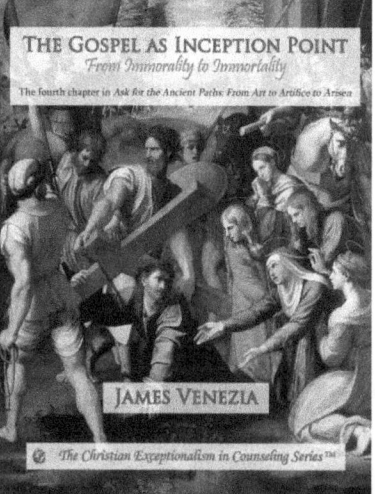

Chapter four (here shown in booklet form) offers a comprehensive exposition of the gospel.

Chapter eight presents a biblical response to psychology.

Chapter ten examines the concept of sanctification.

The second book, *What Agreement Is There Between the Temple of God and Idols?*, is an in-depth study of sin and idolatry.

Chapter two introduces the triple concept - the world, the flesh, and the devil.

Chapter six introduces the issue of idolatry.

Chapter nine investigates the modern construal of the self.

The third book, *The Days of Reckoning Are at Hand,* focuses on application of the biblical counseling paradigm.

Chapter two analyzes suffering from a biblical perspective.

Chapter three considers the issue of loneliness.

Chapter four argues for living relationship with Jesus himself, the life-blood of the Christian faith.

A Summary of *The Christian Exceptionalism in Counseling Series*™

Textbook	Textbook Chapter in Booklet Form[1]
Ask for the Ancient Paths *From Art to Artifice to Arisen*	**The Gospel as Inception Point** *From Immorality to Immortality* (chapter 4)
	What Has Jerusalem To Do With Vienna? *The Case Against Psychology* (chapter 8)
	The Third-Way of Sanctification *From Abominable to Indomitable* (chapter 10)
What Agreement Is There Between the Temple of God and Idols? *The Accidence of Sin and Idolatry*	**Uncovering Idols of the Heart** *Make Us Gods to Go Before Us* (chapter 6)
	Marauding Visigoths *The Autocratic Self* (chapter 9)
The Days of Reckoning Are at Hand *From Fig Leaf to Olive Branch to Laurel Wreath*	**Suffering** *The Kintsugi Objective* (chapter 2)
	The Hobgoblin in the Inglenook *Assessing Loneliness* (chapter 3)
	The Umbilicus of Personal Relationship with Christ (chapter 4)

All materials in *The Christian Exceptionalism in Counseling Series*™ available for sale at Amazon bookseller

---

[1] Please note that each booklet is an exact reprinting of its respective chapter in the textbook.

Also by the Author

*The Lord Kept Vigil That Night:
An Exposition of the Parable of the Lost Son*

*Rescue Us from the Present Evil Age:
Array of Hope*

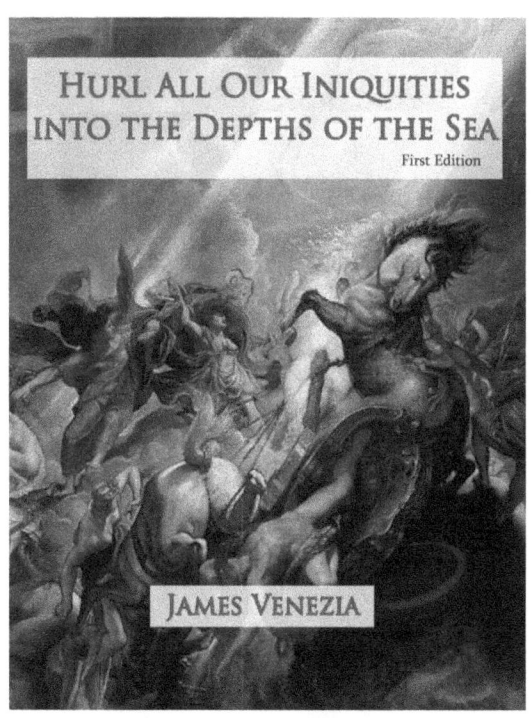

*Hurl All Our Iniquities
into the Depths of the Sea*

www.ingramcontent.com/pod-product-compliance
Lightning Source LLC
Chambersburg PA
CBHW081123170426
43197CB00017B/2733